iii

To the Reader

In publishing ANNUAL EDITIONS we recognize the enormous role played by the magazines, newspapers, and journals of the public press in providing current, first-rate educational information in a broad spectrum of interest areas. Many of these articles are appropriate for students, researchers, and professionals seeking accurate, current material to help bridge the gap between principles and theories and the real world. These articles, however, become more useful for study when those of lasting value are carefully collected, organized, indexed, and reproduced in a low-cost format, which provides easy and permanent access when the material is needed. That is the role played by ANNUAL EDITIONS.

New to ANNUAL EDITIONS is the inclusion of related World Wide Web sites. These sites have been selected by our editorial staff to represent some of the best resources found on the World Wide Web today. Through our carefully developed topic guide, we have linked these Web resources to the articles covered in this ANNUAL EDITIONS reader. We think that you will find this volume useful, and we hope that you will take a moment to visit us on the Web at *http://www.dushkin.com* to tell us what you think.

According to the results of a 1994 survey by Veronis, Suhler, and Associates, the average American spends 3,295 hours each year—the equivalent of 137 days or 82 40–hour work weeks—consuming mass media messages. Of these hours, 1,539 are spent watching television, 1,061 listening to the radio, 261 listening to recorded music, 168 reading newspapers, 99 reading books, 84 reading magazines, 51 watching videos at home, 11 watching movies in theaters, and 21 playing video games. Along with schools, the church, and the family, mass media have great potential for shaping American society. And, just as schools and families have been blamed for a variety of society's ills, these media have taken their fair share of heat.

The mass media are a part of the fabric of American society. Learning how to critically evaluate media messages—asking, Who created this message? What is its intent? How objective is it? How does what I am seeing or hearing reflect and/or shape real-world realities?—is a part of being literate in today's society. The organization of these readings reflects this media literacy perspective. Unit 1 introduces concerns that have been raised about the impact of mass media use and content on children, on daily living, and on society. Unit 2 explores media as sources of news and information, along with the public's changing attitude toward news coverage. Unit 3 introduces questions of media ethics. Unit 4 addresses the relationships among advertisers, media content, and popular culture. Finally, unit 5 takes a look ahead at the shape of tomorrow's media.

This edition also lists relevant *World Wide Web* sites that can be used to further explore the topics. These sites are cross-referenced by number in the *topic guide*.

You will find that the writers included in this collection frequently use television as a reference point in describing how mass media messages are shaped and interpreted. This is a reflection of the media focus of the public press and of television's rapid acceptance and continuing presence as the "massest" of mass media. Most of the articles, even those that are primarily descriptive, include an editorial viewpoint and draw conclusions or make recommendations with which you may disagree. These editorial viewpoints are more fre-

quently critical than they are complimentary. They are not necessarily my opinions and should not necessarily become yours. I encourage you to debate these issues, drawing from the information and insights provided in the readings as well as from your own experiences as a media consumer. If you are an "average" American, you have spent a great deal of time with mass media. Your own observations have as much value as those of the writers whose work is included in these pages.

The articles selected for inclusion in this sixth edition of *Annual Editions: Mass Media* reflect three issues of particular concern in the late 1990s. The first is the ongoing debate over the degree to which the U.S. government and legal system should rightfully be involved in regulating either media messengers or media messages. The second is a rekindled debate over ethics in news coverage, over how news is selected and packaged, and over the appropriate response to rising disinterest in "hard news" among media consumers. The third is a heightened awareness of a media landscape profoundly altered by corporate mergers and technological change.

As always, those involved in producing this anthology are sincerely committed to including articles that are timely, informative, and interesting reading. We value your feedback and encourage you to complete and return the postage-paid *article rating form* on the last page of the book to share your suggestions and let us know your opinions.

Joan Gorham
Editor

ANNUAL EDITIONS

Mass Media

Sixth Edition

99/00

EDITOR

Joan Gorham
West Virginia University

Joan Gorham completed her undergraduate work at the University of Wisconsin and received master's and doctoral degrees from Northern Illinois University. She is currently associate dean for academic affairs in the Eberly College of Arts and Sciences and a professor of communication studies at West Virginia University. Dr. Gorham is the author of *Commercial Media and Classroom Teaching* and has published numerous articles on communication in instruction. She has taught classes dealing with mass media and media literacy at the high school and college levels, as well as for teachers throughout the state of West Virginia.

Dushkin/McGraw-Hill
Sluice Dock, Guilford, Connecticut 06437

Visit us on the Internet
http://www.dushkin.com/annualeditions/

Credits

1. Living with Media
Facing overview—Dushkin/McGraw-Hill illustration by Mike Eagle.
2. Covering News
Facing overview—Courtesy of Cheryl Greenleaf.
3. Defining the Rules
Facing overview—EPA-Documerica photo. 111-112—National Archives photos.
4. A Word from Our Sponsor
Facing overview—© 1998, Cleo Freelance Photo. 155—Gillette illustration. 157—Photo by Harry Matthei.
159—Westinghouse photo. 161—Kraft Foods photo. 162—Colgate-Palmolive illustration.
5. The Shape of Things to Come
Facing overview—© 1998 by PhotoDisc, Inc.

Copyright

Cataloging in Publication Data
Main entry under title: Annual Editions: Mass media. 1999/2000.
    1. Mass media—Periodicals. I. Gorham, Joan, *comp.* II. Title: Mass media.
ISBN 0–07–041133–6   301.16'05   ISSN 1092–0439

Sixth Edition

Cover image © 1999 PhotoDisc, Inc.

Printed in the United States of America   1234567890BAHBAH5432109   Printed on Recycled Paper

Contents

UNIT 1

Living with Media

Eight articles discuss the
impact of mass media on
daily living and on society.

The concepts in bold italics are developed in the article. For further expansion please refer to the Topic Guide and the Index.

Covering News

UNIT 2

The twelve articles in this
unit provide critical perspectives on news gathering and
how it is delivered to the public.

The concepts in bold italics are developed in the article. For further expansion please refer to the Topic Guide and the Index.

The concepts in bold italics are developed in the article. For further expansion please refer to the Topic Guide and the Index.

UNIT 3

Defining
the Rules

Seven selections explore
how presenting newsworthy
information can be complicated
by considerations of what
is ethically right and wrong.

The concepts in bold italics are developed in the article. For further expansion please refer to the Topic Guide and the Index.

UNIT 4

A Word from Our Sponsor

In this section, seven selections explore relationships among financial backers, advertising, and media content.

The concepts in bold italics are developed in the article. For further expansion please refer to the Topic Guide and the Index.

ix

UNIT 5

The Shape of
Things to Come

Five selections explore new media
technologies and the changing
landscape of mass media forms,
consumption, and regulation.

The concepts in bold italics are developed in the article. For further expansion please refer to the Topic Guide and the Index.

The concepts in bold italics are developed in the article. For further expansion please refer to the Topic Guide and the Index.

Topic Guide

This topic guide suggests how the selections and World Wide Web sites found in the next section of this book relate to topics of traditional concern to students and professionals involved with the study of mass media. It is useful for locating interrelated articles and Web sites for reading and research. The guide is arranged alphabetically according to topic.

The relevant Web sites, which are numbered and annotated on pages 4 and 5, are easily identified by the Web icon (◎) under the topic articles. By linking the articles and the Web sites by topic, this ANNUAL EDITIONS reader becomes a powerful learning and research tool.

TOPIC AREA	TREATED IN	TOPIC AREA	TREATED IN
Advertising/ Target Marketing	4. Gendered Media 5. Boys Will Be Girls 28. Inventing the Commercial 29. Blowing Up the Wall 30. Sex, Lies, and Advertising 31. Squeeze 32. Television Is Losing 33. Last Gasp of Mass Media? 34. "But First, a Word from Our Sponsor" 35. Now It's Your Web 39. New Ratings Game ◎ *1, 5, 15, 25, 27, 28*		25. Intervention Dilemma 26. Starr Turn 27. Spot News 29. Blowing Up the Wall 36. Without a Rulebook ◎ *10, 11, 13, 15, 19, 20, 21, 22, 23*
		Family Values	1. TV without Guilt 2. Context of Television Violence 3. Anything Goes 6. TV's Frisky Family Values ◎ *5, 6, 8, 29*
Agenda Setting	2. Context of Television Violence 5. Boys Will Be Girls 7. So Big: The Telecommunications Act 8. Global Media Giants 9. "You News" 15. Tell It Long, Take Your Time 16. Rise of Solutions Journalism 22. Consumer Alert 29. Blowing Up the Wall ◎ *5, 6, 8, 11, 19, 20*	**Federal Communications Commission (FCC)**	3. Anything Goes 7. So Big: The Telecommunications Act ◎ *17, 20, 22, 23*
		Gatekeeping	8. Global Media Giants 10. Do You Believe What Newspeople Tell You? 14. Parachute Journalism 16. Rise of Solutions Journalism 20. Myths of the Global Information Village 21. Missing on the Home Front 22. Consumer Alert 31. Squeeze 37. Daily Me ◎ *9, 10, 11, 12, 13, 16, 17, 19, 20, 23, 24, 28, 29*
Cable	7. So Big: The Telecommunications Act 8. Global Media Giants 11. Matter of Trust 13. Rise and Rise of 24-Hour Local News ◎ *4, 6, 9, 11, 26*		
Credibility	10. Do You Believe What Newspeople Tell You? 11. Matter of Trust 14. Parachute Journalism 15. Tell It Long, Take Your Time 16. Rise of Solutions Journalism 22. Consumer Alert 23. Secrets and Lies 29. Blowing Up the Wall ◎ *6, 9, 10, 13, 15, 19, 20, 21, 23*	**Gender Stereotypes**	4. Gendered Media 5. Boys Will Be Girls ◎ *1, 6, 7*
		Government Influence	2. Context of Television Violence 7. So Big: The Telecommunications Act 20. Myths of the Global Information Village 21. Missing on the Home Front 38. X-Rated Ratings? ◎ *4, 10, 17, 22, 24, 29*
Cultivation Theory	2. Context of Television Violence 3. Anything Goes 4. Gendered Media 5. Boys Will Be Girls 14. Parachute Journalism 22. Consumer Alert ◎ *1, 5, 6, 7, 8, 10, 20, 21*	**Internet/New Technologies**	20. Myths of the Global Information Village 35. Now It's Your Web 36. Without a Rulebook 37. Daily Me 39. New Ratings Game ◎ *2, 5, 6, 12, 17, 18, 19, 20, 22, 24, 27, 29, 30, 31*
Ethics	7. So Big: The Telecommunications Act 10. Do You Believe What Newspeople Tell You? 14. Parachute Journalism 16. Rise of Solutions Journalism 21. Missing on the Home Front 22. Consumer Alert 23. Secrets and Lies 24. Too Much Information?	**Magazines**	4. Gendered Media 5. Boys Will Be Girls 8. Global Media Giants 11. Matter of Trust 15. Tell It Long, Take Your Time 21. Missing on the Home Front 30. Sex, Lies, and Advertising 33. Last Gasp of Mass Media?

AE: Mass Media

The following World Wide Web sites have been carefully researched and selected to support the articles found in this reader. If you are interested in learning more about specific topics found in this book, these Web sites are a good place to start. The sites are cross-referenced by number and appear in the topic guide on the previous two pages. Also, you can link to these Web sites through our DUSHKIN ONLINE support site at *http://www.dushkin.com/online/*.

The following sites were available at the time of publication. Visit our Web site—we update DUSHKIN ONLINE regularly to reflect any changes.

General Sources

1. The Media and Communications Site
http://www.aber.ac.uk/~dgc/media.html
This huge British site suggests many Internet resources covering everything from advertising to the impact of the media on perceptions of gender, ethnicity, and class. Access the home page of the Association for Media, Communication and Cultural Studies, a British organization, and the online International Journal of Media and Communication Studies.

2. MediaWeb/Rice University
http://nt.riceinfo.rice.edu/outreach/MediaWeb/web.cfm?Title=A
This site is a varied and vast alphabetical guide to media-related Web sites from all over the world. Many links to professional mass media organizations are included.

3. Netcomtalk/Boston University
http://web.bu.edu/COM/communication.html
Bookmark this site, an online, multimedia publication of the College of Communication at Boston University, for your daily perusal of a wide variety of news items and topics in media and communications. Click on "COMNews Today" for the latest happenings in mass media.

4. NewsPlace
http://www.niu.edu/newsplace/
This site of Professor Avi Bass from Northern Illinois University will lead you to a wealth of resources of interest in the study of mass media, such as international perspectives on censorship. Links to government, corporate, and other organizations are provided.

Living with Media

5. Center for Media Education
http://epn.org/cme/
Open this site to explore the impact on society of television and other electronic media through discussion of such topics as the effects of television violence, television and online advertising, and media images.

6. Children and the Media Program
http://www.dnai.com/~children/media/media.html
Open this site for access to a variety of views on the impact of media on children. Read about public opinion surveys of young people, independent research on television and print media, industry conference proceedings, and more. An Internet resource list is included.

7. Geocities
http://www.geocities.com/Wellesley/1031/#media/
This site presents a negative perspective on how the media portray women. By clicking on its many links, you can find such varied resources as an archive on misogynistic quotes and a discussion of newspeak and doublethink.

8. National Coalition on Television Violence
http://www.nctvv.org
The home page of the NCTV will lead you to definitions of the problem of television violence, explanations of how it affects people and what can be done about it, a bibliography, and a list of related organizations.

Covering News

9. Cable News Network
http://www.cnn.com
This is CNN's interactive site, which many people consider to be the best news site online.

10. Fairness and Accuracy in Reporting
http://www.fair.org
FAIR, a U.S. media watch group, offers well-documented criticism of media bias and censorship. It advocates structural reform to break up the dominant media conglomerates. Parts of the site are currently under construction.

11. Media & Democracy Congress
http://www.igc.apc.org/an/Congress.html
At this site, sponsored by the Institute for Alternative Journalism, find out the purpose and findings of the Media & Democracy Congress. You can get reports and audios of the Congress's proceedings, meant to build a stronger, more vibrant independent media community and to encourage citizenship over consumerism in an age in which public interest journalism is at risk.

12. Media Source
http://www.mediasource.com
This online service was created exclusively to help journalists find the information they need through the Internet. It includes such interesting features as a page for biographies, photos, and contact numbers of industry experts for a journalist's story.

13. Organization of News Ombudsmen
http://www5.infi.net/ono/
This ONO page provides links to journalism Web sites. The ONO works to aid in the wider establishment of the position of news ombudsmen on newspapers and elsewhere in the media and to provide a forum for the interchange of experiences, information, and ideas among news ombudsmen.

14. Television News Archive
http://tvnews.vanderbilt.edu
By browsing through this Vanderbilt University site, you can review national U.S. television news broadcasts from 1968 onward. It will give you insight into how the broadcast news industry has changed over the years and what trends define the industry today.

15. What Local TV News Doesn't Want You to Know!
http://www.tfs.net/personal/gbyron/tvnews1.html
Open this page to read perspectives on local TV news from someone who has been there—Greg Byron, a former radio and television newsman. He addresses such topics as the ratings- and advertising-driven nature of local news and the qualifications and training of anchors.

Defining the Rules

16. The Electronic Journalist
http://spj.org
This site for *The Electronic Journalist*, an online service of the Society of Professional Journalists (SPJ), will lead you to a number of articles having to do with journalistic ethics, accuracy, and other topics.

17. Federal Communications Commission
http://www.fcc.gov
This is the home page of the FCC, an independent U.S. government agency whose mission "is to encourage competition in all communications markets and to protect the public interest." Open the site to find information about such topics as laws regulating the media.

18. Index on Censorship
http://www.oneworld.org/index_oc/
This site from Great Britain provides information and many international links to show, it explains, "how free speech affects the political issues of the moment."

19. International Television Association
http://www.itva.org
This home page of the International Television Association, which describes itself as "the premier association for video, multimedia and film professionals," is useful for links to other media resources, discussions of ethical topics, explanation of such issues as "fair use," and debate over the impact of the Internet.

20. Media Watchdog
http://theory.lcs.mit.edu/~mernst/media/
This site lists extensive international links to media watch resources, including specific media-criticism articles and information about media watch groups. The emphasis here is on critiquing the accuracy and exposing the biases of the mainstream media.

21. Michigan Press Photographers Association
http://www.mppa.org
Ethical issues in photojournalism are featured at this site sponsored by the MPPA.

22. Pepper & Corazzini, L.L.P
http://www.commlaw.com/pepper/Memos/memos.html
Reading the materials at this site, of a firm that specializes in communications, telecommunications, Internet, and online services law, will give you a sense of the enormous complexity of media law today. Attorneys' reports on such topics as rules governing children's television are presented.

23. Poynter Online: Research Center
http://www.poynter.org/research/research.htm
The Poynter Institute for Media Studies provides extensive links to information and resources on media ethics, media writing and editing, visual journalism, and much more. Many bibliographies and Web sites are included.

24. World Intellectual Property Organization
http://www.wipo.org/eng/
Click on the links at WIPO's home page to find general information on WIPO and intellectual property, publications and documents, international classifications, and more.

A Word from Our Sponsor

25. Advertising Age
http://adage.com
Gain access to articles and features about media advertising, such as a history of television advertising, at this site.

26. History of Cable
http://www.pcta.com/histcabl.html
This site will give you information as to how and why cable television was started. Go from here back to the Pennsylvania Cable & Telecommunication Association home page.

27. Niche E-Zine
http://www.hsr.com/niche/index.html
Search through this online journal for articles and excerpts from speeches for a sense of how one international advertisement agency, Hensley Segal Rentschler Inc., views narrowcasting, target marketing, and the role of advertising in various media in the digital era.

28. USA DATA
http://www.usadata.com/usadata/general.htm
Browse through this site of a "media reporting" company to get a sense of the elements involved in programming and advertising decisions made for television and other media. USA DATA notes its ability to provide clients "with reliable market and consumer behavior-specific data."

The Shape of Things to Come

29. Citizens Internet Empowerment Coalition
http://www.ciec.org
The CIEC is a broad group of Internet users, library groups, publishers, online service providers, and civil liberties groups working to preserve the First Amendment and ensure the future of free expression. Find discussions of the Communications Decency Act and Internet-related topics here.

30. Educause
http://www.educause.edu
Open this site for an e-mailed summary of info-tech news from various major publications and for many other resources meant to facilitate the introduction, use, access to, and management of information resources in teaching, learning, scholarship, and research.

31. Link, Digital Campus
http://linkmag.com
This interactive "campus magazine" provides current news in education, analysis of current events, and much more of interest to students.

32. Marshall McLuhan Studies
http://www.beaulieuhome.com/McLuhan/mcweb.html
Open this Canadian site for links to a number of interesting articles about the information age, such as the origin of the term "Global Village," and how editors' mindsets must change in order to be effective in the electronic era.

We highly recommend that you review our Web site for expanded information and our other product lines. We are continually updating and adding links to our Web site in order to offer you the most usable and useful information that will support and expand the value of your Annual Editions. You can reach us at: *http://www.dushkin.com/annualeditions/.*

www.dushkin.com/online/

Unit Selections

1. **TV without Guilt: Group Portrait with Television,** David Finkel
2. **The Context of Television Violence,** Ellen A. Wartella
3. **Anything Goes: Moral Bankruptcy of Television and Hollywood,** Joe McNamara
4. **Gendered Media: The Influence of Media on Views of Gender,** Julia T. Wood
5. **Boys Will Be Girls,** Liza Featherstone
6. **TV's Frisky Family Values,** *U.S. News & World Report*
7. **So Big: The Telecommunications Act at Year One,** Neil Hickey
8. **The Global Media Giants,** Robert W. McChesney

Key Points to Consider

❖ After reading the unit's first article, compare your family's use of television with the way television was used in the Delmar household. Beyond the question of quantity of television watching, how accurately do you feel this portrait reflects the typical family's relationship with television?

❖ In your opinion, does media content primarily reflect social reality or does it significantly shape social reality? Should it do otherwise?

❖ Do you agree with criticisms of media portrayals of women, men, minorities, sexuality, and violence? To what degree can scientific research resolve questions of effects of such portrayals? What positive examples of each can you think of?

 **Links** | **www.dushkin.com/online/**

5. **Center for Media Education**
   http://epn.org/cme/
6. **Children and the Media Program**
   http://www.dnai.com/~children/media/media.html
7. **Geocities**
   http://www.geocities.com/Wellesley/1031/#media/
8. **National Coalition on Television Violence**
   http://www.nctvv.org

These sites are annotated on pages 4 and 5.

The media have been blamed for just about everything from a decrease in attention span to an increase in street crime to undoing our capacity to think. In *Amusing Ourselves to Death* (Penguin, 1986), social critic Neil Postman suggests that the cocktail party, the quiz show, and popular trivia games are reflections of society's trying to find a use for the abundance of superficial information given us by the media—and are useful for little else than attempts to impress one another with small talk. Peggy Noonan, a former network writer who worked as a speechwriter during the Reagan administration, has observed that experiences are no longer "real" unless they are ratified by television (which is why, she says, half the people in a stadium watch the game on monitors rather than the field). Marie Winn's memorable description of a child transfixed by television, slack-jawed, tongue resting on the front teeth, eyes glazed and vacant (*The Plug-In Drug*, Penguin, 1985) has become an often-quoted symbol of the passivity encouraged by television viewing. We, as a nation, have a distinct love-hate relationship with mass media.

Questions of whether or not and to what extent media influence our behaviors, values, expectations, and ways of thinking are difficult to answer. While one bibliographer has compiled a list of over 3,000 citations of English-language articles focusing just on children and television (and all written within the last 40 years), the conclusions drawn in these articles vary. Isolating media as a causal agent in examining human behavior is a difficult task, complicated by the challenge of understanding the complexities of the mind, differences in the context in which media are consumed (e.g., the personal, nonmedia experiences of the consumer and the extent to which media content is actively versus passively processed), the difficulty of finding representative control groups who have not been exposed to media, and the challenge of determining long-range effects.

Media messages serve a variety of purposes: they inform, they influence public opinion, they sell, and they entertain. They frequently do all of these things, sometimes below the level of consumers' conscious awareness. Children watch *Sesame Street* to be entertained, but they also learn to count, to share, to accept physical differences among individuals, and (perhaps) to desire a Sesame Street lunch box. Adults watch crime dramas to be entertained, but they also learn that they have the right to remain silent when arrested, how (accurately or inaccurately) the criminal justice system works, and that the world is an unsafe place.

Nicholas Johnson, a former chairman of the Federal Communications Commission, has noted, "Every moment of television programming—commercials, entertainment, news—teaches us something." How such incidental learning occurs is most often explained by two theories. Social Learning (or Modeling) Theory suggests that the behavior of media consumers, particularly children, is affected by their imitating role models presented via media. The degree to which modeling occurs depends upon the presence of *inhibitors,* lessons learned in real life that discourage imitation, and *disinhibitors,* experiences in real life that reinforce imitation. Cultivation Theory holds that media shape behavior by influencing attitudes. Media provide a "window to the world," exposing consumers to images of reality that may or may not jibe with personal experience.

Mainstreaming effects occur when media introduce images of things with which the consumer has no personal experience. *Resonance* effects occur when media images echo personal experience. Thus, a television viewer who has never been in a hospital will be more likely to believe that doctors are like those on *ER* than a viewer who has logged hours in real-world emergency rooms, and a television viewer who has had real-world experiences similar to those seen on *ER* may find that watching the show reinforces their belief that all doctors and hospitals are like those on *ER*. However, a television viewer who has had personal experiences in hospitals that differ from the images portrayed on *ER* is not likely to believe what is on television over what has been observed in real life. Heavy media consumers are more likely to be affected than light consumers, since they spend more time absorbing information from media (and, presumably, have less time available for first-person life experiences).

The first six articles in this section examine media use, media content, and media effects. The first essay "TV without Guilt: Group Portrait with Television" provides a candid look at how television has become ingrained in the rituals of one family's daily life. The Delmars are unquestionably heavy media consumers. They also consider themselves very normal people—and perhaps they are. The average television household tunes in to over 7 hours of TV per day, compared with 4.4 hours in the 1950s. In "The Context of Television Violence," Ellen Wartella challenges the television industry "to own up to the role it has played in lowering the threshold for real violence in our society." Joe McNamara ("Anything Goes: Moral Bankruptcy of Television and Hollywood") argues that the humor in contemporary situation comedies "influences as well and perhaps more effectively because it is not perceived as a form of violence or even attempted influence." Julia Wood ("Gendered Media: The Influence of Media on Views of Gender") contends that media are harmfully perpetrating stereotypical expectations and attitudes about male/female roles and interactions. In contrast, Liza Featherstone ("Boys Will Be Girls") finds more similarities than differences in the images of what we "should be" as they are reinforced by contemporary men's and women's magazines, and the essay "TV's Frisky Family Values" claims that television has a significant impact on our society.

The final two articles in this section examine the sources who create media messages. "So Big: The Telecommunication Act at Year One" analyzes the 1996 Telecommunications Act and its impact on diversity of choice. We are in an era of "vertical integration" among media producers; nine powerful, mostly U.S.-based media corporations, dominate the global commercial media system. "The Global Media Giants" describes their reach.

Each of the writers whose views are included in this section agrees that media have the potential of influencing behavior and values. Each also agrees that media content has changed over the years. They differ in the degree to which they believe that individual media consumers, particularly children, are shaped by what they encounter through media. Some argue that changes in media content primarily reflect changes in social norms and attitudes; others claim that media provide role models and cultivate attitudes that make us who we are.

Living with Media

TV Without Guilt

Group Portrait With Television

One family's love affair with the tube

David Finkel

The first TV to come on is the one in the master bedroom, a 13-inch Hitachi. The time is 8:20 a.m. The alarm clock goes off, and Bonnie Delmar opens her eyes and immediately reaches over to the night stand for the remote. Her husband, Steve, has already left for work. The children are still asleep. The house is quiet. On comes CBS because Bonnie was watching the David Letterman show when she drifted off the night before. She watches "This Morning" for a few minutes, catching up on what has happened in the last seven hours in the world beyond her Gaithersburg home, and then she switches to NBC in time for the weather and Willard Scott. Later in the day, she will tell about a dream she once had. "I dreamt I was married to Willard Scott," she will say. "I was going to my 10th high school reunion, and I was excited that everyone was going to see that I was married to a celebrity, but then I wasn't excited because it was Willard Scott. You know?"

The second TV to come on is the 19-inch Zenith in the bedroom of Bonnie's daughter, Ashley, age 7 years and 10 months. The time is now 8:45, 40 minutes before school begins, and Ashley and her younger brother, Steven, get dressed while watching "The Bozo Show." The Zenith is the newest TV in the house, purchased a few weeks before to replace the 26-inch Sony console that had been in Ashley's room until the color picture tube went bad. "She threw a fit when the console broke," Bonnie says of Ashley's initial reaction. "She was, like, 'I won't watch TV in my room anymore,' so Steve and Steven went out and got her a new TV, and she wasn't at all happy about it. I mean, she went in her room and cried about it. She actually cried. She wanted a big screen. I actually laughed at her. I said, 'You've got to be kidding,' and that made her more furious. She was saying, 'How can you give me such a small TV?' But, anyway, that's over. She's fine now." On the screen this morning, Bozo is standing next to a child who is attempting to throw a ping-pong ball into a succession of six buckets. She does this and wins several prizes, and Ashley and Steven jump around the bedroom cheering while Bonnie, who has been watching with them, claps her hands. "Wow!" she says. "What a great day."

The third TV to come on is the 27-inch Hitachi by the kitchen table. It's now a few minutes after 9, time for "Live—Regis & Kathie Lee." This Hitachi has an especially complex remote, but Steven has mastered it, despite being only 6. He picks it up

and changes the channel to "Barney and Friends." "I love you, you love me," the Barney theme song begins, but Steven sings his own variation, learned from Ashley, who learned it at school. "I hate you, you hate me, he sings, "let's kill Barney one two three, with a great big knife, stab him in his head, pull it out and then he's dead." "Steven!" Bonnie says, laughing. "How's it really go?" "I don't know," Steven says. He picks up the remote again and switches to cartoons, while Bonnie, who wants to watch "Regis & Kathie Lee," goes over to the counter by the sink and turns on the five-inch, black-and-white, battery powered Panasonic.

It is now 9:10 a.m. in the Delmar house. Fifty minutes have gone by since the alarm. Four TVs have been turned on. It will be another 16 hours before all the TVs are off and the house is once again quiet.

By the sink, Bonnie continues to watch "Regis & Kathie Lee."

At the table, Ashley and Steven watch Speedy Gonzales in "Here Today, Gone Tamale."

Looking at them, it's hard to imagine three happier people.

"Mom," Ashley says later, after she has gone to school and come home and resumed watching TV, "I'm going to watch TV in Heaven."

"You're going to watch TV in Heaven?" Bonnie says.

"Yeah," Ashley says.

"Well," Bonnie says, "let's hope they have it on up there."

Of all the relationships of modern civilization, none is more hypocritical than the relationship between an American family and its television set.

We say we don't watch TV except occasionally, and yet, according to Nielsen figures, we have it on an average of 7½ hours a day. We worry that TV causes violent behavior, and yet we keep watching violent shows. We complain that TV is getting too graphic, and yet we are buying sets with sharper pictures and larger screens. We insist we have better things to do than watch TV, and yet every night, on every street, shooting through the gaps in closed blinds or around the edges of drawn curtains is the electric blue glow that is the true color of our lives.

TV is our angst. TV is our guilt. We watch it. We worry about it. We blame it. We watch it some more. We feel bad about how much we really watch it. We lie.

Except for the Delmars.

"I just don't buy it that too much TV is bad for you," says Steve, 37, the chief financial officer of a company that makes automated telephone answering systems, who gets home from work around 7, eats dinner while watching Dan Rather and Connie Chung, settles down in the den by the 19-inch Sony, watches a few hours of sports, goes back to the bedroom, turns on the Hitachi and falls asleep with it on because Bonnie can't fall asleep if it's off. "Nobody wants to admit they watch television—it's got the connotation: 'the boob tube'—but all these people, what are they doing? I'm not sure if they have any more intellect. It's not like they're all going to the Smithsonian or anything."

"Let's see," says Bonnie, 35, a housewife and former restaurant hostess with a bachelor's degree in elementary education, totaling up how much TV she watches a day. "It just depends on if I'm home or not. Almost always, the TV is on from 4 o'clock to the end of 'David Letterman.' It depends, though. If I'm home, I'm watching. Probably nine hours a day is average. There are some days I might actually watch 16, 17 hours, but there are some days I'm out and about, and I don't get to watch as much."

At the Delmars', there are six TVs, counting the old Sony console that is now in the guest room, and plans are to refinish the basement and add two more. At the Delmars', not only is the TV always on, it is virtually a member of the family, part of nearly every significant moment in their lives.

Bonnie remembers her honeymoon. "The cable went out," she says. "It wasn't out for long, six hours maybe, but I was pretty mad."

She remembers Steven's birth. "Steven was born during the halftime of a Redskins game," she says. "It was a Monday night, "Monday Night Football," a big game. I was actually pushing, and Steve and the doctor were watching the game right down to the last second."

She remembers Ashley's birth. "I cut out the TV guide the day she was born," she says. "I thought that would be interesting." She gets Ashley's baby book. "Look—'Webster' was on, in first run. 'Mr. Belvedere.' 'Diff'rent Strokes.' 'Falcon Crest.' 'Fall Guy.' 'Miami Vice.' 'Dallas.' 'Dynasty.' 'Knight Rider.' God, can you believe it? Wow."

She remembers when Ashley and Steven were conceived. "I don't watch TV during sex, if you want to know," she says, laughing. "I'm capable of turning it off for five minutes."

But not much longer than that. Certainly not for an entire day, Bonnie says. In fact, she says, she can't remember the last time a day passed without her watching something. "It would be very hard for me to make it through a day," she says. "It's almost an automatic reflex at this point."

The same goes for the kids, who, until recently, were allowed to watch as much TV as they wanted. Then came the night when Steve awakened well after midnight—Bonnie says it was toward 4 a.m.—and found Ashley sitting up in bed watching the Cartoon Network. Now the rule for the kids is no TV after 11 p.m. on school nights, but other than that, anything goes. "The kids watch everything from 'Barney' to 'Beavis and Butthead,'" Bonnie says. There is no embarrassment in the way she says this, not even the slightest hint of discomfort. There is nothing other than brightness and happiness, for that is what she feels about TV.

"I love it. I love it. I can't help it. I love it," she says. "Why should I be ashamed of saying that?"

3 p.m. The 27-inch Hitachi is on. Time for "Maury Povich." So far this day, Bonnie has watched parts of "Regis & Kathie Lee," "Jerry Springer," "Broadcast House Live," "Geraldo," "American Journal," "Loving," "All My Children," "One Life to Live" and "John & Leeza," and now she is watching Povich talk from his New York studio to a woman named Happy Leuken who weighs more than 600 pounds and is in a Boston hospital weight-loss program. "God, it's so sad," Bonnie says, looking at Happy, who is spread over her hospital bed like raw dough, chatting away. Now she and the rest of the viewing audience see what Happy can't, that Happy's hero, exercise guru Richard Simmons, is standing outside the door to Happy's room, poised to dash in and surprise her with a bouquet of flowers. "Watch," Bonnie says. "He loves to cry. He'll come in. He'll cry. She'll cry. The audience will cry. I might cry too." In he runs. Happy looks surprised. The studio audience applauds. He embraces her. The studio audience cheers. He kisses her big neck. The cheers get louder. She kisses him on the lips. "There he goes," Bonnie says. "He's working up to it. He's starting to blink."

She keeps watching. "Did you know he was on 'General Hospital?'" she says. "It was years and years ago. He was running an exercise class. There was one character, a heavyset character, who was in the class, and I thought they were going to transform her into something beautiful, but I guess she wouldn't lose any weight because they dropped the story line."

Bonnie not only knows this about Richard Simmons, she knows everything about everybody. To her, TV is more than entertainment, it's a family of actors who share histories and links.

Earlier in the day, when she was showing off some school lunch boxes she has collected over the years, she got to the "Get Smart" lunch box and found herself thinking about Dick Gautier, who played Hymie the Robot, and Julie Newmar, who she thinks played opposite Gautier in one or two episodes and definitely played Catwoman in "Batman," as did Eartha Kitt and Lee Meriwether, who was also in "The Time Tunnel" and whose daughter was a model on "The Price Is Right." "Kyle. Kyle Meriwether," she said. "She used to substitute when one of the other girls, like Janice, couldn't make it." A little later, when the soap opera "Loving" came on, Bonnie said of an actress: "That woman is married to Michael Knight, who plays Tad in 'All My Children,' and she was married to David Hasselhoff, who played a character named Michael Knight in that show 'Knight Rider.' Isn't that weird?" Now, looking at Maury Povich, she says, "Can you believe Maury Povich is married to Connie Chung?"

So of course she knows about Richard Simmons, who is now sitting on Happy's bed, congratulating her on the 50 or so pounds she has lost, absently rubbing his thumb up and down her exposed lower leg. Over the years, there's been all kinds of research done on the effects of television on viewers, including, fairly recently, a study on the effects of the TV set itself, which showed that the bigger the screen is, the more involved a viewer feels. It also noted that people are buying bigger TVs all the time, something that Steve, who has looked at a 35-inch Mitsubishi, is considering for the basement. For now, though, the 27-inch Hitachi is the biggest screen in the house, which, as Simmons keeps rubbing Happy's leg, rubbing it, rubbing it, rubbing it, seems plenty big enough. "That kind of grosses me out," Bonnie says, and she leaves the house to pick up the kids from school.

The school is just down the street. In fact lots of things in Bonnie's life are just down the street: the toy store where she buys Ninja Turtle dolls for Steven and "Beverly Hills, 90210" dolls for Ashley; the pizza place that is always advertising two pizzas with up to five toppings each for $7.99; the grocery store where she buys Cap'n Crunch, and Flintstone Push Ups in Yabba Dabba Doo Orange, and all the other things the kids want after seeing them on TV. The school is closest of all, so close that when Bonnie has the windows open and the TV volume down she can hear the kids squealing and laughing on the playground.

She is back in a few minutes. The TV is still on, and as the car doors open and close, Happy Leuken is still chatting away, talking now about how the hospital allows conjugal visits. Now Happy's husband is talking about their own conjugal visit, about how exciting it was that, for the first time in years, his wife was able to lift her legs onto the bed by herself, and how much he's liking her body, really *really* liking it—and that's what Ashley and Steven come home to.

They run into the house, stop by the TV, listen. Some parents might worry about this, but not Bonnie. She simply goes into the kitchen and begins getting out snacks. If the kids have a question, she figures, they'll ask it, and if they don't they'll probably get bored and change the channel. Sure enough, Steven picks up the remote and changes to cartoons. He and Ashley sit at the kitchen table. Bonnie pours them sodas. She gets them Rice Krispies treats. She defrosts some Ball Park Fun Franks—"Michael Jordan endorses these," she says—and serves them with potato chips, which Ashley dips in ketchup. The kids keep watching. Eating. Watching. Then they run back to Ashley's room to watch cartoons on her TV, and Bonnie changes the channel to Sally Jessy Raphael, where the topic is "moms who share their daughters' boyfriends."

"Don't you love watching this?" she asks during a commercial. "Can you tell me you're not enjoying this? I love seeing how people live." Even the worst shows, she says, have value if for no other reason than she gets to see what other lives are like. "Lesbians. Homosexuals. Transvestites," she says, listing people she has met through TV. "Spiritualists. Occultists. Teenage runaways. Teenage drug addicts. Teenage alcoholics. Child stars who are in trouble. Politicians. Bald men. People with physical problems. Cancer survivors. Siamese twins." Now she will learn about moms and daughters who share the same boyfriends, and tomorrow, according to a commercial, she will meet "a man who had his private parts enlarged—on the next Maury."

She agrees it's a strange group of people. Nonetheless, she keeps watching as one of the moms on the show says she and her daughter run a phone sex line and pretend to have orgasms while actually eating donuts and painting their nails.

"You know, TV really does open up your eyes about how many people in the world there are, and how different they are," Bonnie says. "I mean without TV, who would exist? Just these middle-class people I see every day. I wouldn't know anything else was going on."

She watches to the end.

Then, with the kids, she watches "Full House."

Then they watch "Saved by the Bell."

Then she watches the local news.

Then Steve comes home and the entire family eats dinner and watches Dan Rather and Connie Chung.

Then, sometimes with Steve, sometimes with the kids, sometimes by herself, Bonnie watches "Jeopardy," "Mad About You," "Wings," "Seinfeld," "Frasier," "The Mary Tyler Moore Show," "The Dick Van Dyke Show," "The Tonight Show" and "The Late Show With David Letterman. Toward the end of "Letterman" she falls asleep, awakens long enough to turn off the TV and falls back asleep until 8:20 a.m., when she reaches woozily for the remote and starts all over again.

Not that TV is the only thing Bonnie does. "I don't just sit and watch TV," she says. "I'll clean while I watch. I'll read the paper. I'll work on crafts. I like making doll-house furniture with Ashley. I'll fold laundry." She also reads books, volunteers at the school several times a week and works on the yard.

But almost all of this involves TV, at least peripherally. The crafts are done in front of the Hitachi, and whenever she cleans the house she takes the portable Panasonic along to the rooms that don't have a TV. The book she is reading at the moment is by Howard Stern, and the book she's reading with Ashley, which came from a school book club, is about Stephanie, one of the characters on "Full House."

From time to time, her friends poke fun at her about all of this, but she doesn't mind. Sometimes Steve does too—"the walking TV Guide," he calls her—but she doesn't mind that either. They've been married nearly 10 years now, and even though she once turned down a free weekend in Jamaica with Steve in part because the hotel room didn't have a TV, he says of her, "If everybody was like Bonnie, the world would be a helluva lot better place."

"I'd definitely like to have a perfect family," she is saying one evening.

"She'd like to have the Beaver Cleaver family," says Steve.

"I would. You know I've had people tell me that Steven looks like Beaver," she says, adding that she always tells them, "Thank you."

"You do?" says Steve.

"Yeah," says Bonnie. "It's a compliment."

"Bonnie's life tends to be dictated by what she sees on television," Steve says, rolling his eyes.

"You think a lot of stuff on television is ridiculous," Bonnie says to him.

"Yeah, I do. For instance, talk shows. Why would anyone want to watch these shows all the time?"

"You learn a lot," Bonnie says.

"Like what?"

"About everything."

"Like enlarged sex organs?"

"Yeah," Bonnie says.

"It's like the National Enquirer," Steve says. "Pretty soon there'll be a show on two-headed cabbages."

"But you know what?" Bonnie says. "I always have something to talk about at parties."

"That's true," Steve says.

"For instance," Bonnie says, "do you know how many women the average man sleeps with in his lifetime?"

"What's your source for this?"

"Geraldo."

"The man who put skin from his butt on his head?"

"Seven. The answer is seven," Bonnie says. "Don't you find that interesting?"

So there is conversation in the Delmar house too, as well as family time, when everyone watches a show together. "We all watch 'Home Improvement,' " Bonnie says. "We all watch 'Seinfeld.' " They also watch "Married . . . With Children," a show that has been called sexist, misogynous, soft pornography and worse. But it also has about 20 million regular viewers, including the Delmars, who try to watch it every week.

This week, however, Bonnie announces she wants to watch a special on CBS, "a show that was on when I was little, and I want to watch it very much."

"What is it?" Steve asks.

" 'The Waltons Reunion,' " Bonnie says.

"Oh, God. I thought they died," Steve says.

"I *loved* that show," Bonnie says.

"But Mom . . . " Ashley says.

"Mom . . . " Steven says.

"If you want to sit quietly, you can sit here and watch," Bonnie says. "But be quiet. Mommy wants to watch this."

And so Ashley and Steven go off to watch "Married . . . With Children" by themselves.

"Channel Two Five," Bonnie calls to them as they run down the hallway, so they'll know what to press on the remote.

They go to Ashley's room, a room in which they spend a couple of hours every day, just them and whatever they want to watch. Steven has his own bedroom a few steps away, but because he doesn't yet have a TV he is in Ashley's room more than his own, usually falling asleep and spending the night in her queen-sized bed. The bed has a heart-shaped pillow on it with a picture of Zack, from "Saved by the Bell," along with the inscription "Sweet Dreams." "Ashley loves Zack," Steven says about that. "He's her love muffin." There is also a dresser drawer filled with videotapes of children's movies—"We probably have a hundred," Steven says—as well as a Super Nintendo game, a VCR, a videotape rewinder, a cable outlet and of course, the new 19-inch Zenith, on which Al Bundy, one of the "Married . . . With Children" characters, is saying to his wife, Peg, as their neighbor Marcy listens, "I'm telling you, Peg, I'm so hot, if Marcy wasn't here I'd take you on the floor right now."

To which Peg says, "Get out, Marcy."

To which Ashley and Steven, hearing every word of this exchange, say nothing. They just keep listening as Al and Peg get in an argument about sex, and Peg says to Al that TV is the "only thing you've turned on in 20 years," and Al says to a Peg, "Well, if you came with a remote and a mute button, I might turn you on too."

Wordlessly, Ashley and Steven watch the show until it ends and then run back out to Bonnie. "How was it?" she asks, and that's all she asks—not so much because she doesn't care what her children watch but because she and Steve don't see any reason to worry about it.

"You know why?" Bonnie says the next day, when the kids are in school and she is making them a surprise for when they get home, a concoction of cereal, pretzel sticks, butter and brown sugar. "Because I really trust my kids. If there's anything bad, they'll tell me about it."

She puts the pan in the oven. On the Hitachi, Maury Povich is about to show a videotape of a convenience store clerk being shot during a robbery. "It's so as graphic, you might not want to watch," he warns.

If TV's so bad, Bonnie says, why are her kids doing so well? If it's so bad, why is Steven so happy, and why is Ashley excelling in school? Just the other day, at a parent-teacher conference, Ashley's teacher called her a terrific student and concluded by saying to Bonnie, "You will be seeing great things from Ashley"—and to Bonnie's way of thinking TV is one of the reasons why. As she said after the conference, "I have friends who think it's terrible that I let my kids eat candy, that I let my kids watch TV, that I don't have a lot of rules, but I'll tell you what: Set my kids and their kids in the same room and see who's better behaved. They're really, really sweet kids. And a lot of these parents who try to do everything right—no TV, lots of reading, lots of rules, trying to do everything perfectly—let's face it. Their kids can be real pains in the neck."

The smell of melting butter and brown sugar fills the kitchen. On the Hitachi, the convenience store clerk is on the ground, bleeding, yelling for help.

"I think they're doing good," she says of her kids. "I don't think TV has corrupted them at all. Who knows, you know? We won't know for 15, 20 years. But right now, they seem okay."

3:20. Time to go pick them up.

Once, last year, when Ashley was in first grade and Steven was still at home, Bonnie decided to let Ashley walk to school, just as she had done when she was child growing up. That's when she lived in Wheaton, in a split-level, in a time when she and everyone else felt absolutely, unquestionably safe. Year after year she would walk to school, walk home at lunch time to eat a peanut butter sandwich and watch "The Donna Reed Show," walk back to school, walk back home. The first day Ashley did this, though, the very first day, she came home with a note alerting parents that a man in a van had been seen loitering near certain bus stops, taking photographs of little children. So that was the end of that. For some reason the world has changed, Bonnie says, although she doesn't think the reason is TV.

The kids run in and plop down at the kitchen table. At this time of day, the decision about what to watch on the Hitachi is theirs, and they switch to Daffy Duck as they dig into the cereal-and-pretzel mix.

Another day, they decide to stick with "Maury Povich." "That lady is so skinny you can see her bones," Ashley says as the camera focuses on a woman who is almost skeletal.

"That lady has an eating disorder," Bonnie says.

"What's an eating disorder?" Ashley asks.

And so, because of TV, Ashley and Steven learn about eating disorders.

Later, they watch "Beverly Hills, 90210," in which the plot revolves around a boy who forces himself on a girl.

And so Ashley and Steven learn about date rape.

Eleven o'clock comes. Time to turn off the Zenith, according to the new rule of house. The night before, Ashley cried when Bonnie did this—"It's not *fair*," she yelled—but this night, in the darkened room, Bonnie sits on the edge of the bed and traces her fingers over her children's faces in light, lazy circles, and soon their eyes are shut.

And so Ashley and Steven learn to go sleep without TV.

Thirty years ago: Bonnie is small. The TV is black and white. There is one TV in the entire house, no cable, no remote, no VCR, just a TV in the corner of the living room with an antenna on top and Red Skelton on the screen, and Bonnie is laughing so hard she is rolling around on the carpet. She is allowed to stay up as late as she wants, and watch as much TV as she wants, and there has never been a happier child.

Thirty years later: Ninety-eight percent of American households have TV, according to Nielsen Media Research; 66 percent have at least two TVs; 77 percent have at least one VCR; 62 percent get cable; and TV is under scrutiny by everyone from politicians who are proposing ratings for TV shows and video games, to academicians and sociologists who produce study after study about its dulling effects on developing brains, to a group of 20 worried women who come together one evening at an elementary school in Silver Spring, not far at all from the neighborhood where Bonnie grew up.

Bonnie isn't among them. Bonnie, in fact, would never go to such a meeting, and neither would Steve, who says of such things, "These people who get so rabid, they should be taking it easy." The women, though, feel exactly the opposite. Members of a loosely organized group called the Mothers Information Exchange, they have come to hear about the effects of TV from Amy Blank, who is with the Maryland Campaign for Kids' TV, an organization that monitors children's programming on area TV stations. All of the women have children. All see TV as something to be concerned about. Several of the women go so far as to say they feel truly afraid of what TV might be doing to their children, and what they hear over the next 90 minutes doesn't make them feel any less anxious.

"As we'll learn this evening, we have an incredible relationship with that box over there," says Blank, an edge of direness in her voice, motioning toward a TV that is hooked up to a VCR. "We can't remember when we didn't have it in our lives. That's really profound. We don't have people in our lives this long, some of us. We've had this thing in our lives all our lives. It's incredible."

She asks the women how many TV sets they own.

"We have five."

"We have four."

She asks how many hours a day the TVs are on.

"Six."

"Three-and-a-half."

"Oh God, this is embarrassing."

"Are you including Barney videos?"

"Do you have to include your husband?"

She turns on the TV and shows a videotape, in which the announcer says that "in a typical television season, the average adolescent views 14,000 instances of sexual contact or sexual innuendo in TV ads and programs."

She turns on an opaque projector and shows a chart that says: "Most children will see 8,000 murders and 10,000 acts of violence before they finish elementary school."

"They won't do any other thing, other than eat or sleep, that many times," she says. "That's what we're teaching them. It's okay to kill 8,000 people. It's okay to hurt or maim 10,000 people. It's okay. TV does it, so it's okay."

She shows another chart of what parents should do, a list that includes limiting the amount of time children watch TV.

"I think we're seeing tremendous effects on our kids and on our society," she says. "I mean, we're a broken society. We really are. We're struggling. There's so much incredible pain out there. And many of us just don't know where to hide, and don't know what to do."

"I want to show you one last thing," she says, and on the TV comes a clip from "The Simpsons," a show she detests so much that, earlier in the evening, when one of the mothers said she thought "The Simpsons" could be funny at times, she said, "Bart should be shot."

This clip, though, she likes. It is of Marge Simpson, the mother, writing a letter to a TV station.

"Dear Purveyors of Senseless Violence," she begins.

"I know this may sound silly at first, but I believe that the cartoons you show to our children are influencing their behavior in a negative way. Please try to tone down the psychotic violence in your otherwise fine programming.

"Yours truly, Marge Simpson."

"Dear Valued Viewer," the station manager writes back. "In regards to your specific comments about the show, our research indicates that one person cannot make a difference, no matter how big a screwball she is."

"I'll show them what one screwball can do!" Marge says to that. Blank snaps off the TV.

"Well," she says, "I don't think any of us are screwballs," and with those words and the vision of 8,000 murders in their minds, the women head off into the darkness of prime time.

Meanwhile, back in Gaithersburg, where the Delmars are watching TV, life is as untroubled as usual.

Thursday, 8 p.m. Time for "The Simpsons." But it's also time for "Mad About You," which Bonnie, Steve and Steven want to watch, so Ashley goes back to her room by herself.

She turns on her TV. She sits at her desk, takes out some paper and pastels and starts to draw. Five minutes go by. Ten minutes.

On the screen, a character named Krusty the Klown is reciting a limerick: "There once was a man from Enis . . . "

Now Bart is sticking the leg of a chair in the garbage disposal, turning it on and riding it like a bronco.

Now he is talking about how something "sucks."

But Ashley doesn't notice. She is completely involved in getting what she sees at the moment in her mind down on paper. She draws some white clouds in a blue sky. Now she draws a flower with blue petals and a pink center, and now she writes under the flower, "This is Steven."

She puts down her pastels, looks at what she has done, holds it up, explains the title:

"I think he looks like a flower."

She runs out to the kitchen table and climbs onto the lap of Bonnie, who is, of course, busy watching TV, but not so busy that she can't give her daughter a hug, and in this way another evening passes by. Around 9, Ashley lies on the floor in front of the TV and does her spelling homework. At 10, she is back on Bonnie's lap. "I love you," she says to Bonnie as 10:30 comes and goes. "Kiss me."

Sometimes, Bonnie says, she thinks her life could be a TV show, although she isn't quite sure what kind of show it would be.

She knows it wouldn't be a drama, she says, not yet anyway, because not enough dramatic things have happened, at least not directly to her. There have been friends with cancer, friends with bad marriages, friends who have suffered all kinds of traumas, but the only drama in her own life came a few years ago, when she found herself engaged in an escalating internal dialogue about mortality. For reasons she is still unsure of, she would make a dentist's appointment and wonder if she would live long enough to go, or she would buy milk and wonder if she would make it through the expiration date. Finally, in tears one day, she told her mother about this, and gradually the thoughts went away, bringing an end to a time that was certainly interesting, Bonnie says, and even momentarily disturbing, but hardly the stuff of TV.

So it wouldn't be a drama, she says, and neither would it be a talk show. There is, of course, plenty of talking in the Delmar house, but it's the talk of any family rather than of TV. The phone rings. It's Steve. "Hi," Bonnie says. "What time will you be home?" At the table, Steven takes a big bite out of a sandwich. "Chew carefully," Bonnie says. "Peanut butter can make you choke." There are, on occasion, longer, deeper, more philosophical discussions, but those too are internal dialogues that usually come into her mind late at night, when everyone is asleep except Bonnie, who's trying one more time to go to sleep without being lulled there by TV. "I think that's the reason I have to have the TV on," she says. "If it's not on, I think. I think, I think, I think." About: "Everything. I know this sounds weird, but I think about ways the economy could be solved. Really. I think about NAFTA. I think about how my life could be better. I think about TV. It's an intense thing. I won't think about one solution, I'll think about 20. I get into all these ideas,

and then I think I'll write a letter to Bill Clinton, or to Dear Abby, or someone else. And then . . . then I'll think no one wants to hear what I'm thinking, so I'll just turn the TV on, and eventually I'll drift off.

"That's the thing about TV," she says. "You don't have to think."

So: not a drama, not a talk show.

Obviously, then, it would have to be a situation comedy, which Bonnie says is fine with her because, after all, "isn't everybody's life a sitcom kind of life?"

True enough, a lot of what goes on at the Delmars' seems exactly that. Days almost always begin brightly and end with hugs, and in between there's no telling what exactly will happen.

Like the time Bonnie went out to mow the lawn, got on the rider mower, started picturing Eddie Albert "bouncing on that tractor" and began singing the theme song to "Green Acres." Not once did she sing it, not twice, but over and over, for more than an hour, until she realized the kid across the street was looking at her like she was from another planet. Which is why whenever she has mowed the lawn since, she has hummed.

Or how about the time she was actually on TV? It was right after Ashley was born, and she had to make a fast trip to the grocery store. She grabbed a sweat shirt out of the dryer, hurried through the store with her baby and was in line to pay, thinking how big and unattractive she must look, when she noticed the checkout guy kind of smiling at her. How nice, she thought, suddenly feeling better about herself. "And then I came home and realized I had a pair of underwear and a sock stuck to my back," she says. "Static cling. I had walked through the whole store that way. Well, okay, I can handle that. But the next week one of the local TV stations had some cameras in the store, and they asked if they could talk to me and film me walking with my baby, and I said sure, and I'll bet all the Giant people were watching that night, and the checkout guy said, 'Hey! That's the lady who had the underwear stuck to her back!' "

So: a situation comedy.

" 'Life With the Delmars,' " Bonnie says it could be called, and it would have four characters:

The dad.

"He'd be hard-working," she says. "He'd be a character who's in and out, one of those characters where you don't see too much of him, but funny. And fun."

The son.

"Kindergarten student. Enthusiastic. Mischievous. Rambunctious."

The daughter.

"Definitely precocious. She'd act like a teenager, a teenager wannabe. Stubborn. Funny."

And the mom.

"Let's see," she says. "Who am I?"

She thinks. Thinks some more. Can't come up with a description, so she thinks instead about who might watch such a show.

"*I'd* watch it," she says.

THE CONTEXT OF TELEVISION VIOLENCE

Ellen A. Wartella

Ellen A. Wartella is Dean of the College of Communication and Walter Cronkite Regents Chair in Communication at University of Texas at Austin.

I am delighted to be here this evening and to be invited to make the second Carroll Arnold lecture. It is an honor to follow David Zarefsky who last year talked about the state of public discourse. This year I want to examine television violence.

The debate about media violence has followed the history of media in this century as well as the history of our field. I wish to acknowledge my colleagues on the National Television Violence Study from whom I have learned much and with whom I am privileged to work: at Texas, Wayne Danielson, Nick Lasorsa and Chuck Whitney; at UC-Santa Barbara: Ed Donnerstein, Joel Federman, Dale Kunkel, Dan Linz, Jim Potter and Barbara Wilson; at Wisconsin-Madison: Joanne Cantor and at North Carolina: Jane Brown and Frank Biocca. In addition there are more than two dozen graduate students around the country with whom we have worked. This is truly a collaborative project and one which resides in a particular historical context. Tonight I take as my theme just this notion of "context" for our understanding of television violence.

In these remarks the notion of "context" of violence has multiple meanings: I want to talk about the social and cultural context for the current round of criticism and inquiry into television violence. Second, the National Television Violence Study monitoring of television is premised on the notion that not all television violence is the same—that the context of a violent act or portrayal is crucial to distinguishing among portrayals—and so I will engage in a discussion of how the context of violence varies across the television landscape. Finally, I will address the particular political and public policy context within which this project is situated and the upcoming policy decisions concerning potential remedies for television violence. That context matters and how it matters is the overarching theme I want to talk about.

Let me say at the outset that I consider myself to be a non-violent person. I am not particularly radical in that belief, but I prefer non-violence to violence by the same token that I prefer reasonableness to irrationality, or peace to war, or life to death. I concede that there are times at which violence may be necessary, but I do not find violence preferable to non-violence. As a critic of violence on television, I am not absolutely opposed to showing violence in all instances. That is far too narrowing, for some televised depic-

> "The debate about media violence has followed the history of media . . . as well as the history of our field."

 From *Carroll C. Arnold Distinguished Lecture*, November 23, 1996, pp. 1-11. © 1996 by Allyn & Bacon. Reprinted by permission.

"That germinal violence leading to the birth of our nation provides the benchmark against which we may contrast other violence in American history . . . ."

tions of violence do have educational or social value. The crux of my concerns is not so much with the fact of violence, always, but with the quality of violence as depicted on television today. However, because I am also a firm believer in free speech and the First Amendment, I am apt to argue for more responsibility from industry, and for public and government expression of concern in order to hold the industry to account.

Let me try to unfold an analysis of the state of violence on television in America, and its interplay with real violence in our world. In short, I want to set the stage on which television is projected. I will say this again and again: context is important. The context in which violence takes place, or is viewed, matters dearly.

As Americans, we live in a violent society. We have always lived in a violent society. Indeed, America celebrates the outcome of a democratic revolution, which like all revolutions, was at least for a time inseparable from a certain accepted violence. To have stood the ground at the bridge in Concord as a Minuteman and fired the shot heard round the world was to be cast into history as a hero. That germinal violence leading to the birth of our nation provides the benchmark against which we may contrast other violence in American history and differentiate between degrees of violence and American morality.

All violence is not the same. Any violent episode or era will reveal a complex set of causes, effects, means and ends buried within it. My entire generation, for example, was indelibly shaped by the violence of the 1960s. We witnessed JFK and RFK and MLK and Malcolm

X all gunned down while images of violence in the streets of Newark, Watts, Chicago, Detroit and elsewhere played into our view of the world, never to recede from it. The Vietnam war was our living room war.

In trying to sort out human behavior, the significance of surrounding, or contextual, factors is unavoidable. Circumstances surrounding acts of violence deserve extra attention. Moral, legal, religious and social issues, and sometimes mitigating facts, are bound within the specific context in which human beings act under life's real terms. This is evident across contemporary American experience. Contextual concerns framed the trial of Lt. Calley and his role in the My Lai Massacre, the beating of Rodney King by officers of the LAPD (and the trial and riots which followed), or the prosecution of a wife who kills her abusive husband. A framework, part reality and part morality, surrounds each picture of violence extracted from the real world. In any event, these frames are nearly always essential for the pictures themselves to be comprehensible.

What startles us completely about some violence is its entirely extraneous nature: the shooting spree of a Charles Whitman atop the University of Texas bell tower, or the random mayhem in a Scottish schoolroom. The utterly unreal nature of such extreme violence leaves us gasping and groping. It leaves us with a fear, for it is a violence that fits no frame, no intelligible explanation.

In the past 15 or so years, a remarkably cavalier, vicious, wanton and senseless pattern of violence entered society and the American psyche. Drive-by shootings and gangbanger crimes, fueled by a trade in handguns and crack cocaine, ushered in fears of an epidemic of violence we may not fully comprehend. The violence panic of this time, unlike that of the 1960s, seems much more to surround children and youth, as both the victims and the perpetrators of violence.

When hip-hop artist Tupac Shakur was shot to death in Las Vegas in Fall, 1996, sadly enough, many people weren't surprised. After all, he was a successful, pure product of a deadly culture. Reverend Jesse Jackson made this comment: "Sometimes the lure of violent culture is so magnetic that even when one overcomes it with material success, it continues to call. He couldn't break the cycle." Shakur died as he lived, walking the walk, talking the talk, of violence glamorized.

That cycle of violence has helped us become the most violent industrialized nation on the earth. A lot of numbers gird that conclusion. But the numbers that tell the most tragic story concern children and adolescents:

• Among young people in the age group from 15-24 years old, homicide is the second leading cause of death and for African American youth murder is number one.

• Adolescents account for 24 percent of all violent crimes leading to arrest. The rate has increased over time for those in the 12-19 year old age group, while it is down in the 35 and older age group.

• Every 5 minutes a child is arrested in America for committing a violent crime; gun related violence takes the life of an American child every three hours.

• A child growing up in Washington DC or Chicago is 15 times more likely to be murdered than a child in Northern Ireland.

What could account for this? Most of us generally accept the notion that violent behavior is a complex, multivariable problem, formed of many influences. Racism, poverty, drug abuse, child abuse, alcoholism, illiteracy, gangs, guns, mental illness, a decline in family cohesion, a lack of deterrents, the failure of positive role models . . . all interact to affect antisocial behavior. As Rowell Huesmann has argued: aggression is a syndrome, an enduring pattern of behavior that can persist through childhood into adulthood.

In simple terms, violence may be less mysterious than some think. I only suggest this rhetorically, for of course, I have few doubts that violence is nothing if not insidious and intractable in many ways. But consider the context not of one act of violence, but of the persistent fact of violence.

Violence pays. Only violence pays. In those three words Frantz Fanon, psychiatrist, political theorist and revolutionary, summarizes a lesson from history all too familiar to oppressed classes. The simple utterance, violence pays, is a lesson straight from life itself: we live in a world shaped by the exercise of power where violence itself is the most extreme form of power. In Fanon's analysis, historical colonialism informs the oppressed that the oppressor's violence is, if not justifiable, then at least lucrative, as a means to gain and hold power. Fanon's "wretched of the earth" dream of the riches to be gotten by revolution, a counter force to the experience of colonial oppression.

> " 'Sometimes the lure of violent culture is so magnetic that even when one overcomes it with material success, it continues to call.' "

> " . . . violence has helped make American entertainment products the second largest export of this nation."

Violence pays. It certainly does—at the box office, for Hollywood and New York movies and television. Moreover, violence has helped make American entertainment products the second largest export of this nation. Violence is a staple, in particular, of movies that attract adolescent males. PG-13 and R-rated movies serve to attract such boys like forbidden fruit, with their conflation of action-adventure-guns-sex and excessive, explicit graphic violence wielded by powerful heroes. This violence resides in a context different from portrayals of violence as a last ditch effort to escape an impending harm.

Violence in the media may not be the most important contributor to violence in the real world but it is surely one of the multiple, overlapping causes. Social scientists first began studying media violence in the 1920s, and evidence of a causal relationship between media violence and real violence has been accumulating for at least 40 years. The Centers for Disease Control, the National Academy of Science, the American Psychological Association, the American Medical Association—all have examined violence in our society and traced these connections. Today, we find wide consensus among the experts that, of all the factors contributing to violence in our society, violence on television may be the easiest to control, the most tractable.

The National Television Violence Study, with which I'm associated, is the most comprehensive scientific assessment yet conducted of the context of televised violence. As an indication of the scope of the study, in its first year of monitoring television in the 1994-95 season, we analyzed about 2500 hours of television programming, including more than 2700 programs; we sampled television programs across 23 cable channels during the TV season. This is the largest, most representative sample of television ever examined using scientific content analysis techniques.

We began with two goals:

One, to identify the contextual features associated with violent depictions on television.

Two, to analyze the television environment in-depth in order to report on the nature and extent of violent depictions. We focused, in particular, on the relative presence of the most problematic portrayals.

Why contextualize TV violence? Because we understand that all violence is complex. The problem isn't round like an orb, it isn't monolithic; an act of violence is one tile in a mosaic.

Violence on television is presented in many different forms and settings. In some cases, heroes may be rewarded for acting violently as when the central authority-figure on a police show shoots a murderer, while in other cases, violent characters may go unpunished. Violence may be depicted without much attention to the pain and suffering (both immediate and long-term) for victims and their families; a gunshot wound, for example, may be shown in close-up without elaborating on the agony, physical pain, or often debilitating effects of gunshot wounds when people survive them. Or, conversely they may show that violence causes pain and suffering for the victim, the victim's family, and the community. Anti-violence themes may be embedded in the overall narrative of a program that contains violent acts as a part of the message. Or, we may see multiple acts of violence depicted in such graphic ways as to suggest that shooting to kill is another of life's mundane aspects, a banality, to be approached with indifference or even humor. In short, violence on television is contextualized in so many different ways that we believed the time had come for a thorough examination of these contexts in which depictions of violence are presented.

First, we had to define violence. Violence is defined in our study as any overt depiction of the use of physical force—or credible threat of physical force—intended to physically harm an animate being or group. Violence also includes certain depictions of physically harmful consequences suffered by an animate being or group as a result of unseen violent force. It is important to note that with this definition we kept our focus on acute physical aggression directed against living beings. I believe this is a conservative definition of violence. I believe we could have widened it to focus on psychological aggression or acts of nature as some other studies have done.

The contextual factors we examine in portrayals of television violence are derived from the previous effects research literature. These context variables include pain/harm cues, the nature of rewards and punishments, graphicness of portrayals, the presence of guns and weapons, the attractiveness of the perpetrators and targets, the presence of humor, and the degree to which violence is fantasized or realistic. These characteristics of violent portrayals have all been found to differentially influence the effects of such images on viewers, particularly children.

When looking at the entire body of existing effects research, as we did, you find three major effects of televised violence 1) viewers learn the aggressive attitudes and behaviors depicted in the programs they see (known as the learning effect); 2) prolonged viewing of media violence can lead to emotional desensitization toward real violence and real victims, which may result in callous attitudes and a decreased likelihood that desensitized individuals will take action to help victims when real violence occurs (the desensitization effect); and 3) viewing violence may increase our fear of being victimized, leading toward self-protective behavior and an increased mistrust of others (the fear effect).

This past February we released our report of the 1994-95 television season. We found violence on TV does indeed vary by context.

• Violence is a predominant theme on television. However, some genres, police shows, tabloid news shows and movies, for instance, are more violent then others. Other reality-based shows and comedies are not so violent. While more than half of all the programs we studied contained at least some violence, one-third contained more than nine violent interactions and each violent interaction may itself consist of numerous individually violent acts.

• In most cases the perpetrator engages in repeated violence. More than half of the violence (58 percent), is committed by characters who engage not in isolated acts of violence but in a pattern of repeated aggression.

• Warnings about violence on TV are almost nonexistent. Among the programs that contain violence in the 1994-95 season, only 15 percent are preceded by any sort of advisory

" . . . we may see multiple acts of violence depicted in such graphic ways as to suggest that shooting to kill is another of life's mundane aspects . . . . "

> " . . . prolonged viewing of media violence can lead to emotional desensitization toward real violence and real victims . . . . "

or content code. Most of these are placed on movies. Other genres, including children's programs with substantial amounts of problematic violence, rarely include a warning label.

• Television violence often involves the use of a gun. In one quarter of violent interactions a gun is used and presentation of visual cues such as the image of a weapon tend to activate aggressive thought in viewers. These later serve to facilitate aggression or act as cognitive filters to influence the interpretation of neutral events as possibly threatening or aggressive.

• On television, perpetrators go unpunished. In about three quarters of all violent scenes, the perpetrators get away with what they've done. One of the clearest findings of this study is that the world of television is not only violent—it also consistently sanctions its violence. The message: violence pays. A very high proportion of violent scenes lack any form of punishment for the perpetrators. This is troubling, and our concern is exacerbated by the finding that this pattern is consistent across all channel types and all genres.

• The consequences of violence are often not realistically portrayed. Less than half of television's violent interactions show the victims experiencing any signs of pain. Only about one in six programs depict any long-term negative consequences such as physical suffering (limping, the wearing of bandages, or other evidence of a prolonged effect), or financial or emotional harm.

• Violence is often presented as humorous. More than a third of all violent scenes involve a humorous context, trivializing or undermining

the seriousness with which violence ought to be regarded.

• Violent programs rarely employ a strong anti-violence theme. With as much violence as there is on television, you might think that a reasonable portion of it would stress an anti-violence message. Only 4 percent of all violent programs do so. This represents a huge missed opportunity for television to counter-balance the more common depictions that show violence as attractive, effective, and socially acceptable.

Those are our findings from the 1994-95 television season which we released in February of this year. We are currently analyzing the 1995-96 season and will release new findings in winter 1997.

The February report—by coincidence—was released the day before President Clinton signed into law the 1996 Telecommunications Act. Indeed he mentioned our findings at the bill signing to underscore the V-Chip clause of the 1996 Act.

That raises yet another set of contextual concerns. The entire monitoring project we are conducting is situated within a particular political and historical context: monitors were urged on the broadcast and cable television industries in 1994 by Congress and the President. That was an extraordinary step in a series of government policy initiatives regarding television violence that began in 1990 and will continue to unfold over the next few months. Let me trace some of those steps:

The 1990 Children's Television Act (the first piece of federal legislation regarding children's television in our nation's history) asked the major broadcast networks to find a way to voluntarily limit the amount of violence on television, and to do so by

1993. Essentially the law put aside anti-trust rules to allow the networks to deliberate.

By summer of 1993, it became clear that ABC, NBC, CBS and Fox had not met—even once to discuss the issue. Senator Paul Simon of Illinois then held hearings in LA and in Washington later that fall during which he castigated the industry for not voluntarily reducing violence. Most remarkably, the hearings gave voice to social science researchers who had concluded that television violence is a social problem, if not a public health problem, and that the television industry has a responsibility to do something about it. The Clinton Administration supported our call for self-regulation by the industry.

During the summer of 1994, both the cable television industry and the broadcast networks hired independent monitors to provide an annual assessment of violence on television for the American people. The National Cable Television Association hired our group, the NTVS, and Jeff Cole of UCLA was hired by the four major broadcast networks. Both Cole's report (which is released annually in the fall) and our report (released later in the winter) are thus the result of government pressure on the industry.

However, public pressure did not let up after monitors were hired. Throughout 1994 and 1995, bipartisan criticism of media violence was picking up steam: President Clinton's 1995 State of the Union address deplored media violence and then Senator Robert Dole criticized media violence later that spring when announcing his candidacy for president. And the recurring public and government criticism of television violence,

slasher films, rap music and violent videos, turned up at least weekly, if not more often, in the press and on Capitol Hill. Clearly, the industry's hiring of independent monitors alone was not enough to quell public concern over media violence, violence bashing has become a way for political liberals to insert themselves into the family values argument that had been the province of the political and religious right.

During that period, Congress was developing the landmark Telecommunications Act that would outline the nature of government regulation in the new landscape of digital communications. By the time the Act passed and became law, on February 7, 1996, it contained the requirement that all television receivers made after February 1998 must contain a V-chip or "violence-chip"—a blocking device that parent's can use to filter out programs with objectionable violence, language or sexuality. However, in order to activate the blocking device, programs must be rated by some system that will help parents identify which programs contain objectionable features.

At the end of February, President Clinton held a summit with television industry executives who agreed to develop this ratings system to be used in conjunction with the V-chip. Jack Valenti, head of the MPAA, along with Eddie Fritts of the National Association of Broadcasters and Decker Angstrom of the National Cable Television Association are heading the industry ratings group.

This group should be reporting, within the next month or so, their suggestion for a ratings system, a system that will then be reviewed by the FCC and most likely put into

"... the hearings gave voice to social science researchers who had concluded that television violence is a social problem, if not a public health problem, and that the television industry has a responsibility to do something about it."

"... the chip offers a technological fix—a limited fix— to a large and complicated human, moral, and social problem."

effect within the next year, before the V-chip comes on line.

The V-chip and the ratings system it requires, are coming under considerable scrutiny. No one is quite sure how the whole system will work. What shows will and won't be rated (the industry has said it will not rate news or sports)? Will the ratings system be a prescriptive, age related system like the film industry's G, PG, PG-13 and R ratings? Or will it be a more descriptive system that describes the actual content on the air (e.g. no violence, mild violence, graphic violence)? Public advocacy groups prefer the latter, but Mr. Valenti and the industry and their advertisers prefer the less-descriptive, letter-coded ratings. Who will rate the shows? Each network, some industry wide group, or outside raters?

Those are questions of implementation, there are also many questions about the effects of this system. Will the V-chip actually be used by parents to block objectionable programs for children? Or will it just sit there unused, like the flashing clocks no one sets on so many VCRs? Will the existence of such a rating system affect advertiser support for the production of more daring, adult television programs that risk receiving negative ratings? Or will the ratings system have a boomerang effect and lead to even more graphic and explicit violence on some television shows just because the individual broadcaster no longer has to exercise social responsibility? And will the presence of a V-chip and ratings system excuse the industry from providing more advisories and anti-violent messages on violent programs?

I have no doubt that the next few months and even years will see more not less public discussion of television violence and how our society can and should deal with it. It is within this context that the television monitoring project was initiated and will continue. As communication researchers, we will have great opportunity to provide evidence regarding the ways in which programming will be affected and how the V-chip and ratings system will be used by families. Indeed, there is considerable research to be done as a consequence of the enactment of public policies regarding television violence.

But, will this technological fix, the V-chip, put to rest the public's concern about television violence? Will it affect, at all, the nature of violence in American life? These are important questions about which I can only speculate, but which are the real and important business of moments like this. So let me speculate:.

First, I predict that the V-chip won't settle the debate, and may only marginally alter the television landscape. Why? Because the chip offers a technological fix—a limited fix— to a large and complicated human, moral, and social problem. Hollywood movies didn't become less violent after a ratings system was installed. It's clear that parents want a more helpful and descriptive warning label on violent television than a simple age-based code.

At the same time, parents and children will need more than a television blocking device and a code to navigate the television landscape. I predict that educators and parents will increase the demand for more information and education about media, so that we'll be able to use the chip intelligently and know what we're filtering out or in. We have an appalling lack of media education in this country; indeed the United States is the only English-speaking nation in the world without media education in its public schools. Media education is desperately needed in order to develop more literate audiences. And a literate viewership, I suggest, is necessary for any technological fixes to be effective.

Second, I believe that violence in the media won't abate until the industry producing these portrayals A) understands the effects of media violence, B) admits that what it produces does contribute to real violence, and C) demonstrates greater responsibility by moderating the violent nature of its programming. Once a ratings system is in place, the television industry cannot walk away from the debate. They will have to constantly examine, question and be willing to explain the sort of violence being portrayed. If not all violence is the same, as we've shown, and some portrayals are more harmful than others, then producers, writers, directors and programmers have a responsibility, I believe, to try to show violence in the least harmful manner. But this will require the industry to move beyond the position that violence on TV does no real harm, that it does not contribute to real world violence. We know it does.

Third, I predict there will be increasing opportunities for communications researchers to work with the industry, to share our knowledge and help create less harmful programming. We can't expunge violence altogether from dramatic and reality-based TV, since violence is, after all, a very true dimension of human existence. But we can suggest ways in which television can be socially responsible in portraying the realities of violence. I predict—I hope—we will have many chances to do that.

In conclusion, let me return to the theme of my remarks tonight and see if I can't extract at least a few hard-gained kernels of optimism from this whole troubling business. This lecture is but a window in the context of ongoing work. The point of our research isn't to condemn; but to discover and learn, and ideally to teach. Television has value. Television proves its value by the many good programs produced every year.

Television shows need not be sanitized or insipid, they need not be all smiley-faced or falsely optimistic about the worlds they depict. All we should hope for is that they be more honest, truthful, realistic, and sensitive to the very impressionable young minds upon whom television has such a great effect. Which is to say, I do hope they will become less sensational and stop glamorizing violence, stop making it seem as if violence is an ordinary and acceptable human response to a difficult world.

At the very least, we need television which elevates and celebrates a more refined sense of justice—justice based on reason instead of revenge, on laws instead of guns, on deliberation instead of impulse, and finally, which holds perpetrators of violence accountable for their actions. Let me add my voice to those calling upon the television industry to be accountable for its actions—to own-up to the role it has played in lowering the threshold for real violence in our society.

Let us imagine a television industry so responsible that its dramatic depictions of violence serve to repel viewers from ever committing violence, rather then seducing them into acting on dangerous fantasies, or leaving them with over-heightened anxieties and fears. Let us imagine television working harder to portray violence, suffering or inhumanity accurately in context, to put it in proper historical or social perspective. Some portrayals of violence can be so powerful, so hideous, but so moving, that they stop us and make us think deeply about ourselves as a people. The movie "Schindler's List" comes to mind. I would rather that movie actors spill stage blood than leave any new generation ignorant of the devastation of true violent epochs and run the risk of reliving history.

I return to Fanon's lesson: violence pays. We must devalue violence and teach our children that no, indeed, it does not pay. We must devalue it and teach them that violence is not a valid currency for ordinary exchange; it doesn't get us where we need to go; it is a last resort, only a means of mere survival, and even then, it has grave consequences.

The power of television in modern life is clear. To quote Edward R. Murrow: "This instrument can teach. It can illuminate. Yes, and it can even inspire. But it can do so only to the extent that humans are determined to use it to those ends. Otherwise, it is merely wires and lights in a box."

I disagree—television also holds the power to harm, to instill fear, and to render us callous to suffering. It can bring ugliness into the world.

We are at a moment in which the television industry and the future members of that industry we educate can influence the moral climate of television production. This is the context of today's debate and context matters.

What an honor this has been, I thank you very much.

ANYTHING GOES:

Moral Bankruptcy of Television and Hollywood

One network executive sums it up: "Little by little, everybody has gotten a little less afraid of the old taboos. . . . It seems we're able to go a lot further than we have, even considering the conservative swing the country has taken."

by Joe McNamara

IN 1961, Newton N. Minow, chairman of the Federal Communications Commission, challenged executives of the television industry "to sit down in front of your television set when your station goes on the air and stay there without a book, magazine, newspaper, profit-and-loss sheet or rating book to distract you—and keep your eyes glued to that set until the station signs off. I can assure you that you will observe a vast wasteland. . . .

"Is there one person in this room who claims that broadcasting can't do better? Your trust accounting with your beneficiaries is overdue."

More than three decades later, an intelligent teenage viewer laughs uncontrollably as a dog gnaws on a brain growing outside the head of a young man, who then embraces a number of women dressed in white, spattering them with blood. When asked why he's laughing, the viewer—my son—replies, "Because it's funny."

Jerry Seinfeld claims that dropping candy into an incision in an operating room after saying, "All right, just let me finish my coffee and we'll go watch them slice this fat bastard up," was a turning point on "Seinfeld" because, "Once that happened, it was like the horses were out of the barn. We thought, if we can get away with *this* . . ." (emphasis his). The series' acme, according to critic Jay McInerney (who called the episode "brilliant"), involved doing an entire show about masturbation without ever referring to it by

---

Dr. McNamara is executive director of marketing communications, Hillsdale (Mich.) College.

name as "four friends compete to see who can remain 'master of [their] domain' the longest."

In a bowling alley, Homer Simpson's decapitated head rolls slowly down the lane towards pins impaled with spikes, driving one of them into the skull, which pops open to reveal a note: "I owe you one brain. Signed, God." Bart Simpson's grace before meals runs, "Hey, God, we did all this ourselves, so thanks for nothing." Lisa Simpson mockingly describes prayer as "the last refuge of the scoundrel."

To all of these incidents, and countless others, my 12-year-old son, with the nodding agreement of his three brothers, proclaims: "Don't worry, Dad, none of that is real; it's just television."

Yet, it is real, very real, and much, much more than "just television." For those in their early teens, it is seeing 15,000 sexual acts or innuendoes and a total of 33,000 murders and 200,000 acts of random violence in a single year, according to the American Family Association.

While more than 3,000 studies have documented the inexorable nexus between TV violence and socially aggressive behavior, no one has described the relationship between humor and disappearing moral standards, though the behavioral keys involved are identical. According to psychologists, these are observational learning (attention, retention, motivation, and potential reproduction) and the selection of a model one chooses to imitate.

Studies conducted in Oak Park, Mich., in

1977 and followed up in 1992 showed that "women who watched violent television shows as children in the 1970s are more physically aggressive and more capable of committing criminal acts today." The women who scored at the top of categories "watched aggressive female heroines in the media as children and continued to do so as adults." These results "confirmed some of our worst fears," indicates L. Rowell Huesman, a psychology professor and researcher in the Aggression Research Group at the University of Michigan Institute for Social Research, Ann Arbor.

Another study by the same institute documented the rise of and rationale for playground bullies. After studying the viewing habits of a group of children for 30 years, the researchers concluded that TV violence desensitizes the very young and noted that television "played a larger role in children's aggression than poverty, race, or parental behavior."

Demeaning an important American art form may be bad enough, but abusing children to make a profit at the same time defies comprehension. Syndicated columnist Suzanne Fields noted that "Our children face an unusual enemy of childhood today, grownups who conduct a carpet bombing of information and images against kids who simply don't have the maturity to understand what they see and hear." Understand it they may not, but enjoy it they do, and remarkably few major critics—with the exception of Diane and Michael Medved; William Bennett; columnists Bob Herbert and Kirk Nicewong-

From *USA Today Magazine*, January 1998, pp. 62-64. © 1998 by the Society for the Advancement of Education. Reprinted by permission.

er; and Harvard University's Alvin F. Pouissant—will say a word.

Humor has become a form of psychological violence, but Hollywood's lethal silence among the writers, producers, studios, and critics who lack the courage to face the truth and do what is right remains virtually intact. There are, after all, millions of dollars to be made in exploiting the vulnerabilities of children whose values are not yet formed and who are looking for leadership and role models.

In the case of situation comedies, their laughter directed towards premarital or extramarital sex constitutes positive reinforcement with documentable—some would say detestably corrosive—consequences. Apparently, the worst mistake young men or women can make involves choosing abstinence when everything around them reflects the sexual obsession that supposedly typifies life in America.

"With sex-starved Amandas and out-of-the-closet 'Friends' crowding early prime time, would homespun TV characters stand a chance today?," asks *TV Guide*, already knowing the answer. "Friends" has the concept of the traditional family squarely and effectively in its sights. "Living Single" offers racial and ethnic stereotypes that might even shock Archie Bunker, as well as the thousands who have invested their lives in something called the civil rights movement. The characters on "Melrose Place," as someone once said of an oft-married Hollywood figure, "could find sex in the crotch of a tree." "Melrose Place" producer Frank South, choosing an unfortunate metaphor for his show's promotion of homosexuality, says, "We'll keep pushing." Do the songs of fools now outweigh the rebukes of the wise? Check out "sweeps" months and find out.

In fact, Hollywood's advocacy of gays and lesbians exposes a glaring double standard. The author of *The Celluloid Closet* proudly boasts that "Hollywood . . . taught straight people what to think about gay people and gay people what to think about themselves. No one escaped its influence:" United Features Syndicate critic Kirk Nicewonger notes, "Aren't many of those who would nod solemnly in agreement with these sentiments the same people who scoff at concerns about movie violence influencing real-life behavior?" Humor influences as well and perhaps more effectively because it is not perceived as a form of violence or even as attempted influence.

By 1980, the out-of-wedlock birth rate reached a total of 18% of annual births and then jumped to slightly over 30% by 1992. While the percentages are frightening enough, the real numbers are numbing: in 1992, 1,224,876 babies were born to single women, and white females between the ages of 20 and 30 constitute the fastest-growing group. At this rate, by 2015, 50% of all chil-

dren born will be born out of wedlock. No "Murphy Brown" this, but the reflection of a generally acidic attitude toward the traditional views of marriage and morality.

Situation comedies can not be singled out as the sole cause of such a decline, but the attitudes they spawn and constantly reinforce contribute directly to the problem. Researcher Robert Maginnis reports that, when individuals between the ages of 18 and 30 were "asked to assess the degree to which today's movies, television, and music lyrics encourage teenage sex," 63% said "a great deal" or "quite a lot."

Raunchily destructive comic attitudes toward traditional virtues and families did not assume center stage overnight. For centuries, laughter was seen as a method of teaching, following French playwright Moliere's belief that the comic sought "to correct through amusement." Philosopher Jean-Jacques Rousseau, according to author J.Y.T. Grieg, thought that "comedy performed no useful social function even at its best, and might at its worst lead directly to corruption and immorality."

Yet, Grieg also mentions, and partially endorses, Max Eastman's *The Sense of Humor.* Eastman sees humor as an instinct and claims that there is "a certain range of feelings which can be enjoyed playfully, just as certain wave-lengths can be perceived as light, and if you pass beyond this laugh spectrum at either end the humor disappears." He goes on to assert that "Aggression jokes derive their peculiar delightfulness from the fact that we have cruel impulses which we *cannot* unleash in serious life, cultural standards being here at variance with our instincts, and they sneak forth and take a drink of satisfaction when we play." Moreover, "Jests often liberate the surging wishes prisoned in us. They remove the lid of our culture, and let us be, in fun at least and for a second, animals."

Traditional cultural standards do supply the guidelines that make civilized life possible and safe, sometimes even despite our own instincts. However, when Eastman sees the function of comedy as some sort of relief valve which can "remove the lid of our culture" and allow us to be animals "in fun at least and for a second," he has put his finger on the dilemma. The second has been stretched into minutes, to half-hour shows, to entire years of television production, and, for some, to a way of life.

Humor as a basically harmless interchange between equals has given way to brutal vulgarizations with no end in sight. As Rabbi Daniel Lapin of Toward Tradition once explained to me, if a British barrister falls down once, it may be funny. Repeated falls, though, must contain increasingly bizarre elements to keep the audience "entertained." The same may be said for American humor and its attendant profanity and vulgarity, set on a deliberately downward course by writers, directors, ex-

ecutives, and actors. The real matter here is money, and some in the entertainment industry, driven by fear of failure, will do anything, even—or perhaps especially—to vulnerable children to boost the bottom line.

Screenwriter John Gregory Dunne's lunch with a Hollywood producer took an odd turn when the producer pretended to grab a small animal from under the table and asked Dunne if he saw "the monster" and recognized it. Stunned, Dunne replied that he neither could see nor name the imaginary animal, and the producer exclaimed, "It's *our money.*" Dunne describes the resultant six years, four contracts, and 27 drafts of one movie script in his book, *Monster: Living Off the Big Screen.* The script concerned the tortured life of TV newswoman Jessica Savitch, up to her drowning in the muck of the Delaware Canal. The finished version, six years later, "though it bore absolutely no resemblance to the raw material from which it had been wrenched, did what [the Disney studio] wanted it to do: It made money, thereby feeding the monster."

Apparently, Hollywood has little or no compunction about feeding kids to the monster. Michael and Diane Medved's book, *Saving Childhood: How to Protect Your Children from the National Assault on Innocence,* argues forcefully that youngsters need to be protected from the pessimism that dominates television and motion pictures. The Medveds acknowledge the inevitability of observational learning: "The deepest problem with this material isn't the possibility that children will imitate the behavior they see on screen, though we know that this sort of imitation does occur. The more universal threat involves the underlying message conveyed by these ugly, consistently dysfunctional images, encouraging self-pity and fear." Although they refer here to Hollywood's staccato drumbeat that things always will get worse, they base their conclusions on the notion that "prolonged exposure to the dysfunctional elements in our culture" will cause viewers to "lose faith, confidence and resistance . . . to the plague of pessimism."

More often than not, situation comedies celebrate dysfunctionality by rejecting the very things that make civilized life possible: discipline, self-control, hard work, delayed gratification, faith, and a commitment to genuine families. Yet, one network executive recently claimed: "Little by little, everybody has gotten a little less afraid of the old taboos. . . . It seems we're able to go a lot further than we have, even considering the conservative swing the country has taken." These executives have ravaged the roots of cultural traditions, professing not dismay, but dollar-driven self-satisfaction at the moral mudslides that inevitably follow such deliberate destruction of America's religious roots.

The writers and producers responsible for such destruction could give their audiences much more, but they choose not to. They have opted for the dollar-laden low road, competing to see who can get away with the most first, afraid not to follow the pack for fear of being characterized as out of step with Hollywood leadership. Instead of intelligence, integrity, and inspiration, viewers get what one producer ordered: "We were told to lose the contrived plot stuff . . . and [add] . . . more big hair and breasts." What drives some of the most talented people in the world to such demi-moronic nihilism? These very same people have shown, time and again, they can produce laughter combined with sophistication and optimism, but they will not. Instead, we get the boobonic plague.

There are exceptions, but their ranks are thinning. Actor Michael J. Fox won't let his own children watch his new show, "Spin City." Everyone in the industry could learn a lesson from director Spike Lee: "Sometimes art should be about elevation, not just wallowing in the same old [crap]. . . . Life is valued cheaply. I definitely wanted to offer another view."

Given time, however, those writers and executives who lower the level of intelligence and discourse with brainless sex, profanity, nudity, and vulgarity have anesthetized, and eventually will annihilate, the ability of an audience to react positively to anything higher or ennobling. "I don't think audiences know how to be audiences anymore," producer Norman Lear told Nancy Hass of *The New York Times*. "They just want to hoot and make sounds." Lear still doesn't get it, because he insists that television's sexual saturation is not a moral issue: "The biggest problem with how much sex there is on TV isn't whether it's offensive. . . . It's that most [of it] just isn't funny. It's stupid and boring." Hass agrees that "many people within the industry—and no doubt many viewers" think that the real issue is variety, not morality. No wonder she entitled her article, "Cheap, Easy, and Moronic."

Prominent industry leaders know they are destroying the medium for those who will follow, but they simply refuse to acknowledge that reality. When they talk about "pushing the envelope," they really mean filling it. The money's too good and the audience too easy to exploit, so executives, writers, and producers follow the very same predatory practices that they, in their scripts and lives, usually attribute to business executives and religious figures. Favorite targets include corporate officials, Roman Catholic priests and nuns, and evangelical leaders.

We have gone from stand-up comics Mort Sahl and Lenny Bruce to the literate sophistication of Mike Nichols and Elaine May, through roundly mocked, "sugar-coated" Jackie Gleason and Lucille Ball to the brainless profanity of Dennis Miller and sexually laden and insulting racist, ethnic, and religious stereotypes. Humor on many shows has become a form of cultural and psychological violence, but no one looks at it that way because vulnerable young audiences respond, corporate sponsors chuckle and congratulate themselves, and everyone associated with the industry laughs all the way to the bank.

A half-mile wide and 27 miles long, Malibu, Calif., justifiably can claim that "nowhere in the world is there such a concentration of wealth and stardom," a belief few would refute. Those five beaches and six canyons hold the future of an art form with a generation of viewers and an important aspect of America's cultural integrity in them, but the occupants are in debt and refuse to admit it. An entire generation of youngsters has been taken hostage and doesn't know it. There will be no ransom note, only commercials from corporations who apparently care more about market share than our children's future.

Accountability

No one has the courage to offer the "trust accounting" demanded by Newton Minow more than 35 years ago or to address his most recent concerns: "In 1961, I worried that my children would not benefit much from television, but in 1991, I worry that my grandchildren will actually be harmed by it. . . . In 1961, they didn't make PG-13 movies, much less NC-17. Now, a six-year-old can watch them on cable."

In his 1991 Gannett Foundation Media Center revisiting of the "vast wasteland" speech of 1961, Minow quoted journalist E.B. White's reaction in 1938 when he first saw the new technological then-oddity called television: "We shall stand or fall by television, of that I am sure. I believe television is going to be the test of the modern world, and that in this new opportunity to see beyond the range of our vision, we shall discover there either a new and unbearable disturbance to the general peace, or a saving radiance in the sky."

Must television and motion pictures remain Minow's "reactive mirror of the lowest common denominator" of society? Must the men and women invested with such power pursue only their dollar-denominated death-spiral? Must they continue to degrade, deny, and eventually destroy White's "new opportunity to see beyond the range of our vision"? Must there be "a new and unbearable disturbance to the general peace" because those responsible for it haven't the courage to see the source of the disturbance in their Malibu mirrors? Imagine trying to justify applying the phrase "saving radiance in the sky" to the morals of today's situation comedies.

There is plenty viewers can do to protest this trend. Just three of the 25 best-selling videos of all times have an "R" rating. Go buy the other 22 and show them repeatedly. Watch many of the classics made before the first "R" rating in 1968, because 60% of the films made after that were "R" or worse. Look for the Dove Foundation's blue-and-white label on videos the Grand Rapids, Mich., organization rates as "family friendly," or sponsor a low-cost, multi-film festival they can help you set up.

Open that most radical of books, the Bible, and talk about the revelations of Revelation. Get some of the best of PBS, like "Shadowlands" and Ken Burns, and ignore most of the ideology-laden glop they throw at you. Explain to your kids that masterpieces teach you something new about yourself every time you see them, and then watch them again. Revisit older musicals and newer versions (after viewing the latter yourself first). Watch historical footage, especially of combat, with older kids, and explain that all this was done in the name of freedom. Convert your church social hall or service club to a mini-theater and offer a weekly film festival of your own. Keep cheesy film-gossip magazines out of your house and out of your life.

Work to establish a money-back guarantee at motion picture theaters. Most honest merchants have one. If you leave the movie within the first 20 minutes, you should have a right to get your money back because you were dissatisfied with what your ticket bought you.

The real trick is how to do this without seeming to be overbearing and out of touch with your children and their friends. There are usually no fanfares or overtures for unsung heroes. The best music comes later.

Gendered Media: The Influence of Media on Views of Gender

Julia T. Wood

Department of Communication, University of North Carolina at Chapel Hill.

THEMES IN MEDIA

Of the many influences on how we view men and women, media are the most pervasive and one of the most powerful. Woven throughout our daily lives, media insinuate their messages into our consciousness at every turn. All forms of media communicate images of the sexes, many of which perpetuate unrealistic, stereotypical, and limiting perceptions. Three themes describe how media represent gender. First, women are underrepresented, which falsely implies that men are the cultural standard and women are unimportant or invisible. Second, men and women are portrayed in stereotypical ways that reflect and sustain socially endorsed views of gender. Third, depictions of relationships between men and women emphasize traditional roles and normalize violence against women. We will consider each of these themes in this section.

Underrepresentation of Women

A primary way in which media distort reality is in underrepresenting women. Whether it is prime-time television, in which there are three times as many white men as women (Basow, 1992 p. 159), or children's programming, in which males outnumber females by two to one, or newscasts, in which women make up 16% of newscasters and in which stories about men are included 10 times more often than ones about women ("Study Reports Sex Bias," 1989), media misrepresent

actual proportions of men and women in the population. This constant distortion tempts us to believe that there really are more men than women and, further, that men are the cultural standard.

Other myths about what is standard are similarly fortified by communication in media. Minorities are even less visible than women, with African-Americans appearing only rarely (Gray, 1986; Stroman, 1989) and other ethnic minorities being virtually nonexistent. In children's programming when African-Americans do appear, almost invariably they appear in supporting roles rather than as main characters (O'Connor, 1989). While more African-Americans are appearing in

---

MEDIA'S MISREPRESENTATION OF AMERICAN LIFE

The media present a distorted version of cultural life in our country. According to media portrayals:

White males make up two-thirds of the population. The women are less in number, perhaps because fewer than 10% live beyond 35. Those who do, like their younger and male counterparts, are nearly all white and heterosexual. In addition to being young, the majority of women are beautiful, very thin, passive, and primarily concerned with relationships and getting rings out of collars and commodes. There are a few bad, bitchy women, and they are not so pretty, not so subordinate, and not so caring as the good women. Most of the bad ones work outside of the home, which is probably why they are hardened and undesirable. The more powerful, ambitious men occupy themselves with important business deals, exciting adventures, and rescuing dependent females, whom they often then assault sexually.

---

prime-time television, they are too often cast in stereotypical roles. In the 1992 season, for instance, 12 of the 74 series on commercial networks included large African-American casts, yet most featured them in stereotypical roles. Black men are presented as lazy and unable to handle authority, as lecherous, and/or as unlawful, while females are portrayed as domineering or as sex objects ("Sights, Sounds, and Stereotypes," 1992). Writing in 1993, David Evans (1993, p. 10) criticized television for stereotyping black males as athletes and entertainers. These roles, wrote Evans, mislead young black male viewers into thinking success "is only a dribble or dance step away," and blind them to other, more realistic ambitions. Hispanics and Asians are nearly absent, and when they are presented it is usually as villains or criminals (Lichter, Lichter, Rothman, & Amundson, 1987).

Also underrepresented is the single fastest growing group of Americans—older people. As a country, we are aging so that people over 60 make up a major part of our population; within this group, women significantly outnumber men (Wood, 1993c). Older people not only are underrepresented in media but also are represented inaccurately. In contrast to demographic realities, media consistently show fewer older women than men, presumably because our culture worships youth and beauty in women. Further, elderly individuals are frequently portrayed as sick, dependent, fumbling, and passive, images not borne out in real life. Distorted depictions of older people and especially older women in media, however, can delude us into thinking they are a small, sickly, and unimportant part of our population.

The lack of women in the media is paralleled by the scarcity of women in charge of media. Only about 5% of television writers, executives, and producers are women (Lichter, Lichter, & Rothman, 1986). Ironically, while two-thirds of journalism graduates are women, they make up less than 2% of those in corporate management of newspapers and only about 5% of newspaper publishers ("Women in Media," 1988). Female film directors are even more scarce, as are executives in charge of MTV. It is probably not coincidental that so few women are behind the scenes of an industry that so consistently portrays women negatively. Some media analysts (Mills, 1988) believe that if more women had positions of authority at executive levels, media would offer more positive portrayals of women.

Stereotypical Portrayals of Women and Men

In general, media continue to present both women and men in stereotyped ways that limit our perceptions of human possibilities. Typically men are portrayed as active, adventurous, powerful, sexually aggressive, and largely uninvolved in human relationships. Just as consistent with cultural views of gender are depictions of women as sex objects who are usually young, thin, beautiful, passive, dependent, and often incompetent and dumb. Female characters devote their primary energies to improving their appearances and taking care of homes and people. Because media pervade our lives, the ways they misrepresent genders may distort how we see ourselves and what we perceive as normal and desirable for men and women.

Stereotypical portrayals of men. According to J. A. Doyle (1989, p. 111), whose research focuses on masculinity, children's television typically shows males as "aggressive, dominant, and engaged in exciting activities from which they receive rewards from others for their 'masculine' accomplishments." Relatedly, recent studies reveal that the majority of men on prime-time television are independent, aggressive, and in charge (McCauley, Thangavelu, & Rozin, 1988). Television programming for all ages disproportionately depicts men as serious, confident, competent, powerful, and in high-status positions. Gentleness in men, which was briefly evident in the 1970s, has receded as established male characters are redrawn to be more tough and distanced from others (Boyer, 1986). Highly popular films such as *Lethal Weapon, Predator, Days of Thunder, Total Recall, Robocop, Die Hard,* and *Die Harder* star men who embody the stereotype of extreme masculinity. Media, then, reinforce long-standing cultural ideals of masculinity: Men are presented as hard, tough, independent, sexually aggressive, unafraid, violent, totally in control of all emotions, and—above all—in no way feminine.

Equally interesting is how males are *not* presented. J. D. Brown and K. Campbell (1986) report that men are seldom shown doing housework. Doyle (1989) notes that boys and men are rarely presented caring for others. B. Horovitz (1989) points out they are typically represented as uninterested in and incompetent at homemaking, cooking, and child care. Each season's new ads for cooking and cleaning supplies include several that caricature men as incompetent buffoons, who are klutzes in the kitchen and no better at taking care of children. While children's books have made a limited attempt to depict women engaged in activities outside of the home, there has been little parallel effort to show men involved in family and home life. When someone is shown taking care of a child, it is usually the mother, not the father. This perpetuates a negative stereotype of men as uncaring and uninvolved in family life.

Stereotypical portrayals of women. Media's images of women also reflect cultural stereotypes that depart markedly from reality. As we have already seen, girls and women are dramatically underrepresented. In prime-time television in 1987, fully two-thirds of the speaking parts were for men. Women are portrayed as significantly younger and thinner than women in the population as a whole, and most are

JILL

I remember when I was little I used to read books from the boys' section of the library because they were more interesting. Boys did the fun stuff and the exciting things. My mother kept trying to get me to read girls' books, but I just couldn't get into them. Why can't stories about girls be full of adventure and bravery? I know when I'm a mother, I want any daughters of mine to understand that excitement isn't just for boys.

depicted as passive, dependent on men, and enmeshed in relationships or housework (Davis, 1990). The requirements of youth and beauty in women even influence news shows, where female newscasters are expected to be younger, more physically attractive, and less outspoken than males (Craft, 1988; Sanders & Rock, 1988). Despite educators' criticism of self-fulfilling prophesies that discourage girls from success in math and science, that stereotype was dramatically reiterated in 1992 when Mattel offered a new talking Barbie doll. What did she say? "Math class is tough," a message that reinforces the stereotype that women cannot do math ("Mattel Offers Trade-In," 1992). From children's programming, in which the few existing female characters typically spend their time watching males do things (Feldman & Brown, 1984; Woodman, 1991), to MTV, which routinely pictures women satisfying men's sexual fantasies (Pareles, 1990; Texier, 1990), media reiterate the cultural image of women as dependent, ornamental objects whose primary functions are to look good, please men, and stay quietly on the periphery of life.

Media have created two images of women: good women and bad ones. These polar opposites are often juxtaposed against each other to dramatize differences in the consequences that befall good and bad women. Good women are pretty, deferential, and focused on home, family, and caring for others. Subordinate to men, they are usually cast as victims, angels, martyrs, and loyal wives and helpmates. Occasionally, women who depart from traditional roles are portrayed positively, but this is done either by making their career lives invisible, as with Claire Huxtable, or by softening and feminizing working women to make them more consistent with traditional views of femininity. For instance, in the original script, Cagney and Lacey were conceived as strong, mature, independent women who took their work seriously and did it well. It took 6 years for writers Barbara Corday and Barbara Avedon to sell the script to CBS, and even then they had to agree to subdue Cagney's and Lacey's abilities to placate producer Barney Rosenzweig, who complained, "These women aren't soft enough. These women aren't feminine enough" (Faludi, 1991, p. 150). While female

viewers wrote thousands of letters praising the show, male executives at CBS continued to force writers to make the characters softer, more tender, and less sure of themselves (Faludi, 1991, p. 152). The remaking of Cagney and Lacey illustrates the media's bias in favor of women who are traditionally feminine and who are not too able, too powerful, or too confident. The rule seems to be that a woman may be strong and successful if and only if she also exemplifies traditional stereotypes of femininity—subservience, passivity, beauty, and an identity linked to one or more men.

The other image of women the media offer us is the evil sister of the good homebody. Versions of this image are the witch, bitch, whore, or nonwoman, who is represented as hard, cold, aggressive—all of the things a good woman is not supposed to be. Exemplifying the evil woman is Alex in *Fatal Attraction*, which grossed more than $100 million in its first four months (Faludi, 1991, p. 113). Yet Alex was only an extreme version of how bad women are generally portrayed. In children's literature, we encounter witches and mean stepmothers as villains, with beautiful and passive females like Snow White and Sleeping Beauty as their good counterparts.

Prime-time television favorably portrays pretty, nurturing, other-focused women, such as Claire Huxtable on "The Cosby Show," whose career as an attorney never entered storylines as much as her engagement in family matters. Hope in "Thirtysomething" is an angel, committed to husband Michael and daughter Janey. In the biographies written for each of the characters when the show was in development, all male characters were defined in terms of their career goals, beliefs, and activities. Hope's biography consisted of one line: "Hope is married to Michael" (Faludi, 1991, p. 162). Hope epitomizes the traditional woman, so much so in fact that in one episode she refers to herself as June Cleaver and calls Michael "Ward," thus reprising the traditional family of the 1950s as personified in "Leave It to Beaver" (Faludi, 1991, p. 161). Meanwhile, prime-time typically represents ambitious, independent women as lonely, embittered spinsters who are counterpoints to "good" women.

Stereotypical Images of Relationships Between Men and Women

Given media's stereotypical portrayals of women and men, we shouldn't be surprised to find that relationships between women and men are similarly depicted in ways that reinforce stereotypes. Four themes demonstrate how media reflect and promote traditional arrangements between the sexes.

Women's dependence/men's independence. Walt Disney's award-winning animated film *The Little Mermaid* vividly embodies females' dependence on males for identity. In this feature film, the mermaid quite literally gives up her identity as a mermaid in order to become acceptable to her human lover. In this children's story, we see a particularly obvious illustration of the asymmetrical relationship between women and men that is more subtly conveyed in other media productions. Even the Smurfs, formless little beings who have no obvious sex, reflect the male-female, dominant-submissive roles. The female smurf, unlike her male companions, who have names, is called only Smurfette, making her sole identity a diminutive relation to male smurfs. The male dominance/female subservience pattern that permeates mediated representations of relationships is no accident. Beginning in 1991, television executives deliberately and consciously adopted a policy of having dominant male characters in all Saturday morning children's programming (Carter, 1991).

Women, as well as minorities, are cast in support roles rather than leading ones in both children's shows and the commercials interspersed within them (O'Connor, 1989). Analyses of MTV revealed that it portrays females as passive and waiting for men's attention, while males are shown ignoring, exploiting, or directing women (Brown, Campbell, & Fisher, 1986). In rap music videos, where African-American men and women star, men dominate women, whose primary role is as objects of male desires (Pareles, 1990; Texier, 1990). News programs that have male and female hosts routinely cast the female as deferential to her male colleague (Craft, 1988; Sanders & Rock, 1988). Commercials, too, manifest power cues that echo the male dominance/female subservience pattern. For instance, men are usually shown positioned above women, and women are more frequently pictured in varying degrees of undress (Masse & Rosenblum, 1988; Nigro, Hill, Gelbein, & Clark, 1988). Such nonverbal cues represent women as vulnerable and more submissive while men stay in control.

In a brief departure from this pattern, films and television beginning in the 1970s responded to the second wave of feminism by showing women who were independent without being hard, embittered, or without close relationships. Films such as *Alice Doesn't Live Here Anymore, Up the Sandbox, The Turning Point, Diary of a Mad Housewife,* and *An Unmarried Woman* offered realistic portraits of women who sought and found their own voices independent of men. Judy Davis's film, *My Brilliant Career,* particularly embodied this focus by telling the story of a woman who chooses work over marriage. During this period, television followed suit, offering viewers prime-time fare such as "Maude" and "The Mary Tyler Moore Show," which starred women who were able and achieving in their own rights. "One Day at a Time," which premiered in 1974, was the first prime-time program about a divorced woman.

By the 1980s, however, traditionally gendered arrangements resurged as the backlash movement against feminism was embraced by media (Haskell, 1988; Maslin, 1990). Thus, film fare in the 1980s included *Pretty Woman,* the story of a prostitute who becomes a good woman when she is saved from her evil ways by a rigidly stereotypical man, complete with millions to prove his success. Meanwhile, *Tie Me Up, Tie Me Down* trivialized abuse of women and underlined women's dependence on men with a story of a woman who is bound by a man and colludes in sustaining her bondage. *Crossing Delancey* showed successful careerist Amy Irving talked into believing she needs a man to be complete, a theme reprised by Cher in *Moonstruck.*

Television, too, cooperated in returning women to their traditional roles with characters like Hope in "Thirtysomething," who minded house and baby as an ultratraditional wife, and even Murphy Brown found her career wasn't enough and had a baby. Against her protests, Cybill Shepherd, who played Maddie in "Moonlighting," was forced to marry briefly on screen, which Susan Faludi (1991, p. 157) refers to as part of a "campaign to cow this independent female figure." Popular music added its voice with hit songs like "Having My Baby," which glorified a woman who defined herself by motherhood and her relationship to a man. The point is not that having babies or committing to relationships is wrong; rather, it is that media virtually require this of women in order to present them positively. Media define a very narrow range for womanhood.

Joining the campaign to restore traditional dominant-subordinate patterns of male-female relationships were magazines, which reinvigorated their focus on women's role as the helpmate and supporter of husbands and families (Peirce, 1990). In 1988, that staple of Americana, *Good Housekeeping,* did its part to revive women's traditional roles with a full-page ad ("The Best in the House," 1988) for its new demographic edition marketed to "the new traditionalist woman." A month later, the magazine followed this up with a second full-page ad in national newspapers that saluted the "new traditionalist woman," with this copy ("The New Traditionalist," 1988): "She has made her commitment. Her mission: create a more meaningful life for herself and her family. She is the New Traditionalist— a contemporary woman who finds her fulfillment in traditional values." The long-standing dominant-submissive model for male-female relationships was largely restored in the 1980s. With only rare exceptions, women are still portrayed as dependent on men and subservient to them. As B. Lott (1989, p. 64) points out, it is women who "do the laundry and are secretaries to men who own companies."

Men's authority/women's incompetence. A second recurrent theme in media representations of relationships is that men are the competent authorities who save women from their incompetence. Children's litera-

PAUL

I wouldn't say this around anyone, but personally I'd be glad if the media let up a little on us guys. I watch those guys in films and on TV, and I just feel inadequate. I mean, I'm healthy and I look okay, and I'll probably make a decent salary when I graduate. But I am no stud; I can't beat up three guys at once, women don't fall dead at my feet; I doubt I'll make a million bucks; and I don't have muscles that ripple. Every time I go to a film, I leave feeling like a wimp. How can any of us guys measure up to what's on the screen?

ture vividly implements this motif by casting females as helpless and males as coming to their rescue. Sleeping Beauty's resurrection depends on Prince Charming's kiss, a theme that appears in the increasingly popular gothic romance novels for adults (Modleski, 1982).

One of the most pervasive ways in which media define males as authorities is in commercials. Women are routinely shown anguishing over dirty floors and bathroom fixtures only to be relieved of their distress when Mr. Clean shows up to tell them how to keep their homes spotless. Even when commercials are aimed at women, selling products intended for them, up to 90% of the time a man's voice is used to explain the value of what is being sold (Basow, 1992, p. 161; Bretl & Cantor, 1988). Using male voice-overs reinforces the cultural view that men are authorities and women depend on men to tell them what to do.

Television further communicates the message that men are authorities and women are not. One means of doing this is sheer numbers. As we have seen, men vastly outnumber women in television programming. In addition, the dominance of men as news anchors who inform us of happenings in the world underlines their authority ("Study Reports Sex Bias," 1989). Prime-time television contributes to this image by showing women who need to be rescued by men and by presenting women as incompetent more than twice as often as men (Boyer, 1986; Lichter et al., 1986).

Consider the characters in "The Jetsons," an animated television series set in the future. Daughter Judy Jetson is constantly complaining and waiting for others to help her, using ploys of helplessness and flattery to win men's attention. *The Rescuers,* a popular animated video of the 1990s, features Miss Bianca (whose voice is that of Zsa Zsa Gabor, fittingly enough), who splits her time evenly between being in trouble and being grateful to male characters for rescuing her. These stereotypical representations of males and females reinforce a number of harmful beliefs. They suggest, first, that men are more competent than women. Compounding this is the message that a woman's power lies in her looks and conventional

femininity, since that is how females from Sleeping Beauty to Judy Jetson get males to assist them with their dilemmas (McCauley, Thangavelu, & Rozin, 1988). Third, these stereotypes underline the requirement that men must perform, succeed, and conquer in order to be worthy.

Women as primary caregivers/men as breadwinners. A third perennial theme in media is that women are caregivers and men are providers. Since the backlash of the 1980s, in fact, this gendered arrangement has been promulgated with renewed vigor. Once again, as in the 1950s, we see women devoting themselves to getting rings off of collars, gray out of their hair, and meals on the table. Corresponding to this is the restatement of men's inability in domestic and nurturing roles. Horovitz (1989), for instance, reports that in commercials men are regularly the butt of jokes for their ignorance about nutrition, child care, and housework.

When media portray women who work outside of the home, their career lives typically receive little or no attention. Although these characters have titles such as lawyer or doctor, they are shown predominantly in their roles as homemakers, mothers, and wives. We see them involved in caring conversations with family and friends and doing things for others, all of which never seem to conflict with their professional responsibilities. This has the potential to cultivate unrealistic expectations of being "superwoman," who does it all without her getting a hair out of place or being late to a conference.

Magazines play a key role in promoting pleasing others as a primary focus of women's lives. K. Peirce's (1990) study found that magazines aimed at women stress looking good and doing things to please others. Thus, advertising tells women how to be "me, only better" by dyeing their hair to look younger; how to lose weight so "you'll still be attractive to him"; and how to prepare gourmet meals so "he's always glad to come home." Constantly, these advertisements empha-

JOANNE

I'd like to know who dreams up those commercials that show men as unable to boil water or run a vacuum. I'd like to tell them they're creating monsters. My boyfriend and I agreed to split all chores equally when we moved in together. Ha! Fat chance of that. He does zilch. When I get on his case, he reminds me of what happened when the father on some show had to take over housework and practically demolished the kitchen. Then he grins and says, "Now, you wouldn't want that, would you?" Or worse yet, he throws up Hope or one of the other women on TV, and asks me why I can't be as sweet and supportive as she is. It's like the junk on television gives him blanket license for doing nothing.

size pleasing others, especially men, as central to being a woman, and the message is fortified with the thinly veiled warning that if a woman fails to look good and please, her man might leave (Rakow, 1992).

There is a second, less known way in which advertisements contribute to stereotypes of women as focused on others and men as focused on work. Writing in 1990, Gloria Steinem, editor of *Ms.*, revealed that advertisers control some to most of the *content* in magazines. In exchange for placing an ad, a company receives "complimentary copy," which is one or more articles that increase the market appeal of its product. So a soup company that takes out an ad might be given a three-page story on how to prepare meals using that brand of soup; likewise, an ad for hair coloring products might be accompanied by interviews with famous women who choose to dye their hair. Thus, the message of advertisers is multiplied by magazine content, which readers often mistakenly assume is independent of advertising.

Advertisers support media, and they exert a powerful influence on what is presented. To understand the prevalence of traditional gender roles in programming, magazine copy, and other media, we need only ask what is in the best interests of advertisers. They want to sponsor shows that create or expand markets for their products. Media images of women as sex objects, devoted homemakers, and mothers buttress the very roles in which the majority of consuming takes place. To live up to these images, women have to buy cosmetics and other personal care products, diet aids, food, household cleaners, utensils and appliances, clothes and toys for children, and so on. In short, it is in advertisers' interests to support programming and copy that feature women in traditional roles. In a recent analysis, Lana Rakow (1992) demonstrated that much advertising is oppressive to women and is very difficult to resist, even when one is a committed feminist.

Women's role in the home and men's role outside of it are reinforced by newspapers and news programming. Both emphasize men's independent activities and, in fact, define news almost entirely as stories about and by men ("Study Reports Sex Bias," 1989). Stories about men focus on work and/or their achievements (Luebke, 1989), reiterating the cultural message that men are supposed to do, perform. Meanwhile the few stories about women almost invariably focus on their roles as wives, mothers, and homemakers ("Study Reports Sex Bias," 1989). Even stories about women who are in the news because of achievements and professional activities typically dwell on marriage, family life, and other aspects of women's traditional role (Foreit et al., 1980).

Women as victims and sex objects/men as aggressors. A final theme in mediated representations of relationships between women and men is representation of women as subject to men's sexual desires. The irony of this representation is that the very qualities women are encouraged to develop (beauty, sexiness, passivity, and powerlessness) in order to meet cultural ideals of femininity contribute to their victimization. Also, the qualities that men are urged to exemplify (aggressiveness, dominance, sexuality, and strength) are identical to those linked to abuse of women. It is no coincidence that all but one of the women nominated for Best Actress in the 1988 Academy Awards played a victim (Faludi, 1991, p. 138). Women are portrayed alternatively either as decorative objects, who must attract a man to be valuable, or as victims of men's sexual impulses. Either way, women are defined by their bodies and how men treat them. Their independent identities and endeavors are irrelevant to how they are represented in media, and their abilities to resist exploitation by others are obscured.

This theme, which was somewhat toned down during the 1970s, returned with vigor in the 1980s as the backlash permeated media. According to S. A. Basow (1992, p. 160), since 1987 there has been a "resurgence of male prominence, pretty female sidekicks, female homemakers." Advertising in magazines also communicates the message that women are sexual objects. While men are seldom pictured nude or even partially unclothed, women habitually are. Advertisements for makeup, colognes, hair products, and clothes often show women attracting men because they got the right products and made themselves irresistible. Stars on prime-time and films, who are beautiful and dangerously thin, perpetuate the idea that women must literally starve themselves to death to win men's interest (Silverstein et al., 1986).

Perhaps the most glaring examples of portrayals of women as sex objects and men as sexual aggressors occur in music videos as shown on MTV and many other stations. Typically, females are shown dancing provocatively in scant and/or revealing clothing as they try to gain men's attention (Texier, 1990). Frequently, men are seen coercing women into sexual activities and/or physically abusing them. Violence against women is also condoned in many recent films. R. Warshaw (1991) reported that cinematic presentations of rapes, especially acquaintance rapes, are not presented as power-motivated violations of women but rather as strictly sexual encounters. Similarly, others (Cowan, Lee, Levy, & Snyder, 1988; Cowan & O'Brien, 1990) have found that male dominance and sexual exploitation of women are themes in virtually all R- and X-rated films, which almost anyone may now rent for home viewing. These media images carry to extremes long-standing cultural views of masculinity as aggressive and femininity as passive. They also make violence seem sexy (D. Russell, 1993). In so doing, they recreate these limited and limiting perceptions in the thinking of another generation of women and men.

In sum, we have identified basic stereotypes and

themes in media's representations of women, men, and relationships between the two. Individually and in combination these images sustain and reinforce socially constructed views of the genders, views that have restricted both men and women and that appear to legitimize destructive behaviors ranging from anorexia to battering. Later in this chapter, we will probe more closely how media versions of gender are linked to problems such as these. . . .

Pathologizing the Human Body

One of the most damaging consequences of media's images of women and men is that these images encourage us to perceive normal bodies and normal physical functions as problems. It's understandable to wish we weighed a little more or less, had better developed muscles, and never had pimples or cramps. What is neither reasonable nor healthy, however, is to regard healthy, functional bodies as abnormal and unacceptable. Yet this is precisely the negative self-image cultivated by media portrayals of women and men. Because sex sells products (Muro, 1989), sexual and erotic images are the single most prominent characteristic of advertising (Courtney & Whipple, 1983). Further, advertising is increasingly objectifying men, which probably accounts for the rise in men's weight training and cosmetic surgery. Media, and especially advertising, are equal opportunity dehumanizers of both sexes.

Not only do media induce us to think we should measure up to artificial standards, but they encourage us to see normal bodies and bodily functions as pathologies. A good example is the media's construction of premenstrual syndrome (PMS). Historically, PMS has not been a problem, but recently it has been declared a disease (Richmond-Abbott, 1992). In fact, a good deal of research (Parlee, 1973, 1987) indicates that PMS affected very few women in earlier eras. After the war, when women were no longer needed in the work force, opinion changed and the term *premenstrual tension* was coined (Greene & Dalton, 1953) and used to define women as inferior employees. In 1964, only one article on PMS appeared; in 1988–1989, a total of 425 were published (Tavris, 1992, p. 140). Drug companies funded research and publicity, since selling PMS meant selling their remedies for the newly created problem. Behind the hoopla, however, there was and is little evidence to support the currently widespread belief that PMS is a serious problem for a significant portion of the female population. Facts aside, the myth has caught on, carrying in its wake many women and men who now perceive normal monthly changes as abnormal and as making women unfit for positions of leadership and authority. Another consequence of defining PMS as a serious problem most women suffer is that it leads to labeling women in general as deviant and unreliable (Unger & Crawford, 1992), an image that fortifies long-held biases against women.

Menopause is similarly pathologized. Carol Tavris (1992, p. 159) notes that books describe menopause "in terms of deprivation, deficiency, loss, shedding, and sloughing," language that defines a normal process as negative. Like menstruation, menopause is represented as abnormalcy and disease, an image that probably contributes to the negative attitudes toward it in America. The cover of the May 25, 1992, *Newsweek* featured an abstract drawing of a tree in the shape of a woman's head. The tree was stripped of all leaves, making it drab and barren. Across the picture was the cover-story headline "Menopause." From first glance, menopause was represented negatively—as desolate and unfruitful. The article focused primarily on the problems and losses of menopause. Only toward the end did readers find reports from anthropologists, whose cross-cultural research revealed that in many cultures menopause is not an issue or is viewed positively. Women in Mayan villages and the Greek island of Evia do not understand questions about hot flashes and depression, which are symptoms often associated with menopause in Western societies ("Menopause," 1992, p. 77). These are not part of their experience in cultures that do not define a normal change in women as a pathology. Because Western countries, especially America, stigmatize menopause and define it as "the end of womanhood," Western women are likely to feel distressed and unproductive about the cessation of menstruation (Greer, 1992).

Advertising is very effective in convincing us that we need products to solve problems we are unaware of until some clever public relations campaign persuades us that something natural about us is really unnatural and unacceptable. Media have convinced millions of American women that what every medical source considers "normal body weight" is really abnormal and cause for severe dieting (Wolf, 1991). Similarly, gray hair, which naturally develops with age, is now something all of us, especially women, are supposed to cover up. Facial lines, which indicate a person has lived a life and accumulated experiences, can be removed so that we look younger—a prime goal in a culture that glorifies youth (Greer, 1992).

Body hair is another interesting case of media's convincing us that something normal is really abnormal. Beginning in 1915, a sustained marketing campaign informed women that underarm hair was unsightly and socially incorrect. (The campaign against leg hair came later.) *Harper's Bazaar,* an upscale magazine, launched the crusade against underarm hair with a photograph of a woman whose raised arms revealed clean-shaven armpits. Underneath the photograph was this caption: "Summer dress and modern dancing combine to make necessary the removal of objectionable hair" (Adams, 1991). Within a few years, ads promoting removal of underarm hair appeared in most women's magazines, and by 1922, razors and depilatories were firmly ensconced in middle America as evidenced by their inclusion in the women's section of the Sears Roebuck catalog.

Media efforts to pathologize natural physiology can be very serious. As we have seen in prior chapters, the emphasis on excessive thinness contributes to severe and potentially lethal dieting, especially in Caucasian women (Spitzack, 1993). Nonetheless, the top female models in 1993 are skeletal, more so than in recent years (Leland & Leonard, 1993). Many women's natural breast size exceeded the cultural ideal in the 1960s when thin, angular bodies were represented as ideal. Thus, breast reduction surgeries rose. By the 1980s, cultural standards changed to define large breasts as the feminine ideal. Consequently, breast augmentation surgeries accelerated, and fully 80% of implants were for cosmetic reasons ("The Implant Circus," 1992). In an effort to meet the cultural standards of beautiful bodies, many women suffered unnecessary surgery, which led to disfigurement, loss of feeling, and sometimes death for women when silicone implants were later linked to fatal conditions. Implicitly, media argue that our natural state is abnormal and objectionable, a premise that is essential to sell products and advice for improving ourselves. Accepting media messages about our bodies and ourselves, however, is not inevitable: We can reflect on the messages and resist those that are inappropriate and/or harmful. We would probably all be considerably happier and healthier if we became more critical in analyzing media's communication about how we should look, be, and act.

Normalizing Violence Against Women

Since we have seen that media positively portray aggression in males and passivity in females, it's important to ask whether media messages contribute to abuse of and violence against women. There is by now fairly convincing evidence (Hansen & Hansen, 1988) that exposure to sexual violence through media is linked to greater tolerance, or even approval, of violence. For instance, P. Dieter (1989) found a strong relationship between females' viewing of sexually violent MTV and their acceptance of sexual violence as part of "normal" relationships. He reasoned that the more they observe positive portrayals of sexual violence, the more likely women are to perceive this as natural in relationships with men and the less likely they are to object to violence or to defend themselves from it. In short, Dieter suggests that heavy exposure to media violence within relationships tends to normalize it, so that abuse and violence are considered natural parts of love and sex.

Dieter's study demonstrates a direct link between sexual aggression and one popular form of media, MTV. Research on pornography further corroborates connections between exposure to portrayals of violence against women and willingness to engage in or accept it in one's own relationships (Russell, 1993). Before we discuss this research, however, we need to clarify what we will mean by the term pornography, since defining it is a matter of some controversy. Pornography is not simply sexually explicit material. To distinguish pornography from erotica, we might focus on mutual agreement and mutual benefit. If we use these criteria, pornography may be defined as materials that favorably show subordination and degradation of a person such as presenting sadistic behaviors as pleasurable, brutalizing and pain as enjoyable, and forced sex or abuse as positive. Erotica, on the other hand, depicts consensual sexual activities that are sought by and pleasurable to all parties involved (MacKinnon, 1987). These distinctions are important, since it has been well established that graphic sexual material itself is not harmful, while sexually violent materials appear to be (Donnerstein, Linz, & Penrod, 1987).

Pornographic films are a big business, outnumbering other films by 3 to 1 and grossing over $365 million a year in the United States alone (Wolf, 1991). The primary themes characteristic of pornography as a genre are extremes of those in media generally: sex, violence, and domination of one person by another, usually women by men (Basow, 1992, p. 317). More than 80% of X-rated films in one study included scenes in which one or more men dominate and exploit one or more women; within these films, three-fourths portray physical aggression against women, and fully half explicitly depict rape (Cowan et al., 1988). That these are linked to viewers' own tendencies to engage in sexual violence is no longer disputable. According to recent research (Demare, Briere, & Lips, 1988; Donnerstein et al., 1987; Malamuth & Briere, 1986), viewing sexually violent material tends to increase men's beliefs in rape myths, raises the likelihood that men will admit they might themselves commit rape, and desensitizes men to rape, thereby making forced sex more acceptable to them. This research suggests that repeated exposure to pornography influences how men think about rape by transforming it from an unacceptable behavior with which they do not identify into one they find acceptable and enticing. Not surprisingly, the single best predictor of rape is the circulation of pornographic materials that glorify sexual force and exploitation (Baron & Straus, 1989). This is alarming when we realize that 18 million men buy a total of 165 different pornographic magazines every month in the United States (Wolf, 1991, p. 79).

It is well documented that the incidence of reported rape is rising and that an increasing number of men regard forced sex as acceptable (Brownmiller, 1993; Soeken & Damrosch, 1986). Studies of men (Allgeier, 1987; Koss & Dinero, 1988; Koss, Dinero, Seibel, & Cox, 1988; Koss, Gidycz, & Wisniewski, 1987; Lisak & Roth, 1988) have produced shocking findings: While the majority of college men report not having raped anyone, a stunning 50% admit they have coerced, manipulated, or pressured a woman to have sex or have had sex with her after getting her drunk; 1 in 12 men at some colleges has engaged in behaviors meeting the legal definition of rape or attempted rape; over 80% of men who admitted to acts that meet the definition of rape did not believe they had committed rape; and fully one-third of college men said they would commit rape if they believed nobody would find out.

Contrary to popular belief, we also know that men who do commit rape are not psychologically abnormal. They are indistinguishable from other men in terms of psychological adjustment and health, emotional well-being, heterosexual relationships, and frequency of sexual experiences (Segel-Evans, 1987). The only established difference between men who are sexually violent and men who are not is that the former have "hypermasculine" attitudes and self-concepts—their approval of male dominance and sexual rights is even stronger than that of nonrapists (Allgeier, 1987; Koss & Dinero, 1988; Lisak & Roth, 1988; Wood, 1993a). The difference between sexually violent men and others appears to be only a matter of degree.

We also know something about women who are victims of rape and other forms of sexual violence. Between 33% and 66% of all women have been sexually abused before reaching age 18 (Clutter, 1990; Koss, 1990). The majority of college women—up to 75%—say they have been coerced into some type of unwanted sex at least once (Koss, Gidycz, & Wisniewski, 1987; Poppen & Segal, 1988; Warshaw, 1988). A third of women who survive rape contemplate suicide (Koss et al., 1988). It is also clear that the trauma of rape is not confined to the time of its actual occurrence. The feelings that accompany rape and sexual assault—fear, a sense of degradation and shame, anger, powerlessness, and depression—endure far beyond the act itself (Brownmiller, 1975; Wood, 1992b, 1993f). Most victims of rape continue to deal with the emotional aftermath of rape for the rest of their lives (Marhoefer-Dvorak, Resick, Hutter, & Girelli, 1988).

What causes rape, now the fastest growing violent crime in the United States (Doyle, 1989; Soeken & Damrosch, 1986)? According to experts (Costin & Schwartz, 1987; Koss & Dinero, 1988; Koss, Gidycz, & Wisniewski, 1987; Scott & Tetreault, 1987; Scully, 1990), rape is not the result of psychological deviance or uncontrollable lust. Although rape involves sex, it is not motivated by sexual desire. Authorities agree that rape is an aggressive act used to dominate and show power over another person, be it a man over a woman or one man over another, as in prison settings where rape is one way inmates brutalize one another and establish a power hierarchy (Rideau & Sinclair, 1982). Instead, mounting evidence suggests that rape is a predictable outcome of views of men, women, and relationships between the sexes that our society inculcates in mem-

bers (Brownmiller, 1975; Costin & Schwartz, 1987; Scott & Tetreault, 1987; South & Felson, 1990).

Particularly compelling support for the cultural basis of rape comes from cross-cultural studies (Griffin, 1981; Sanday, 1986), which reveal that rape is extremely rare in cultures that value women and feminine qualities and that have ideologies that promote harmonious interdependence among humans and between them and the natural world. Rape is most common in countries, like the United States, that have ideologies of male supremacy and dominance and a disrespect of women and nature. Cultural values communicated to us by family, schools, media, and other sources constantly encourage us to believe men are superior, men should dominate women, male aggression is acceptable as a means of attaining what is wanted, women are passive and should defer to men, and women are sex objects. In concert, these beliefs legitimize violence and aggression against women.

While the majority of media communication may not be pornographic, it does echo in somewhat muted forms the predominant themes of pornography: sex, violence, and male domination of women. As we have seen, these same motifs permeate media that are part of our daily

MYTHS AND FACTS ABOUT RAPE

Myth	Fact
Rape is a sexual act that results from sexual urges.	Rape is an aggressive act used to dominate another.
Rapists are abnormal.	Rapists have not been shown to differ from nonrapists in personality, psychology, adjustment, or involvement in interpersonal relationships.
Most rapes occur between strangers.	Eighty percent to 90% of rapes are committed by a person known to the victim (Allgeier, 1987).
Most rapists are African-American men, and most victims are Caucasian women.	More than three-fourths of all rapes occur within races, not between races. This myth reflects racism.
The way a woman dresses affects the likelihood she will be raped.	The majority—up to 90%—of rapes are planned in advance and without knowledge of how the victim will dress (Scully, 1990).
False reports of rapes are frequent.	The majority of rapes are never reported (Koss, Gidycz, & Wisniewski, 1987). Less than 10% of rape reports are judged false, the same as for other violent crimes.
Rape is a universal problem.	The incidence of rape varies across cultures. It is highest in societies with ideologies of male dominance and a disregard for nature; it is lowest in cultures that respect women and feminine values (Griffin, 1981).

lives, which generally portray males as dominating in number, status, authority, and will. Substantial violence toward women punctuates movies, television—including children's programming—rock music, and music videos, desensitizing men and women alike to the *unnaturalness* and unacceptability of force and brutality between human beings. Thus, the research that demonstrates connections between sex-stereotypical media and acceptance of sexual violence is consistent with that showing relationships between more extreme, pornographic media and acceptance of and use of violence. . . .

REFERENCES

Adams, C. (1991, April). The straight dope. *Triangle Comic Review*, p. 26.

Allgeier, E. R. (1987). Coercive versus consensual sexual interactions. In V. P. Makosky (Ed.), *The G. Stanley Hall Lecture Series* (Vol. 7, pp. 7–63). Washington, DC: American Psychological Association.

Baron, L., & Straus, M. A. (1989). *Four theories of rape in American society.* New Haven, CT: Yale University Press.

Basow, S. A. (1992). *Gender: Stereotypes and roles* (3rd ed.). Pacific Grove, CA: Brooks/Cole.

The best in the house. (1988, October 19). *New York Times*, p. 52Y.

Boyer, P. J. (1986, February 16). TV turns to the hard-boiled male. *New York Times*, pp. H1, H29.

Bretl, D., & Cantor, J. (1988). The portrayal of men and women in U.S. commercials: A recent content analysis and trend over 15 years. *Sex Roles, 18,* 595–609.

Brown, J. D., & Campbell, K. (1986). Race and gender in music videos: The same beat but a different drummer. *Journal of Communication, 36,* 94–106.

Brown, J. D., Campbell, K., & Fisher, L. (1986). American adolescents and music videos: Why do they watch? *Gazette, 37,* 9–32.

Brownmiller, S. (1975). *Against our wills: Men, women, and rape.* New York: Simon and Schuster.

Brownmiller, S. (1993, January 4). Making female bodies the battlefield. *Newsweek*, p. 37.

Carter, B. (1991, May 1). Children's TV, where boys are king. *New York Times*, pp. A1, C18.

Clutter, S. (1990, May 3). Gender may affect response and outrage to sex abuse. *Morning Call*, p. D14.

Costin, F., & Schwartz, N. (1987). Beliefs about rape and women's social roles: A four-nation study. *Journal of Interpersonal Violence, 2,* 46–56.

Courtney, A. E., & Whipple T. W. (1983). *Sex stereotyping in advertising.* Lexington, MA: D. C. Heath.

Cowan, G., Lee, C., Levy, D., & Snyder, D. (1988). Dominance and inequality in X-rated videocassettes. *Psychology of Women Quarterly, 12,* 299–311.

Cowan, G., & O'Brien, M. (1990). Gender and survival vs. death in slasher films: A content analysis. *Sex Roles, 23,* 187–196.

Craft, C. (1988). *Too old, too ugly, and not deferential to men: An anchorwoman's courageous battle against sex discrimination.* Rockland, CA: Prima.

Davis, D. M. (1990). Portrayals of women in prime-time network television: Some demographic characteristics. *Sex Roles, 23,* 325–332.

Demare, D., Briere, J., & Lips, H. M. (1988). Violent pornography and self-reported likelihood of sexual aggression. *Journal of Research in Personality, 22,* 140–153.

Dieter, P. (1989, March). *Shooting her with video, drugs, bullets, and promises.* Paper presented at the meeting of the Association of Women in Psychology, Newport, RI.

Donnerstein, E., Linz, D., & Penrod, S. (1987). *The question of pornography: Research findings and policy implications.* New York: Free Press.

Doyle, J. A. (1989). *The male experience* (2nd ed.). Dubuque, IA: William C. Brown.

Evans, D. (1993, March 1). The wrong examples. *Newsweek*, p. 10.

Faludi, S. (1991). *Backlash: The undeclared war against American women.* New York: Crown.

Feldman, N. S., & Brown, E. (1984, April). *Male vs. female differences in control strategies: What children learn from Saturday morning television.* Paper presented at the meeting of the Eastern Psychological Association, Baltimore, MD. (Cited in Basow, 1992.)

Foreit, K. G., Agor, T., Byers, J., Larue, J., Lokey, H., Palazzini, M., Patterson, M., & Smith, L. (1980). Sex bias in the newspaper treatment of male-centered and female-centered news stories. *Sex Roles, 6,* 475–480.

Gray, H. (1986). Television and the new black man: Black male images in prime-time situation comedies. *Media, Culture, and Society, 8,* 223–242.

Greene, R., & Dalton, K. (1953). The premenstrual syndrome. *British Medical Journal, 1,* 1007–1014.

Greer, G. (1992). *The change: Women, aging, and menopause.* New York: Alfred Knopf.

Griffin, S. (1981). *Pornography and silence: Culture's revenge against nature.* New York: Harper and Row.

Hansen, C. H., & Hansen, R. D. (1988). How rock music videos can change what is seen when boy meets girl: Priming stereotypic appraisal of social interactions. *Sex Roles, 19,* 287–316.

Haskell, M. (1988, May). Hollywood Madonnas. *Ms.*, pp. 84, 86, 88.

Horovitz, B. (1989, August 10). In TV commercials, men are often the butt of the jokes. *Philadelphia Inquirer*, pp. 5b, 6b.

The implant circus. (1992, February 18). *Wall Street Journal*, p. A20.

Koss, M. P. (1990). The women's mental health research agenda: Violence against women. *American Psychologist, 45,* 374–380.

Koss, M. P., & Dinero, T. E. (1988). Predictors of sexual aggression among a national sample of male college students. In V. I. Quinsey & R. Orentky (Eds.), *Human sexual aggression* (pp. 133–147). New York: Academy of Sciences.

Koss, M. P., Dinero, T. E., Seibel, C. A., & Cox, S. L. (1988). Stranger and acquaintance rape: Are there differences in the victim's experience? *Psychology of Women Quarterly, 12,* 1–24.

Koss, M. P., Gidycz, C. J., Wisniewski, N. (1987). The scope of rape: Incidence and prevalence of sexual aggression and victimization in a national sample of higher education students. *Journal of Consulting and Clinical Psychology, 55,* 162–170.

Leland, J., & Leonard, E. (1993, February 1). Back to Twiggy. *Newsweek*, pp. 64–65.

Lichter, S. R., Lichter, L. S., & Rothman, S. (1986, September/October). From Lucy to Lacey: TV's dream girls. *Public Opinion*, pp. 16–19.

Lichter, S. R., Lichter, L. S., Rothman, S., & Amundson, D. (1987, July/August). Prime-time prejudice: TV's images of blacks and Hispanics. *Public Opinion*, pp. 13–16.

Lisak, D., & Roth, S. (1988). Motivational factors in nonincarcerated sexually aggressive men. *Journal of Personality and Social Psychology, 55,* 795–802.

Lott, B. (1989). Sexist discrimination as distancing behavior: II. Prime-time television. *Psychology of Women Quarterly, 13,* 341–355.

MacKinnon, C. A. (1987). *Feminism unmodified: Discourses on life and law.* Cambridge, MA: Harvard University Press.

Malamuth, N. M., & Briere, J. (1986). Sexual violence in the media: Indirect effects on aggression against women. *Journal of Social Issues, 42,* 75–92.

Marhoefer-Dvorak, S., Resick, P., Hutter, C., & Girelli, S. (1988). Single-versus multiple-incident rape victims: A comparison of psychological reactions to rape. *Journal of Interpersonal Violence, 3,* 145–160.

Maslin, J. (1990, June 17). Bimbos embody retro rage. *New York Times*, pp. H13, H14.

Masse, M. A., & Rosenblum, K. (1988). Male and female created they them: The depiction of gender in the advertising of traditional women's and men's magazine's. *Women's Studies International Forum, 11,* 127–144.

Mattell offers trade-in for "Teen Talk" Barbie. (1992, October 13). *Raleigh News and Observer*, p. A3.

McCauley, C., Thangavelu, K., & Rozin, P. (1988). Sex stereotyping of occupations in relation to television representations and census facts. *Basic and Applied Social Psychology, 9,* 197–212.

Menopause. (1992, May 25). *Newsweek*, pp. 71–80.

Mills, K. (1988). *A place in the news: From the women's pages to the front page.* New York: Dodd, Mead.

Modleski, T. (1982). *Loving with a vengeance: Mass-produced fantasies for women.* New York: Methuen.

Muro, M. (1989, April 23). Comment: New era of eros in advertising. *Morning Call*, pp. D1, D16.

The new traditionalist. (1988, November 17). *New York Times*, p. Y46.

Nigro, G. N., Hill, D. E., Gelbein, M. E., & Clark, C. L. (1988). Changes in the facial prominence of women and men over the last decade. *Psychology of Women Quarterly, 12,* 225–235.

O'Connor, J. J. (1989, June 6). What are commercials selling to children? *New York Times*, p. 28.

Pareles, J. (1990, October 21). The women who talk back in rap. *New York Times*, pp. H33, H36.

Parlee, M. B. (1973). The premenstrual syndrome. *Psychological Bulletin, 80,* 454–465.

Parlee, M. B. (1979, May). Conversational politics. *Psychology Today*, pp. 48–56.

Peirce, K. (1990). A feminist theoretical perspective on the socialization of teenage girls through *Seventeen* magazine. *Sex Roles, 23,* 491–500.

Rakow, L. F. (1986). Rethinking gender research in communication. *Journal of Communication, 36,* 11–26.

Richmond-Abbott, M. (1992). *Masculine and feminine: Gender roles over the life cycle.* New York: McGraw-Hill.

Rideau, W., & Sinclair, B. (1982). Prison: The sexual jungle. In A. Scacco, Jr. (Ed.), *Male Rape* (pp. 3–29). New York: AMS Press.

Russell, D. E. H. (Ed.). (1993). *Feminist views on pornography.* Colchester, VT: Teachers College Press.

Sanday, P. R. (1986). Rape and the silencing of the feminine. In S. Tomaselli & R. Porter (Eds.), *Rape* (pp. 84–101). Oxford, UK: Basil Blackwell.

Sanders, M., & Rock, M. (1988). *Waiting for prime time: The women of television news.* Urbana, IL: University of Illinois Press.

Scott, R., & Tetreault, L. (1987). Attitudes of rapists and other violent offenders toward women. *Journal of Social Psychology, 124,* 375–380.

Scully, D. (1990). *Understanding sexual violence: A study of convicted rapists.* Boston, MA: Unwin Hyman.

Segel-Evans, K. (1987). Rape prevention and masculinity. In F. Abbott (Ed.), *New men, new minds: Breaking male tradition* (pp. 117–121). Freedom, CA: Crossing Press.

Sights, sounds and stereotypes. (1992, October 11). *Raleigh News and Observer*, pp. G1, G10.

Silverstein, B., Perdue, L., Peterson, B., & Kelly, E. (1986). The role of the mass media in promoting a thin standard of bodily attractiveness for women. *Sex Roles, 14,* 519–532.

Soeken, K., & Damrosch, S. (1986). Randomized response technique: Application to research on rape. *Psychology of Women Quarterly, 10,* 119–126.

South, S. J., & Felson, R. B. (1990). The racial patterning of rape. *Social Forces, 69,* 71–93.

Spitzack, C. (1993). The spectacle of anorexia nervosa. *Text and Performance Quarterly, 13,* 1–21.

Stroman, C. A. (1989). To be young, male and black on prime-time television. *Urban Research Review, 12,* 9–10.

Study reports sex bias in news organizations. (1989, April 11). *New York Times*, p. C22.

Tavris, C. (1992). *The mismeasure of woman.* New York: Simon and Schuster.

Texier, C. (1990, April 22). Have women surrendered in MTV's battle of the sexes? *New York Times*, pp. H29, H31.

Unger, R., & Crawford, M. (1992). *Women and gender: A feminist psychology.* New York: McGraw-Hill.

Warshaw, R. (1988). *I never called it rape.* New York: Harper and Row.

Wolf, N. (1991). *The beauty myth.* New York: William Morrow.

Women in media say career's hit "glass ceiling." (1988, March 2). *Easton Express*, p. A9.

Wood, J. T. (1992b). Telling our stories: Narratives as a basis for theorizing sexual harassment. *Journal of Applied Communication Research, 4,* 349–363.

Wood, J. T. (1993a). Engendered relationships: Interaction, caring, power, and responsibility in close relationships. In S. Duck (Ed.), *Processes in close relationships: Contexts of close relationships* (Vol. 3). Beverly Hills, CA: Sage.

Wood, J. T. (1993c). *Who cares: Women, care, and culture.* Carbondale, IL: Southern Illinois University Press.

Wood, J. T. (1993f). Defining and studying sexual harassment as situated experience. In G. Kreps (Ed.), *Communication and sexual harassment in the workplace.* Cresskill, NJ: Hampton Press.

Woodman, S. (1991, May). How super are heros? *Health*, pp. 40, 49, 82.

BOYS WILL BE GIRLS

Men's magazines have a new reader: meet Cosmo Guy

BY LIZA FEATHERSTONE

YOUR CLOCK IS TICKING
Q: HOW DO I KNOW IF I'M A GOOD KISSER?
FOODS THAT FIGHT FAT!

Sound like the parade of neurotic women's magazines at your supermarket counter? Close. All three headlines appeared recently in top-selling men's magazines, which are increasingly indistinguishable from their female counterparts. A new male reader has emerged, one whom people in the magazine business sardonically — and accurately — have dubbed the "Cosmo Guy."

Cosmo Guy is consumed with insecurity about his appearance, and *Men's Health* is his bible. The cover of *Men's Health* — a nearly full-body shot of a model — looks just like *Cosmo*'s. Cover lines that exhort physical self-improvement seem to emanate from his body. *Cosmo* has long rallied its readers with battle cries like "Big Butt Be Gone!"; this April *Men's Health* prods similar soft spots: "Banish Your Potbelly."

Launched ten years ago, *Men's Health* only recently became the business success that it is today. "No one took us too seriously for the first six or seven years," says founding and current editor Michael Lafavore, 45. "It's a boring

Liza Featherstone is a free-lance writer who lives and reads in Brooklyn.

name." Now *Men's Health* boasts a monthly circulation of 1.5 million and climbing — more than its two closest competitors, *GQ* (688,000) and *Esquire* (658,000) combined — and in the past five years its ad revenues have increased by 150 percent, to $52.9 million in 1997.

Cosmo Guy has other suitors, too. *Esquire*, *GQ*, and *Details* have always had fashion pages, but now they're all attending to the man under the clothes. *GQ*, which takes in more money in ad sales — $75.7 million in 1997 — than any other men's magazine, recently posed, to a handful of guys, this burning question: If you were stuck on a desert island, what would be the one grooming product

you couldn't live without? Passionate testimonials ensued, about Tweezerman tweezers — to combat that "unibrow . . . Movie Stars, they all pluck" — and Christian Dior's firming night treatment: "Who cares if it's made for sixty-year-old ladies?" *Esquire* recently featured a first-person essay by a guy who, hair waning, decided to shave it all off, accompanied by before/after pics and instructions about how to follow suit.

All the men's magazines cajole the reader to attend to his abs, however reluctant he might be (fast-growing downmarket newcomer *Maxim* offers workout tips "For Guys Who Hate Gyms"). Last June, when Michael Caru-

Reprinted from *Columbia Journalism Review*, May/June 1998, pp. 60-63. © 1998 by Columbia Journalism Review.

so, 36, became editor-in-chief of *Details* (which, with a half-million buyers, lags just behind *Esquire*), he announced his intention to devote more pages to health, fitness, and grooming.

Men's Health editor Lafavore says the new preoccupation with men's appearance is due largely to the aging of the baby boomers: "We're getting old. As a generation we kind of decided we weren't going to grow up, so now we're completely shocked." Then there's the American health and fitness mania, which *Self* editor-in-chief Judith Daniels calls "the great equalizer" because it has seized women and men alike.

Men's magazines used to present the reader with a world away from women. Life-style magazines all sell fantasies, and theirs was generally a fishing trip with the buddies, away from the wife — or in *GQ*'s case, with the Log Cabin boys. *GQ* used to mention women so infrequently that it was regarded as a (discreetly) gay maga-

love letter (concluding with a reminder to make sure it's welcome — John Hinckley to Jodie Foster being the classic Don't). The magazine also mercilessly ribs men for their self-defeating behavior ("Five Reasons Why You're Not Going to Get Lucky Tonight" — written, like many of *Details*'s sex pieces, by a woman).

Indeed, like some women's magazines — *Cosmo* often reads like a scary focus-group session in which men hold forth on women — men's magazines now often present interviews with members of the opposite sex as a blueprint for self-improvement. Women (some 5,000 of them, we're to understand) told *Men's Health* what they want in the sack (forty-something guys, preliminary massages, flattery) and what they don't want (too much back hair, dumb questions like "Was it good for you?"). For a recent *GQ* piece redefining "The New Gentleman," the author "went straight to the experts . . . Ladies?"

magazines have always done." Of course, the rise of service journalism in men's magazines is part of a larger genderless trend too. As Daniels observes: "Service is creeping into the mainstream. Even daily newspapers have finally caught on to the fact that people want to know how to do something better, cheaper, faster."

Zealous coverage of celebrities is nothing new for men's magazines; in its heyday, *Esquire* sent an editor to India for a week to hang out with Allen Ginsberg. But then the articles tended to focus on the famous person's work or character. Now, like women's magazines, men's magazines are hen houses of celebrity gossip, obsessed with the personal lives of the rich and famous. *GQ*'s food critic Alan Richman, in February's "My Dinner with Sharon Stone," irks the star by criticizing her taste in men. Other examples include *Details*'s "Matt Dillon: The Original Wild Thing," a profile that highlights Dillon's relationship with the

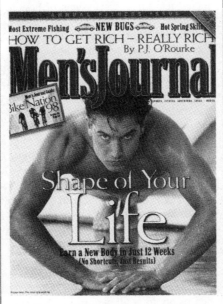

zine. Now sex and relationships — always the straight kind — have a regular presence in its pages (albeit a tormented one. Typical passage: "She's naked and sprawled across his bed — but is this necessarily a good thing?" In a recent personal essay, a married writer wondered if he should go to an amusement park with the cute chick from his office).

Increasingly, men's magazines, like women's, serve as field guides to the rocky terrain of heterosexual mating and relating. "Ask Jimmy the Bartender," *Men's Health*'s new feature, is an advice column on "women, sex, and other stuff that screws up men's lives." *Details* instructs men on how to write a winning

Steven Cohn, editor of *Media Industry Newsletter*, thinks this new concern with sex and relationships has much to do with the mainstreaming of the women's movement and men's consequent confusion. "In the old days, the caveman days before *Ms.*, men just grabbed women by the hair. This has changed, so men need help."

Our New Man is also a shopaholic; men's magazines are awash in products. *Men's Health* recently featured — this is editorial content, not advertising — six different shampoos to pouf up thinning hair, and tells where to buy them. *Self*'s Judith Daniels points out that evaluating products, "sorting out the hooey from the good stuff — that's what women's

actress Cameron Diaz, and *Esquire*'s infamous "'Kevin Spacey Has a Secret," a murkily allegoric profile ("My mom said: 'I hear he's gay.'") by Tom Junod, packaged as a celebrity outing. *Esquire* dispatched reporter Celia Farber to slink around O.J.'s house.

While Cosmo Guy reflects a welcome cultural shift toward greater sexual equality, one wonders how much more appearance-consciousness society needs. For that matter, both women's and men's magazines would probably be better if they devoted more space to ideas and stories and less to shameless panting after products. *Esquire*'s Dubious Achievement issue was pretty dismal this year: "I, Stalkerazzi," an odd and rambling first-person account of John Richardson's stint as a paparazzo, the thrills and the moral dilemmas, was the only piece that could accurately be called journalism. *GQ* averages about two strong pieces a month. Senior writer Mary A. Fischer, for instance, regularly investigates real outrages, like the U.S. government's School of the Americas, which, she reports, has trained some of Latin America's worst human-rights abusers. But with all the fussing about readers' butts, there seems to be increasingly less room for such writing in men's magazines. And their coverage of sex and women — though abundant — generally fails to offer much real insight. It tends to be whiney, in fact, as well as defensive and conventional. References to homosexuality are nervous, and women are consistently typed as possessive, frigid, and mysteriously cranky — or worse. In the April issue, Greg Donaldson describes a four-year marriage to a six-foot-two Amazon who physically assaulted him on a regular basis.

But it's still possible that, in the long run, broadly re-defining men's interests could make men's magazines more layered and diverse. Thus, the next logical question — with all the top-selling men's magazines cross-dressing, can women's magazines be far behind? Will women's magazines become more like men's magazines?

There's no stampede just yet. The long-established, high-grossing women's

WITH TOP-SELLING MEN'S MAGAZINES CROSS-DRESSING, CAN WOMEN'S MAGAZINES BE FAR BEHIND?

magazines — from *Good Housekeeping* to *Mademoiselle* — aren't about to overhaul their profitable formulas. In 1996, women's magazines pulled in $2,884,328,000 in ad revenues, four times as much as men's magazines. It's no wonder men's magazines are imitating them so studiously. Nearly all

women's magazines acknowledge a more intelligent, feminist, career-oriented reader than they did twenty years ago. Yet this imagined reader's interests — looks, shopping, sex, men — remain recognizably feminine in the most old-fashioned sense of the word.

Still, several mavericks recently have been offering a different vision of the future. Though it is less deserved recently, men's magazines have always had a more literary reputation than women's magazines. But *Mirabella* now might appeal to the old *Esquire* reader reincarnated as a woman, publishing hot novelist A.M. Homes on artist Cindy Sherman, and Alain de Boton and David Mamet on "men without women." Not only is the books section long and relatively highbrow, the whole magazine reflects a bookish sensibility: a film piece muses at length on the novels of Henry James, and words like "eponymous" pop up in discussions of how to style your frizzy hair.

Recent start-ups are even bolder. Fairchild's *Jane*, launched last year by former *Sassy* editor Jane Pratt, storms the tree fort on a number of fronts, with coverage of cars and rock 'n' roll. (Music has traditionally been left to young men's magazines like *Details*, as well as historically male-targeted magazines like *Rolling Stone* and *Spin*.) *Jane* is also funny. While men's magazines, even when obnoxious, have usually been good for a laugh, women's magazines tend to be deadly earnest about everything from seducing men to the merits of liquid eyeliner. But irony — even self-mockery — pervades *Jane*.

Then there's sports. The female sports fan, for a few months last year, had plenty to read; new women's magazines that tackled classic men's magazine material — bonefishing, boxing, people who die trying to take photos while heli-skiing.

Jump, a new magazine for teenage girls, despite tips on quick-dry nail polishes and tinted hair mousses, is more *Men's Journal* than *YM*, with articles on hockey, ice-climbing, and life in Homer, Alaska. At press time, *Jump* survives, but the future of its grown-up counterparts is uncertain at best. Condé Nast kicked off the monthly Condé Nast *Sports for Women*, a women's life-style magazine about sports, only to buy *Women's Sports and Fitness* four months later and announce that it will fold the two into one bimonthly — clearly

a less ambitious project. Time Inc. floated two test issues of *Sports Illustrated Woman/Sport* (essentially *Sports Illustrated* with a sex change) but has indefinitely postponed the launch.

For one thing, advertising was questionable. Beauty and fashion features prime the reader's material desires; reading a women's magazine really does make you want to go out and buy lipstick. That is why advertisers love women's magazines, and why any deviation from the formulas is seen as a risk.

Advertising also limits the potential success of men's magazines. Though products for men — from insoles that make you look taller to anti-snoring gadgets — are steadily proliferating, there may never be as many things to sell to men as there are to women. Cohn, of *Media Industry Newsletter*, thinks men's magazines' financial potential has been "overhyped. Until more men are house husbands, it's a very limited advertising marketplace." He's probably right, but it sure looks like a good time to experiment: U.S. magazines, overall, pulled in $13 billion from ads last year, up 14 percent from 1996.

Meanwhile, every month it gets harder to separate the men from the girls. Did I read about snowboarding in *Jump*? *Men's Health*? *Condé Nast Sports for Women*? *Men's Journal*? *Maxim*? All of the above, actually. Increasingly, women and men — or focus groups representing us — want the same things: to stay fit, look good, have agreeable relationships and hot sex, and to worship celebrities with the appropriate degree of irony.

This winter I was beginning to make sense of all this when the newly launched issue of *Men Are From Mars and Women Are From Venus* appeared on my newsstand. Founded by John Gray, author of the best-selling book of the same dispiriting title, this new monthly seems to retort: snowboarding be damned. You have as much in common with a person of the opposite sex as you do with an extraterrestrial. It was a bleak vision, and even, perhaps, a harbinger of backlash.

But winter is over and I feel better. Here's the April *Details*, with all the dish on Courtney Love, not to mention Monica Lewinsky's high school friends. It may be too warm for snowboarding and ice-climbing, but it's never bad weather for gossip.

TV's frisky family values

*In prime time, there is more sex and sex talk
than ever and Americans fear the consequences*

If you want to send a message," the old Hollywood adage has it, "use Western Union." But the reality is that television teaches lessons aplenty—about sex, marriage, relationships, law and order and decency. As Homer Simpson, the cartoon patriarch of one of the nation's favorite dysfunctional families, puts it: "The answers to life's problems aren't at the bottom of a bottle. They're on TV."

But most of the answers proffered by entertainment television do not sit well with Americans. A new poll by *U.S. News* shows two thirds of the public thinks TV shows have a negative impact on the country and huge majorities believe TV contributes to social problems like violence, divorce, teen pregnancy and the decline of family values. Ed Goeas, who conducted the poll along with Celinda Lake, notes that the greatest anxieties are expressed by women and by those who are religious, but the anger "is overwhelming and across the board."

A separate mail-in survey by *U.S. News* and the UCLA Center for Communication Policy to Hollywood leaders shows them to be far less worried than the public about the impact of TV on the nation, especially on matters relating to sex and family values. But entertainment figures are still surprisingly dour about the impact of their product. The survey is not scientific. But half of the 570 Hollywood elite who responded said TV had a negative impact on the country, and strong majorities said TV only did a fair or poor job in encouraging such things as lawful behavior, sexual abstinence and respect for police.

The level of concern in the public and industry surely will encourage critics. Republican presidential candidate

Bob Dole vowed in an interview with *U.S. News* to continue to criticize Hollywood fare. "I don't want legislation" to force a cleanup of movies and TV, he insisted. "But if they'd make good movies, they wouldn't have to worry about anything else. The problem is that they make lousy movies, and they're filled with things that young people shouldn't see."

To examine the kinds of messages TV's fantasy factory manufactures, *U.S. News* looked at a week's worth of prime-time entertainment on the ABC, CBS, NBC and Fox networks in mid-March. Admittedly, the sample ignores much that critics find objectionable on TV today: cable fare, talk shows, soap operas, tabloid news shows and vio-

CASUAL SEX

FRIENDS (NBC, THURSDAY, 8 P.M.) is one of the most popular shows and is laden with plots that portray or refer to casual sex.

61% of Hollywood leaders think TV places too much emphasis on sex, and 92% say TV does a fair or poor job of encouraging sexual abstinence.

lence-ridden theatrical movies. But the sitcoms and dramas on network prime time still offer a revealing glimpse into TV's moral universe.

SEX

On NBC's popular sitcom "Friends," Phoebe has a problem: Her boyfriend won't sleep with her. "The guy still won't put out, huh?" a pal commiser-

ates. The gang speculates he must be gay. But Phoebe rules that out because when she was dancing with him recently, "I felt it on my hip." Later, she can barely contain her glee: She finally "made it" with her boyfriend. The trick, she explains, was to make clear to him that she wasn't expecting a commitment just because they'd had sex.

Sex has replaced violence as prime time's obsession. Of the 58 shows monitored by *U.S. News,* almost half contained sexual acts or references to sex. That's no anomaly. In an extensive study, Robert Lichter, Linda Lichter, Stanley Rothman and Daniel Amundson found that a sexual act or reference occurred every four minutes on average during prime time.

Sexual innuendo and scatological humor are rampant even during the 8 p.m to 9 p.m. slot that used to be reserved for family-friendly programming. Actor Tom Selleck, who has appeared on five episodes of "Friends," summarizes the angst of many parents. "I do have the dilemma: Can my daughter watch it?" The prevailing attitude on comedies, says liberal producer Norman Lear, is this: "They seek to get away with as much as they can." A sample from mid-March:

■ On NBC's "Caroline in the City," penis size is a running joke. A male character asks: "Does size matter?" A female responds: "Give women some credit. Of course it doesn't matter. Unless you're having sex."

■ On ABC's "Grace Under Fire," Grace promises to pay off her boyfriend with "Mother Nature's credit card" if he watches her kids.

■ On NBC's "Mad About You," a neighbor asks Paul for permission to "loosely cup your dog's testicles" to prove a point.

The National Institute for Mental Health has called entertainment TV an "important sex educator." If so, the main lesson seems to be: Go for it. "It is absolutely taken for granted that you date somebody a couple of times and sleep with them," says Michael Josephson, president of the California-based Josephson Institute of Ethics. Consider these episodes: On Fox's "Melrose Place," an inebriated Jake takes a stranger to his hotel room. "No strings, attached, right?" he asks her. "None but these," she says, dropping the spaghetti straps of her slip from her shoulders by way of an answer. And on NBC's "Seinfeld," a minicrisis erupts because of a shortage of contraceptive sponges. With supplies limited, Elaine interviews her date to decide if he is "spongeworthy." He passes muster.

These plot lines mirror a recent report on the family hour by the conservative Media Research Center, which found that portrayals of premarital sex outnumbered sex within marriage by 8 to 1. Moreover, casual sex was "almost always condoned." That makes viewers uneasy. "If the public had its way, there would be few examples of any kind of sex on television, even though the situation comedies and dramas with sexual references or themes have the highest ratings," notes Jeffrey Cole, director of the UCLA center that worked with *U.S. News.*

Another source of concern is that TV does not dwell much on the biological consequences of sex, although AIDS was mentioned twice and gonorrhea once in the prime-time shows in mid-March. Lichter and his co-authors found in their study that only 1 in 85 sexual references on TV concerned birth control, abortion or sexually transmitted diseases. "Producers and writers tell audiences one part of the truth: that sex feels good," says the Rev. Ellwood Kieser, head of the Humanitas Prize Organization, which honors TV programs that promote human values. "But in the real world, sex involves commitment and responsibility." Respondents to *U.S. News*'s Hollywood elite survey agreed: Fifty-eight percent said there should be more discussions of abstinence and 75 percent said there should be more talk of safe sex and contraceptive use.

TEEN SEX

MELROSE PLACE (FOX, MONDAY, 8 P.M.) a show popular with youths, is one of several programs in the time slot that used to be the "family hour" that raise lots of sexual themes.

76% of Americans think TV contributes to the problem of teen pregnancy, while only 37% of Hollywood leaders agree.

FAMILY

On ABC, Roseanne's son and daughter place her new baby and a turtle in the center of a circle made of socks. They then place bets on which—the baby or the turtle—will break the boundary first. Roseanne's older daughter walks in and urges them to stop lest they traumatize the baby. "Every grownup in the household is going to traumatize the kid," the younger sister replies. "Beating the turtle is the only shot at self-esteem." Their father walks in and slaps down a $5 bet on the turtle.

In the past, the issues confronting TV families tended to be trivial—not unlike the recent "Home Improvement" episode in which Tim Allen and his fictional son feud over the boy's haircut. But the trend in sitcoms today is toward ever more daunting and controversial issues, from spousal abuse to teen pregnancy. The star of NBC's "The John Larroquette Show," for example, is a recovering alcoholic with a teenage son he abandoned as a baby and a grown daughter from a different mother. He hadn't known he'd sired her until recently.

There is obviously something laudable about the embrace of such realism, but some, like *New York Times* TV critic Caryn James, believe sitcoms have plunged into a state of "dysfunctional overload." A procession of social ills beamed into living rooms can make such maladies seem normal, some con-

tend. In *U.S. News*'s sampling, the episode of Fox's "Beverly Hills, 90210" found Kelly's mom struggling to get her daughter back on her feet after a drug addiction; on ABC's "Murder One," three women describe how a doctor they were paying to help end their drug addiction actually drugged and raped them during his evening rounds. Darlene, Roseanne's 19-year-old unmarried daughter, also turned up pregnant on a recent episode.

The good news is that father—and mother—still know best. From June Cleaver to Roseanne, "television has taken a fairly traditional approach to family authority, consistently portraying parents in firm control of their children," notes media critic Lichter. None of the shows from the mid-March sample showed kids flouting parental authority or parents "doing their own thing" and ignoring the needs or behavior of their kids.

In facing the kinds of daunting issues that afflict TV families, a real-world family might turn to its faith. Not the case on prime time. A report by the Media Research Center last week noted that the network coverage of faith is "virtually nonexistent." But that might soon be changing because a surprise hit this year is the CBS show "Touched by an Angel," in which Della Reese and Roma Downey play angels who help out lost souls on Earth. "The message is that God exists, which for television is revolutionary," says executive producer Martha Williamson. "We're breaking the rules that say God has no place on TV and God doesn't bring in the numbers [good ratings]."

The success of the show is likely to spawn clones. "There's a call out at the big three networks for feel-good stories," says Williamson. And it's being heeded: One show in development for the WB Network is "Seventh Heaven," featuring a big family headed by a minister dad.

Percentage of those who expressed concern that portrayals of sex or sexual references contribute to these problems:		
	ALL AMERICANS	HOLLYWOOD ELITE
■ Extramarital sex	84%	43%
■ Casual sex	83	56
■ Young people having sex	90	63
■ Violence against women	94	61

Percentage of those who think these solutions are an appropriate way to handle worrisome issues on TV:	ALL AMERICANS	HOLLYWOOD ELITE
■ Industry self-regulation	73%	80%
■ Technical devices such as the V-chip	83	62
■ Parental supervision	95	96

VIOLENCE

On ABC's "World's Funniest Videos" with a laugh track on, a skier tumbles 20 feet down a wall of sheer rock; a couple on a speeding motorcycle crash into a building; a French groom digging in his back yard accidentally smashes his bride in the face with a shovel.

Contrary to popular perception, violence is not ubiquitous in prime time. A UCLA report last fall found that theatrical movies and on-air promotions are the real trouble spots. Only 10 of 121 prime-time shows monitored in that study had frequent problems with violence. One of the main offenders, argued UCLA researchers, was "America's Funniest Home Videos," which shows violence devoid of context.

In the *U.S. News* sample, just a handful of shows seemed excessive: On Fox's "The X-Files," a "death fetishist" clipped hair and pulled the fingernails off of corpses, the results of which were shown in graphic detail; and on CBS's "Walker, Texas Ranger," there was the usual barrage of karate kicks and flying fists that did nothing to advance the plot.

Most cop shows, though, treated violence in an intelligent fashion. On one episode of NBC's "Homicide: Life on the Street," for example, the arrest of a teen drug dealer leads detectives to uncover a series of gruesome murders. The program did not show the brutish acts being committed, though grisly corpses were shown; the only act of violence on the program involved the police making an arrest.

The problem is the long-term one that crime on TV still outstrips real-life mayhem and there still is too little emphasis on the consequences of violence. In their report on four decades of entertainment TV, Lichter and his co-authors counted about 50 crimes—including a dozen murders—in every hour of prime time. "Since 1955, TV characters have been murdered at a rate one thousand

times higher than real-world victims," they write. In the *U.S. News* sample, Fox's "New York Undercover" featured five shootings in an hour, for example. The straight-from-the-headlines show was about the assassination of a Nation of Islam-like character to avenge the murder of a fellow Islamic group member 20 years earlier.

VIOLENCE

THE X-FILES (FOX, FRIDAY, 9 P.M.) is a cult favorite; it can also be pretty gruesome at times. Americans rank the impact of TV on real-life violence as a major concern.

92% of Americans think TV contributes to violence in the country, and 78% of Hollywood officials agree with that view.

The cumulative impact of the video crime wave may be one reason Americans are more worried about crime than ever, despite a drop in the actual crime rate. Media critic George Gerbner contends that those who watch TV often see the world as more vicious than those who don't watch as much TV. This "heightens perceptions of danger and risk" that heavy TV watchers feel. Other academic studies indicate that hard-core watchers have a higher fear of victimization than do infrequent viewers.

RACE RELATIONS

On Fox's "New York Undercover," a white woman lieutenant discusses affirmative action with a Det. J. C. Williams, who's black. "We both get perks. I get them because I'm white; you get them because you're male," she says. Williams responds: "I'll try to remember that the next time that I am passed up by a cab or when a woman who sees me holds her purse closer to her." The lieutenant shakes her head: "How will we ever get past this?"

Prime time is far more heterogeneous than before. An unpublished study of the 1994–95 television season by the Washington-based Center for Media and Public Affairs found that 9 out of 10 prime-time episodes included a black character and that over half of the shows featured an African-American character in a continuing role. The proportion of Latinos on prime time is about 2 percent.

Another salutary development is that negative stereotypes of minorities have decreased. The bad news, according to critics, is that Hollywood has gone to the other extreme. One issue is that on entertainment shows, "It's hard to find a member of a minority group that does something wrong," says actor Selleck, who denounces the trend as Hollywood "tokenism." On news-related shows, of course, the opposite is true, because minorities are portrayed disproportionately as scary wrongdoers.

Several hour long dramas—ABC's "NYPD Blue," NBC's "ER" and Fox's "New York Undercover," for example—tackle racial problems in a serious fashion. But the tendency in TV shows is to trivialize racial problems or pretend they don't exist. Cultural critic Benjamin DeMott argues that "race deleting" themes on TV add to the nation's confusion about race. It's the reason, he argues,

Percentage of those who expressed concern about the portrayal of these things on TV:	ALL AMERICANS	HOLLYWOOD ELITE
■ Verbal references to sex	82%	38%
■ Visual images of nudity or seminudity	83	42
■ Homosexual activity	75	31
■ Passionate encounters and heavy kissing	75	28
■ Premarital sex	83	38
■ Extramarital sex	85	56

that Americans were shocked at the different reactions of whites and blacks to the O. J. Simpson verdict.

It's also true that blacks and whites watch completely different worlds on TV—and race isn't a reference point in those worlds. Jannette Dates, acting dean of communications at Howard University and co-editor of *Split Image: African Americans in the Mass Media,* argues that in the increasingly splintered world of TV, the races are being "ghettoized" as whites watch such things as "Seinfeld" and blacks such things as "Martin." She argues that middle-class values tend to be promoted on white shows and that black families are demeaned on too many black shows.

One major area where Hollywood officials and the public think alike is that parents must take a larger role in monitoring what their kids watch—more than

FAMILIES

HOME IMPROVEMENT (ABC, TUESDAY, 9 P.M.) is one of the shows that portray families wholesomely. But many still worry about TV's impact on values.

81% of Americans think TV contributes to the decline of family values, and 46% of Hollywood leaders agree with that sentiment.

95 percent of both groups feel that way. And recent events show that viewers hold the power to change TV. Just a handful of the 42 shows introduced last fall have been renewed. Both sides claim they want better programming. And the reasons may have been best summed up by Bart Simpson. "It's just hard not listening to TV," he told his

father. "It's spent more time raising us than you have."

BY JIM IMPOCO WITH ROBIN M. BENNEFIELD, KENAN POLLACK, RICHARD BIERCK, KAREN SCHMIDT AND STEPHEN GREGORY

The U.S. News poll of the general public was of 1,000 American adults conducted by Celinda Lake of Lake Research and Ed Goeas of the Tarrance Group March 16–18, 1996. Margin of error: plus or minus 3.1 percent. The poll of the Hollywood leaders was a mailed survey that went to 6,059 persons and for which there were 570 responses. Among those who helped at the UCLA Center for Communication Policy on the Hollywood poll are Jeffrey Cole, Michael Suman, Phoebe Schramm, Marde Gregory, James Reynolds, Scott Davis and Jeff Shore. Percentages listed in each of the surveys may not add up to 100 because some respondents answered "Don't know."

SO BIG

The Telecommunications Act at Year One

by Neil Hickey

Backslapping. Glee. Jubilation. High fives. "A Victory for Viewers," the *New York Times* headlined its lead editorial. A "landmark" bill, wrote *The Wall Street Journal.* "This is the first major overhaul of telecommunications law since Marconi was alive and the crystal set was state of the art," trumpeted Thomas Bliley, chairman of the House Commerce Committee. Broadcasters, cablecasters, and telephone executives all declared themselves tickled pink. Four often bitter years of mule-trading, bickering, and take-no-prisoners lobbying by some of the most powerful corporations in America had come to a triumphal end. The architects of the 1996 Telecommunications Act, a trade journal reported, were sure it would create millions of jobs and "unleash a torrent of competition heralding nothing less than the dawn of a new information age." The bill was "the best overall blueprint that any country in the world has ever come up with," said Congressman Edward Markey. President Clinton proclaimed that consumers will enjoy more choice and lower prices and that they'll "continue to benefit from a diversity of voices and viewpoints in radio, television, and the print media. . . . Today with the stroke of a pen, our laws will catch up with the future," he intoned at the signing ceremony on February 8, [1996].

Now, twelve months into the new law's life, seems a good moment to pull into a rest stop off the information superhighway to check our road maps and

Neil Hickey is a CJR *contributing editor.*

From *Columbia Journalism Review,* January/February 1997, pp. 23-28. © 1997 by Columbia Journalism Review. Reprinted by permission.

learn where we've been and where we think we're going and if that highly acclaimed bridge to our telecommunications future is rickety or sound. One veteran observer called the new law "The Full Employment Act for Telecommunications Lawyers," and that tag has proved prophetic, as the massed legal talent of the affected industries, the Federal Communications Commission, the Justice Department, and dozens of consumer activist groups conduct a talmudic analysis to puzzle out how to tilt the statute their way. At the heart of it is a commendable goal: to haul down the Berlin Wall of barriers that have created de facto monopolies in the cable and telephone industries. It sets the stage for an unbuttoned, free-for-all rivalry between local phone companies, long distance companies, and cable system operators, which holds out the promise, at least, of reducing prices significantly for all three of those services.

How is it possible for fewer and fewer owners to generate greater and greater competition?

Other parts of the law have drawn fire from independent analysts. For example, it removed all limitations on the number of radio stations one company can own nationally, and allowed up to eight per company locally (instead of only four); relaxed the rules about how many TV stations one company can operate; ordered the FCC to consider easing the rule limiting ownership to one TV station per market, as well as the bar to ownership of a newspaper and a broadcast outlet in the same city; permitted common ownership of cable systems and broadcast networks; ended all rate regulation of smaller cable TV systems and promised the same for large ones later on; extended the license term of TV and radio stations to eight years from four; allowed TV networks to start and own another broadcast network if they choose; required that all TV sets come equipped with a V-chip to help screen out violent and sexually explicit shows; imposed prison terms and fines on anybody who transmits pornography over the Internet. Enough loopholes and wiggle room were built into the legislation, however, to keep the FCC staff fully engaged for years.

But far and away the splashiest effect of the new law during the last year has been the historic, unprecedented torrent of mergers, consolidations, buyouts, partnerships, and joint ventures that has changed the face of Big Media in America. A bare few examples:

• Westinghouse/CBS bought Infinity Broadcasting for $4.9 billion, creating a radio colossus of 77 stations and achieving dominant power in the nation's top ten radio markets, with multiple stations in each.

• Time Warner Inc. and Turner Broadcasting system merged in a $6.7 billion deal that created the world's largest media company.

• Nynex bought Bell Atlantic for $22.1 billion, making the new entity the largest regional telephone company in the U.S.

• Two other Baby Bells, SBC and Pacific Telesis, joined forces in a $16.7 million merger.

• Rupert Murdoch's News Corp. acquired full ownership of New World Communications Group Inc. for $3 billion, making it the nation's leading television-station owner with 22 outlets.

• U.S. West, a regional Bell company, paid $10.8 billion for control of Continental Cablevision, the third-largest cable operator in the United States.

• Tribune Company of Chicago purchased Renaissance Communications for $1.13 billion, making it a 16-station giant with access to a third of America's TV households.

• Worldcom Inc., the fourth-largest long-distance phone company, bought MFS Communications (the leading provider of alternative local phone service to businesses) for $12.4 billion, creating the first one-stop local/long distance phone company since the Bell System broke up in 1984.

• The A. H. Belo Corporation of Dallas bought the Providence Journal Company for $1.5 billion, fashioning a media empire of 16 TV stations plus the Food TV Network (a cable network) and such newspapers as *The Dallas Morning News* and the Providence *Journal-Bulletin*.

• Clear Channel Communications boosted its radio station line-up to more than 100 stations, giving it a total audience second only to that of Westinghouse.

• Chancellor Broadcasting Co. bought twelve radio stations from Colfax Communications for $365 million, giving it 53 stations in 15 markets.

• Gannett acquired Multimedia Entertainment for $1.7 billion, thereby gaining 10 newspapers (for a total of 92), 5 TV stations (new total: 15), 2 radio stations (for a chain of 13), and a cable operation with subscribers in 5 states.

Factor into those deals the famous $18.5 billion sale of Cap Cities/ABC to the Walt Disney Co.; Westinghouse's $5.4 billion takeover of CBS Inc.; Viacom's ingestion of Paramount Communications (which earlier had absorbed Simon & Schuster); and Rupert Murdoch's swallowing up of Twentieth Century Fox, HarperCollins, and *TV Guide*. And to that add the largest and most dramatic foreign takeover of any American company: the $23 billion buyout of MCI by British Telecommunications announced in November, which will give the U.S. long-distance company a pocketful of cash to lay siege to local phone companies, which is now allowed under the 1996 act.

Virtually all the coverage of this unprecedented deluge of consolidations appeared on the business pages of newspapers (if it appeared at all) and on cable channels (CNBC, CNNFN) devoted to business news, and thus flew under the radar of most Americans — even though collectively the deals have a prodigious impact on most people's lives and change irrevocably the very shape and texture of the nation's media. While the new law was making its way through Congress to the president's desk, the word "competition," like a Tibetan mantra, was a thunderous accompaniment to the negotiations. President Clinton threatened to veto it because, he insisted, instead of promoting "competition it promotes mergers and concentrations of power." Congress tweaked the bill to get his OK, but it's still the most potent instrument in legislative history for promoting megamergers and consolidations, and for fostering giantism in media companies by relaxing ownership rules and hauling down barriers to inter-industry matrimony.

Thus the question presents itself like a Japanese koan (the scrupulous contemplation of which may or may not lead to enlightenment): how is it possible for fewer and fewer owners to generate greater and greater competition?

And the implications for journalism: how much news will be suppressed and self-censored by news executives and reporters reluctant to invoke the wrath (or even the raised eyebrow) of their corporate overseers who don't want eager-beaver newspeople mucking around in the dealings of the parent companies? Would CBS News give full play to any malfeasance by Westinghouse in a disaster at the power-generation plant in Shanghai, China, where Westinghouse owns a $100 million, 35 percent interest? It's doubtful, since the Chinese government is famously sensitive to criticism. In August NBC abjectly apologized to China after sportscaster Bob Costas in his on-air commentary at the Olympics referred to "problems with human rights, property rights . . . and the threat posed to Taiwan," as well as to the well-documented use by Chinese athletes of performance-enhancing drugs. NBC parent GE, one needs to know, has huge investments in China (lighting, hospital equipment, plastics), and NBC operates a pair of satellite channels (NBC Asia and CNBC Asia) which aspire to serve the whole Chinese mainland; and GE has an agreement with China Telecom to build a data transmission network. "We didn't intend to hurt their feelings," an NBC vice president explained meekly, in justifying the apology. One trade journal wondered: since when does a network have to apologize for reporting the truth? The answer: ever since news departments have become smaller and smaller potatoes in an ever larger mulligan stew of corporate expansionism. In late November, China threatened to ax all of the

Disney company's massive business interests in China if it went ahead with plans to distribute a Martin Scorsese movie about Tibet's spiritual leader, the Dalai Lama. Disney sells toys, clothing, and other Disneyana in China, and exhibits films such as *Toy Story* and *Jumanji*. "If Disney distributes [the movie called *Kundun*], China won't be happy and that means Disney's business in China will be terminated," warned an official in Beijing. "It's very serious." Disney, to its credit, decided that it would indeed distribute the film. But we may confidently predict that neither ABC, CBS, NBC, nor Fox — nor any cable network connected with them — will ever broadcast a tough documentary on China's brutal treatment of Tibet or its ruthless suppression of the Tiananmen Square democracy movement or its sale of nuclear materials to rogue nations or its expected crackdown on democracy in Hong Kong when it assumes control there on July 1.

This year's merger of Time Warner Inc. and Turner Broadcasting System Inc. has boosted to a whole new level the concerns about how consumers can be caught in the crossfire between emerging media behemoths. That's been dramatized, entertainingly, in New York City recently, where Time Warner (the second biggest cable operator, nationally) is the gatekeeper to the hearts and minds of most cable subscribers. From the moment the TW-Turner nuptials won the blessing of Washington, Time Warner refused to carry Rupert Murdoch's newly minted 24-hour Fox News Channel on its New York City system. Ted Turner in his new seat of power as vice-chairman of TW — so the very logical supposition goes — wanted no further competition for his own all-news channels (CNN, CNNFN, Headline News) and certainly none from Murdoch, whom he loudly and obsessively disdains. One need not be an admirer of Rupert Murdoch to find something "bothersome" in all this, as Mark Cooper of the Consumer Federation of America puts it. No new entry into cable programming can be fully successful nationally without acceptance by both TW and the number one cable giant, TeleCommunications Inc. (which owns 9.9 percent of TW), since together they control access to almost half of all cable subscribers in the U.S. Their interlocking ambitions create "a chilling concentration of common economic interests," Cooper points out. "On the one hand the public understands that concentrated ownership creates problems. On the other, it doesn't know what it's not getting. So when it doesn't receive an additional news channel, it doesn't complain. The difficulty of proving a negative creates a problem for public policy."

Virtually all the coverage of this unprecedented deluge of consolidations appeared as business news, and thus flew under the radar of most Americans

Ruminating on the TW-Turner versus Murdoch shootout in an editorial on October 24 ("Mr. Murdoch's Rage"), *The New York Times* decided: "It is unsettling enough to contemplate a world dominated by a few giant media companies without imagining them being run by spiteful egomaniacs" — calling to mind Murdoch's own history of exclusionary practices: he cancelled the BBC from his Hong Kong-based Star satellite network to appease Chinese bureaucrats who were annoyed with its coverage and has kept CNN off Star as well. On November 10, the *Times* wrote that the TW/Murdoch sideshow proves that the government "has little chance of controlling — or even fully understanding — the newly deregulated communications industry."

Constructing lists of what might be called "hypothetical unethicals" by emerging megamedia is a new parlor game, and a too-easy one. Will TW's *Sports Illustrated* write favorably about any players' strike, now that that lucrative Atlanta Braves franchise is a new member of the family? Will the Providence *Journal-Bulletin* in reviewing The Food TV Network write that its recipes are tasteless and boring, at the risk of annoying the A. H. Belo parent of both of them? Now that Westinghouse owns *both* all-news radio stations in New York (WCBS and WINS), will it eventually merge their newsrooms to save money, thus neutralizing those historically hotly competitive stations and denying New Yorkers one of their sources of news?

None of those things — and plenty more like them — may ever happen. But for the first time the fields are now tilled and fertilized to make the growth of such weeds not only possible but likely. "What scares me most," says Gene Kimmelman, co-director of the Consumers Union in Washington, "is that eventually we may have most of the big players in cahoots with each other and there will be no one who has a major ownership stake in dissemination of information with a market incentive to criticize. Who's going to blow the whistle? The way the public gets its information will be predominantly controlled by those who are benefiting from a monopolistic environment." William Small, the Larkin Professor of Communications at Fordham (and former president of NBC News) says that, during the act's first year, he has seen no "horrendous examples" of news suppression growing out of the consolidations. "But self-censorship is always the greatest concern. If you're an investigative reporter or producer do you hesitate to do a piece on GE's dealings with the Pentagon? Do you say: why should I get GE mad at the news division, or at me? We'll never know."

Time magazine went out of its way in October to acknowledge this minefield in a prologue by managing editor Walter Isaacson to an article about "the strains" caused by TW's union with Turner. Since Time Inc.'s original merger with Warner seven years ago, wrote Isaacson, (which, he confessed, the magazine "initially failed to cover") *Time* faces "a lot more suspicions....[B]ut we learned our lesson quickly..." He went on:

Among the trends in the media world is consolidation, with sprawling corporations owning news organizations and raising the specter of conflicting interests and a less diverse babble of journalistic voices. . . . [I]ndividual press baron[s] can be insidious meddlers. . . . If any readers or watchdog groups discern a pattern of dishonest judgments, they can (and should) flail us. . . . But we promise that the mistakes we make will be due to our editorial fallibility rather than to corporate kowtowing.

Some of the most worrisome fallout of the 1996 act is occurring in the radio industry, where all limitations on how many stations one company can own nationally have been repealed, and the local cap increased to eight. In Memphis, Clear Channel Communications Inc. (which now operates 121 stations nationwide) owns seven outlets, and four of those are targeted at the city's predominantly African-American listeners — giving them a near monopoly voice to that segment of the local population. Art Gilliam, president of WLOK-AM in Memphis (a black-oriented station and one of the few remaining independents in the city), complains he's being squeezed out. "The old Communications Act mandated service to the community by station owners. Local ownership is more likely to provide good community service because those owners are more familiar with their communities and have a vested interest in them. The big change with the new act is in the philosophical approach to what best serves a local community." In Rochester, New York, the American Radio Systems Corp. (ARS) was ordered by the Justice Department in October to slash its ownership from eight stations to four, thereby reducing its stranglehold on the city's radio advertising revenues. That came as a great relief to Andrew Langston, owner of a small, independent African-American-oriented station (WDKX-FM) which he and his wife started from scratch in 1974. The big conglomerated radio chains make it extremely hard "for folks who are black and Hispanic to have a place in radio," he maintains. "Large corporations like ARS are such a dominant force that they can eliminate the small entrepreneur." The Justice Department is embarked on a nationwide review of how mammoth radio chains are exploiting the new law to grab a preemptive share of local radio ad rev-

Of all the provisions of the 1996 act, the one that seemed most promising for consumers at the outset is now the one most in tatters

enues — and forcing divestitures where anti-trust violations seem apparent.

A contrarian view has it that one company owning eight radio stations in a single city can be good for radio news. How's that? Well, says David Bartlett, president of the Radio-Television News Directors Association, an affluent string of stations in the same town creates a deep pool of cash that can be tapped for news and public affairs programs. "There's no shortage of interest on the part of the audience in radio news. But there have been very few stations big enough to afford it," he claims. "I'd much rather have a good news operation that serves six or eight stations in the same city than have none of those stations doing any news because they're owned by separate owners and can't afford to do it. So you may discover in the short and medium term that consolidation may actually lead to a revival of radio news, and that's much to be wished."

Or, another scenario, offered by an urban radio reporter: "If you're a newsperson in, let's say, Kansas City, would you prefer that your owner be the big local fatcat, or a station group with headquarters a thousand miles away — which would give you more freedom to cover local news? It depends on who the local fatcat is and how committed he is to independent news. A lot of local owners don't want their golf pals, who run the city, covered in a bad light."

But of all the provisions of the 1996 Telecommunications Act, the one that seemed most promising for consumers at the outset is now the one most in tatters. At the very core of the act was the so-called "two-wire world": no longer would cable TV and regional telephone companies have monopolies, respectively, on video service and local phone service into the home. In a gesture of thrilling *aggiornamento*, the act allowed cable to supply phone service and phone companies to deliver cable programs — so that the resulting hot competition nationwide would drive down the prices of both. But — except for test runs in places like Dover Township, New Jersey, and Alexandria, Virginia — no such boon to consumers is visible anywhere on the horizon. In fact, astonishingly, it never was on the horizon, according to a Clinton administration official who spoke to CJR on condition of anonymity:

"One of the real dilemmas we had while this act was being debated was: 'At what point do we admit that the notion of cable and telephony attacking each other's markets is bullshit?' We knew, because we study these things, that this was a lie. It wasn't going to happen. The costs on both sides, and the technological hurdles, are too high. Oh, maybe twenty years from now, but probably not even then. This bill was supposed to promote competition now, not twenty years from now. My point to you is that everybody in Washington so badly wanted this to happen that they didn't ask the cable and phone companies: 'How much is this going to cost you? How do you plan to finance the crushing costs? How will you conduct a business about which you now know nothing?'" That was the big story that never got written, the source insists. "Everybody missed it. I never saw an article that said categorically, 'This bill is based on a two-wire world and it's not going to happen.' In fact, it was supposed to bring more competition, lower prices, and more services. But so far we've seen more consolidation, higher prices, and no new services."

The handwriting finally appeared on the wall in October when Gerald Levin, the Time Warner c.e.o., told investors that — after spending billions gearing up for telephony — his company was "not interested" in the phone business anymore. A few Wall Streeters are guessing that Time Warner will, in fact, eventually sell off all or parts of its cable TV holdings to reduce its $17.5 billion debt. And TCI's fabled c.e.o. John Malone is also thinking the formerly unthinkable, according to reports: He "has made the decision that the cable business is not where he wants to be," a Schroder Wertheim analyst told *Business Week* in October. Meanwhile, the phone companies, in spite of grandiose announcements, show zero progress in invading cable's turf. Their proudest initiative was a joint venture of Nynex, Bell Atlantic, and Pacific Telesis, to cobble together a new entity called Tele-TV and to hire away Howard Stringer, CBS's top broadcast executive, to run it and teach them how to get into television. But so far that grandstand play has shown no visible results, and the chances of consumers ever receiving news broadcasts and sports and *Seinfeld* from their local phone companies grow ever slimmer. Nonetheless, some experts continue to believe that cable and telephony will go after each other's business. Greg Simon, chief domestic policy adviser to Vice President Al Gore, told CJR that it's going to happen — eventually — but not as fast as many imagined when the act was in preparation.

One big roadblock to cable and long-distance getting into the vastly profitable $100 million local phone business has been the so-called "interconnection" controversy: namely, how far can the Baby Bells go in blocking those two giant potential competitors from hitchhiking on the local phone lines into consumers' homes? Outfits like AT&T and Sprint need that access — as the law permits — if they are ever to compete for local phone customers. But the Bells have resisted, and it's now in the lap of the courts. It's a rumpus that the public is virtually totally igno-

> "The act was supposed to bring more competition, lower prices, and more services. But so far we've seen more consolidation, higher prices, and no new services"

rant about, even though, as Andrew Jay Schwartzman of the Media Access Project puts it: "The interconnection is the single most important internal building block of this whole telecommunications transformation, and dramatically affects the rate at which a lot of this change will take place."

With the Republicans once again in control of Congress, a new phase begins in teasing out the 1996 act's ramifications for consumers. Among the large open questions: should common ownership of a newspaper and a broadcast station in the same market be permitted (except for already-existing situations, e.g., the *Chicago Tribune*-WGN and the *New York Post*-WNYW); and should any one entity be allowed to own more than one TV station in the same area? The White House and the Democratic minority will publicly resist any such liberalizations as tending to concentrate more media influence in fewer hands. But one administration insider, speaking off the record, mused that blanket newspaper/broadcasting restrictions are "a totally counterproductive idea" because they prevent a thriving radio or TV station from buying a sickly newspaper and restoring it to health. That could be crucial in a two-newspaper town, the source argues, "where there's one dominant paper and another on its last legs. The rule as it stands contributes to the death of small papers and the creation of newspaper monopolies." Similarly — so goes the theory — there's a potential silver lining in changing the rules to allow one entrepreneur to own two TV outlets in the same market, if that owner promised (for example) to format his second channel as a local all-news station for C-SPAN-like coverage of community affairs, along with live town hall meetings and free political time for office seekers.

As the new telecommunications law blows out the first candle on its birthday cake, the payout benefits are still a mixed bag and its ultimate net rewards for consumers are visible only through a glass darkly. George Gerbner, founder and chairman of the newly formed Cultural Environment Movement, complains that the act passed "in virtual secrecy, without any discussion of its long-range consequences." It "legitimizes monopolies" and "unleashes them on a global market," he insists. Television journalism has become "an adjunct of marketing and thus must be more entertaining and more adjusted to the fantasy world of drama and fiction." Jeff Chester, director of the Center for Media Education, says: "We really have to look at this as rebuilding the communications system from the ground up. It's going to be dominated by a handful of very large, powerful players." Among

big players who own news organizations, the focus "is going to be more on merchandising and entertainment than news." And the stage is set, more so than ever in U.S. media history, for corporate bosses to suppress unwelcome news and otherwise meddle in editorial decisions. The American Society of Magazine Editors meeting in Bermuda in October issued a policy statement — after alleged intrusive actions by owners — declaring that "editors need the maximum possible protection from untoward commercial or other extra-journalistic pressures. It seems appropriate now to make that standard explicit and precise." Broadcast and newspaper journalists are in need, more than ever, of similar explicit and precise assurances.

If there is bad and ambiguous news imbedded in the act, there's good news as well.

• The new law affirms the rights of citizens, as well as schools, hospitals, museums and libraries, to have affordable access to these emerging advanced communications networks.

• Digital broadcasting — which will drastically expand the number of TV signals in every community — holds out at least the promise of vastly greater diversity from our television service.

• Local and long distance phone rates will decline eventually as companies like AT&T, the newly-forged MCI-British Tel and the regional Bells gird for battle against each other.

In truth, diversity of choice for consumers is coming from technology and marketplace forces as much as from governmental tinkering. The direct broadcast satellite industry (DBS), for example, is emerging as the main competitor of cable; from a standing start barely eighteen months ago it now has 5 million subscribers and will have about 20 million soon after the year 2000. And the Internet continues as the most varied and democratic medium yet invented.

Meanwhile, the revolutionary Telecommunications Act of 1996 is being massaged, tickled, vivisected, and anatomized by the administration, Congress, the courts, the Justice Department, and the FCC to discover how its (often very unspecific) provisions ought to work out in the real world. That involves a lot of heavy lifting. In early November, *Broadcasting & Cable* magazine editorialized that nine months after passage of the Act, "the new landscape looks remarkably moribund. . . . All the competition that was to ensue from the most ambitious rewriting of communications law has yet to occur. . . . That's not to say that competition won't come along, but . . . by then today's marketplace may be unrecognizable."

All those high-fives of last February were way premature.

The stage is set, more so than ever in U.S. media history, for corporate bosses to suppress unwelcome news and otherwise meddle in editorial decisions

The Global Media Giants

The nine firms that dominate the world

By Robert W. McChesney

A specter now haunts the world: a global commercial media system dominated by a small number of super-powerful, mostly U.S.-based transnational media corporations. It is a system that works to advance the cause of the global market and promote commercial values, while denigrating journalism and culture not conducive to the immediate bottom line or long-run corporate interests. It is a disaster for anything but the most superficial notion of democracy—a democracy where, to paraphrase John Jay's maxim, those who own the world ought to govern it.

The global commercial system is a very recent development. Until the 1980s, media systems were generally national in scope. While there have been imports of books, films, music and TV shows for decades, the basic broadcasting systems and newspaper industries were domestically owned and regulated. Beginning in the 1980s, pressure from the IMF, World Bank and U.S. government to deregulate and privatize media and communication systems coincided with new satellite and digital technologies, resulting in the rise of transnational media giants.

How quickly has the global media system emerged? The two largest media firms in the world, Time Warner and Disney, generated around 15 percent of their income outside of the United States in 1990. By 1997, that figure was in the 30 percent–35 percent range. Both firms expect to do a majority of their business abroad at some point in the next decade.

The global media system is now dominated by a first tier of nine giant firms. The five largest are Time Warner (1997 sales: $24 billion), Disney ($22 billion), Bertelsmann ($15 billion), Viacom ($13 billion), and Rupert Murdoch's News Corporation ($11 billion). Besides needing global scope to compete, the rules of thumb for global media giants are twofold: First, get bigger so you dominate markets and your competition can't buy you out. Firms like Disney and Time Warner have almost tripled in size this decade.

Second, have interests in numerous media industries, such as film production, book publishing, music, TV channels and networks, retail stores, amusement parks, magazines, newspapers and the like. The profit whole for the global media giant can be vastly greater than the sum of the media parts. A film, for example, should also generate a soundtrack, a book, and merchandise, and possibly spin-off TV shows, CD-ROMs, video games and amusement park rides. Firms that do not have con-glomerated media holdings simply cannot compete in this market.

The first tier is rounded out by TCI, the largest U.S. cable company that also has U.S. and global media holdings in scores of ventures too numerous to mention. The other three first-tier global media firms are all part of much larger industrial corporate powerhouses: General Electric (1997 sales: $80 billion), owner of **NBC**; Sony (1997 sales: $48 billion), owner of Columbia & TriStar Pictures and major recording interests; and Seagram (1997 sales: $14 billion), owner of Universal film and music interests. The media holdings of these last four firms do between $6 billion and $9 billion in business per year. While they are not as diverse as the media holdings of the first five global media giants, these four firms have global distribution and production in the areas where they compete. And firms like Sony and GE have the resources to make deals to get a lot bigger very quickly if they so desire.

Behind these firms is a second tier of some three or four dozen media firms that do between $1 billion and $8 billion per year in media-related business. These firms tend to have national or regional strongholds or to specialize in global niche markets. About one-half of them come from North America, including the likes of Westinghouse

From *Extra*, November/December 1997, pp. 11-18. © 1997 by Robert W. McChesney. Reprinted by permission.

(CBS), the New York Times Co., Hearst, Comcast and Gannett. Most of the rest come from Europe, with a handful based in East Asia and Latin America.

In short, the overwhelming majority (in revenue terms) of the world's film production, TV show production, cable channel ownership, cable and satellite system ownership, book publishing, magazine publishing and music production is provided by these 50 or so firms, and the first nine firms thoroughly dominate many of these sectors. By any standard of democracy, such a concentration of media power is troubling, if not unacceptable.

But that hardly explains how concentrated and uncompetitive this global media power actually is. In addition, these firms are all actively engaged in equity joint ventures where they share ownership of concerns with their "competitors" so as to reduce competition and risk. Each of the nine first-tier media giants, for example, has joint ventures with, on average, two-thirds of the other eight first-tier media giants. And the second tier is every bit as aggressive about making joint ventures. (See chart below for the extent of joint ventures between media giants.)

We are the world

In some ways, the emerging global commercial media system is not an entirely negative proposition. It occasionally promotes anti-racist, anti-sexist or anti-authoritarian messages that can be welcome in some of the more repressive corners of the world. But on balance the system has minimal interest in journalism or public affairs except for that which serves the business and upper-middle classes, and it privileges just a few lucrative genres that it can do quite well—like sports, light entertainment and action movies—over other fare. Even at its best the entire system is saturated by a hyper-commercialism, a veritable commercial carpetbombing of every aspect of human life. As the C.E.O. of Westinghouse put it (**Advertising Age**, 2/3/97), "We are here to serve advertisers. That is our *raison d'etre.*"

Some once posited that the rise of the Internet would eliminate the monopoly power of the global media giants. Such talk has declined recently as the largest media, telecommunication and computer firms have done everything within their immense powers to colonize the Internet, or at least neutralize its threat. The global media cartel may be evolving into a global communication cartel.

But the entire global media and communication system is still in flux. While we are probably not too far from crystallization, there will likely be considerable merger and joint venture activity in the coming years. Indeed, by the time you read this, there may already be some shifts in who owns what or whom.

What is tragic is that this entire process of global media concentration has taken place with little public debate, especially in the U.S., despite the clear implications for politics and culture. After World War II, the Allies restricted media concentration in occupied Germany and Japan because they noted that such concentration promoted anti-democratic, even fascist, political cultures. It may be time for the United States and everyone else to take a dose of that medicine. But for that to happen will require concerted effort to educate and organize people around media issues. That is the task before us.

This article and the following corporate profiles are based on The Global Media: The New Missionaries of Corporate Capitalism *(Cassell, 1997), co-authored with Edward S. Herman.* The Global Media *can be ordered by calling 1-800-561-7704.*

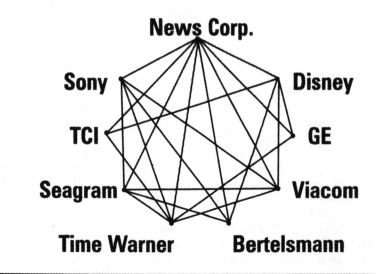

With Friends Like These...

JUST HOW uncompetitive is the global media system? Consider the rampant use of equity joint ventures highlighted in the chart below. Rupert Murdoch said it best when asked how he regards direct competition with one of the other giants when entering a new market: "We can join forces now, or we can kill each other and then join forces." (**Business Week**, 3/25/96) Murdoch and the other giants know there is only one rational choice.

To hear TCI major-domo John Malone, this is hardly the sort of ruthlessly competitive market that Milton Friedman and Jack Kemp lecture about. "Nobody can really afford to get mad at their competitors, because they are partners in one area and competitors in another." (**Financial Times**, 5/28/96) And the largest media giants are also prime customers for each other.   —*R.M.*

News Corp.

Sony   **Disney**

TCI   **GE**

Seagram   **Viacom**

Time Warner   **Bertelsmann**

Time Warner
$25 billion
1997 sales

Time Warner, the largest media corporation in the world, was formed in 1989 through the merger of Time Inc. and Warner Communications. In 1992, Time Warner split off its entertainment group, and sold 25 percent of it to U.S. West, and 5.6 percent of it to each of the Japanese conglomerates Itochu and Toshiba. It regained from Disney its position as the world's largest media firm with the 1996 acquisition of Turner Broadcasting.

Time Warner is moving toward being a fully global company, with over 200 subsidiaries worldwide. In 1996, approximately two-thirds of Time Warner's income came from the United States, but that figure is expected to drop to three-fifths by 2000 and eventually to less than one-half. Time Warner expects globalization to provide growth tonic; it projects that its annual sales growth rate of 14 percent in the middle 1990s will climb to over 20 percent by the end of the decade.

Music accounts for just over 20 percent of Time Warner's business, as does the news division of magazine and book publishing and cable television news. Time Warner's U.S. cable systems account for over 10 percent of income. The remainder is accounted for largely by Time Warner's extensive entertainment film, video and television holdings. Time Warner is a major force in virtually every medium and on every continent.

Time Warner has zeroed in on global television as the most lucrative area for growth. Unlike News Corporation, however, Time Warner has devoted itself to producing programming and channels rather than developing entire satellite systems. Time Warner is also one of the largest movie theater owners in the world, with approximately 1,000 screens outside of the United States and further expansion projected.

The Time Warner strategy is to merge the former Turner global channels—**CNN** and **TNT/Cartoon Channel**—with their **HBO International** and recently launched **Warner** channels to make a four-pronged assault on the global market. **HBO International** has already established itself as the leading subscrip-

tion TV channel in the world; it has a family of pay channels and is available in over 35 countries. **HBO** President Jeffrey Bewkes states that global expansion is **HBO**'s "manifest destiny."

CNN International, a subsidiary of **CNN**, is also established as the premier

TIME WARNER

global television news channel, beamed via ten satellites to over 200 nations and 90 million subscribers by 1994, a 27 percent increase over 1993. The long-term goal for **CNN International** is to operate (or participate in joint ventures to establish) **CNN** channels in French, Japanese, Hindi, Arabic and perhaps one or two other regional languages. **CNN** launched a Spanish-language service for Latin America in 1997, based in Atlanta. **CNN International** will also draw on the Time Warner journalism resources as it faces new challenges from news channels launched by News Corporation and NBC-Microsoft.

Before their 1996 merger, Turner and Time Warner were both global television powers with the **TNT/Cartoon Network** and **Warner** channels, drawing upon their respective large libraries of cartoons and motion pictures. Now these channels will be redeployed to better utilize each other's resources, with plans being drawn up to develop several more global cable channels to take advantage of the world's largest film, television and cartoon libraries.

Time Warner selected holdings

- Majority interest in **WB**, a U.S. television network launched in 1995 to provide a distribution platform for Time Warner films and programs. It is carried on the Tribune Company's 16 U.S. television stations, which reach 25 percent of U.S. TV households;
- Significant interests in non-U.S. broadcasting joint ventures;
- The largest cable system in the United States, controlling 22 of the largest 100 markets;
- Several U.S. and global cable television channels, including **CNN**, **Headline News**, **CNNfn**, **TBS**, **TNT**, **Turner Classic Movies**, **The Cartoon Network** and **CNN-SI** (a cross-production with **Sports Illustrated**);
- Partial ownership of the cable channel **Comedy Central** and a controlling stake in **Court TV**;

- **HBO** and **Cinemax** pay cable channels;
- Minority stake in PrimeStar, U.S. satellite television service;
- Warner Brothers and New Line Cinema film studios;
- More than 1,000 movie screens outside of the United States;
- A library of over 6,000 films, 25,000 television programs, books, music and thousands of cartoons;
- Twenty-four magazines, including **Time**, **People** and **Sports Illustrated**;
- Fifty percent of DC Comics, publisher of **Superman**, **Batman** and 60 other titles;
- The second largest book-publishing business in the world, including Time-Life Books (42 percent of sales outside of the United States) and the Book-of-the-Month Club;
- Warner Music Group, one of the largest global music businesses with nearly 60 percent of revenues from outside the United States;
- Six Flags theme park chain;
- The Atlanta Hawks and Atlanta Braves professional sports teams;
- Retail stores, including over 150 Warner Bros. stores and Turner Retail Group;
- Minority interests in toy companies Atari and Hasbro.

Disney
$24 billion
1997 sales

Disney is the closest challenger to Time Warner for the status of world's largest media firm. In the early 1990s, Disney successfully shifted its emphasis from its theme parks and resorts to its film and television divisions. In 1995, Disney made the move from being a dominant global content producer to being a fully integrated media giant with the purchase of Capital Cities/ABC for $19 billion, one of the biggest acquisitions in business history.

The Walt Disney Company

Disney now generates 31 percent of its income from broadcasting, 23 percent from theme parks, and the balance from "creative content," meaning films, publishing and merchandising. The ABC deal provided Disney, already regarded as the industry leader at using cross-selling and cross-promotion to maximize revenues, with a U.S. broadcasting network and widespread global media holdings to incorporate into its activities.

Consequently, according to **Adver-**

tising Age (8/7/95), Disney "is uniquely positioned to fulfill virtually any marketing option, on any scale, almost anywhere in the world." It has already included the new Capital Cities/ABC brands in its exclusive global marketing deals with McDonald's and Mattel toymakers. Although Disney has traditionally preferred to operate on its own, C.E.O. Michael Eisner has announced Disney's plans to expand aggressively overseas through joint ventures with local firms or other global players, or through further acquisitions. Disney's stated goal is to expand its non-U.S. share of revenues from 23 percent in 1995 to 50 percent by 2000.

Historically, Disney has been strong in entertainment and animation, two areas that do well in the global market. In 1996 Disney reorganized, putting all its global television activities into a single division, Disney/ABC International Television. Its first order of business is to expand the children- and family-oriented **Disney Channel** into a global force, capitalizing upon the enormous Disney resources. Disney is also developing an advertising-supported children's channel to complement the subscription **Disney Channel.**

For the most part, Disney's success has been restricted to English-language channels in North America, Britain and Australia. Disney's absence has permitted the children's channels of News Corporation, Time Warner and especially Viacom to dominate the lucrative global market. Disney launched a Chinese-language **Disney Channel** based in Taiwan in 1995, and plans to launch **Disney Channels** in France, Italy, Germany and the Middle East. "The **Disney Channel** should be the killer children's service throughout the world," Disney's executive in charge of international television states.

With the purchase of ABC's **ESPN,** the television sports network, Disney has possession of the unquestioned global leader. **ESPN** has three U.S. cable channels, a radio network with 420 affiliates, and the ESPN Sports-Zone website, one of the most heavily used locales on the Internet. One Disney executive notes that with **ESPN** and the family-oriented **Disney Channel,** Disney has "two horses to ride in foreign markets, not just one."

ESPN International dominates televised sport, broadcasting on a 24-hour basis in 21 languages to over 165 countries. It reaches the one desirable audience that had eluded Disney in the past: young, single, middle-class men. "Our plan is to think globally but to customize locally," states the senior VP of **ESPN International.** In Latin America the emphasis is on soccer, in Asia it is table tennis, and in India **ESPN** provided over 1,000 hours of cricket in 1995.

Disney plans to exploit the "synergies" of ESPN much as it has exploited its cartoon characters. "We know that when we lay Mickey Mouse or Goofy on top of products, we get pretty creative stuff," Eisner states. "**ESPN** has the potential to be that kind of brand." Disney plans call for a chain of ESPN theme sports bars, ESPN product merchandising, and possibly a chain of ESPN entertainment centers based on the Club ESPN at Walt Disney World. ESPN has released five music CDs, two of which have sold over 500,000 copies. In late 1996, Disney began negotiations with Hearst and Petersen Publishing to produce **ESPNSports Weekly** magazine, to be a "branded competitor to **Sports Illustrated.**"

Disney selected holdings

- The U.S. **ABC** television and radio networks;
- Ten U.S. television stations and 21 U.S. radio stations;
- U.S. and global cable television channels **Disney Channel, ESPN, ESPN2** and **ESPNews;** holdings in **Lifetime, A & E** and **History** channels;
- Americast, interactive TV joint venture with several telephone companies;
- Several major film, video and television production studios including Disney, Miramax and Buena Vista;
- Magazine and newspaper publishing, through its subsidiaries, Fairchild Publications and Chilton Publications;
- Book publishing, including Hyperion Books and Chilton Publications;
- Several music labels, including Hollywood Records, Mammoth Records and Walt Disney Records;
- Theme parks and resorts, including Disneyland, Disney World and stakes in major theme parks in France and Japan;
- Disney Cruise Line;
- DisneyQuest, a chain of high-tech arcade game stores;

- Controlling interests in the NHL Anaheim Mighty Ducks and major league baseball's Anaheim Angels;
- Consumer products, including more than 550 Disney retail stores worldwide.

Bertelsmann
$15 billion
1996 sales

Bertelsmann is the one European firm in the first tier of media giants. The Bertelsmann empire was built on global networks of book and music clubs. Music and television provide 31 percent of its income, book publishing 33 percent, magazines and newspapers 20 percent, and a global printing business accounts for the remainder. In 1994 its income was distributed among Germany (36 percent), the rest of Europe (32 percent), the United States (24 percent) and the rest of the world (8 percent).

Bertelsmann's stated goal is to evolve "from a media enterprise with international activities into a truly global communications group." Bertelsmann's strengths in global expansion are its global distribution network for music, its global book and music clubs, and its facility with languages other than English. It is working to strengthen its music holdings to become the world leader, through a possible buyout of—or merger with—EMI and through establishing joint ventures with local music companies in emerging markets. Bertelsmann is considered to be the best contender of all the media giants to exploit the Eastern European markets.

Bertelsmann has two severe competitive disadvantages in the global media sweepstakes. It has no significant film or television production studios or film library, and it has minimal involvement in global television, where much of the growth is taking place. The company began to address this problem in 1996 by merging its television interests (Ufa) into a joint venture with Compagnie Luxembourgeoise de Telediffusion (CLT), the Luxembourg-based European commercial broadcasting power. According to a Bertelsmann executive, the CLT deal was "a strategic step to become a major media player, especially in light of the recent European and American mergers."

Bertelsmann selected holdings

- German television channels **RTL**, **RTL2**, **SuperRTL** and **Vox**;
- Part ownership of **Premiere**, Germany's largest pay-TV channel;
- Stakes in British, French and Dutch TV channels;
- 50 percent stake in CLT-Ufa, which owns 19 European TV channels and 23 European radio stations;
- Eighteen European radio stations;
- Newspaper and magazine publishing, including more than 100 magazines;
- Book publishing, with some 40 publishing houses, concentrating on German-, French- and English-language (Bantam and Doubleday Dell) titles;
- Major recording studios Arista and RCA;
- Leading book and record clubs in the world.

Viacom
$13 billion
1997 sales

C.E.O. Sumner Redstone, who controls 39 percent of Viacom's stock, orchestrated the deals that led to the acquisitions of Paramount and Blockbuster in 1994, thereby promoting the firm from $2 billion in 1993 sales to the front ranks. Viacom generates 33 percent of its income from its film studios, 33 percent from its music, video rentals and theme parks, 18 percent from broadcasting, and 14 percent from publishing. Redstone's strategy is for Viacom to become the world's "premier software driven growth company."

Viacom's growth strategy is twofold. First, it is implementing an aggressive policy of using company-wide cross-promotions to improve sales. It proved invaluable that **MTV** constantly plugged the film *Clueless* in 1995, and the same strategy will be applied to the Paramount television program based on the movie. Simon & Schuster is

establishing a Nickelodeon book imprint and a "Beavis and Butthead" book series based on the **MTV** characters. Viacom also has plans to establish a comic-book imprint based upon Paramount characters, it is considering creating a record label to exploit its **MTV** brand name and it has plans to open a chain of retail stores to capitalize upon its "brands" à la Disney and Time Warner. In 1997 Paramount will begin

producing three Nickelodeon and three MTV movies annually. "We're just now beginning to realize the benefits of the Paramount and Blockbuster mergers," Redstone stated in 1996.

Second, Viacom has targeted global growth, with a stated goal of earning 40 percent of its revenues outside of the United States by 2000. As one Wall Street analyst puts it, Redstone wants Viacom "playing in the same international league" with News Corporation and Time Warner. Since 1992 Viacom has invested between $750 million and $1 billion in international expansion. "We're not taking our foot off the accelerator," one Viacom executive states.

Viacom's two main weapons are **Nickelodeon** and **MTV**. **Nickelodeon** has been a global powerhouse, expanding to every continent but Antarctica in 1996 and 1997 and offering programming in several languages. It is already a world leader in children's television, reaching 90 million TV households in 70 countries other than the United States—where it can be seen in 68 million households and completely dominates children's television.

MTV is the preeminent global music television channel, available in 250 million homes worldwide and in scores of nations. In 1996 Viacom announced further plans to "significantly expand" its global operations. **MTV** has used new digital technologies to make it possible to customize programming inexpensively for different regions and nations around the world.

Viacom selected holdings

- Thirteen U.S. television stations;
- A 50 percent interest in the U.S. **UPN** television network with Chris-Craft Industries;
- U.S. and global cable television networks, including **MTV**, **M2**, **VH1**, **Nickelodeon**, **Showtime**, **TVLand** and **Paramount Networks**;
- A 50 percent interest in **Comedy Central** channel (with Time Warner);
- Film, video and television production, including Paramount Pictures;
- 50 percent stake in United Cinemas International, one of the world's three largest theater companies;
- Blockbuster Video and Music stores, the world's largest video rental stores;
- Book publishing, including Simon & Schuster, Scribners and Macmillan;
- Five theme parks.

News Corporation
$10 billion
1996 sales

The News Corporation is often identified with its head, Rupert Murdoch, whose family controls some 30 percent of its stock. Murdoch's goal is for News Corporation to own multiple forms of programming—news, sports, films and children's shows—and beam them via satellite or TV stations to homes in the United States, Europe, Asia and South America. Viacom CEO Sumner Redstone says of Murdoch that "he basically wants to conquer the world."

And he seems to be doing it. Redstone, Disney CEO Michael Eisner,

 The News Corporation Limited

and time Warner CEO Gerald Levin have each commented that Murdoch is the one media executive they most respect and fear, and the one whose moves they study. TCI's John Malone states that global media vertical integration is all about trying to catch Rupert. Time Warner executive Ted Turner views Murdoch in a more sinister fashion, having likened him to Adolf Hitler.

After establishing News Corporation in his native Australia, Murdoch entered the British market in the 1960s and by the 1980s had become a dominant force in the U.S. market. News Corporation went heavily into debt to subsidize its purchase of Twentieth Century Fox and the formation of the **Fox** television network in the 1980s; by the mid-1990s News Corporation had eliminated much of that debt.

News Corporation operates in nine different media on six continents. Its 1995 revenues were distributed relatively evenly among filmed entertainment (26 percent), newspapers (24 percent), television (21 percent), magazines (14 percent) and book publishing (12 percent). News Corporation has been masterful in utilizing its various properties for cross-promotional purposes, and at using its media power to curry influence with public officials worldwide. "Murdoch seems to have Washington in his back pocket," observed one industry analyst after News Corporation received another favorable ruling (**New**

York Times, 7/26/96). The only media sector in which News Corporation lacks a major presence is music, but it has a half-interest in the **Channel V** music television channel in Asia.

Although News Corporation earned 70 percent of its 1995 income in the United States, its plan for global expansion looks to continental Europe, Asia and Latin America, areas where growth is expected to be greatest for commercial media. Until around 2005, Murdoch expects the surest profits in the developed world, especially Europe and Japan. News Corporation is putting most of its eggs in the basket of television, specifically digital satellite television. It plans to draw on its experience in establishing the most profitable satellite television system in the world, the booming **British Sky Broadcasting** (**BSkyB**). News Corporation can also use its U.S. **Fox** television network to provide programming for its nascent satellite ventures. News Corporation is spending billions of dollars to establish these systems around the world; although the risk is considerable, if only a few of them establish monopoly or duopoly positions the entire project should prove lucrative.

News Corporation selected holdings
- The U.S. **Fox** broadcasting network;
- Twenty-two U.S. television stations, the largest U.S. station group, covering over 40 percent of U.S. TV households;
- **Fox News Channel**;
- A 50 percent stake (with TCI's Liberty Media) in several U.S. and global cable networks, including **fx, fxM** and **Fox Sports Net**;
- 50 percent stake in Fox Kids Worldwide, production studio and owner of U.S. cable **Family Channel**;
- Ownership or major interests in satellite services reaching Europe, U.S., Asia, and Latin America, often under the Sky Broadcasting brand;
- Twentieth Century Fox, a major film, television and video production center, which has a library of over 2,000 films to exploit;
- Some 132 newspapers (primarily in Australia, Britain and the United States, including the **London Times** and the **New York Post**), making it one of the three largest newspaper groups in the world;
- Twenty-five magazines, most notably **TV Guide**;
- Book publishing interests, including HarperCollins;
- Los Angeles Dodgers baseball team.

Sony
$9 billion
1997 sales (media only)

Sony's media holdings are concentrated in music (the former CBS records) and film and television production (the former Columbia Pictures), each of which it purchased in 1989. Music accounts for about 60 percent of Sony's media income and film and television production account for the rest. Sony is a dominant entertainment producer, and its media sales are expected to surpass $9 billion in 1997. It also has major holdings in movie theaters in joint venture with Seagram. As Sony's media activities seem divorced from its other extensive activities—Sony expects $50 billion in company-wide sales in 1997—there is ongoing speculation that it will sell its valuable production studios to vertically integrated chains that can better exploit them.

Sony was foiled in its initial attempts to find synergies between hardware and software, but it anticipates that digital communication will provide the basis for new synergies. Sony hopes to capitalize upon its vast copyrighted library of films, music and TV programs to leap to the front of the digital video disc market, where it is poised to be one of the two global leaders with Matsushita. Sony also enjoys a 25 percent share of the multi-billion-dollar video games industry; with the shift to digital formats these games can now be converted into channels in digital television systems.

TCI
$7 billion
1996 sales

TCI (Tele-Communications Inc.) is smaller than the other firms in the first tier, but its unique position in the media industry has made it a central player in the global media system. TCI's foundation is its dominant position as the second biggest U.S. cable television system provider. C.E.O. John Malone, who has effective controlling interest over TCI, has been able to use the steady cash influx from the lucrative semi-monopolistic cable business to build an empire.

Malone understands the importance of the U.S. cable base to bankroll TCI's expansion; in 1995 and 1996 he bought several smaller cable systems to consoli-

date TCI's hold on the U.S. cable market. TCI faces a direct and potentially very damaging challenge to its U.S. market share from digital satellite broadcasting. It is responding by converting its cable systems to digital format so as to increase channel capacity to 200. TCI is also using its satellite spin-off to position itself in the rival satellite business and retain some of the 15 to 20 million Americans expected to switch from cable broadcasting to satellite broadcasting by 2000. In addition to owning two satellites valued at $600 million, TCI holds a 21 percent stake in Primestar, a U.S. satellite television joint venture with the other leading U.S. cable companies, News Corporation and General Electric, which already had 1.2 million subscribers in l996.

TCI has used its control of cable systems to acquire equity stakes in many of the cable channels that need to be carried over TCI to be viable. TCI has significant interests in **Discover, QVC, Fox Sports Net, Court TV, E!, Home Shopping Network** and **Black Entertainment TV**, among others. In 1996, TCI negotiated the right to purchase a 20 percent stake in News Corporation's new **Fox News Channel** in return for access to TCI systems. Through its subsidiary Liberty Media, TCI has interests in 92 U.S. program services.

Nor does TCI restrict its investments to cable channels and content producers. It has a 10 percent stake in Time Warner as well as a 20 percent stake in Silver King Communications, where former **Fox** network builder Barry Diller is putting together another U.S. television network.

TCI has applied its expansionist strategy to the global as well as domestic media market. On the one hand, TCI develops its core cable business and has become the global leader in cable systems, with strong units in Britain, Japan and Chile. Merrill Lynch estimates that TCI International's cable base outside of the United States will increase from 3 million subscribers in 1995 to 10 million in 1999.

On the other hand, TCI uses its cable resources to invest across all global media and to engage in numerous non-cable joint ventures. "When you are the largest cable operator in the world," a TCI executive states, "people find a way to do business with you." It already has 30 media deals outside of the United States, including a venture with Sega Enterprises to launch computer game channels, a joint venture with News Corporation for a global sports channel, and a 10 percent stake in Sky Latin America.

Universal (Seagram) $7 billion

1997 sales

Effectively controlled by the Bronfman family, the global beverage firm Seagram purchased Universal (then MCA) from Matsushita for $5.7 billion in 1995. Matsushita was unable to make a success of MCA and had refused to go along with MCA executives who had wanted to acquire CBS in the early 1990s. Universal is expected to account for approximately half of Seagram's $14 billion in sales in 1997.

Over half of Universal's income is generated by the Universal Studios' production of films and television programs. Universal is also a major music producer and book publisher and operates several theme parks. As many of the broadcast networks and cable channels vertically integrate with production companies, Universal has fewer options for sales and is less secure in its future. It owns the cable **USA Network** and the **Sci-Fi Network**, after buying out its uneasy partner Viacom.

NBC (GE) $5 billion

1996 sales

General Electric is one of the leading electronics and manufacturing firms in the world with nearly $80 billion in sales in 1996. Its operations have become increasingly global, with non-U.S. revenues increasing from 20 percent of the total in 1985 to 38 percent in 1995, and an expected 50 percent in 2000. Although NBC currently constitutes only a small portion of GE's total activity, after years of rapid growth it is considered to be the core of

GE's strategy for long-term global growth.

NBC owns U.S. television and radio networks and 11 television stations. It has been aggressive in expanding into cable, where it now owns several cable channels outright, like **CNBC**, as well as shares in some 20 other channels, including the **A&E** network. The most dramatic expression of GE's media-centered strategy is its 1996 alliance and joint investment with Microsoft to produce the cable news channel **MSNBC**, along with a complementary on-line service. From this initial $500 million investment, NBC and Microsoft plan to expand **MSNBC** quickly into a global news channel, followed perhaps by a global entertainment and sports channel. NBC and Microsoft are also developing a series of TV channels in Europe aimed at computer users.

The Second Tier

Below the global giants in the media food chain is a second tier of corporations that fill regional or niche markets. Some of these firms are as large as the smaller global companies, but lack their world-wide reach. A few second-tier companies may attempt, through aggressive mergers and acquisitions of like-sized firms, to become full-blown first-tier global media giants; others will likely be swallowed by larger companies amassing ever greater empires.

U.S.

Westinghouse $5 billion
Advance Publications $4.9 billion
Gannett $4.0 billion
Cox Enterprises $3.8 billion
Times-Mirror $3.5 billion
Comcast $3.4 billion
McGraw Hill $3 billion
Reader's Digest $3 billion
Knight Ridder $2.9 billion
Dow Jones $2.5 billion
New York Times Co. $2.5 billion
Tribune Co. $2.2 billion
Hearst $2 billion
Washington Post Co. $1.8 billion
Cablevision $1.1 billion
DirecTV (Owned by General Motors)
DreamWorks

Canada

Thomson $7.3 billion
Rogers Communications $2 billion
Hollinger

Latin America

Cisneros Group (Venezuela) $3.2 billion
Globo (Brazil) $2.2 billion
Clarin (Argentina) $1.2 billion
Televisa (Mexico) $1.2 billion

Europe

Havas (France) $8.8 billion
Reed Elsevier (Britain/Netherlands) $5.5 billion
EMI (Britain) $5.4 billion
Hachette (France) $5.3 billion
Reuters (Britain) $4.1 billion
Kirch Group (Germany) $4 billion
Granada Group (Britain $3.6 billion
BBC (Britain) $3.5 billion
Axel Springer (Germany) $3 billion
Canal Plus (France) $3 billion
CLT (Luxembourg) $3 billion
Pearson PLC (Britain $2.9 billion
United News & Media (Britain) $2.9 billion
Carlton Communications (Britain) $2.5 billion
Mediaset (Italy) $2 billion
Kinnevik (Sweden) $1.8 billion
Television Francais 1 (France) $1.8 billion
Verlagsgruppe Bauer (Germany) $1.7 billion
Wolters Kluwer (Netherlands) $1.7 billion
RCS Editori Spa (Italy) $1.6 billion
VNU (Netherlands) $1.4 billion
Prisa Group (Spain)
Antena 3 (Spain)
CEP Communications (France)

Asia/Pacific

NHK (Japan) $5.6 billion
Fuji Television (Japan) $2.6 billion
Nippon Television Network (Japan) $2.2 billion
Cheil Jedang (Korea) $2.1 billion
Tokyo Broadcasting System (Japan) $2.1 billion
Modi (India) $2 billion
Asahi National Broadcasting Co. (Japan) $1.6 billion
Toho Company (Japan) $1.6 billion
PBL (Australia) $750 million
TVB International (China)
Chinese Entertainment Television (China)
Asia Broadcasting and Communications Network (Thailand)
ABS-CBN (Philippines)
Doordarshan (India)
Chinese Central Television (China)

Most sales figures are for 1996, but some are as early as 1993.

Unit Selections

Key Points to Consider

❖ To what extent do you agree with criticisms of the news media? Is current disinterest in news the media's fault? Should making news more interesting/appealing be a priority of news media? Why or why not?

❖ The issue of liberal versus conservative bias in news reporting is raised in a few articles in this unit. How is it that media consumers can have such opposite opinions about the direction of perceived bias? Analyze an issue of a newspaper or news magazine, noting examples of liberal and/or conservative bias in the selection and presentation of article topics.

❖ Watch newscasts on two different networks on the same evening (in many markets, you can find one network's early evening news airing on the half hour and another on the hour, or you can videotape one network while watching another). Record the stories covered, in the order in which they are reported, and the time devoted to each. Did you notice any patterns in the reporting? Were there any differences in the way stories on the same topic were presented? Did you note any instances in which editorial or entertainment values were reflected in story selection or coverage? What conclusions do you draw from your findings?

 **Links**   **www.dushkin.com/online/**

9. **Cable News Network**
   http://www.cnn.com
10. **Fairness and Accuracy in Reporting**
    http://www.fair.org
11. **Media & Democracy Congress**
    http://www.igc.apc.org/an/Congress.html
12. **Media Source**
    http://www.mediasource.com
13. **Organization of News Ombudsmen**
    http://www5.infi.net/ono/
14. **Television News Archive**
    http://tvnews.vanderbilt.edu
15. **What Local TV News Doesn't Want You to Know!**
    http://www.tfs.net/personal/gbyron/tvnews1.html

These sites are annotated on pages 4 and 5.

With the advent of television, media scholar Marshall McLuhan predicted the coming of a "global village" in which communication media would transcend the boundaries of nations: "Ours is a world of allatoneness. 'Time' has ceased, 'space' has vanished. We now live in . . . a simultaneous happening." In naming CNN founder Ted Turner its 1991 Man of the Year, *Time* noted that, a generation later, CNN had begun to make McLuhan's prophecy come to pass. The availability of a worldwide, 24-hour news network has changed news from something that *has happened* to something that *is happening*. As president, George Bush was quoted as having said to other world leaders, "I learn more from CNN than I do from the CIA."

The reporting of news and information was not, in the beginning, considered an important function within media organizations. The first newspapers focused more on political advocacy and editorializing than on attempting to provide a comprehensive or objective overview of newsworthy events. Television news was originally limited to 15-minute commercial-free broadcasts presented as a public service. Over the years, however, the news business has become big business. Television news operations are intensely competitive, locked in head-to-head popularity races in which the loss of one ratings point can translate into a loss of $10 million in advertising revenue.

Perceptions of news sources vary among consumer groups. According to a recent Harris Poll, college graduates overwhelmingly rate newspapers as being more accurate and providing more complete news coverage than television. However, 47 percent of adult Americans pick television news as providing greater variety and completeness of coverage, and the share of consumers who rely on television alone for news has grown steadily for three decades.

The articles in this section explore the changing landscape of contemporary news and information coverage. News, by definition, is timely: It is "news," not "olds." Decisions regarding what stories to play and how to play them are made under tight deadlines. Media expert Wilbur Schramm has noted that "hardly anything about communication is so impressive as the enormous number of choices and discards and interpretations that have to be made between [an] actual news event and the symbols that later appear in the mind of a reporter, an editor, a reader, a listener, or a viewer. Therefore, even if everyone does his job perfectly, it is hard enough to get the report of an event straight and clear and true." Schramm's comments point to the tremendous impact of selectivity in crafting news messages. What gets into the media and what does not are influenced by choices made by individuals with personal opinions, causes, and biases. The process of making these decisions is called *gatekeeping*.

Gatekeeping is necessary. News operations cannot logistically cover or report every event that happens in the world from one edition or broadcast to the next. The concerns associated with the reality of gatekeeping relate to whether or not the gatekeepers abuse the privilege of deciding what information or viewpoints the mass audience receives. Simply being selected for media coverage lends an issue, an event, or an individual a certain degree of celebrity—the "masser" the medium, the greater the effect. Thus, the privilege of choice grants considerable power (see "Tales from the Trail" by James McCartney).

In his novel *The Evening News,* Arthur Hailey observed: "People watch the news to find out the answers to three questions, Is the world safe? Are my home and family safe? and, Did anything happen today that was interesting?" Given cursory answers to those questions, viewers are satisfied that they are "keeping up," although the total amount of news delivered in a half-hour newscast would, if set in type, hardly fill the front page of a daily newspaper. Despite the growing number of news sources and the around-the-clock availability of news information, many adults report that they are too busy to follow the news, or are suspicious of the media, or find the news too depressing. "Do You Believe What Newspeople Tell You?" "A Matter of Trust," and "Challenging the 'Liberal Media' Claim" provide differing perspectives on public perceptions of news sources. " 'You News' " analyzes network news's shift to what Dan Rather has called "news lite": soft features with entertainment value and consumer "relevance" that compete for air time with hard-hitting (but less interesting) coverage of politics or international news.

News media are under enormous pressure to fill time and space with quality visuals under tightened budgets. The competitive nature of news media values gatekeeping choices inherently influenced by profit motives. Some critics contend that there is a sensationalist bias in news coverage. Some note that tight deadlines deprive reporters and editors of time to adequately investigate, reflect, and evaluate before filing their stories (see "Parachute Journalism"). Some worry that media ownership megadeals pose a major challenge to providing objectivity and diversity in viewpoints, while others are concerned with the potentially limitless ability for unchecked gossip and paranoid news to reach mass audiences via the Internet.

There are, however, exceptions to these negative characterizations of contemporary news coverage. In "Tell It Long, Take Your Time, Go in Depth," Steve Weinberg reports that a significant number of journalists are breaking the "keep it short, write it fast" canons of contemporary reporting, instead devoting extensive time to researching in-depth, well-written stories that reflect the lives of ordinary people. Susan Benesch puts a positive spin on soft news coverage, describing "The Rise of Solutions Journalism" as an antidote to traditional bad news bias. And David Lieberman reports on the increase in 24-hour local cable news channels that cover breaking news, weather, traffic, sports, and leisurely reports about local politics and events.

The percentage of people reporting that they regularly watch a nightly network newscast dropped from 60 to 42 percent between 1993 and 1996. Over the same period of time, the percentage of people who reported they *never* watch a nightly news broadcast more than doubled, from 6 to 14 percent, and 38 daily newspapers went out of business. News veteran Walter Cronkite, long retired from CBS, has noted, "We've always known that you can gain circulation or viewers by cheapening the product, and now you're finding the bad driving out the good." But is a consumer orientation to gatekeeping necessarily misdirected? It is arguable that news media have let a marketplace orientation get in the way of their serving their rightful role as careful and credible reporters of what the public should know. It is equally arguable that they are simply listening to public feedback and responding to what they hear.

Covering News

"You News"

by Andie Tucher

om Brokaw comes to our telephone interview loaded for bear. To my boilerplate question — "How do you respond to the critics who say your newscast has become softer?" — he snaps back that many of the critics are also competitors with agendas of their own.

"There is an elitist, myopic point of view about what these broadcasts have been and what they should be," he says, "and I'm getting a little weary of it. There are no important stories we have missed." After we hang up, he calls me back to say I had overstated the length of a piece I had mentioned as an example of a softer story — two minutes on the Oregon death-penalty laws for sheep-chasing dogs — and to

Andie Tucher is an associate editor at CJR. *For three years ending in April 1996 she worked in a special-project unit at ABC News.*

remind me that critics have their own agendas.

Of course they do. Some of the criticism does come from rivals at CBS and ABC, who fear that NBC may be taking over as the new top dog in the ratings war among the Big Three. From mid-December through mid-March, Brokaw's half-hour evening broadcast consistently edged out — barely but visibly — the seven-year ratings leader, ABC's *World News Tonight with Peter Jennings*, winning ten times, tying three, and placing second once in fourteen weeks. (During the week ending March 7, for instance, NBC had an 8.8 rating, an 18 share, and an average of 12.01 million viewers; ABC came in at 8.5/17 with 11.16 million viewers; and CBS at 7.6/16 with 9.95 million viewers.)

And this advance comes at a time when the market for network evening news is inexorably shrinking: throughout the 1970s, the three net-

work newscasts together would routinely attract up to three-quarters of the viewing audience, but Nielsen reports that the combined audience share for the three has now slipped under 50 percent.

But edgy rivals aside, Brokaw's slicked-up newscast would still be ripe for reassessment. While all the networks have been tinkering with their programs, *The Nightly News with Tom Brokaw* has given itself an inside-and-out makeover. NBC's broadcast now sports a hipper, more high-tech feel, with a new video-wall backdrop, Brokaw's face in a monitor mirroring Brokaw's face on Brokaw himself, Brokaw's face appearing suddenly on the giant video screen overlooking Times Square as he signs off. Where once the airtime was full of congressional wrangles and Middle East peace talks, now it's heavy with medical news and features from fly-over country. NBC has indeed gone

It's not your father's newscast anymore

Call it "News Lite" or "News you can use" — by whatever name, TV is racing for relevance. But what gets lost along the way?

softer and more user-friendly — "populist," NBC executives like to call it — and Brokaw argues urgently that "what we're attempting to do is to cover the important news of the day and the news that is relevant to our viewers, and that news now has a much different woof and warp than it did twenty-five years ago."

Brokaw's competitors detect a betrayal of journalistic standards in all this. CBS anchor Dan Rather told *The Philadelphia Inquirer* in February that NBC was purveying "News Lite." In late March, when Paul Friedman, ABC's executive vice president for news, also took back his old job as the newscast's executive producer, he told *The Washington Post* that ABC would "cover serious news that the others can't manage."

But the old polarity between "soft" and "hard" news is itself something of a red herring. That's because NBC's *Nightly News* is not simply replacing

POLITICIANS AND TELEVISION JOURNALISTS ALIKE WANT YOU TO KNOW THEY ARE JUST FOLKS WHO FEEL YOUR PAIN

coverage of world events with traditional soft features on heroic rescues or celebrity comebacks. NBC's producers, not unlike their fellows at the other networks, have discovered that, in addition to the old categories of the news you need and the news you want, they can add a third type of news that's flourishing in the '90s: news about you

— news to use at your next doctor's visit, PTA meeting, or family dinner-table discussion.

The special problems of the network news in the '90s are legion. It's not just that many people are too busy, too cynical, or too turned off by public life to enjoy the evening-news habit. It's also that so many have been able to go elsewhere — and everywhere — for their news, from CNN to all-news radio to the Internet to local television news to tabloid TV to paid political ads, free political time, and even the late-night comedians, a favorite "news source" for a reported one-third of television-watchers under thirty, according to the Freedom Forum's Media Studies Center. "This is a fact of life," says ABC's Jennings. "I don't know how any evening news broadcast could now cast itself in such a way as to suddenly command the attention of vastly greater numbers of people."

What's more, the newscasts' core viewers tend to be older; The Pew Research Center reckons that almost two-thirds of people over sixty-four watch a network newscast "regularly," while less than a quarter of GenXers do. So "sooner or later the current news audience is all going to die," says Andrew Tyndall, editor of the *Tyndall Weekly*, which tracks and times the stories covered on the evening news. "And that's sooner rather than later."

In some fundamental ways the three newscasts haven't broken far from tradition — or from each other. All pay due attention to the obvious breaking stories: none could have been accused of ignoring either the verdict against O.J. Simpson or the death of Deng Xiaoping. After some initial foot-dragging all have recently been doing a "pretty good job" covering the hot political story of the day — the campaign fund-raising scandals — says Bill Hogan, director of investigative projects at The Center for Public Integrity in Washington, a watchdog group that monitors political spending.

All include, as they always have, bright bits of the "news you want" — softer stories like the return of *Star Wars* and mushy little tributes to Valentine's Day. And all air a weekly slate of regular segments, ranging from "Your Money" and "Eye on America" to the often lightweight, even gossamer "Travels with Harry" on CBS (correspondent Harry Smith visits the stars of girls' basketball) and "Person of the Week" (people who have made positive social contributions) on ABC.

But these days, all three networks are paying as much attention to health problems as any scriptwriter for *E.R.* During just the first two and a half months of 1997 a steady channel surfer through the three broadcasts would have been provided with "news you can use" about, among other topics, clot busters, osteoporosis, memory loss, macular degeneration, allergies, diabetes, male menopause, estrogen, blood transfusions, brain injuries, Alzheimer's, flu, antihistamines, panic attacks, arthritis, beta blockers, grapes as cancer fighters, uterine fibroids, obesity, drinking and driving, car-phoning and driving, and

mammograms. "The *New England Journal of Medicine* should be charging," says Sandy Socolow, a former executive producer for Walter Cronkite at CBS. "All three broadcasts are mesmerized by anything that involves the human body — and I'm not talking about sex."

What distinguishes NBC now is that both the gossamer and the useful often outweigh the grit. Its *Nightly News* tends to air fewer stories each evening

AN AD IN THE NEW YORK TIMES TOUTED THE EVENING'S HOTTEST STORY: "MARRIAGE 'BOOT CAMP': COULD IT SAVE YOUR RELATIONSHIP?"

than ABC or CBS, and far fewer of those come from the national capitals, whether Moscow, Belgrade, or, yes, Washington. More of them focus on trends, life-style and consumer issues, pop culture, and heartland America — and NBC isn't hiding its Lite under a bushel, either. An ad for the newscast appearing in *The New York Times* on March 28 touted what was obviously considered the evening's hottest story: "Marriage 'Boot Camp': Could it Save Your Relationship?" (The story was bumped by the news of the California cult suicide and actually aired April 4.)

Brokaw says he's simply "trying to be less of a wire service of the air" because it's clear people have already heard the major news of the day by the time they click on the evening news. "I travel across this country a lot," he says, "and everywhere I go I hear what people are talking about and what interests them and what they are desperate to know about. And a whole lot

of that has very little to do with what we would routinely put on the air ten-fifteen years ago."

Last year, according to Tyndall, viewers were apparently most desperate to know about the summer Olympics, which were broadcast by NBC Sports and which got more airtime on NBC News than any other story in 1996 (CBS's biggest story was TWA Flight 800 and ABC's was the Dole campaign, which included the entire primary season; see box). At the same time, NBC's attention to such hard-news topics as the presidential campaign and the Middle Eastern peace process was drastically lower than its competitors'.

And NBC has figured out the pleasures and profits of packaging. Tyndall calculates that during the first two and a half months of 1997, NBC gave over a total of 351 minutes of its weeknight broadcasts to named feature segments, compared with 197 minutes on CBS and 185 on ABC. On any given evening as much as a third or more of the twenty-two-minute news hole might be devoted to such segments. Some of the features were shorter specials like "Sleepless in America," "Starting Over" (on keeping New Year's resolutions), "The Plane Truth" (airline safety), or "Going Home" (NBC newspeople return to their roots); others were established regulars like "In Their Own Words," "In Depth," "The Family," "The Fleecing of America" (governmental and institutional corruption and waste), "The American Dream," and "Norman Schwarzkopf's America."

All this translates into a "potpourri," as Brokaw would have it, a "rich mix of different kinds of stories." It's a mix, anyway. In the first months of 1997 NBC's "In Depth" segment, which usually runs some three or four minutes, examined everything from finding jobs for welfare recipients to the aging process. Under the other labels came a jumble of the informative, the you-focused, and the fluffy: reports on the meaning of daydreams, the genealogy craze, absent fathers, oversupply rip-offs at the Pentagon, no-fault divorce, Debbie Reynolds's comeback, getting out of debt, managing one's time, overcoming the fear of flying, coarse behavior among athletes, senior citizens on stage in Las Vegas, and how life has changed for women in Yankton, South Dakota (pop. 12,703), where Brokaw grew up.

The other networks have made changes that are similar, though somewhat smaller. As its own ratings trembled, ABC added a three-times-weekly "Solutions" segment in place of the eight-year-old "American Agenda," which had explored a wide range of issues in health, education, religion, and the environment. The new feature, introduced last September, also falls heavily into the utilitarian mold. It has focused on successful efforts around the country, many of them small in scale and private or local in scope, to address common problems and predicaments of daily life: how to cure chronic pain, find good day care, cut neighborhood crime, motivate children to learn, reduce accidents among teenage drivers.

"Solutions" has come in for its share of criticism, too. After the segment looked at cures for snoring, the *Wall Street Journal* television critic, Dorothy Rabinowitz, wrote savagely of a broadcast "that has begun confusing itself with a social agency whose mission it is to advise citizens on all manner of personal concerns."

Jennings maintains that "Solutions" marks no radical departure for the broadcast; it's simply a way to emphasize a feature that had already been an important and popular part of "American Agenda." "I think we're paying a little price because of what it's called," he says. The segment on snoring "would have been fine if it had been on 'Your Health.' It's a national problem and a thing we spend money on, and if we'd done it on 'Your Health' — well, Dorothy would just have waited for another one," Jennings continues, laughing.

"Our critics just don't like it because it's deemed to be pandering," he says. "But we get more response to 'Solutions' on the Internet than anything else we've ever done."

CBS's *Evening News*, meanwhile,

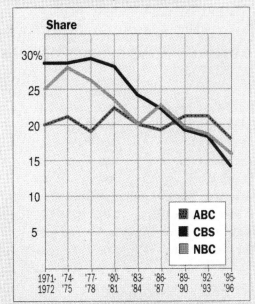

Nielsen's Numbers:

How the Three Network Evening Newscasts Have Scored with U.S. Audiences, 1971-1996

Share

Audience share, shown above, measures the percentage of the households *actually* watching television that was tuned to each program. Ratings, listed below, take *potential* viewers into account, showing the percentage of all households with television tuned to each program. Years run from September to April. In '95-'96 a single ratings point represented 959,000 U.S. households.

Rating	1971-1972	'74-'75	'77-'78	'80-'81	'83-'84	'86-'87	'89-'90	'92-'93	'95-'96
ABC	9.6	11.1	9.9	12.6	11.1	10.7	11.0	11.3	8.6
CBS	14.7	15.0	15.1	15.4	13.8	12.1	10.1	9.8	7.2
NBC	12.9	14.4	13.6	13.2	11.2	12.1	9.9	9.4	8.1

MOFFETT CECIL

after dominating the airwaves for years as the newscast of the "Tiffany" network, slid into third place in the ratings after Larry Tisch's cost-cutting years of the late '80s. Ratings don't always tell the whole story, of course. Some of NBC *Nightly News*'s current strength

may be attributable to "bounce" from the network's other successes — the thriving thrice-weekly newsmagazine *Dateline*, the slick new cable-and-online partner MSNBC, and the hot prime-time schedule. And CBS is quick to point out that some of its newscast's present weakness derives from intra-network "splat": CBS traded twenty-six affiliated stations with other networks after losing the broadcast rights to pro football, often ending up with weaker partner stations.

Dan Rather maintains that it's a "miracle" the *Evening News* is doing as well as it is in the face of the network's crumbled delivery system. "Because we have a reputation for being a hard-news outfit, we manage to stay in the hunt," he says. "I believe if we go the soft-news route we fall farther behind. I don't hear anybody among our viewers complaining that we run too much foreign news. I do find viewers complaining when we run something they feel is a waste of their time — like a soft feature."

CBS's lineup does indeed include noticeably more international stories than the other two newscasts. Last year the *Evening News* spent more time than either competitor on both Bosnia and the Middle Eastern conflict. It has aired a series of pieces by Bob Simon on the adjustments to black rule in South Africa, and no other network had a correspondent filing reports from Albania weeks before the country imploded in mid-March. But CBS, too, airs such small-focus features as "The Class of 2000" on teenagers' lives, and it has certainly done its bit for the *New England Journal of Medicine.*

As the newscasts continue to warm up and soften up, it's easy to romanticize the golden age when television news did, supposedly, have a soul. It's never been entirely, unrelentingly devoted to "hard" news: on a single randomly selected evening in 1971, CBS gave five minutes to Charles Kuralt's visit to a rally of Airstream-trailer fanciers and NBC's David Brinkley bade a leisurely welcome to spring.

And sometimes the evening news mistook ponderousness for heft. There was that hot night in August 1977 when ABC and NBC led their broadcasts with the death of Elvis Presley and the Tiffany network began with six minutes on an event it considered more newsworthy: negotiations over the Panama Canal Treaty. "A lot of the foreign coverage ten years ago was deathly dull," says Tyndall. "A lot of the vaunted foreign news coverage that NBC is *not* now doing used to be Marvin Kalb reading a press release from the secretary of state."

But critics point to other artifacts of the golden age that now seem just as quaint as an Airstream. "In the good old days you never even raised the issue of cost," says Marty Koughan, a sixteen-year veteran of CBS News who is now the executive producer for Mother Jones Television, "and if you raised the question of ratings you were mocked. At *CBS Reports* I worked on an hour on litigation in America — just try that today."

Sandy Socolow remembers when a sort of intellectual elitism was considered not just normal among newspeople, but healthy. "The mandate used to be to tell people what they needed to know — but they often don't know what they need to know until someone tells them," he says. "The newsperson's job is to hunch out what's important, what's significant, and to *make* that interesting."

But that, says Brokaw, is exactly what's changed — the sense of what's really important to people — and a broadcast that doesn't notice isn't going to last long. "One of the things that I want not to happen is for us to all commit suicide," he says. Everything from education to the automobile busi-

ness has also been changing, and "they could have been rigid and said 'I don't want to be demeaning to the institution,' and they'd have gotten left behind."

Brokaw could have added the rest of the press to his list of evolving institutions, too, as it grapples with the glut of information and what surveys suggest is an unshakable resistance among most of the audience to serious, "hard" news. The print press, long since displaced as the medium of first resort by the evening newscasts and more

recently by the omnipresent CNN and C-SPAN, has for years been adapting by substituting service stories, lifestyle features, and analysis for the urgent scoop. The "newspaper of record," *The New York Times*, now puts on its front page leisurely stories about the plight of bored wealthy Russian wives or the overelaborate caution labels on, for instance, children's Batman capes. The muckraking bimonthly *Mother Jones* recently started a health column. And the best-selling issue on domestic newsstands for both *Time* and *Newsweek* in 1996 was devoted to new interpretations of the life of Jesus. Among *Newsweek*'s top ten covers only number nine, on the crash of TWA Flight 800, was pegged to a breaking news story. Other top sellers featured John F. Kennedy's new wife ("Carolyn Style"), gay parenting, the cartoon character Dilbert on why "Work is Hell," and "The Biology of Beauty."

TOP 10 EVENING-NEWS STORIES OF 1996

	Total Minutes	ABC	CBS	NBC
1. TWA Flight 800 crash	363	105	141	117
2. Bob Dole campaign	338	120	122	95
3. Yugoslavia war	301	117	134	49
4. O.J. Simpson trial	252	72	89	92
5. Israeli-Palestinian conflict	244	88	104	52
6. Whitewater investigations	216	78	82	55
7. Atlanta Olympic games	207	39	28	140
8. ValuJet Flight 592 crash	184	48	61	74
9. GOP San Diego convention	178	62	68	49
10. Bull market	174	54	59	61

Source: ADT Research/Andrew Tyndall. Subtotals may not add up due to rounding.

MOFFETT CECIL

So, the argument goes, why should the newscasts be exempt from reorienting themselves as best they can, too? Why should the public require this one medium to be stuck with playing Norma Desmond when everyone else gets to be Madonna?

One reason is precisely that: everyone else *is* doing it. If the goal is really to give people news they haven't already heard, it's hard to believe that without NBC on the case, viewers would never find out that families work better if Dad's around or that not getting a good night's sleep can be bad for your health. The more any broadcast strives to be "not your father's evening news," the more indistinguishable it is from the "everything else" that is its most feared competition — the local television news, the tabloid shows and newsmagazines, the slick print magazines, Oprah, even the late-night comedians.

Yet there's a larger question at stake here, too, one that goes well beyond any critique rooted in Tyndall's numbers of minutes devoted to this or that. It's a question of the mood, the tone, the underlying message of the stories that do make air — and of the ones that don't. How long can an evening news program emphasize the fulfillment of viewers' needs, work to provide exactly what they are "desperate" to hear — and continue to function as a *national* newscast at all?

No one will argue that news about helping your child do better in school is less worthy on some cosmic scale than yet more news about Bosnia, or that it's not a journalist's business to give your sister the information she needs to discover her breast cancer early. If the evening news once had room for all those Panama Canal negotiations, it should certainly be able to find some place for stories of more immediate human interest.

Nor will anyone contend that the newscasts have entirely given up on stories that connect viewers to a larger world than their own home or community, introducing them to issues they didn't necessarily know they didn't know about. Everything from ABC's backgrounder on a Supreme Court religious-freedom case involving the rebuilding of a church, to CBS's exploration of China's intentions in Hong Kong, to NBC's look at the debate over executing a mentally ill criminal in Texas has managed to do that.

But the danger is very real now that as any national newscast edges closer in tone and subject to local-news and newsmagazine programs, it will make more of its journalistic decisions and consume more of its twenty-two minutes based on local-news and newsmagazine standards. That it will choose personal relevance instead of national importance, it will prefer soft soap to hard truths, and, given a choice between raising ratings and raising hell, it will look up and not down.

It's already happening. Take foreign news. From January 1 to mid-March, the civil war in Zaire, the second largest country in sub-Saharan Africa, was almost entirely off the map for every one of the network newscasts. And on March 13, after marine helicopters moved in to evacuate several hundred Americans from Albania, Brokaw led his broadcast with a dramatic description of the "meltdown" in a country whose name had first been breathed on the weeknight newscast just the previous evening. The chaotic little country had, apparently, been of no interest whatsoever without an American angle.

While some of this inattention to foreign news obviously reflects the end of cold-war tensions, much of it is also clearly due to fear — of low ratings and high cost. Brokaw, while arguing that NBC has not missed a major foreign story, also bluntly points out that when Bryant Gumbel took *Today* to black Africa and did "a really distinguished piece of work," it got "almost no ratings." In consequence, he says, "I knew immediately it would be harder for us to go back to Africa ourselves."

Or consider political news. For all their emphasis on clot busters and mammograms, all three newscasts have just about forgotten an entire class of sick people whose plight was a hot topic four years ago when Clinton proposed his health-care reform measures — those who are uninsured.

Even the biggest stories are often smaller than they used to be. In June 1991 ABC's *World News Tonight* went on the air with a huge project: every night for two weeks it devoted at least one significant segment to examining child poverty — its causes, consequences, and possible remedies. Throughout the late '80s NBC devoted

WHY SHOULD THE PUBLIC REQUIRE THE EVENING NEWS TO BE STUCK WITH PLAYING NORMA DESMOND WHEN EVERYONE ELSE GETS TO BE MADONNA?

its "Special Segment," sometimes lasting as long as five or six minutes, to topics like the loss of the rain forests, racism in the military, and — for two weeks — a look at the lives of Vietnamese citizens and Vietnam veterans a decade after the fall of Saigon.

But ABC's big project this spring resonated much differently. Throughout the entire month of March *World News Tonight* joined with ABC's entertainment and sports divisions to focus on one question: how parents can talk to children about drugs. It is a topic of great concern, of course, but one with a very circumscribed focus — on *you*, *your* family, *your* children, not someone else's who may be in need. And while Brokaw defends NBC's regular "Fleecing of America" segment as "an investigative piece in the richest old mainline tradition of journalism," its title betrays its preoccupation with investigating only a

pinched and personal victimology: how the government is out to cheat *you*.

Like everything else, the evening news goes through cycles and fashions, and this trend, too, will doubtless cycle on. "The evening news is not this font of perceived wisdom that our critics say we think we are," says Jennings. "We are another institution on the national playing field and we respond in some considerable measure to how the really powerful institutions in the country operate — the executive branch, the Congress, the Pentagon, the Federal Bureau of Investigation, in the old days the CIA.

"There are tons of people out there," Jennings goes on, "who say 'Well, just do this, do that, you should be doing this, you shouldn't be doing that.' But journalism is nothing if not a rolling experiment. We get up every day trying to figure out what is relevant to people in the country, and we very often don't know the answer in any immediate sense."

In fact the trend toward the personalizing and softening of news is very much a response to — if not an outright imitation of — the way other "really powerful institutions in the country" have themselves been working to woo an alienated and restive public.

Between the politicians who won in the last election and the warmed-up segments of the evening news, the parallels are particularly striking. Like the journalists, the politicians have focused on small, personalized promises of a better life, not for your country, but for you and your family: Airplane flights without butterflies! Time off from work for PTA meetings! A good night's sleep for all!

Both talk in the cadences of a manufactured populism that replaces the inspiriting tones of leadership with a comforting patois of service and infotainment. Politicians and television journalists alike want us to know they are just folks like us, just folks who understand our concerns, just folks who feel our pain, just folks who know what we're desperate to hear.

And what might get enough votes — or ratings points — to win.

A survey conducted by the Roper Center in conjunction with the Newseum reveals surprising findings about what Americans may think of the news: what's wrong, what's right, whom to trust.

Do You Believe What Newspeople Tell You?

BY JUDITH VALENTE

A NATIONAL SURVEY SUGGESTS THAT AMERICANS may need and depend on the news but have serious misgivings about the reporters who present it. Survey respondents said that journalists are far too closely allied with special interests, that they go overboard to play up the sensational aspects of a story and that they put far too much emphasis on the private lives of their subjects.

Basically, the survey indicates that while there is a strong need for and an attachment to news, there is a distrust of newspapers, television and radio as a whole.

The strong feelings expressed in the survey "reflect a general antipathy toward bigness—big government, big business, big media," says David Lawrence Jr., publisher of *The Miami Herald.*

While 34% of those surveyed said that "freedom of the press should be protected under all circumstances," 65% agreed that "there are times when the press should not be allowed to publish or broadcast certain things."

At the same time, 80% said that the press—meaning newspapers, magazines, TV and radio—was crucial to the functioning of a free society. And 71% said the news was useful in helping them make practical decisions in their lives, in such matters as investing, voting, health and education.

What's News

- 95% want to know about crime.
- 94% are interested in local news.
- 92% express an interest in the environment.
- 88% want to know what the national government is doing.
- 87% are interested in news from around the world.
- 67% are interested in the arts.
- 63% are interested in sports.

What's Wrong

- 82% think reporters are insensitive to people's pain when covering disasters and accidents.
- 64% think the news is too sensationalized.
- 64% think reporters spend too much time offering their own opinions.
- 63% think the news is too manipulated by special interests.
- 60% think reporters too often quote sources whose names are not given in news stories.
- 52% think the news is too biased.
- 46% think the news is too negative.

When it comes to trust, while 22% said they believed all of what a minister, priest or rabbi had to say, only 2% said the same about newspaper reporters, and just 5% said they totally trusted network TV news anchors. Local TV anchors got a 7% trust rating, while radio talk-show hosts got just 1%. (The President got 4%, and members of Congress and lawyers got 3%.)

More than 70% said they read a local paper several times a week, and about 25% said they listened to political talk radio at least once a week. As for journalistic pundits such as the McLaughlin Group, the public message seems to be: Put a lid on it. "We don't care what their opinion is," says Mary Sorenson, 22, a survey participant and nursing assistant from Verona, Wis.

"The public's standard for news is higher than ever," notes Al Neuharth, chairman of The Freedom Forum and the founder of *USA Today*. "The truth is, mainstream journalism as a profession has improved dramatically since I started out in the business 50 years ago. Many consumers of news don't realize that, just as many journalists don't understand the higher standards to which we are being held."

Tom Brokaw, the *NBC Nightly News* anchor, says the amount of news coverage of big stories "can give the impression of a feeding frenzy." He adds: "You have all these cable systems, the Internet. People feel bombarded." Likewise, the process of news gathering "can appear quite discomforting," he says. "Most people are polite. The press is often not polite when it's trying to get at the bottom of something."

Joseph Dupont, 42, a survey participant and quality-control technician from Leominister, Mass., expresses a strong reaction to the "feeding frenzy" atmosphere: "It makes me want to tear their necks out when they approach a survivor 30 minutes after their loved one is dead and ask, 'How do you feel?' They want to be first with the story. There should be some common decency." A resounding 82% of those surveyed agreed that the press was insensitive to people's pain when covering disasters and accidents.

"A lot of that comes from TV," David Lawrence says. "It's the intrusive nature of the medium. People lump [TV and newspapers] together. I always argue, 'Judge us separately.' " Reporters aren't necessarily insensitive, Lawrence adds. "They're skeptical. We pay them to be."

Richard Oppel, editor of the *Austin (Tex.) American-Statesman*, says most journalists don't "exploit the lurid or the tasteless." But he adds, "We haven't done an adequate job covering news that builds community, inspires people and offers solutions. We must do better on this."

The survey found that people generally pay attention to the news 30 minutes to two hours daily. Where do they get their news? Most said from their local newspaper and local television stations. Local TV anchors were their most trusted sources of information. "It may be a sense of proximity," says Carol Marin, co-anchor of the nightly news on WMAQ, the NBC-TV affiliate in Chicago. "You are a part of the community in which people live. There's a relationship."

Network news has lost half of its audience in the last 20 years. In 1975, about 48% of all households tuned in to one of the three networks' nightly newscasts; the number is now down to about 26%.

What respondents said they were interested in runs counter to conventional wisdom. More wanted to know about international news and about the environment than about sports or political campaigns. Two-thirds said there was too little coverage of subjects of interest to youth. A full 42% complained that journalists don't ask

What Anchors Say About the News

High-profile television news anchors share some of the same concerns as their critics.

"[Coverage of big stories] can give the impression of a feeding frenzy. People feel bombarded."
—Tom Brokaw, anchor, *NBC Nightly News*

"We have to stop underestimating the intelligence of people."
—Carol Marin, co-anchor, the evening news, WMAQ, Chicago

"This survey refutes those cynical voices who say the public does not take our work seriously."
—Dan Rather, anchor, *CBS Evening News*

"I feel, as any citizen, that more and more media in fewer hands, in the abstract, is reason to be concerned."
—Peter Jennings, anchor, *ABC World News Tonight*

elected officials the kinds of questions that are important to most Americans, and 76% said the press spent too much time reporting on the private lives of public officials.

Joseph Dupont says he sees the press as fixated on sensational crime stories, such as the murder of Bill Cosby's son in Los Angeles and of 6-year-old JonBenét Ramsey in Boulder, Colo. "What I'd like to see is more of the good side of humanity," he adds. "Bad stuff happens all the time."

"There are enough high-profile cases where we might have gone too far," acknowledges N. Christian Anderson, publisher of the Colorado Springs *Gazette Telegraph*. "I think people are saying, 'Back off.' "

However, reporters have complained that it's disingenuous for the public to rail against sensational coverage of crime and controversy, and then still tune in to TV shows such as *Hard Copy* and *Inside Edition*, which blur the line between news and entertainment. "I don't see how trash TV can prosper in a climate that people profess to abhor." says Carol Marin. "Readers and viewers have their end to hold up too."

David Lawrence insists the press often does take the high road. "We don't always print everything we know," he says. "There might be something genuinely grisly in a crime of violence, and we'll make a decision as to whether it ought to be in the paper."

Though survey participants cited Tom Brokaw as their favorite TV anchor, he's no stranger to the debate over press ethics. In December, NBC reportedly was forced to pay more than $500,000 to Richard Jewell, the Atlanta security guard wrongly implicated in the Olympic Park bombing last summer—all because Brokaw had announced on the air last July that authorities "probably

What Do *You* Say?

What can newspeople do to increase your trust in them? We'd like to know. Please send your comments to: News Survey, P.O. Box 5099, Grand Central Station, New York, N.Y. 10163-5099.

America's First Newseum

DID YOU EVER PICTURE YOURSELF READING the evening news on camera, like Dan Rather or Connie Chung? Well, you can do exactly that beginning April 18 at a brand-new, three-story interactive museum devoted strictly to the news in all forms from all times and all places. It's in Arlington, Va., just a few subway stops from the Washington Mall, it's free and, yes, it's called the Newseum.

"We hope this Newseum will help the press and the public both understand each other better—it's that simple," declared Al Neuharth, founder of *USA Today* and currently head of The Freedom Forum, the non-profit foundation that built the $50 million structure.

If you go to the Newseum, you will be able to see yourself as a network anchor reading the evening news on camera, write your own news story, even see your face on the cover of PARADE. A state-of-the-art broadcast studio will show how news programs are produced.

The Newseum is more broadly dedicated to informing the public about the First Amendment, which guarantees a free press, and to presenting information about the news from ancient times to the present. The permanent collection will exhibit objects associated with news events and people, including a printed version of Columbus' letter to the Spanish court about the discovery of the New World, Paul Revere's glasses, Ernie Pyle's typewriter, Sumerian tablets from 2400 B.C., and a Civil War-era camera used by Mathew Brady.

Designed largely by Ralph Appelbaum, who has won recognition for the Holocaust Memorial Museum in Washington, D.C., the Newseum stands beside what is now Freedom Park. The park contains, among other exhibits, three sections of the Berlin Wall, a replica of the door to the Birmingham jail cell that detained the Rev. Martin Luther King Jr. and the small kayak that brought an escaping Cuban couple across the Gulf Stream to Florida. There is also a memorial to 934 reporters killed on the job.

"The Newseum will be an educational and entertaining experience for all," said Peter Prichard, the Newseum's executive director. Quoting Thomas Jefferson, he added: " 'Our liberty depends on freedom of the press, and that cannot be limited without being lost.' "

The Newseum, in Arlington, Va., opens April 18. For more information: write, Newseum, 1101 Wilson Blvd., Dept. P, Arlington, Va. 22209; call 1-888-NEWSEUM, or visit *http://www.newseum.org* on the Web.

have enough to arrest [Jewell] right now [and] probably enough to prosecute him."

Brokaw says he was citing information from law-enforcement sources at the time. NBC never issued an apology or a retraction. (CNN paid Jewell an undisclosed amount in a separate settlement. Jewell, meanwhile, is seeking reparation from the *Atlanta Journal-Constitution*, which he says libeled him.)

Juries also have taken aim at the press. A North Carolina jury recently awarded $5.5 million in punitive damages against ABC over a 1992 *Primetime Live* report that accused the Food Lion supermarket chain of selling spoiled meat. The accuracy of the report wasn't at issue. The jury seemed troubled by ABC's practice of sending reporters undercover with hidden cameras.

Erosion of confidence in the press isn't new. Public opinion of the press reached a high point following Watergate but began declining soon after. A 1996 poll by the National Opinion Research Center at the University of Chicago found that only 11% of those surveyed felt "a great deal" of confidence in the press.

Peter Jennings, the anchor of *ABC World News Tonight*, sees a double standard in what viewers want. "They can be offended by what they perceive as a press frenzy," he says. "Yet pity the poor reporter who doesn't get the story that night." He cites TV's coverage of the O. J. Simpson criminal trial. ABC News, then first in the ratings, decided not to air nightly segments on the trial, but NBC did. The ABC broadcast has since dropped to second place, and NBC is on top. "Frankly, I think it cost us," says Jennings. "Are any of us proud of the way the Simpson case grabbed the media by the throat? Of course not."

Reporters nonetheless bristle at the notion that they aren't sensitive to people's pain. "I challenge anyone to tell me the last time they saw somebody stick a microphone in a grieving person's face," says Carol Marin. "Yes, we talk to people about their pain. But it's almost never in an ambush interview."

The public may think journalists insensitive, says the editor Richard Oppel, but "most people go into journalism because they care deeply about people and believe they can change the ills of society."

"We make decisions all day long on what's not going to get put in the newspaper," says N. Christian Anderson. "Almost invariably, we rely on the public's right to know."

A vast majority of those surveyed (88%) said they believed corporate owners improperly influenced news reporting—and that the big corporations seemed to keep getting bigger. "Americans have a healthy disrespect for the concentration of power," says Richard Oppel, "and they see media ownership becoming more and more concentrated." In the last two years, Westinghouse took over CBS, Disney acquired ABC, and Turner merged with the media giant Time Warner.

An overwhelming 90% said the media's desire to make profits improperly influenced the news, and the same number said advertisers did. Peter Jennings disagrees. "Journalists will be the first to scream if they feel they are being manipulated or suppressed in any way," he says, noting that ABC News has covered stories unflattering to its corporate parent, Disney, in recent months.

Still, the public's concern about the influence of special interests is rooted in reality. In 1995, ABC issued an apology and agreed to pay $16 million in legal expenses to Philip Morris and R. J. Reynolds, rather than fight a lawsuit the tobacco companies had brought over a report alleging that they had raised nicotine levels to hook smokers.

"The media, which historically has served as a check on society, is now looked upon as part of the establishment," says Jonathan C. Klein, executive vice president of CBS News.

Far more insidious than corporate oversight, says Carol Marin, is the attention paid to viewer demographics or so-called "target marketing." "If you are a female 20 to 35 years old, do you only need to know about issues that are of concern to women 20 to 35 years old?" she asks. "We have to stop underestimating the intelligence of people."

How can the press win a better report card from the public? Richard Oppel suggests listening more to what the public has to say about how the news is covered. Readers, he says, have urged the press to look at the "profoundly ordinary" as a way of giving a balanced picture of community life. "There was a feeling that we stay so focused on the fringe, we miss what is happening in the center," says Oppel.

Peter Jennings is optimistic that the press can bridge the gap with its public. "If we have anything in this country, it is a capacity for self-correction," he says.

Dan Rather, the *CBS Evening News* anchor, is also heartened: "If nothing else, this survey refutes those cynical voices who say that the public does not take our work seriously. For those of us who are trying to be worthy of the name 'independent American journalist,' we can only be encouraged by these results and use them to remind us to avoid the kinds of abuses that are reflected in the public's concerns."

About the Survey

The survey of 1500 individuals from around the U.S. was conducted in January by the Roper Center in Storrs, Conn. Commissioned by the Newseum, the survey has a sampling error of plus or minus 2.5%, according to Ken Dautrich, assistant director of the Roper Center. Detailed survey results are available at *http://www.newseum.org* (the Newseum site) on the World Wide Web.

T RADITIONAL NEWS MEDIA ARE BESIEGED BY significant challenges. Most recently, the negative public reaction to this year's coverage of the Monica Lewinsky/White House situation raised significant image and credibility issues. Other challenges derive from longer term trends, most importantly, the rise of an astonishingly varied number of new sources of news and information including those that offer news, at best, indirectly and dressed up as entertainment, and those that make no pretense of offering news at all, but instead only provide unfiltered information.

As exhilarating as these challenges to the media might be, the potential downside they present for journalists is enormously disquieting. If Americans increasingly distrust the media, get their news essentially by osmosis through talk

has made a wholesale swing toward reliance on non-traditional sources of news.

T WENTY-ONE SOURCES OF NEWS AND INFORMATION were used by Gallup in its recent major assessment of the public's use and view of the media. The survey of 1,009 Americans was conducted in March and has a plus-or-minus 3 percent margin of error. It measured the frequency with which each news outlet is used by the public as a source of news and the perception of each source in terms of accuracy and objectivity.

The list ranges from hard news sources (national newspapers, network and local TV news, local newspapers), to media that straddle the line between news and information (C-SPAN and the Internet), to media that blur the distinction between news and entertain-

A MATTER OF TRUST

A new Gallup Poll shows Americans have more confidence in TV news than print, trust the nightly newsmagazines more than the network newscasts (and the print news magazines), believe CNN—and don't rely on the Internet for news.

shows and infotainment programming, or get it directly from the source through C-SPAN or the Internet, the old style gatekeeper breed of journalist could be poised to follow the slide rule and buggy whip into oblivion.

New survey data, however, go a long way toward assuaging some of the fears held by the guardians of traditional media. A recent Gallup Poll shows that Americans continue to rely on and report faith in many of the traditional hard news sources they have long used for news and information. Use of the "new" media as sources for news is much lower, and so is trust in its accuracy. There appears to be, in short, little evidence of a public backlash against the mainstream media based on their coverage of what has happened (or at least what has been alleged to have happened) in the White House, and there is even less evidence that the public

ment (morning TV news shows, talk radio and infotainment programs).

What the survey found: Americans have generally high levels of trust in many of the major sources of news and information to which they are exposed, but are quite discriminating, and negative, in their views of others. Broadcast news has higher credibility than print. Prime time TV newsmagazines are both popular and highly trusted, as are local television newscasts. And both are more trusted than the networks' nightly newscasts. The direct-to-the-public information sources such as C-SPAN and the Internet have yet to register much of an impression of any kind with the bulk of the American population.

Here are the key findings:

■ The highest levels of trust are reserved for electronic news sources: CNN,

**BY FRANK NEWPORT
AND LYDIA SAAD**

public television news, local television news and prime time TV newsmagazines. All four of these have "net trust" (trust minus distrust) levels above 50 percent, with about 70 percent of the public, overall, saying they trust their accuracy, compared to about 15 percent who say they don't. Conspicuously missing from the top tier for perceived credibility is the nightly network news, with a net trust rating of only 43 percent.

While CNN gets the highest trust ratings in the survey, local TV newscasts would have to be viewed as the heavyweight champion on the list, in that they receive high trust ratings and, according to the survey, are one of America's two most frequently used sources of news.

Other traditional news sources—local and national newspapers and weekly news magazines—rank significantly lower in terms of their perceived credibility, with the national print news magazines coming in lowest of the group.

When Bill Clinton appeared on Arsenio Hall and MTV in 1992 to promote his presidential campaign, he gave birth to a whole school of thought about the new media. Oprah sells hundreds of thousands of books, Don Imus hosts a radio talk show based on a virtual Who's Who of American politics, the Wall Street Journal breaks stories on its Internet site, Matt Drudge is sued because of the supposed negative impact of allegations published on his Web site, and half-hour infotainment shows dominate the pre-prime time hours in most American TV markets.

None of this seems to matter. These outlets are not used with any great frequency specifically as sources of news and information. Despite its enormous potential, the Internet has at best only a narrow, niche audience that uses it for news. Radio and TV talk shows and the infotainment shows do only slightly better.

Moreover, all of these sources rate particularly low on trust. In the case of talk shows and the infotainment programs, the lack of credibility is overwhelming. Fifty percent or more of those with an opinion say they can't trust the accuracy of what they see or hear there. On the Internet, the "can't trust" figure is 45 percent.

Prime time TV newsmagazines constitute a burgeoning source of news and information. These shows will continue to metastasize until they are on every network every night of the week, and eventually—as some observers have noted—may well replace the early evening network newscasts altogether.

The public could easily become reliant on these shows as their primary source of news and information, which have among the highest levels of trust of any of the news sources tested. And, sure to rankle the editors of the more traditional print news magazines, TV newsmagazines are now used much more frequently by the public than Time, Newsweek and U.S. News & World Report. Not only do the print news magazines get lower scores for accuracy than their distant cousins on TV, but in fact they score among the lowest on trust.

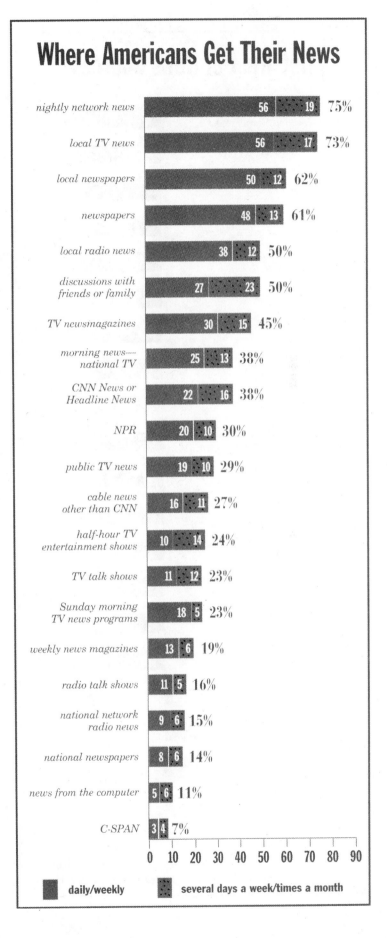

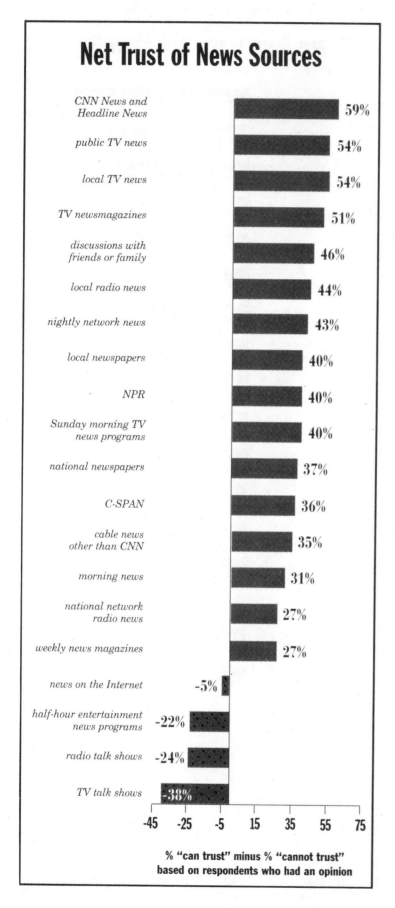

Net Trust of News Sources

CNN News and Headline News	59%
public TV news	54%
local TV news	54%
TV newsmagazines	51%
discussions with friends or family	46%
local radio news	44%
nightly network news	43%
local newspapers	40%
NPR	40%
Sunday morning TV news programs	40%
national newspapers	37%
C-SPAN	36%
cable news other than CNN	35%
morning news	31%
national network radio news	27%
weekly news magazines	27%
news on the Internet	-5%
half-hour entertainment news programs	-22%
radio talk shows	-24%
TV talk shows	-38%

-45 -25 -5 15 35 55 75

% "can trust" minus % "cannot trust" based on respondents who had an opinion

■ "Direct to the audience" sources of news are supposed to revolutionize the way we get and use news, eventually obviating the need for journalists to select, edit and interpret what we see and read. Two such sources were measured by Gallup, and neither has fulfilled the prophecies. Neither C-SPAN nor the Internet is heavily used for news, and C-SPAN, in fact, is the least used source of any of those tested. The Internet is only marginally more frequently used.

There are, however, differences between the two. C-SPAN is more trusted than the Net, but for a medium that does almost no filtering of the news it presents, it receives only a relatively modest level of trust from those who have an opinion.

■ In the local arena, television news wins out over newspapers in both frequency of use and trust. Americans, particularly young people, say they use local television as a source of news more than they use local newspapers, and the public also has more trust in the accuracy of what it sees on TV newscasts than in what it reads in local newspapers.

Still, local papers have a significant leg up over other print sources of news. Almost two-thirds of Americans read a local newspaper for news and information at least several times a week, compared to only 14 percent who say they frequently get their news from a national newspaper and only 19 percent who cite weekly news magazines. Although they are among the most prestigious news outlets in journalism, public reliance on publications such as the New York Times, Time and Newsweek is low—and on par with talk radio and infotainment shows.

Several electronic mass media sources of news and information are more trusted than the oldest source of news of all, word-of-mouth, described in the Gallup research as "discussions with your friends or family." Only 64 percent of Americans say they can trust what they hear from friends and family, while 18 percent say they can't. This net trust level is below that of CNN, public television news, local television news and prime time TV newsmagazines, suggesting that the news anchors Americans see on TV are considered more reliable as sources of accurate information than personal acquaintances.

IS THERE AN INCOMPATIBILITY BETWEEN THE HIGH levels of expressed trust in many frequently used sources of news and information and the more critical reaction generated by these same sources in terms of their coverage of the White House crisis earlier this year?

Yes and no. Some of the complaining as measured in Gallup polls earlier this year seemed to focus on the amount of Monica/Paula/Kathleen coverage, which is not necessarily inconsistent with positive impressions about its accuracy. In fact, Gallup polling has suggested all year that Americans do not overwhelmingly believe Bill Clinton is innocent. It would seem that Americans don't think the news media are barking up the wrong tree in the White House crisis as much as it thinks that the media should not be barking up any of these types of trees at all.

The Gallup survey also touched on the issue of an alleged liberal bias in news coverage. There is, to our knowledge, no systematic or universally agreed upon way to determine the presence or absence of bias in news coverage. The survey asked Americans to evaluate the major news sources as "fair and impartial," as having a liberal bias or as having a conservative bias.

The results: More Americans perceive bias of one stripe or another than believe the various media are fair and impartial—the ratio being about 55 percent to 45 percent across all media. Additionally, the plurality who do sense a bias tend to think that news is too liberal rather than too conservative, although this tendency is not pronounced. There seem to be four dynamics that drive these findings:

1) One person's poison is another's cup of tea, meaning that bias is strongly related to personal ideology; 2) while conservatives tend to see liberal bias and liberals tend to see conservative bias, this tendency is much stronger among the conservatives surveyed; 3) self-identified conservatives outnumber liberals by about three-to-two in the Gallup media survey—thus their perceptions of bias carry more weight; and 4) the large group of moderates in America tend to perceive somewhat more of a liberal bias than a conservative bias.

The perception of a liberal bias is strongest—but still not overwhelming—for national news sources. At the local level those who see either left- or right-wing bias in print or TV essentially cancel each other out. In other words, the direction of the perceived bias for local news sources (both newspapers and TV news) is split almost exactly the same—down the middle. Conservatives, in particular, are significantly less apt to say that local television news has a liberal bias than any of the other news sources tested.

Of additional interest is the fact that the one medium that distributes every conceivable type of news and information, from every conceivable perspective—the Internet—has the highest "net liberal" bias of any major news source tested.

Although each major news event—O.J. Simpson, the White House crisis, the death of Princess Diana—seems to bring with it new criticisms of the news media, it appears that the American public still has a good deal of trust in what it sees and reads in the daily news. Although new ways of disseminating news will continue to develop in the years ahead, the public currently seems most content with the old-fashioned way of getting their news. And, electronic news media dominate as trustworthy sources of news for the average American.

Frank Newport is editor in chief of The Gallup Poll. Lydia Saad is The Gallup Poll's managing editor.

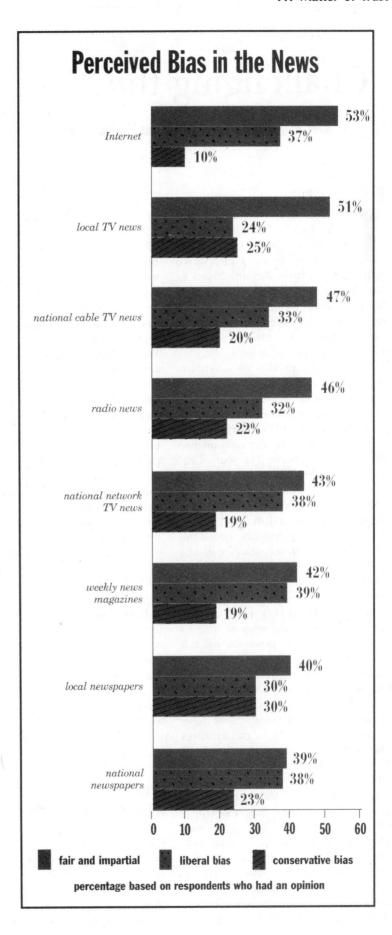

Perceived Bias in the News

	fair and impartial	liberal bias	conservative bias
Internet	53%	37%	10%
local TV news	51%	24%	25%
national cable TV news	47%	33%	20%
radio news	46%	32%	22%
national network TV news	43%	38%	19%
weekly news magazines	42%	39%	19%
local newspapers	40%	30%	30%
national newspapers	39%	38%	23%

percentage based on respondents who had an opinion

Challenging the "Liberal Media" Claim

On economics, journalists' private views are to right of public

By David Croteau

The idea that the mainstream media have a "liberal bias" has long been conventional wisdom. At various times, conservative public figures from Richard Nixon to Newt Gingrich have all taken refuge in the claim that the "liberal" media were out to get them. A legion of conservative talk show hosts, pundits and media-watch groups pound away at the idea that the media exhibit an inherently "liberal" tilt. But the assertion is based on little evidence and is repeatedly made in the face of contradictory facts.

In particular, the conservative critique of the news media rests on two general propositions: (1) journalists' views are to the left of the public, and (2) journalists frame news content in a way that accentuates these left perspectives. Researchers and analysts have discovered persuasive evidence against the latter claim. Content analyses of the news media have, at a minimum, shown the absence of any such systematic liberal/left tilt; some studies have found a remarkably consistent press usually reflecting the narrow range of views of those in positions of power, as well as a spectrum of expert opinion that tilts toward the right. (See Croteau and Hoynes, *By Invitation Only*; Soley, *The News Shapers*.)

But even some progressives have been willing to cede to conservatives the first point: that journalists hold views that are to the left of the public. Professionals in general, they observe, often have "liberal" leanings on social issues, and there is no reason to expect journalists to be any different. However, they have also argued convincingly that the norms of "objective journalism" and the powerful corporate interests that own and sponsor the news media ensure that news content never strays too far, for too long, from

protecting the status quo.

You don't understand the corporate ideology of General Motors by studying the personal beliefs of the assembly-line workers, the argument goes. Ideological orientation is introduced and enforced by those high in the organizational hierarchy who have the power to hire and fire, to reward and punish. Working journalists, despite their sometimes high visibility, usually do not call the shots in the nation's media corporations. (The documentary *Fear and Favor in the Newsroom* provides vivid illustrations of this situation.) Consequently, the private views of individual journalists often matter little.

Such an analysis of organizational dynamics is fundamental to understanding the news process. It, indeed, is a crucial argument that kicks the legs out from the conservative critique and gets at the more fundamental structural elements that set the news agenda. Still, this approach begs the question: Are journalists *really* to the left of the public? This element of the conservative critique has not been adequately addressed; it's one reason why the "liberal media" charge gets repeated without serious scrutiny.

To examine this essential underpinning of the "liberal media" claim, as well as other matters, FAIR commissioned a survey of journalists of the Washington press corps.

Journalists' Economic Policy Views: A Comparison With the Public

The survey included a series of questions regarding recent policy debates. Most questions were taken from, or very closely modeled after, questions that had been asked in national random surveys of the general public. That way rough comparisons could be made

between how journalists and the general public saw these issues.

Political Orientation

One of the basic findings of this survey is that most journalists identify themselves as centrists on both social and economic issues.

On *social* issues, how would you characterize your political orientation?

Center	57%
Left	30%
Right	9%
Other	5%

On *economic* issues, how would you characterize your political orientation?

Center	64%
Right	19%
Left	11%
Other	5%

When asked to characterize their political orientation on social and economic issues, most journalists self-identify as centrists. Of the minority who do not identify with the center, most have left leanings concerning social issues and right leanings concerning economic ones. This is consistent with a long history of research on profit-sector professionals in general (Brint, *The Political Attitudes of Professionals*; Derber et al., *Power in the Highest Degree*). High levels of education tend to be associated with liberal views on social issues such as racial equality, gay rights, gun control and abortion rights. High levels of income tend to be associated with conservative views on economic issues such as tax policy and federal spending. Most journalists, therefore, would certainly not recognize themselves in the

From *Extra*, July/August 1998, pp. 4-9. © 1998 by David Croteau. Reprinted by permission.

"liberal media" picture painted by conservative critics.

These identifications may explain why an earlier survey of journalists (Roper Center/Freedom Forum, 1996) found that respondents had voted for Bill Clinton in large numbers. Clinton's centrist "new Democrat" orientation combines moderately liberal social policies (which bring criticism from conservative anti-gay, anti-abortion and other activists) with moderately conservative economic policies (which bring criticism from labor unions, welfare rights advocates and others). This orientation fits well with the views expressed by journalists.

State of the Economy

The Washington press corps has often been accused of being an "elite" that is out of touch with mainstream Americans. Journalists responding to this survey certainly did have very high household incomes, with over half living in households with $100,000 or more in income, and one-third in households with income of $150,000 or more. By comparison, the Census Bureau reports that the 1996 median household income was $35,492. Eighty percent of U.S. households had incomes below $68,015; 95 percent

made less than $119,540.

Perhaps it should come as no surprise, then, that journalists have a much more positive assessment of the state of the economy than the general public. Choosing from a list of options, 34 percent of journalists said they thought economic conditions were "excellent" and another 58 percent said "good." Only 4 percent saw them as fair, and 1 percent rated them "poor."

When pollsters ask the same question of the general public—where the benefits of economic growth have fallen unevenly—far different views are found. A March 1998 Gallup **CNN/USA Today** poll discovered that only 20 percent of the general public see economic conditions as "excellent," while 46 percent say "good." A full 27 percent describe them as "only fair" and 7 percent believe they are "poor."

Economic Priorities

Asked to prioritize various issues for the President and Congress, the surveyed journalists gave answers often starkly at odds with the public, as measured by a nationwide November 1996 poll conducted by Greenberg Research.

Entitlements: Journalists overwhelmingly chose as one of the top few priorities: "reform entitlement programs" by

slowing growth in Medicare and Social Security. Only 12 percent of journalists ranked entitlement reform as a middle or low priority (compared to 38 percent of the public). By contrast, most of the public chose "protect Medicare and Social Security against major cuts" as one of its top few priorities—with 24 percent calling it the "single highest priority." In short, while journalists' gave heavy priority to slowing entitlements, the general public emphasized protecting them.

Health care: 32 percent of journalists felt that requiring employers to "provide health insurance to their employees" should be one of the top few priorities, while a larger 47 percent of the public did.

NAFTA expansion: This issue revealed the biggest gap between journalists and the public. While 24 percent of journalists chose expansion of NAFTA to other Latin American countries as one of the top few priorities, only 7 percent of the public did. A whopping 44 percent of the general public ranked NAFTA expansion as a low priority.

In these issue areas, the claimed economic centrism of journalists is often belied by a series of economic priorities that are actually to the right of the pub-

---

Economic Priorities

Regarding "a few issues facing the country," journalists—and the public in a 1996 Greenberg poll—were asked: "How high a priority do you think each one should receive from Congress and the President?"

NOTE: **Journalists' responses** are listed on the first line in **bold**; the public's responses are on the second line.

	Single Highest Priority	One of Top Few Priorities	Near Top of List	Middle of List	Toward Bottom of List	Don't Know/ Not Sure
a. Protect Medicare and Social Security against major cuts	**13%** 24%	**26%** 35%	**16%** 24%	**13%** 12%	**15%** 5%	**16%** 1%
b. Reform entitlement programs by slowing the rate of increase in spending for programs like Medicare and Social Security	**19%** 10%	**37%** 25%	**15%** 20%	**8%** 26%	**4%** 12%	**17%** 6%
c. Expand the NAFTA trade agreement to include other countries in Latin America	**4%** 2%	**20%** 5%	**24%** 7%	**29%** 33%	**8%** 44%	**16%** 9%
d. Require that employers provide health insurance to their employees	**15%** 16%	**17%** 31%	**19%** 18%	**16%** 20%	**16%** 13%	**17%** 2%

lic, and which would bring opposition from groups on the left: labor unions, health care advocates, senior citizens' advocates.

Environmental Laws

The one area in the survey where journalists could be considered somewhat to the left of the general public was regarding environmental regulation. When asked to choose between whether stricter environmental laws and regulations "cost too many jobs and hurt the economy" or "are worth the cost," 79 percent of journalists said such laws were worth the cost, while 21 percent disagreed. In comparison, in an October 1996 poll by the Pew Research Center, only 63 percent of the public said such laws were worth the cost, while 30 percent disagreed.

This result may not be very surprising since the economic cost of environmental regulation is often perceived to be carried by workers in the form of lost jobs—a problem that may not be of immediate salience for professional journalists. There may be more envi-

ronmental commitment—pro and con—among the general public than among journalists: 51 percent of the public, vs. 32 percent of journalists, agreed "strongly" that stricter environmental laws are "worth the cost"; 22 percent of the public, vs. 8 percent of journalists, strongly took the opposite view.

Corporate Power

The general public is more critical of the concentration of corporate power in the United States than are journalists. When asked whether they felt "too much power is concentrated in the hands of a few large companies," 57 percent of the journalists agreed, while 43 percent felt they did not have too much

---

Corporate Power

Which of the following statements comes closer to your views?

Too much power is concentrated in the hands of a few large companies.

Journalists		The Public
57%		77%
24%	Strongly agree	62%
32%	Not strongly	15%
1%	Not sure	—

The largest companies do NOT have too much power.

Journalists		The Public
43%		18%
12%	Strongly agree	9%
30%	Not strongly	9%
1%	Not sure	—
—	Neither/don't know	5%

Times Mirror, Oct. 1995

Methodology

In consultation with the Survey and Evaluation Research Laboratory at Virginia Commonwealth University, a 24-question self-administered survey was sent by mail to 444 Washington–based journalists. Data was gathered from late February through April 1998.

Journalists were asked a range of questions about how they did their work and about how they viewed the quality of media coverage in the broad area of politics and economic policy. They were asked for their opinions and views about a range of recent policy issues and debates. Finally, they were asked for demographic and identifying information, including their political orientation.

The survey targeted Washington bureau chiefs and Washington-based journalists who cover national politics and/or economic policy at U.S. national and major metropolitan outlets. The intent was to represent the breadth of available media outlets, while realistically focusing on the largest and most influential of these national and major metropolitan outlets.

A survey was sent to every journalist who met the following criteria:
- They were listed in the Spring 1998 *News Media Yellow Book*, a directory of media professionals, under one or more of the following assignment categories: "Congress," "federal government," "national affairs," "politics," "White House," "business," "consumer issues," "economics" or "labor."
- They were based in the Washington, D.C. area.
- They worked for a national or major metropolitan U.S. news organization that potentially reaches the general public.

In addition, Washington-based journalists listed as "bureau chiefs" in the *Yellow Book* were surveyed if they were at a U.S. news organization that potentially reaches the general public and has at least 10 staffers listed in the *Yellow Book*.

These criteria yielded a targeted population total of 33 bureau chiefs and 411 other journalists, all of whom were sent questionnaires.

The targeted population represents a broad range of news outlets, while at the same time focusing on the largest and most influential of these outlets. The criteria used for targeting journalists meant that smaller and less influential news outlets were not over-represented, a problem found in earlier research on Washington–based journalists. The criteria were successful in both generating significant breadth (journalists at 78 different news organizations were surveyed) and keeping the emphasis on the largest and most influential media (half of the surveys were sent to journalists at 14 news organizations).

The 14 news organizations that received more than 10 surveys were (in alphabetical order): **ABC News/ABC Radio, Associated Press/AP Broadcast News, Bloomberg News, CNN, Knight-Ridder Newspapers/Tribune Information Services, Los Angeles Times, NBC News, New York Times, Reuters America, Time, USA Today/USA Weekend, Wall Street Journal, Washington Post** and **Washington Times**.

Of the 444 questionnaires mailed, 141 were returned, for a response rate of 32 percent. In terms of type of position held by the journalist, type of media outlet, and general size of media outlet, there was no statistically significant difference between respondents and non-respondents. (See table opposite.)

power. The numbers were quite different, though, when the Times Mirror Center asked the same question of the general public in October 1995. A full 77 percent of the public felt that corporations had too much power, with only 18 percent feeling that they did not. The public also tended to take a more emphatic position: 62 percent agreed "strongly" that a few corporations have too much power, vs. only 24 percent of journalists who were that definitive.

Taxes

The centrist orientation of journalists comes through clearly when assessing Clinton's 1993 economic plan, which modestly raised tax rates on the wealthy, countering the trend of reduced tax rates that they had enjoyed in previous years. Nearly half (49 per-

cent) of journalists thought this policy was about right, while 14 percent thought it went too far, and 18 percent thought it didn't go far enough. In contrast, when the public was asked a similar question in an **ABC News/Washington Post** poll in April 1993, 15 percent of the general public felt Clinton's policy went too far and an overwhelming 72 percent felt it didn't go far enough. (Ten percent volunteered that they thought it was about right.) Here again, the relative economic privilege of the Washington press corps may partly explain this contrast with the public.

NAFTA and "Fast Track"

Compared to the general public, journalists have a far more positive assessment of NAFTA's impact and are more

likely to support granting the president "fast track" authority to negotiate new trade agreements. Sixty-five percent of journalists feel that NAFTA has had more of a positive impact on the United States, while only 8 percent feel it has had more of a negative impact. But most recent polls find the American public more negative than positive on NAFTA's effect. In a Hart-Teeter **NBC News/Wall Street Journal** poll in July 1997, only 32 percent of the public thought NAFTA's impact on the U.S. was more positive, while 42 percent felt NAFTA had a mostly negative impact.

Perhaps as a result of these differing assessments of NAFTA, journalists are much more likely to favor granting "fast track" authority to the president to negotiate new trade agreements—authority opposed most forcefully by unions. A full 71 percent of journalists favor such a policy, while only 10 percent oppose it. According to an October 1997 Hart-Teeter **NBC News/Wall Street Journal** poll, the rate of opposition to "fast-track" among the general public is over five times that of the rate among journalists: Fifty-six percent of the public say they oppose "fast track," while only 35 percent support it. In the debate over trade, most journalists tend to agree with the position that corporations take on the issue, while most members of the public side with the critical views of labor and many consumer and environmental groups.

Medical Care

As indicated above under "Economic Priorities," journalists are less interested than the general public in requiring that employers provide health insurance to their employees. Journalists are also less likely than the public to believe that the federal government should guarantee medical care for those who don't have health insurance. While 43 percent of journalists felt that the government should guarantee medical care, a similar 35 percent felt that this was not the responsibility of the government. In contrast, a February 1996 **New York Times/CBS News** poll found that the general public supports government guaranteed medical care by more than a two-to-one margin (64 percent to 29 percent).

Targeted Journalists Vs. Respondents

Type of position:	Percent of Targeted Journalists (number)		Percent of Respondents (number)	
Washington bureau chiefs	7%	(33)	6%	(9)
Editors or producers	23%	(100)	19%	(27)
Reporters, correspondents and other	70%	(311)	75%	(105)
Type of media outlet:				
Wires/news services	19%	(86)	14%	(20)
TV	19%	(84)	17%	(24)
Radio	5%	(20)	6%	(8)
Newspaper	41%	(180)	46%	(65)
Magazines, periodicals and other	17%	(74)	17%	(24)
Size of outlet (as indicated by number of surveys sent)				
Sent more than 10 surveys	50%	(223)	50%	(71)
5–10 surveys	34%	(152)	36%	(51)
3–4 surveys	5%	(23)	6%	(9)
1–2 surveys	10%	(46)	7%	(10)

Journalists' Views on Media Coverage

Journalists responding to the survey report high levels of satisfaction with the amount and quality of economic policy coverage provided by their own news organization. A full 76 percent of the journalists thought that their news organization provided "excellent" or "good" quality coverage in terms of giving the public information they need to make informed political decisions. Another 14 percent thought it was "fair" and 9 percent said it was "poor."

Their assessment of other news media, though, was more varied. "Business-oriented news outlets" received the highest grade for the quality of the economic information they give to the public; 80 percent thought it was "excellent" or "good." "Major daily newspapers," too, received a positive assessment, with 65 percent saying their coverage was "excellent" or "good." However, for every other type of media, less than half of the respondents rated its coverage as "excellent" or "good."

A full 92 percent of responding journalists said the quality of economic policy coverage on broadcast TV networks was only "fair" or "poor," with just 6 percent saying it was "good" and not a single respondent saying it was "excellent." (Even of those journalists working in television, 83 percent rated broadcast TV networks as "fair" or "poor.") Cable news services were judged by 63 percent of journalists to provide only "fair" or "poor" coverage of economic policy issues.

Choosing from a list of possibilities, more journalists (58 percent) thought that business misconduct was a topic that received "too little" media attention. This was followed closely by international trade agreements (53 percent), labor misconduct (50 percent) and the federal budget process (49 percent). The stock market (22 percent) was the item that journalists most often cited as being covered "too much," followed by government misconduct (16 percent) and "downsizing" (14 percent).

Work Routines and Information Sources

Technological changes seem to have had an impact on the work routines and information sources of journalists. With contemporary technology, the news cycle is quite short for a large number of journalists. More than a quarter of those who responded to the survey (26 percent) reported having a deadline more than once a day. Another 55 percent usually had daily deadlines.

Electronic data services have become a staple source of information for journalists. Seventy-two percent reported that they consulted Internet or other on-line services during a typical workday. This was surpassed only by wire services (94 percent) and cable TV news (79 percent).

Journalists rely most often on government officials and business representatives as sources for their stories on economic policy issues. Labor representatives are consulted far less frequently than business representatives, and consumer advocates are even less likely to be consulted.

How often do you talk to the following sources in your work on economic policy issues?

	% saying "nearly always"	% saying "often"
Government officials	51%	34%
Business representatives	31%	35%
Think-tank analysts	17%	47%
University-based academics	10%	38%
Wall Street analysts	9%	22%
Labor representatives	5%	30%
Consumer advocates	5%	20%

Conclusion: Beyond the "Liberal Media" Myth

This survey calls into question the conservative claim that journalists' personal views are to the left of the public. On economic issues, the minority of journalists not in the "center" are more likely to identify as having a "right" orientation. When polled on specific economic policies, journalists were often to the right of public opinion. There appear to be relatively few national journalists with left views on questions like corporate power and trade—issues that probably matter more to most media owners and advertisers than social issues like gay rights and affirmative action.

While this survey exposes the right-wing stereotype of the "liberal journalist," one should not replace it with an equally false mirror image of a "conservative journalist." Like profit-sector professionals in general, many journalists hold somewhat liberal social views and conservative economic views. And it's important to remember that a majority of journalists identify as "centrists."

The right's "liberal media" myth has been maintained, in part, by the well-funded flow of conservative rhetoric that focuses attention on journalists' social views and away from their economic views. But the conservative critique is based not only on the proposition that journalists' views are to the left of the general public, but also that these views influence the news content they produce.

There are two key problems with this latter claim. First, it is *sources*, not journalists, who are allowed to express their views in the conventional model of "objective" journalism. Therefore, we learn much more about the political orientation of news content by looking at sourcing patterns rather than journalists' personal views. As this survey shows (see sidebar), it is government officials and business representatives to whom journalists "nearly always" turn when covering economic policy. Labor representatives and consumer advocates were at the bottom of the list.

This is consistent with earlier research on sources. For example, analysts from the centrist Brookings Institution and right-wing think tanks

Policy Scorecard

On these issues journalists appear to be . . .	to the *left* of the public	to the *right* of the public
Protecting Medicare and Social Security		✓
The expansion of NAFTA		✓
Requiring employers to provide health insurance to their employees		✓
Stricter environmental laws	✓	
Concern over concentrated corporate power		✓
Taxing the wealthy		✓
Impact of NAFTA		✓
"Fast track" trade authority		✓
Government guaranteed medical care		✓

Who the Journalists Are

Demographic characteristics of the respondents to FAIR's survey include:

• Male journalists (66 percent) outnumbered female journalists (34 percent) by about two to one.

• Eighty-nine percent of respondents were white, 5 percent black, 3 percent Latino, 2 percent Asian and 2 percent chose the category "other" when describing their race.

• Only 5 percent of the respondents were not college graduates. Fifty percent had bachelor's degrees, 14 percent had some postgraduate training, and a full 31 percent had postgraduate degrees.

• Only 5 percent of respondents reported annual household incomes under $50,000. Forty-three percent had household incomes between $50,000 and $99,999; 21 percent were between $100,000 and $149,999; 17 percent were between $150,000 and $199,999; and 14 percent had household incomes of $200,000 or more.

such as the Heritage Foundation and the American Enterprise Institute are those most quoted in mainstream news accounts; left-wing think tanks are often invisible (**Extra!**, 5–6/98). When it comes to sources, "liberal bias" is nowhere to be found.

Second, journalists do not work in a vacuum. It is crucial to remember the important role of institutional context in setting the broad parameters for the news process. Businesses are not in the habit of producing products that contradict their fundamental *economic* interests. The large corporations that are the major commercial media in this country—not surprisingly—tend to favor style and substance that is consonant with their corporate interests, as do their corporate advertisers.

It is here, at the structural level, that the fundamental ground rules of news production are set. Of course, working journalists sometimes succeed in temporarily challenging some of those rules and boundaries. But in the long run, if they are to succeed and advance in their profession, they must adapt to the ground rules set by others—regardless of their own personal views.

Perhaps it is in this light that journalists' basic centrist orientation should be understood. Their adherence to the middle of the road and conventional wisdom is consistent with media outlets owned and funded by corporations that benefit from the status quo and are threatened by alternative analyses. Unfortunately, this too often leaves citizens with policy "debates" grounded in the shared assumptions of those in positions of power.

David Croteau is a professor of sociology at Virginia Commonwealth University. Tim Mahoney provided administrative assistance on this project.

THE RISE AND RISE OF 24-HOUR LOCAL NEWS

BY DAVID LIEBERMAN

"A whole new genre of local news." That's what Philip Balboni calls his young, twenty-four-hour regional news service and a host of fledgling cable channels like it. These electronic versions of local newspapers aim to be "the highest quality source of news on television," says Balboni, who — as president of Boston-based New England Cable News and chairman of the Association of Regional News Channels — is a pioneer in a journalistic movement that's burgeoning across the country. He's convinced that, for once, good TV journalism is good business. "There's a strong appetite for quality local news."

Many cable operators agree. Companies serving nearly every major market are rushing to create local and regional all-news channels. Nearly thirty of these services reach about 23 million subscribers in or around cities such as New York, Chicago, Washington, D.C., and San Francisco — and regions including New England, the Pacific Northwest, and Southern California's Orange County. Most are less than five years old. More are on the way. In January, A.H. Belo will introduce a statewide service for Texas. It may face a showdown with Time Warner, which recently announced plans to create a regional news channel at the company's cable systems in Austin. And cable giant Tele-Communications Inc. is considering a possible service for Denver.

The low-budget channels eschew helicopters, fancy weather radars, and expensive remote trucks, and usually lay off the happy talk and celebrity gossip. They devote plenty of time instead to breaking news, weather, traffic, and sports, and leisurely reports about local politics, education, transportation, and the environment.

Different agendas are at work here. Some cable news channels, such as Time Warner's New York 1, go after local newspaper and TV ad dollars. Others, like A.H. Belo's Seattle-based NorthWest Cable News Channel, supplement and promote the company's newspapers and TV stations, generating additional revenues and burnishing the companies' images as specialists in community news.

TV stations and newspapers — though their audiences are usually bigger — are beginning to feel the cable channels' hot breath on their necks. The old-line news outlets can no longer blithely assume they'll be the first to report what's happening in their hometowns. Regional cable news has "opened everybody's eyes to the fact that local news can be done around the clock," says Eric Braun, a consultant with Frank N. Magid Associates, Inc. The twenty-four-hour availability appeals particularly to young adults juggling kids and careers, and to commuters who often can't carve out the time to watch a station's evening newscast.

Viewership runs highest on weekdays before 9 A.M., in prime time, and on weekends before noon. Ratings predictably rise dramatically when there's eventful local news. Florida residents tuned in to

Time Warner's channels when massive brush fires spread through parts of the state in July. Viewers are grateful for news having some genuine relevance to their lives — and for an alternative to the grief and gore that dominate many local station newscasts.

Big-city TV stations often reach hundreds of towns, and lack the time, resources, and inclination to cover any one of them in depth. As a result, many newscasts are heavy on crime, a subject that's relatively easy to report, and that grabs viewers who live far from the scene. (Violent stories filled an average of 40 percent of the time devoted to news in the latest annual survey of local broadcasts in fifty-two major markets, conducted by Rocky Mountain Media Watch. New England Cable News was one of four local newscasters praised by the group "for presenting quality programs that provide empowering information to viewers.")

Regional news cable channels attract surprisingly large audiences by taking the high road. At least they are large by the standards of the cable world, where niche-oriented services usually thrive on a fraction of a ratings point. For example, New York 1 gets better ratings locally than CNN, MSNBC, or Fox News Channel, says Time Warner president Richard Parsons. "It's simple human nature. People want to know what their

---

David Lieberman is a media reporter and columnist for USA Today.

Reprinted from *Columbia Journalism Review*, November/December 1998, pp. 54-57. © 1998 by Columbia Journalism Review.

neighbors are up to. People want to know what's going on in their block. People want to know information that touches their lives."

The hard-charging cablers often cause TV stations to cover events they otherwise might not. New England Cable News, for example (co-owned by Hearst and cable operator MediaOne), shook the Boston market when it began gavel-to-gavel coverage of the Louise Woodward nanny trial. "When some of the local stations saw the ratings, they started covering the trial live," says Barbara Cochran, president of the Radio-Television News Directors Association.

Executives at the cable channels also say they notice changes in the way some TV stations deploy their troops. "We sometimes joked that [local stations] wouldn't go into the suburbs unless several people were tragically killed," says Wayne Lynch, vice president of news and programming at Washington, D.C.'s Newschannel 8. "Now we see them covering the suburbs more." And, according to one TV station executive, the obverse is true. "If an atom bomb went off in Hoboken," he jests, "New York 1 wouldn't cover it until the lethal cloud drifted over Manhattan."

Leading the regional news charge are multimedia powers such as Cablevision Systems, Time Warner, Tribune, and Belo. Cablevision Systems' News 12 Group created the nation's first local news channel on Long Island in 1986. It's a big hit with the Island's affluent suburban audiences that often are neglected by New York City stations whose signals sprawl over three states. The original channel has spawned separate, complementary services covering Southwestern Connecticut, New Jersey, Westchester County, and the Bronx.

Those channels stand cheek by jowl with Time Warner, which created the Manhattan-based New York 1 in 1992. Time Warner also built news channels for its systems in Rochester, Tampa, and Orlando. Although the company likes to run its own channels, Time Warner teamed up with Tribune Company's *Orlando Sentinel* at Central Florida News. Tribune, for its part, solidified its hold on the Windy City by creating CLTV (ChicagoLand Television) News, which has cameras in the newsroom of the *Chicago Tribune*.

Belo is the most aggressive about using all-news channels as a form of corporate synergy. Its New Orleans-based

Newswatch 15, a partnership with Cox's cable system, generates an estimated $500,000 in cash flow simply by rebroadcasting news programming from Belo's local CBS affiliate, WWL. The company's NorthWest Cable News Channel uses resources from Belo's TV stations in Seattle, Portland, and Spokane. And its new Texas Cable News draws on Belo's TV stations in Dallas, Houston, and San Antonio, and newspapers in Dallas and Bryan-College Station.

Will Belo's cable channel cannibalize viewing of its existing TV stations? Analyst Paul Sweeney of Salomon Smith Barney doesn't think so. Rather, it will enhance and promote Belo's over-the-air stations and brand identity, he believes. Like North-West Cable News, management estimates that the new Texas channel will be break-even in four to five years.

But cable news channels needn't be part of a giant media company to prosper. TV station owner Joe Albritton created a respected cable news service in Washington, D.C., Newschannel 8, to complement his ABC affiliate, WJLA. The service also helps the network in this market of influential people who often don't make it home in time to catch the evening news: It's the only non-ABC outlet that has the network's blessing to rebroadcast *World News Tonight with Peter Jennings* and *Nightline*.

Federal law has helped broadcasters like Albritton to create news outlets on cable. Lawmakers gave TV station owners the right to demand payments from systems that retransmit their local broadcast signals. Cable operators who didn't want to pay cash accepted a compromise: they made room on the cable dial for regional news channels.

While the services attract strong ratings in the cable universe, few are popular enough yet to pose a major threat to TV stations' newscasts. Their business plan, says Eric Braun, is built on their cumulative audience over the course of a week. "People dip in and dip out."

Viewers almost have to. Even slickly produced cable news programming can become monotonous over long stretches – and few can brag about their pizzazz.

Styles vary, but a typical rundown consists of a half-hour newscast that's repeated and updated throughout the day. Production values are sometimes primitive with little more than an

anchor, over-the-shoulder graphics, and a string of hastily edited video reports from the field. Channels also fill lots of airtime with panel discussions, call-in shows, and live coverage of city council meetings, planning board sessions, and state legislature activities.

Some channels are starting to flex their journalistic muscles by freeing reporters to handle major investigations. News 12 has dug into allegations of HMO overcharging at its Long Island station, and examined the safety, health, and cleanliness of the region's sea shores. New England Cable News won a Peabody Award this year for a documentary that examined hospice care through the experience of a woman dying of breast cancer. But costly labor-intensive reporting is the exception because most of the channels are still short of funds. They make ends meet by closely monitoring operating expenses. Yearly budgets often run less than $10 million. By contrast, top-rated TV stations in major markets, such as New York and Los Angeles, spend as much as $35 million a year to produce five hours of daily news. They pinch pennies by staffing up with young journalists willing to accept low pay for the opportunity to build a reputation in a major market. Reporter and producer salaries range from $26,000 to $45,000. Anchors do better, earning between $35,000 and $70,000.

Asked to assess the quality of the journalism the channels produce, Braun says, "how do you assess the quality of triple-A baseball? You're looking at rising talent who need a few more years to cut their teeth before they go to the big time." Broadcasters eagerly pounce on regional news channel journalists when they're ready for bigger salaries and a higher profile. "It's a good training ground," says WCBS station manager Steve Friedman, former boss of *The Today Show*. "In the old days the O&Os provided the talent for the future. Then came cable news — a lot of people started at CNN. But when you work at a big station, you want people who already know the local market."

The young journalists are versatile. They have to be. Many channels use electronic gear that requires street reporters to juggle several chores. Lightweight High-8 video cameras played a key role in helping news channels get started in the early 1990s: a single reporter can cover a story without additional crew members to lug a separate tape machine and microphone. Some services have writers who report from the scene and editors who shoot. One channel promoted a photographer to associate producer.

The challenge now is to lower expenses even more, so that news channels can operate economically in communities where cable systems have fewer than 500,000 subscribers. "We believe there's a way to do it in cable systems having only 300,000 subscribers, or perhaps even less," says Time Warner Cable's senior vice president for newsgathering, John Newton. "It depends on how competitive you want to be and whether you operate twenty-four hours a day. But the biggest factor is technology."

That's why many executives are watching Cablevision Systems' efforts to incorporate cutting edge gadgetry at the News 12 Group. The company installed a digital system at its new channel in the Bronx that needs just one person to run the control room. That staffer clicks commands into a computer pre-programmed to cue up digitized videos, insert graphics, and control robotic cameras. Now the company has completed a plan to let field reporters feed video back to the control room simply by plugging a lightweight piece of equipment directly into the parent cable system. "That would give us additional live capacity at very low cost," says Fein. "We don't need a microwave truck."

And now suddenly, here comes the digital age. Every TV station in the country has been handed more spectrum space to let them make the transition from the old-fangled analog style transmission. Those digital channels will enable broadcasters to beam out five or six program services in the bandwidth that now accommodates just one. Some TV people are toying with the idea of creating local, all-news channels — just like the cable guys have done. Otherwise, cable news outlets now up and running could easily migrate over to those slots. Eric Braun thinks that local TV stations are, in fact, considering utilizing some of that invaluable new bandwidth to reach viewers who don't subscribe to cable.

Other cablers are hoping to snag people who prefer getting their local news on the Internet. New England Cable News's site, for example, offers a primitive form of video news-on-demand. Users click on selected stories, and see a herky-jerky version of the TV report on their personal computers. The video on PCs will improve, and cable operators will encourage other convergence efforts, as their systems begin to offer subscribers Internet service via cable modems. These devices connect cable wires to PCs, and transmit data as much as 100 times faster than today's conventional telephone modems.

"There's great promise here," says Balboni. "The challenge is to make local cable news excellent, and to bring TV news to a higher level."

PARACHUTE JOURNALISM

Scene pieces can be richly detailed portraits of communities catapulted into the spotlight by news events. But too often they are stereotypical and one-dimensional.

I
T'S THE HEART OF HISTORIC ROUTE 66, SITUATED BETWEEN THE Cerbat and Hualapai mountain ranges, a "hub of activity for history buffs and nature enthusiasts alike."

That's how the Kingman, Arizona, visitors and convention bureau bills its home. The local chamber of commerce's slogan until recently was "Kingman: The Good Life."

Here's how the San Francisco Chronicle described the same place to its readers: a "salubrious climate" for those who have an "almost religious devotion" to the constitutional right to keep and bear arms—the perfect place for a man like Oklahoma City bomber Timothy McVeigh.

Noting bullet holes in nearby cacti and yucca plants in their lead, reporters Bill Wallace and Rob Haeseler painted a grim picture of life in Kingman.

"By all accounts, McVeigh picked a place where he could feel at home: Distrust of the government runs deep here, and people's love of firearms is almost as great as their fear that the government will try to take them away," Wallace and Haeseler wrote. Devotion to weaponry wasn't the only worrisome quality of this area. The fourth paragraph of the story quotes Mary Ann Mauney of the American Jewish Committee: "Arizona is the state that initially refused to recognize Martin Luther King Day as a holiday."

Wallace, who wrote the piece in San Francisco with dispatches from Haeseler in Kingman, says the bullet holes in the foliage were the kind of "small but telling detail" that broadcasts a place's state of mind.

"When you get up into that kind of community, people are very into guns," says Wallace, who volunteers that he grew up in just that sort of small-town environment. "What I always look for is bullet-riddled road

By Sharyn Wizda

signs; some guy driving along in his pickup, pulls off with a .45, just out of boredom, probably because he had a couple of beers, he's a little bit relaxed, so he goes out and shoots a couple of holes in the sign. You see that a lot in these very isolated communities."

The good life or the armed life? Stereotyping or warts-and-all portrayal? It depends on whom you talk to—and whose story you're reading.

Kingman certainly isn't the only place that's been targeted in the name of news. We've read about Waco, Texas (outlaw Branch Davidian territory); Rancho Santa Fe, California (rich and eccentric cultists' enclave); and practically the entire state of Montana (where militia members live). It happens to big-city neighborhoods and metropolitan suburbs when misfortune hits. Indeed, from those snow-capped mountains nestling Boulder, Colorado, to the "land of desperados" out in Kingman's Wild West, every tragedy is a scene piece waiting to happen.

Lured out of town by an event that catapults into the national-news stratosphere, reporters dutifully write the color story telling readers back home just what this close-knit community that has been ripped apart by [insert actual news here] is like.

Done well, such stories offer insight into a place readers aren't familiar with, a thoughtful examination that tells us what's interesting and what's worth noting about a community. Too often, though, they turn into one-dimensional "parachute pieces" that capture only the most popular or newsworthy clichés about a town.

Washington Post media writer Howard Kurtz says that scene pieces too often "are sort of a collection of clichés."

Boulder Daily Camera Publisher Harold Higgins has served as a "sage observer" for many reporters doing scene pieces in connection with the JonBenet Ramsey story.

'L ET ME GUESS. THE ONE THAT CALLED us the 'festering leech on the underbelly of Fort Riley?'"

David Bossemeyer, executive director of the Junction City, Kansas/Geary County Economic Development Commission, knows exactly which story he's being asked about, even though it ran more than two years ago. Hordes of reporters descended on Junction City after federal authorities pinpointed the city of 20,000 people as the place where convicted Oklahoma City bomber Timothy McVeigh picked up the truck that would carry the deadly cargo to Oklahoma City.

Los Angeles Times writers Louis Sahagun and Stephen Braun were two of those reporters. They described Junction City as a dreary Army town that "sits snug like a fattened leech up against Ft. Riley...drawing economic lifeblood" from the military compound.

"It is also a place where church socials and American Legion parades are complementary rites, where the Just For You bridal boutique offers frilly gowns to farm brides while, a few doors down, the Club Malibu features topless shake dancers for GIs out for a good time," they wrote.

Not the sort of place you'd visit unless you had to.

"They were going for some kind of sensationalism," asserts Bossemeyer. "Being a military town, we do have taverns, we do have check-cashing places. Some of them sought out the most unsavory places in town, so naturally they ended up with that kind of story. If you want a bad story, you go out at 10:30 at night and you find a young soldier in a bar who's disgruntled, and you talk to him."

The Chicago-based Braun, who was the primary writer on the Junction City piece, has carefully sketched many communities for Times readers. For example, he reported on a frightened and suspicious Oklahoma City directly after the bombing, describing it as the "mirror image of any small American city. With its highway fast-food oases and its Wal-Marts, its enfeebled downtown and its leisurely pace, it was a perfect target deep in the heartland."

His most successful pieces, Braun says, "give you a sense of place and of people, and in a way it's becoming more and more difficult, in a sense that every town has a McDonald's now. You've got to work a little bit harder to figure out what makes each of these towns a little bit unique or beyond the stereotype."

But many Junction City residents don't think the L.A. Times piece got very far beyond the stereotype. Braun refused to discuss the story.

Braun's description of Junction City as a "fattened leech" was a single phrase in a story tucked away on an inside page. Yet it inspired numerous other reporters, who picked up the phrase and attached it to Junction City: Denver's Rocky Mountain News used it in a March story about the town to preview the McVeigh trial. It still rankles Junction City's residents.

"That's what they're trying to portray, that this is the place where he picked up the truck, and isn't it fitting that it was in Junction City?" says Katie Roche, executive director of the town's chamber of commerce. "I don't want people all over the country thinking that where I'm living is like that."

Roche has a kindred spirit in realtor Jan Leidenberger, a 26-year resident of Kingman. Leidenberger said the Chronicle's "desperado" focus was misguided, as were countless television renditions of Kingman as a deserted yet gun-happy outpost.

"Every time Kingman was portrayed, they would show a desert with a tumble-down shack," she said. "Kingman is by far more than that.... It is not the wild, woolly West. We do not walk around with guns on our hips or over our shoulders."

Equally distressing for Leidenberger was the implication in some stories that McVeigh's anti-government views were honed in Kingman. "McVeigh was not nurtured here," she says. "The town does not reflect him. It just so happened that he lived here."

Of course, a locality's residents usually have a vested interest in promoting their hometown, while reporters are charged with chronicling and analyzing the same place. But when the views of the locals and the reporters are so divergent, it's hard not to wonder how useful scene pieces are.

"The truth is, it's a crusty old formula that attempts to inject a bit of color into some tragic story that lacks hard news at the moment," says Howard Kurtz, who covers the media for the Washington Post. "We in journalism always seem to do these pieces after the initial shock of the shooting/earthquake/kidnapping has worn off.... More often than not, they are sort of a collection of clichés."

The impetus to keep a good story going is often what spurs such pieces, says Stephen Seplow, who writes about television and other media for the Philadelphia Inquirer and was once the paper's metro editor. "That's one way they can be overworked. There is a danger of coming to broad conclusions from two hours walking around a neighborhood. It's a good idea not to rush in and come to some stereotypical conclusion so you can fill 15 inches on the jump page. But it can really put legitimate news stories in context. McVeigh comes out of a certain environment. If you do a piece about this sort of

local community clichés, because they're so easy." Higgins has served as sage observer for reporters across the country since December, when 6-year-old beauty queen and Boulderite JonBenet Ramsey was found murdered.

"The other part of it is that the people that reporters are interviewing are repeating those same things," Higgins says. "That's how people talk about where they live."

And Kurtz points out that reporters' tendency to edit out quotes that don't fit the premise bleeds over into these pieces as well. "Most reporters are honest enough to try to avoid the most heavy-handed typecasting," he says. "What happens more often is you discard all the quotes that sort of don't fit, because maybe half the people in town haven't heard of the suddenly famous person."

That's just the nature of the business, says the San Francisco Chronicle's Wallace. "The whole point of going to a place with a link to the news is not its similarity to other communities across the country—it's the differences and what effect that may have had on the events or people they're reading about. You're going to put things in the story that seem significant to the narrative you're trying to put out...."

> **"T**HERE IS A DANGER *of coming to broad conclusions from two hours walking around a neighborhood," says the Philadelphia Inquirer's Stephen Seplow. "It's a good idea not to rush in and come to some stereotypical conclusion so you can fill 15 inches on the jump page."*

environment from which he emerged, this can be useful to help explain him."

What isn't useful are the pieces that string together the most common of clichés about a place—something that happens "more often than not," according to Kurtz.

Indeed, the typical scene piece tied to a tragedy can be defined through its elements. There's the opening image, which frequently is some colorful local character; there's the description of places that embody the reporter's chosen theme; there's the sage observer, who could be anybody from a small-town newspaper publisher to a professor from a nearby college. Invariably there are references to "this heartland town" (all Midwest locales) or "this close-knit community" (suitable for all areas).

And much of it may be true. What makes a cliché a cliché is its root in reality—there *are* people in Kingman who like to carry guns, after all.

"When you get dropped into a setting...and you're essentially trying to get some descriptive language or descriptive phrases in a few sentences of what a place is like, it's very difficult to do," says Harold Higgins, publisher of the Boulder Daily Camera. "Reporters tend to go for the

"When we're trying to write a story about a guy who is a suspect in the most grisly bombing case in the country, and he has been living this weird lifestyle in the desert, that is the important detail. The reason we were in Kingman was not because half or two-thirds of the population are everyday citizens who get up and go to work and go home and sit down and have a good meal. It's because there was also a community of people like McVeigh in Kingman."

BUT WHAT IF THERE IS NO McVEIGH yet, no personality with which reporters must match environmental clues? The recent spate of JonBenet-related stories datelined Boulder seem to be divided into one of two categories: Boulder as hippie haven or Boulder as yuppie enclave.

St. Louis Post-Dispatch reporter Kristina Sauerwein, who spent four February days in Boulder reporting on the Ramsey case, saw this: "Boulder is wool socks and Birkenstocks on a snowy day. It's dark sunglasses and hot pink Lycra pants. Skiing and rock-climbing. BMWs and bikes. Straight hair—or no hair. Organic food, herbal medicines and cappuccinos." She reels off a list of Boulder-based "institutes" for devotees of psychic phenomena, yoga and healing arts.

Sauerwein says she chose the details she did because they showed that Boulder was a "little different" from most places. "The case is so bizarre, and Boulder is such a bizarre place, I thought it was interesting to make that point," she says.

And that's a view most locals are willing to accept. "This writer managed to get ahold of the usuals and work them. There's nothing wrong with that," the Daily Camera's Higgins says.

"Boulder's a weird town, let's be honest," jokes Tom Clark, chamber of commerce president. "Like many college towns, that's the reality. The town is made up of an entire spectrum, from the most conservative Republicans to anarchists."

But he's not so sanguine about the rich-enclave reports. "What was most disturbing was this cast by the national media that this is a wealthy, affluent, exclusive community that is isolated from the mainstream," Clark says. "The enclave is based on our view of open space. We wanted to create an enclave where people wanted to live. One of the unintended consequences is that the damn cost of housing has gone through the ceiling. To read some of these stories, you'd swear to God we were a bunch of white suburban racists who wanted to squeeze people of color out."

That's the danger of a quickly drawn parachute piece: The details a reporter chooses to highlight—while accurate—fail to capture the true flavor of a town, or, worse, give the wrong impression.

"Especially when it's done as a quick-hit, you are trying to shoehorn a whole community, with all its complexity, into some preconceived storyline. You do the story in one day, you end up with pretty predictable fare," the Post's Kurtz says.

Realistically, though, one day is often the most a reporter has for this kind of story, points out Tim Jones, who covers the media for the Chicago Tribune. "We've all gone through this: We arrive at 10 o'clock in the morning, and the piece needs to be written by 6 p.m., so you've got six or eight hours," Jones says. "It's ridiculous on its face, but an awful lot of daily journalism is ridiculous on its face when you consider the time constraints…. We're in the daily newspaper business, and most of the time we've only got a few hours."

Yet even stripped of the luxury of time, something reporters are the first to complain they don't have, achieving a thoughtful profile of anything takes empathy and understanding—something sources might argue many reporters don't have either.

Done carefully, the scene piece is elevated into a balanced exploration as well as explanation of a community. (That might mean a town, or it might mean a group of people. For the

Inquirer's Seplow, for example, the city of Boulder isn't the scene that puts JonBenet into context; it's the world of kiddie beauty pageants.)

J AMES BROOKE, THE DENVER-BASED ROCKY Mountain bureau chief for the New York Times, says part of the solution is as simple as location: It's a lot easier to write intelligently about an area you've lived in or with which you're at least passingly familiar.

"That's how you avoid that kind of parachutist view of the world. I get 10 newspapers, from every state except for maybe North Dakota, so that when I arrive somewhere I've been able to do a lot of reading. Ideally, as you kind of work the beat, you're going back to places again and again. You have a sense of the evolution of the place, where it's been, where it's going. You don't get that if you have a bunch of national reporters sitting in Boston or New York waiting for something to happen."

True. Still, most papers don't have the resources for bureaus scattered across the country.

Most important, Brooke and others say, is simple old-fashioned openness. Check that big-city arrogance at the door. "The job is to transmit to a larger audience what is new, different, thought-provoking, exciting about this part of the world," Brooke says. "It's not to make fun of it, it's not to trivialize it, not to make it folksy."

Gigi Anders, a reporter for the Raleigh News & Observer, familiarizes herself as much as possible with an area before heading out for interviews—and then tries to put all that out of her mind. "Going into a scene piece—or any other piece—with a fixed, preformed agenda is best reserved for typists and secretaries, not great writers," she says.

Accurately capturing what makes a place tick is a difficult task, particularly when reporters are called on to fly in, capture and file quickly, admits Dirk Johnson, a Chicago-based national correspondent for the New York Times.

"But when people do terrible things in Chicago and New York, we don't say, 'In Chicago they think X and do Y and everybody thinks Z,' " he says. "The truth of the matter is, in some small little town in Kansas, there is also diversity of thought and style. You may have to look harder for it. But it's there….

"When you go to a place and you look at the town, if you think the life there is simple, you're not looking closely enough and you're not talking to enough people. Because life is never simple. Marriage, kids, death, deceit, fear of failure—they all happen in all of these places, no matter how small, no matter how remote and no matter how many people are wearing Birkenstocks."

Sharyn Wizda is features/special projects editor at the Daily Sentinel in Grand Junction, Colorado.

When profiling a locale, says the New York Times' James Brooke, it's important "not to make fun of it, not to trivialize it, not to make it folksy."

ANNE FORD DOYLE

The Raleigh News & Observer's Gigi Anders says writers should approach scene pieces without preconceived notions of what they'll find.

TELL IT LONG TAKE YOUR TIME GO IN DEPTH

Some newspapers are giving writers a wealth of time and space, urging them to get intimate with subjects. They call it Immersion Journalism.

BY STEVE WEINBERG

The standards that guide newspapers have been updated in some newsrooms to better harmonize with the conventional wisdom of the '90s: 1) Keep it short — readers have tiny attention spans. 2) Don't dig too deeply — libel and invasion-of-privacy lawsuits drain profits. 3) Stick to the time-tested definitions of news — crime, politics, sports, celebrities. 4) Keep reporting costs low. Way low.

But some reporters and editors have found an intriguing way to break free from those restraints. A significant and growing number of them are publishing in-depth narratives based on months of high-cost, high-risk immersion journalism. They are injecting real storytelling into their stories, producing memorable narratives, long ones, about the not-so-ordinary aspects of ordinary life.

A case in point is the Baltimore *Sun's* "A Stage in Their Lives," written by Ken Fuson and published in June — a 16,000-word series covering seventeen broadsheet pages over six days.

Earlier, for fifteen years at *The Des*

Steve Weinberg, a CJR contributing editor, is a former executive director of Investigative Reporters and Editors. *He teaches journalism at the University of Missouri, and is working on a biography of Ida Tarbell.*

Moines Register, Fuson worked to perfect this unorthodox brand of newspaper reporting. In 1996 the *Sun's* editors, as part of a concerted effort to alter the daily's tone, lured him to Baltimore. To write "A Stage in Their Lives," he immersed himself for four months in the lives of students playing key roles in their high school's production of *West Side Story*. It was a challenge, and Fuson succeeded. On one level, his series is a tale about the production of a high school musical. On a deeper level it is a masterful story about teenagers coming of age in the complicated 1990s.

Magazines such as *The New Yorker*, *Esquire*, *Sports Illustrated*, and *Rolling Stone* have published this brand of journalism, off and on, for decades. Book publishers in the business of depth journalism have offered outstanding examples from authors such as J. Anthony Lukas, Tracy Kidder, and Nicholas Lemann. Newspapers large enough to publish Sunday magazines occasionally encouraged this kind of writing before the 1990s.

Sunday magazines are shrinking, but this form of newspaper journalism is not. These days immersion journalism is finding a safe home — along with occasional controversy — in the broadsheet pages of such papers as *The Seattle Times*, the *Chicago Tribune*, *Newsday*,

the *St. Petersburg Times*, *The Philadelphia Inquirer*, *The Miami Herald*, and the *Providence Journal-Bulletin*, not to mention the *Sun*.

Newspapers are producing valuable, innovative, and sometimes beautiful examples of this against-the-grain kind of work. Writers are drawing readers into what are sometimes the equivalent of books, testing the notion that readers still like to read.

MISSIONARIES

Immersion journalism has a history at the *Sun*. In 1979, at the *Evening Sun*, the morning paper's now-defunct partner, Jon Franklin won the first of two Pulitzer Prizes for a work of narrative immersion journalism, "Mrs. Kelly's Monster."

Franklin had been working up to such an opportunity. For years at the *Evening Sun* he sought topics that would allow him to use the techniques of fiction "while observing all the journalistic niceties," as he puts it. "I went out and looked for stories that fit that way of doing it. I practiced. I did a story about a day in the life of a dog catcher. I did a day in the life of a profoundly retarded man."

"Mrs. Kelly's Monster" started out to be a feature on a woman undergoing brain surgery. Franklin assumed the surgery

IMMERSION GETS DIGITAL

Lynn Franklin

Jon Franklin

Some of the sages of immersion journalism are taking their story-telling to the World Wide Web. But the nonfiction novellas and literary journalism found at *bylines* (http://www.bylines.org) are not merely For Your Information — they are for sale.

The site is the creation of University of Oregon writing teacher and two-time Pulitzer honoree Jon Franklin; his wife, Lynn, a writer and editor (she publishes WriterL, an internet newsletter for writers of literary nonfiction); and former Baltimore *Evening Sun* projects editor George Rodgers. By December, the *bylines* virtual bookshelf was offering eighteen long pieces for credit-card sale. "Birth of a Steinway," 18,500 words by Michael Lenehan about the making of a piano, for example, goes for 79 cents, and "Comfort Me With Apples," by Lynn Franklin — "How the quest for perfection almost destroyed the perfect fruit" — goes for 99 cents for 28,000 words. Writers get 60 percent of the gross sales, with the rest divided between the editors and the organizations that provide support, including Investigative Reporters and Editors, or IRE.

The *bylines* editors say they want "humanist" journalism — "real" stories about "real" people — as well as fiction and poetry. Selling such fare on the Web fits the philosophy. In an explanation of "the *bylines* ethic on the site, the editors argue that "the entire history of modern publishing is a tale in which publishers have steadily pushed readers and writers further apart," and that one result is that the economics of writing for a living has became so grim that "fewer and fewer talented young people are willing to consider the writing trade . . . . It is our ambitious aim to confront this literary disaster head-on, simplifying the exchange between writer and reader and focusing our business solely on the value of the words we sell."

— **JARRETT MURPHY**

Jarrett Murphy is an intern at CJR.

---

would be successful, ending Mrs. Kelly's fifty-seven years of pain. He interviewed Mrs. Kelly and her husband. He talked to her daughter separately and with Dr. Thomas Barbee Ducker, the surgeon. That was it, he figured, except for showing up at the hospital to look for his ending. Then the surgery went wrong. Mrs. Kelly died.

Franklin assumed that he had lost his story. Later he had a revelation: he would write about the surgery through Dr. Ducker's eyes. The 4,000-word story that emerged opens this way:

In the cold hours of a winter morning Dr. Thomas Barbee Ducker, chief brain surgeon at the University of Maryland Hospital, rises before dawn. His wife serves him waffles but no coffee. Coffee makes his hands shake.

In 1985, Franklin won his second Pulitzer for another long-form piece, "The Mind Fixers," about the new science of molecular psychiatry. Then he left to start a teaching career at the University of Maryland and the University of Oregon. In 1986, his book *Writing*

for Story (Atheneum) explained step by step how to practice the kind of journalism that had won him honors.

In Baltimore, however, Franklin's brand of journalism made only rare appearances in the *Sun* after his departure. Not many reporters knew how to carry it off, and not many editors encouraged them. "Hard news is cheaper," Franklin says. "Event-oriented news is easier for editors to predict and control."

Then, in the early 1990s, John Carroll and Bill Marimow accepted jobs as editor and managing editor of the *Sun*. Carroll, a *Sun* reporter from 1966 to 1972, returned in 1991 after high-level editing jobs at *The Philadelphia Inquirer* and the Lexington *Herald-Leader*. In Kentucky, Carroll had retained Franklin as a consultant to discuss storytelling with the newsroom staff. After becoming the *Sun's* editor, Carroll hired Marimow, who had won two Pulitzers for investigative reporting at the *Inquirer* before becoming a city editor there.

"I love in-depth reporting and writing,

and so does John," Marimow says. "We were looking for people to practice literary journalism based on great reporting." Both men had been influenced by editor Gene Roberts at *The Philadelphia Inquirer*, before he left to teach and then to become managing editor at *The New York Times*. Under Roberts the *Inquirer* had dominated investigative reporting during the 1970s and 1980s. Immersion/narrative journalism had taken something of a back seat to fact-driven exposés, but it was not absent.

In particular, Donald Drake, the *Inquirer's* medical writer, had parlayed his interest in playwriting to develop his narrative storytelling based on immersion reporting. Five years in a row he spent almost half his time chronicling the successes and disappointments of one class at the University of Pennsylvania School of Medicine. Eventually Roberts hired a new medical writer to cover the hard news on the beat so Drake could concentrate on long-form storytelling.

Today, Drake's title at the *Inquirer* is assistant metropolitan editor, and he works with daily reporters, encouraging them to inject storytelling into their quick-turnaround pieces. He also works with veterans such as Stacey Burling and Michael Vitez on their long-term immersion projects. Vitez won a 1997 Pulitzer for his project, "Final Choices: Seeking The Good Death," an extended piece about the choices that dying people and their families make. Drake helped Burling with her "Community of Hope: Waiting for a Heart," in which the readers observed transplant candidates living on the same hospital corridor, wondering daily who would get the next available heart and who would leave in a box.

THE NEXT GENERATION

At the *Sun*, Carroll and Marimow searched for a new generation of Donald Drakes and Jon Franklins. This has led to blockbuster stories like "God's Other Plan," a January 1997 narrative serial by reporter Patricia Meisol about a lawyer going through pregnancy while dying of cancer; "The Umpire's Sons," a December 1996 story by Lisa Pollak about the lives of two boys fathered by John Hirschbeck, the major league baseball umpire spat upon by Roberto Alomar, and the genetic disease that had killed one while afflicting the other; "Witness to Slavery," a June 1996 narrative series by Gregory Kane and Gilbert A. Lewthwaite about the slave trade in Sudan; and

"Spreading the Word," a July 1997 series by Ginger Thompson, who traveled to Peru to immerse herself in the world of two American linguists doubling as missionaries.

Then there is Ken Fuson, who works with Jan Winburn, an editor Carroll and Marimow hired from *The Hartford Courant,* who had been Fuson's editor nearly two decades earlier at the Columbia, Missouri, *Daily Tribune.* Fuson's "A Stage in Their Lives" is perhaps the most counterintuitive of all the *Sun's* recent narrative immersion stories, since a high school play is by definition both chaotic and ordinary.

Indeed, as he hung out with students day after day, Fuson started worrying about how he would organize the sprawling piece. He found himself with at least fifteen characters, too many for a focused narrative. He emerged from his dilemma after a conversation with Lisa Pollak, his *Sun* colleague, who suggested he concentrate on those with the most at stake.

The five students Fuson chose were pictured on each of the six days the story ran, with a soap opera-like caption under each photograph. On day one, the cutline under Angie Guido's picture says, "She has a vision of herself in the starring role. But wait — another girl stands in the way." On day two: "She finds out today — is she Maria? No other role will do." And so on.

Part one of the narrative opens like this:

Spellbound she sits, her mother on one side, her boyfriend on the other, as another young woman performs the role that will someday be hers.

Since she was little, Angie Guido has dreamed of standing on stage, playing the Puerto Rican girl who falls in love with the boy named Tony.

Maria.

She will be Maria in *West Side Story.*

Say it loud and there's music playing.

That's me, mom, she said.

Say it soft and it's almost like praying.

It won't be long, Angie thinks as she delights in a touring company production of *West Side Story* at the Lyric Opera House in Baltimore. She and twenty members of the Drama Club from North County High School in Anne Arundel County attend the December show with a few parents. This is a prelude; there is expectant talk they will stage the same show for their spring musical.

Someday soon, Angie hopes, she will own the role that is rightfully hers. She has been a loyal drama club soldier, serving on committees, singing in the chorus when she yearned for a solo, watching lead roles slip away because she didn't look the part. But Maria is short, as she is, and dark, as she is, and more than that, Angie is a senior. This will be her last spring musical. Her last chance to shine.

But on the very next night, in that very same theater, another girl from North County High School sits spellbound, her mother on one side, her best friend on the other.

She, too, is captivated by the Puerto Rican girl with the pretty voice.

She, too, wonders: What if that were me?

Reader response was overwhelmingly positive. Fuson heard from teenagers who had read every word, from parents who had been captivated. Carroll and Marimow are so certain that their brand of long-form journalism is good business that they are building reporting and editing staffs to do more of it.

WHEN TIME EQUALS TRUTH

For daily newspapers, with a news cycle that seems to spin ever faster, the most revolutionary of the elements of immersion/narrative reporting is the immersion itself — the ability to take the time to get it right.

At the *St. Petersburg Times,* Anne Hull took six months to immerse herself in the lives of a male teenaged assailant and a female Tampa police officer whose fates intertwined on July 4, 1992, when the teenager held a gun to her skull and pulled the trigger, although the gun misfired. Hull had learned immersion journalism from her newspaper colleague Tom French, who used it that year to show day-to-day life at a high school.

G. Wayne Miller at the *Providence Journal-Bulletin* also entered that challenging world of high school, in 1992-1993, by immersing himself in the lives of two students. Among other practitioners and proselytizers who have achieved recognition are Terrie Claflin at the Medford, Oregon, *Mail Tribune,* David Hanners at *The Dallas Morning News,* Richard Ben Cramer and Steve Twomey at *The Philadelphia Inquirer,* Eric Nalder at *The Seattle Times,* David Finkel at three newspapers (the *Tallahassee Democrat,* the *St. Petersburg Times,* and *The Washington Post,*) Jack Hart at the Portland *Oregonian,* and Roy Peter Clark, who has written for the *St. Petersburg Times* while teaching at the Poynter Institute for Media Studies.

Walt Harrington, who left *The Washington Post* last year to free-lance and teach at the University of Illinois in Champaign-Urbana, says his goal is "to understand other people's worlds from the inside out, to portray people as they understand themselves. Not the way they say they understand themselves, but the way they really understand themselves.

The way, as a subject once told me, you understand yourself 'when you say your prayers in a quiet room.'"

That kind of understanding rarely comes quickly. In journalism, time sometimes equals truth. Tom Wolfe, in a 1972 essay, called this patient, deep reporting an "essential first move" because scenes, not just disparate facts, are necessary to write compelling narrative. "Therefore," Wolfe wrote, "your main problem as a reporter is, simply, managing to stay with whomever you are writing about long enough for the scenes to take place before your own eyes . . . . The initial problem is always to approach total strangers, move in on their lives in some fashion, ask questions you have no natural right to expect answers to, ask to see things you weren't meant to see . . . . Many journalists find it so ungentlemanly, so embarrassing, so terrifying even, that they are never able to master this."

Leon Dash almost fell into this trap at the beginning of his work on "When Children Want Children," his 1986 *Washington Post* series (expanded into a 1989 book) on why so many urban teenagers became involved in out-of-wedlock births. It was thirteen years ago that he rented a basement room in an economically depressed District of Columbia neighborhood, struggling to understand a different world by living in it.

He had resisted the suggestion of his *Post* editor, Bob Woodward, at first, because he thought he already knew many of the answers. As he wrote in the prologue of his book, "I assumed that the high incidence of teenage pregnancy among poor, black urban youths nationwide grew out of youthful ignorance both about birth-control methods and adolescent reproductive capabilities. I also thought the girls were falling victim to cynical manipulation by the boys . . . . I was wrong on all counts."

It was not until five weeks after moving to the Highlands that Dash realized that without immersion he would have missed the truth — that so many of these girls chose pregnancy to gain the attention and respect they were desperate for. The realization came during an interview with a sixteen-year-old girl who was beginning to trust him. It took Dash another year of immersion in the neighborhood to fill in the gaps. Part of the process is talking to sources again and again. One young woman who told Dash the truth did so in the fifth hour of her third interview.

From 1988 to 1994, Dash spent considerable time on one family. The result was an eight-part *Post* series titled "Rosa Lee's Story," followed by a book. Dash met Rosa Lee Cunningham in 1988. At age fifty-two, she was serving time in the District of Columbia jail for selling heroin. A mother at age fourteen, Rosa Lee had given birth to eight children by five fathers, and had more than thirty grandchildren when she and Dash started talking. Six of her children had followed her into a life of crime.

When Dash suggested that he spend time with her after her release, she agreed, saying maybe her story would help others avoid her path. In journalistic terms, those years paid off, but Dash had trouble drawing the line between observation and friendship.

He managed to produce outstanding journalism while straddling the line, but others fail. As Tom Wolfe noted in his anthology *The New Journalism* (Harper & Row), "If a reporter stays with a person or group long enough, they — reporter and subject — will develop a personal relationship . . . . They become stricken with a sense of guilt, responsibility, obligation . . . . People who become overly sensitive on this score inevitably turn out second-rate work, biased in such banal ways that they embarrass even the subjects they think they are 'protecting.'"

Not everybody, though. Kidder mentioned a carpenter he saw regularly while researching the book, *House* (Houghton-Mifflin). "I remember his saying at one point that he and the other builders ought to put a bell around my neck, so they'd know where I was at all times."

ORDINARY, EXTRAORDINARY

A cornerstone of this journalism trend is an emphasis on noncelebrities. They could be called "ordinary people," except that journalists choosing them believe part of the job is to find the extraordinary in the ordinary.

Several journalists who focus on noncelebrities cite this quotation from historian Will Durant: "Civilization is a stream with banks. The stream is sometimes filled with blood from people killing, stealing, shouting and doing the things historians usually record; while on the banks, unnoticed, people build homes, make love, raise children, sing songs, write poetry and even whittle statues. The story of civilization is the story of what happened on the banks. Historians are pessimists because they ignore the banks for the river."

Walt Harrington's focus on life along the banks is evident from the titles of the three books collecting his pieces: *American Profiles: Somebodies and Nobodies Who Matter*; *At the Heart of It: Ordinary People, Extraordinary Lives* (both University of Missouri Press); and *Intimate Journalism: The Art and Craft of Reporting Everyday Life* (Sage). Harrington is puzzled by journalists in general, and at many newspapers in particular, who fail to chronicle the "momentous events of everyday life."

But he recognizes that it can be difficult to do. With notable exceptions, Harrington writes in *Intimate Journalism*, "What passes for everyday-life journalism is too often a mishmash of superficial stories about Aunt Sadie cooking pies, unlikely heroes who save people from drowning or drag them from burning buildings, the nice kid next door who turns out to be a serial killer, and poor people who, against the odds, make it to the top. There's nothing wrong with such stories, except that too often they are the end point of everyday-life coverage, reported and edited with the left hand by people unschooled and unaware of the intricate assumptions and techniques of intimate journalism, which results in stories made superficial by both accident and design."

TELLING STORIES

The word "story" is often misused in journalism. Not that many newspaper articles are really stories. They rarely have beginnings, middles, and ends, rarely include foreshadowing, rarely are shot through with narrative drive. That kind of storytelling technique takes years to master.

Tom Wolfe, in a 1972 essay, emphasized four devices: scene-by-scene construction, presenting each scene through the mind of a particular character, extended dialogue between characters, and inclusion of details (how they dress, how they furnish a home, how they treat superiors and subordinates) symbolic of the characters' status lives.

Although Wolfe's precepts are alive, it is Jon Franklin's book *Writing for Story* that almost certainly has influenced the largest number of current newspaper writers, with Harrington's three books further supplementing it. Franklin, in turn, looks to writers of fiction, and writers who describe fiction techniques. His own bible is Robert Meredith and John Fitzgerald's *The Professional Story Writer and His Art* (Crowell, 1963).

HOW LONG, HOW DEEP?

Almost any topic worthy of immersion is worthy of lengthy treatment. But discipline is also key. At the *Evening Sun*, Franklin recalls "writing long" usually meant merely including more detail. Zoning stories "became, well, complete."

G. Wayne Miller, of the *Providence Journal-Bulletin*, says that without a talented, forceful editor, his stories would sometimes be too long. Recalling his seven-part immersion series about the Hasbro toy company, he wrote recently, in the paper's self-published *How I Wrote the Story* collection: "My initial outline was for eight parts, but my editors said 'too much.' They were right. Thus whittled, my concerns became character development, dramatic tension, detail, and subtext — the ironies and paradoxes, some subtle, some not, that told the real story."

Yet the best writers say the real key is the investment of time. An example: journalists profiling professional hockey coach Mike Keenan, while he was with the St. Louis Blues, tended to focus on his volatile temper, his sometimes bizarre behavior during a game. Gary Smith, a magazine writer who started on the sports pages of the *Wilmington Journal* and the *Philadelphia Daily News*, went places other writers had not gone, including the apartment where Keenan lived at the time, as well as the inner landscapes of Keenan's mind. Here is Smith's lead, from May 8, 1995, in *Sports Illustrated*:

His home was a three-bedroom unit on the sixteenth floor, filled with the furniture of forgetting. All whites and blacks and glass and metal; each morning, in such a place, was surely the dawn of a clean, fresh start.

The one old thing was his leather briefcase, worn and cracked as an old fisherman's face. "It's the only thing in my life," he remarked, "that I haven't thrown out."

But, it turned out, that wasn't quite true. Late one night, as he tried to explain himself over Amarettos, he fell silent and knelt in front of a small bookcase in his living room. Finally he stood.

"No one who has ever written about me," Mike Keenan said, "has a _____ clue who I am." Then he handed *The Great Gatsby* to me, as if that were proof.

The paperback book was a quarter-century old, yellowing and marked in a variety of inks — sentences he had underlined, words and exclamation points he had scribbled in the margins at different junctures since he was a teen. His eyes glittered as he watched me leaf through it. "It's much more complicated," he pointed out, "than anyone really thinks."

The Rise of Solutions Journalism

Newspeople often just point to problems and walk away. Lately they've been trying to find what works.

BY SUSAN BENESCH

U.S. News & World Report ran a list of 1998's "Silver Bullets"—putative solutions to problems as diverse as land mines, obesity, and ill-educated college athletes. The magazine featured the list as a year-end cover story, in an effort to "correct a chronic imbalance in journalism," it said. (The first such list ran the year before.) Land mines can be removed efficiently and safely with new "gizmos" that have been little covered in the press, *U.S. News* reported. College athletes can be better educated if they are given academic scholarships to study after they finish playing on their schools' teams. As an antidote to obesity, *U.S. News* suggested (tongue somewhat in cheek) a "Twinkie tax." If fatty foods were taxed like alcohol and cigarettes, people might consume less of them.

In the same vein, the *Los Angeles Times* capped a recent series on the widespread use of assault weapons in the United States with a story datelined Ballarat, Australia. Its subject? Australia's successful program to buy

Susan Benesch is a free-lance journalist based in New Haven, Connecticut.

Karen Lin Clark

back more than 500,000 semiautomatic fire-arms and pump-action shotguns. And the crux of *The New York Times Magazine's* 7,700-word examination of the country's most drastic welfare-to-work program was writer Jason DeParle's implicit question. "Is this a solution?" DeParle gave a thoughtful, complex answer. Wisconsin's welfare rolls fell by 60 percent in a decade, he noted. But because the state is now offering poor families health care and child care, Wisconsin went from paying $9,700 per family on welfare to $15,700 for the same average family off welfare.

This new journalistic hunt for solutions is also being mounted in television, mid-sized and smaller newspapers, and alternative publications.

ABC News' *World News Tonight with Peter Jennings* aired a story on a San Francisco halfway house called Delancey Street that raises its entire $7 million annual budget running its own restaurant, moving company, roller blade rental shop, and two dozen other businesses staffed by the program's ex-convicts. About 9,000 of Delancey Street's 12,000 participants have stayed away from prison and drugs, says Mimi Silbert, a criminologist who, together with a felon and four addicts, started Delancey Street twenty-five years ago.

The San Diego Union-Tribune ran a story about a local group called The Community Music Center, which helps low-income children learn how to play music—one of a series of "solutions" pieces that the paper runs every two weeks. The center offers inexpensive lessons, and then awards each child who attends faithfully for at least two years the instrument that he or she has been learning to play.

Even *The Nation* magazine, that old bastion of indignant wit and gloom, ran a story on how Burlington, Vermont, has revived its downtown by setting up a land trust, a public computer training center, and a cooperative market for food stamp recipients. The story was part of a new series called "What Works." Two keys to Burlington's success, *The Nation* said, were collaboration between city government and nonprofits, and the fact that the city actually asked residents what they wanted. The piece was so upbeat that two Vermont readers wrote to complain that it was too positive.

"I wasn't trying to paint this as the promised land or anything," said Jay Walljasper, who wrote the piece. The point, he said, was to discover what Burlington had done right, and which of the reasons for its success could be borrowed by other cities. "I think it's important that people sense that everything's not futile out there."

As journalists, we often write about a social problem, then let other institutions, like government, worry about the solutions. But in the past year or so, "solutions journalism"—reporting on efforts that seem to succeed at solving particular social problems—has blossomed in news organizations across the board. As that simultaneous growth indicates, this is not just an effort funded by an outside foundation grant or a corporate marketing department's plan to boost circulation. More and more journalists are enthusiastic about solutions stories. Are they going soft, or are they onto something valuable?

Before the *Union-Tribune* started a regular "Solutions" feature two years ago, says Gerald Warren, the retired editor, "we were writing stories about the numbers of teenage drug users and the number of kids who shot each other. We rarely wrote about the community-based organizations and what they were doing to try to correct these problems." Then Karen Lin Clark was assigned to be the paper's first solutions editor. Said she: "My task is to provide hope . . . not only information but help and hope."

Solutions stories Clark has published this year include one on Oregon's adopt-the-coastline project, in which individuals and groups regularly clear litter off every mile of the state's seashore, and watch for erosion or illegal private use of the land. Clark said she hoped California might do the same. Another story described a man who keeps neighborhood kids off the streets by teaching them boxing, at a ring he built at home. Kids can participate if they promise to fight only in the ring.

Around the same time that the San Diego paper began publishing "Solutions," Jon Wilson, a boatbuilder-turned-editor, was pre-

More journalists are now enthusiastic about this type of story, even though some feel it smacks of boosterism. Are they going soft, or are they onto something valuable?

paring the launch of a glossy magazine called *Hope* on an old estate near the remote seacoast village of Brooklin, Maine. The first issue of *YES! A Journal of Positive Futures* came in Spring 1996 from Bainbridge Island, near Seattle. A new wire called The American News Service, bearing the proud slogan "the pioneer of solution-oriented journalism," was being started in Brattleboro, Vermont. And *U.S. News* published its Outlook 1997 issue listing solutions for everything from crime to high college tuition to the soporific pace of baseball, under the headline, "20 Ways to Save the World." In his introduction to the magazine's first list of proposals, editor James Fallows argued that reporters should cover what's right and how to improve what's wrong. "The average journalist," he wrote, "normally so directed and morally self-confident, shrinks instinctively from considering 'solutions.' "

Many readers notice the aversion, have trouble understanding it, and conclude that journalists are just misanthropes. In a 1997 Public Agenda study of attitudes toward the press, the nonprofit polling and research group found that 79 percent of people interviewed said of their local media, "A reporter's job is to cover bad news," and 65 percent said journalists "unfairly dwell upon conflict and failure."

"It's ironic," says Russ Baker, a freelance reporter who has written for *Hope* magazine and for CJR, "that some journalists don't have any problem erring on the side of doing tremendous damage to something or someone, but they're reluctant to err on the side of seeming enthusiastic about something. We're sort of taught to think that way." Pulitzer Prizes are rarely won for solutions stories.

One reason for the skeptical attitude is that many "good news" stories are badly executed. "Positive" pieces are often written quickly, poorly, in a saccharin tone, or they're formulaic. That reinforces some reporters' distaste for the genre. After reading dozens of solutions stories, good and bad, for this piece, I don't want to hear about any more "folks," who are "meeting the needs" of other folks.

"Solutions stuff can very quickly turn into grandmothers helping kittens out of trees, so you have to be careful," says Paul Slavin, a senior producer at ABC News who oversaw the Solutions series that aired two to three times a week on the Jennings show from August 1996 to September 1997. The series was suspended, says Eileen Murphy, head of public affairs for ABC News, partly because producers had trouble coming up with that many good "Solutions" stories (rather than saccharin anecdotes) every week.

Many journalists have a visceral, adverse reaction to solutions journalism "because it seems like boosterism and cheerleading," says a senior reporter at *The San Diego Union-Tribune,* Copley's 376,000-circulation flagship, one of the first papers to devote a full-time editor and a special logo to it. Solutions journalists hasten to claim that their work is not cheerleading, nor is it leading them down a road toward soft news.

Seventy-five newspapers have subscribed to the fledgling American News Service, the wire devoted, as its motto says, to the "search for solutions." Started by Frances Moore Lappé, the activist best known for her book *Diet for a Small Planet,* and her husband Paul Du Bois, ANS is now edited by Peter Seares, a nineteen-year veteran of Reuters. It was free for two years until August, when it began charging an introductory rate of $7.50 a week for an average of two 800 to 1,000-word features. Asked what kind of story she's after, Lappé cited a solid, well-reported ANS piece on a trend toward small schools where students seem to learn better. Most education reporters ignored that story, she said, while they wrote dozens of times on more contentious subjects, like the debates over school vouchers and national education standards. Still, Seares said, "I'm trying very hard to make sure that our stories don't have a rosy glow. They should be real. We don't want everybody living happily ever after. If occasionally they do, that's not the tone that we're aiming for and we don't want to strike it every time."

If, out of all this, there is a valuable new genre emerging, it consists of tough-minded reporting of news that is largely, but not altogether, positive. It's not soft news or puff pieces, and it's not civic journalism, which usually casts journalists in a role of greater involvement with "the community."

"This isn't service journalism," says Katrina vanden Heuvel, editor of *The Nation.* "I consider it reporting on positive developments, all the while reporting on the difficulties. There's not a one hundred percent success rate on anything in life."

The Nation's "What Works" series has focused on the revitalization of cities. Another long Walljasper piece described Dudley Street, a Boston neighborhood where one community development project after another failed, deepening the residents' cynicism, until a resident stood up at a community meeting with yet another panel of outside redevelopment experts, and asked point-blank how many of them lived in the neighborhood. The funding foundation then decided to give up control to a board mostly made up of people from Dudley Street. Ten years later the Dudley Street Neighborhood Initiative has 2,500 members, and the neighborhood is transformed, Walljasper said. The group cleaned up illegal dumps and padlocked their gates to prevent more dumping, took charge of empty lots and built new housing on some of them, rehabilitated existing housing, organized youth activities in local parks, planted gardens, and so on.

Walljasper, who has been an editor of the *Utne Reader* for thirteen years, proposed the "What Works" series to *The Nation* and has been writing it intermittently for a year. "None of these places that I'm writing about for *The Nation* am I setting up as being the complete answer, or perfect," he says. "There are lots of shades of gray. Serious solutions stories are harder to write than traditional pieces."

A good narrative tends to have conflict, so a report from the promised land can easily be a snooze. The search for tension turns many solutions stories into "individual succeeds against the odds" pieces, which often are sentimental. And the fact that many good programs are run by one driven, charismatic person sometimes leads to adoring profiles. The way to avoid those pitfalls, the best solutions reporters say, is to search for the real, structural reasons why a particular program is succeeding, and anchor the narrative there. That's usually harder to write.

Solutions stories can also be harder to report than negative pieces, according to journalists who do both kinds. Right off the bat, it is much easier to discover that one major

> "The greatest single danger is a paint-by-numbers journalism where an editor orders up a feel-good story and the reporter's job is to fill in the blanks."

thing is wrong with a program or an institution than to satisfy yourself that nothing much is wrong. You can criticize just a part, in other words, but you usually have to praise a whole. You might cover a children's program that seems wonderfully successful, only to discover that the kitchen staff are all illegal immigrants, or the assistant director is embezzling. If you wrote a story just criticizing either of those failings, you'd be safe.

As soon as you actually go out there in favor of something, it puts you in a vulnerable position," says David Bornstein, a New York free-lance magazine writer who works mainly on solutions stories. "I'm much more interested in writing about something I think is good, but it takes a lot more time." He recalls that it took him a week to do a spoof of his native Canada for *Details* magazine. But for a piece in *The Atlantic Monthly* on the antipoverty technique of so-called "micro-credit," in which tiny loans from community banks allow women in Bangladesh to start small, self-run businesses, Bornstein sweated so long—seven months—that the 4,500-word story turned into a solutions-oriented book called *The Price of a Dream.* "To write a really good solutions piece, it's not enough to say 'This is a really good school,'" he notes. "It's being able to spot patterns, to pinpoint the keys to success."

Says Walljasper: "You have to dig into what the problems are, how they got that way, and what ideas offer some promise for change." In many cases, he says, projects work because of collaboration between local government and nonprofit community groups, as in Burlington.

Why, given how hard it is, are journalists doing more of this work than ever? Several of them ascribed it to epiphanies that followed bad news, in life or in print. In the spring of 1985, for example, Jon Wilson was doing very well publishing more than 100,000 bimonthly copies of *WoodenBoat,* the magazine he had started eleven years earlier. Then he saw a photo essay on Nicaragua in an issue of *Newsweek* in which a Contra soldier killed a suspected Sandinista spy. Wilson found himself weeping, and then began plans for a magazine that would celebrate humanity. The first issue of *Hope* was published in the spring of 1996. It favors stories about people standing up to adversity, like Marie Runyon, a housing activist who organizes tenants to take over and run their own buildings in Harlem. *Hope*'s circulation is some 13,000, Wilson says, about half of which is newsstand sales. Eighty percent of subscribers are women, according to a survey commissioned by the magazine. Two-thirds are aged 40 to 49, have advanced degrees, and live in the suburbs. Like other solutions publications, Hope focuses on individual and community efforts—relatively small-scale social programs that are mostly private. A solutions story about government is rare, raising the criticism that solutions journalism implies all problems can be solved by hard-working neighbors.

Another journalist who says he was driven to solutions-style reporting by what he forthrightly calls an epiphany is Mike Jacobs, editor of North Dakota's Grand Forks Herald, which continued publishing through a disastrous flood last April. Since then, Jacobs has hired two reporters who try to find constructive stories. Sometimes that means searching far afield to locales that have dealt with difficulties similar to Grand Forks's, whose most obvious problem is the threat of another flood. Reporter Ian Swanson went to Rochester, Minnesota, to report on how that city managed to contain its Zumbro River, with flood walls that are also bicycle and walking paths. The paper is sending another staffer to the Netherlands to study that country's solutions to its famous problems with encroaching floodwaters.

At The San Diego Union-Tribune, solutions editor Clark runs about one piece every two weeks, about thirty-five column-inches with sidebars. Her story about children who are rewarded with the gift of a musical education motivated two readers to donate pianos, and to proclaim they were eager to duplicate the program. "To me," says Clark, "that's the greatest measure of success."

Reporters inside and outside the paper are skeptical. "Journalists have long reported on schemes for solving problems, well before some genius decided to use the rubric of 'solutions,' " says Howard Kurtz, media reporter for The Washington Post. "Using that label still bothers me a little because it signals to the reader that the reporter is going to lead them to magic solutions when the reality may be a lot more muddled. To me, the greatest single danger here is a paint-by-numbers journalism in which an editor orders up a certain kind of feel-good story and a reporter's job is to fill in the blanks."

That's the key. Real, high-quality solutions journalism is worthwhile precisely because it promises no magic bullets, and it doesn't paint by the numbers. It differs from other good journalism in one simple way: instead of pointing out what's wrong in the hope that someone will fix it, solutions journalism points out what's right, hoping that someone can imitate it.

SPOON-FED NEWS

When the nation's television critics make the pilgrimage to Pasadena twice a year, the networks lavish them with heavy doses of propaganda along with free meals, glitzy parties and trinkets. Is this trip necessary?

THERE'S A PILE OF LOOT THAT'S BEEN SITTING IN MY OFFICE FOR MONTHS WHILE I figure what to make of an event I attended for the first time this year—the Television Critics Association conference, a biannual lovefest between network executives, television stars and the press.

What do we have for the lucky journalists who went? Well, let's see, there's a "The Young and the Restless" cookbook (try Victor and Diane's "lemony custard cake clouds with marinated strawberries"), a wool "NYPD Blue" baseball cap, bright blue flannel "Today" show pajamas and a brown denim backpack from ABC to take home the haul. There were several high-quality freebies that I missed, including a toaster from CBS (no kidding),

binoculars from Showtime and an enormous stuffed Rugrats toy from Nickelodeon.

Still, NBC made sure I got my leather-collared denim jacket, which arrived by Federal Express two weeks after the January conference. Then there were books, CDs, T-shirts, workout water bottles—and microwave popcorn to boot.

Veterans of the TV critics press tour are accustomed to the networks' calculated largesse. They are also familiar with the shock of first-timers at these events. Who wouldn't be surprised? When I showed up at CBS' main press conference to cover the event for the Washington Post, journalists were carting around large, cellophane-wrapped-and-bowed baskets of goodies.

No wonder newcomers often write what the regulars call "pigs at the trough" articles.

But this event is a mainstay of coverage of the television industry, and it warrants a look beyond knee-jerk sanctimony—though there's plenty of room for that.

Journalistically, the Television Critics Association press tour is a tough one, an opportunity for journalists to work their sources, but more often an opportunity for those sources to curry favor with journalists. The gifts are only a small part of what is problematic about it. More than 100 television critics and feature writers from publications across the country flock to the Ritz-Carlton in Pasadena for a nonstop, promotional marathon mounted, sponsored and run by the networks. The broadcasters set the agenda, orchestrate access to their stars, provide a press room and even schedule time for journalists to write and file stories.

BY SHARON WAXMAN

But at least the networks show up. Unlike their movie industry counterparts, network brass attending the meetings expose themselves to a forum that is open to discussion, debate and a virtually unlimited number of questions. While some journalists attend news conferences and then spew back the networks' spin to their readers, executives can also be buttonholed and forced to address specific issues. The news conferences inevitably yield some tough questions.

Then there are the parties, thrown by the networks for the journalists, where reporters can luck into relaxed, rewarding discussions with actors, writers and producers, in addition to the suits.

Nevertheless, the critics who faithfully attend the press tour know that there is something distasteful about the constant taking of what the networks have to give. "I won't rationalize the tchotchkes delivered to the room—the T-shirts, the candies—fine, you're right," says Tom Jicha, critic and writer for Fort Lauderdale's Sun-Sentinel. "But all that junk doesn't cost what one lunch costs, and there you are in line, ready to eat."

Indeed I was. What else was there to do? Pop out to McDonald's and be back for the question-and-answer session? I considered it; it seemed ridiculous.

The Wichita Eagle's Bob Curtright is president of the Television Critics Association.

But the effect of this constant face- and pocket-stuffing is insidious. It contributes to an atmosphere of collusion rather than one of skepticism, and it very subtly undermines the credibility of journalists who are there not as guests of the networks, but as (we presume) critical observers of the hows and whys of television programming.

At long last, the TCA seems to have figured this out. At its meeting in July—with rumors flying about this article going to press and the preparation of another for the new magazine Brill's Content—members voted unanimously to "limit outside material to informational uses only." In other words, the networks were being requested to cease and desist from their deluge of freebies, like that handsome wheel-on luggage handed out by Turner during the July tour.

Fort Lauderdale's Tom Jicha says he'd prefer several days of no-frills interviews.

TCA President Bob Curtright of the Wichita Eagle explains that the association could not "ban" gifts outright since the networks organize the press tour. It remains to be seen to what degree the networks will comply.

In addition, the group adopted a code of conduct barring members from soliciting work from the networks or producers during the press tour.

Was the timing of the reforms a coincidence? Hardly. "If you didn't know that AJR and Brill's Content were examining us before the tour, then you certainly did by the time we had our meeting. There's no way that goes unnoticed," says David Glasier, a former TCA president and TV critic for the News-Herald in Willoughby, Ohio. "My feeling was that if getting rid of the trinkets eliminates one possible gray area, then great."

BUT ELIMINATING THE FREEBIES DOES NOT ADDRESS THE BIGGER problem: Worse than eating what the networks serve for lunch (and breakfast and dinner) is swallowing their spoon-fed news. "It's ludicrous," says Nikki Finke, New York maga-

zine's West Coast editor and a veteran Hollywood reporter. Finke refuses to attend the meetings, saying they provide no useful information. "It's always the same. If you're the No. 3 network you're moving up. If you're No. 2 you're almost at the top, and if you're No. 1 you're staying there."

Finke says that many of the journalists who go to the press tour meetings (and the editors who send them) are just plain lazy, content to fill their notebooks with quotes that will provide fodder for a couple of months' worth of feature stories and TV columns.

Gary Dretzka, a senior writer based in Los Angeles for the Chicago Tribune, agrees. "It's filler," he says. "And editors who take television coverage not seriously at all think it's $3,000 well invested." But Dretzka usually attends the news conferences with network executives.

Is this any way to cover the most influential medium of popular American culture? Finke says it isn't. "If you're interested in TV as a business, you'll have sources.... There are agents, managers, producers, lawyers, studios—there is a whole range of people who run the industry," she says. "But those journalists never talk to the other people."

Ouch. She has a point. The meetings seduce journalists into thinking that they're doing real reporting, when in fact real reporting only happens as an adjunct to the main event. The networks keep you so busy with "news conferences" (read: promotional events) that it's easy to forget that the reporter's objective is not the same as the networks'.

But there's another facet to this problem. For many of the critic/feature writers there is little alternative to the network-run meetings. On a practical level, say TCA members, the press tour is the only access journalists from smaller and mid-size newspapers will get to top network brass and TV talent. Sure, New York Times reporters can call up ABC Entertainment chief Stu Bloomberg any time. But what about writers for the Wichita Eagle? Meanwhile, the networks claim (with some justification) that it is far more efficient to present an entertainment schedule to a single group of TV reporters and critics than to call each one on the phone.

Some reporters insist that they can do good reporting at the Pasadena meetings despite the ingratiating atmosphere. "We are spoon-fed by these people, but what we make of it is up to us," says Gail Shister, the Philadelphia Inquirer's TV columnist. "Compare it to a political convention—it depends on your own enterprise as a reporter, how you work it. For me, the real news is not on the podium, it's on the floor. And what the press tour affords you is an enormous floor, seven days a week, and you can work the floor every day, every night. For me it's a gold mine; not only do I file every day, but I always come back with six or seven columns in the can."

As examples, Shister points to an off-the-cuff interview she did with actress Camryn Manheim of "The Practice" during a party for that show and producer David E. Kelley's other program, "Ally McBeal." Manheim spoke openly about being an overweight actress in a model-thin environment, and Shister was able to quickly gather comments from Manheim's colleagues, an exercise that would have taken days of phone work.

"That's why I go to the tour," she says. "It's the Super Bowl of TV coverage. You have to be there."

But Finke scoffs that even the better reporters at the TV meetings are playing the networks' game. She counters: "I've compared interviews I've done with executives and producers on their own, and they have literally said things 180 degrees different than what they said at the TV critics' thing. Because it's bogus. Who's going to speak honestly when all their bosses are standing right there?"

HOWEVER GRAFT-RIDDEN AND STAGE-MANAGED THE TELEVISION critics' press tour seems today, the event used to be much, much worse. Back in the late 1960s when it was first organized by the networks, some 30 television writers were flown in and put up at a Century City hotel. Flights, hotel, meals and parties were provided.

In the early days, no "real" journalism was expected or required. Publicists handed out lists of questions for reporters to ask the actors (there were no sessions with network executives), and complete articles sometimes appeared under the doors of journalists in the morning, courtesy of the networks. Once a network flew the critics to London to interview the actors in "Robin Hood," according to Jicha. Another time they were flown to Hawaii to interview actor Jack Lord from "Hawaii Five-O."

The Chicago Tribune's Gary Dretzka says many writers return from the conferences "with garbage."

Gradually, with the ethical changes in journalism prompted by Watergate and the subsequent questioning of the relationship between reporters and the people on their beat, the rules changed. By the mid-'70s, about a third of the newspapers decided to pay their own way. The percentage gradually grew, but some freeloaders hung on until as late as 1988. In 1977, the television critics began to organize in order to have more control over the press tour proceedings, and so the Television Critics Association was born.

With that came a decision to challenge the networks on the free meals. "It just came down to logistics," says Jicha. The network heads said it was easier to organize a working meal for the journalists, saying, " 'When we pay for lunch, it keeps you here. If we allow you to scatter around Los Angeles, it would be 3 [p.m.] before we reassemble,' " Jicha recalls being told. "We said, 'OK, we'll pay for the meals.' They said, 'No, we don't think you will.' Back then at the Century Plaza lunch was about $35, dinner about $80."

The networks were right. The newspapers wouldn't pay that much. So the networks never stopped footing the bills.

The TCA's recent about-face on the question of freebies may not break the hearts of network executives, who have been scaling back their participation in the press tours. NBC hosted only two days in July rather than three and will host only one in January 1999, while other networks are similarly ramping down.

"What is most disappointing for the whole press tour concept is putting on a session that gets very low

attendance," says Pat Schultz, NBC's vice president for entertainment press and publicity. Some journalists, she continues, "can go to a party and never talk to the people you want them to talk to. People may go to party and not do any work. That's frustrating."

WHEN ALL IS SAID AND DONE, IS THE TELEVISION CRITICS Association press tour a necessary evil? There are two ways to look at this question.

One is to consider whether it would be possible to cover the networks' program schedules any other way. Could diligent television journalists come to Los Angeles for several days of no-frills interviews? Only those newspapers really devoted to serious coverage of the television industry would bother. Says Jicha: "I yearn for it. We'd be there half as long; we'd ask pointed questions."

But this begs another question: Is it really necessary to be writing promotional stories about every new show that passes through the tube? Because let's face it, that is the main point of the press tours.

Would journalists' time be better spent elsewhere? Finke thinks so. "I have six stories planned in the next three months about the TV entertainment business," she says. "Not one of those stories could be reported at the TV critics meetings, or has any relation to the TV critics meetings."

But, some might ask, how important is all of this anyway? After all, it's only television.

The answer is "all of this" is increasingly important. In a universe where entertainment occupies such a huge space in contemporary culture, responsible coverage of the industry is of growing significance. As the media devote ever more column inches and broadcast time to coverage of the entertainment industry, higher standards must be demanded.

The Philadelphia Inquirer's Gail Shister calls the tour "the Super Bowl of TV coverage."

The standards of the critics' association may have been appropriate and even laudable in the late 1970s; today the association itself seems to recognize a need to achieve a greater measure of distance and skepticism.

But there's not an easy solution. Journalists would be stupid to forgo the chance to meet with the network heads out of purist spite. The fact is the press tour provides rare, unfettered access to people at all levels of the television industry; it would be foolish to pass that up.

The problem is when the press tour is not the starting point for coverage of the television industry, but the only point. Instead of being a sideshow providing useful insight into the way television shows are made or how programming decisions are made, it too easily becomes the main event.

"The newspapers have allowed the networks to blow the tune, to control the pace of the dance," says the Chicago Tribune's Dretzka. "A lot of people come back with garbage. They can't help but promote the TV shows. I just don't see how it's worthwhile."

Sharon Waxman, who covers Hollywood for the Washington Post, wrote about the movie industry's relationship with the news media in AJR's June 1997 issue.

ASSEMBLY-LINE JOURNALISM

What's the difference between a news story and a widget?
At today's profit-driven papers, not much

BY DOUG UNDERWOOD

In the bad old days around 1995 and 1996, when journalists at the *Winston-Salem Journal* were laboring under an unpopular "grid system" designed to numerically measure reporters' work, they circulated a newsletter mocking the company's consultant-designed, assembly-line-style evaluation program.

The spoof contained the following codified, "performance-based" categories: use of corporate jargon (5.3 quadrillion); comfort provided to downsized employees (0 degrees Kelvin); and the quality of the news stories (.0000676 percent).

The *Journal*'s real grid system required editors to estimate the time it should take a reporter to produce a story. A reporter was expected, for example, to produce as many as forty stories a week if each piece were based upon a press release and one or two cooperative sources—and about fifteen stories a week if each were based on meetings or police activities. At the end of the week, editorial supervisors would measure the

Doug Underwood, a former reporter for The Seattle Times *and the Gannett News Service, is an associate professor at the School of Communications at the University of Washington. His article, "When MBA's Rule the Newsroom," in the March/April 1998* CJR, *was the basis for a book published in 1993 under the same title.*

lengths of stories and calculate the time it took to do them to see if reporters met the newspaper's weekly output goals.

The *Journal* assessment grid is gone now, deep-sixed in the spring of 1996 by a new managing editor, Carl Crothers, who calls it a "spreadsheet" approach that destroyed morale in the *Journal* newsroom and drove the newspaper toward mediocrity. "It creates a factory mentality," says Crothers. "It left [employees] coming in with the hope that they'd create enough widgets to get their score and get their paycheck each week. Good journalism was left in the trashcan."

Today, the Media General-owned *Journal* uses a more traditional system. Employees receive an annual evaluation that avoids statistical calculation of journalists' work and is written by supervisors in narrative form. But at many other newspapers the trend has been toward systems that codify newsroom employee productivity in numerical terms or that rate employee performance in terms reminiscent of elementary school report cards.

At the Copley-owned *San Diego Union-Tribune*, reporters are ranked by their supervisor in four categories of performance, which may involve calculations of how many stories the journalist produced and where they were played; the rankings are tied to merit pay increases. At the Knight Ridder-owned *News-Sentinel* in Fort Wayne, In-

diana, and the McClatchy-owned *Sacramento Bee*, newsroom employee raises are determined, in part, on the journalist's score in a number of performance categories. And at the Gannett-owned *Cincinnati Enquirer*, story productivity is one of twelve performance gauges that would be factored into a reporter's evaluation under a proposed new job performance plan.

Some performance systems have been used in tandem with cost-cutting campaigns or downsizing schemes. During the six months in 1995 and 1996 when the grid system was in operation at the *Journal*, for example, about a dozen journalists (roughly 10 percent of the 120 newsroom employees) were let go.

Newspaper executives defend the codified evaluations systems as much-needed tools to reduce inefficiency, manage newsroom costs, spur employee performance, root out underperformers, and encourage professional growth. But many reporters bristle at the indignity of having their output rated in statistical ways that they find inappropriate for a creative professional activity. It is particularly galling, they argue, when these systems—which are operated under the guise of scientific objectivity—are manipulated to crank up story productivity and to hold down newsroom expenses.

This is the complaint of Patti Epler, a recently departed veteran political in-

    Reprinted from *Columbia Journalism Review*, July/August 1998, pp. 42-44. © 1998 by Columbia Journalism Review.

vestigative reporter for McClatchy's *News Tribune* in Tacoma, Washington. Epler left the *News Tribune* for the *Phoenix New Times* last year after she was transferred from special projects to a suburban beat during a reorganization of the newsroom and the adoption of a

"two" from their supervisor, for example, are given a company sheet explaining that they are in need of regular management direction and that their contribution is "below most"; a "four" ranking, on the other hand, indicates that the employee is "an exemplary team

dards for supervisors to use in grading newsroom employees in four areas: accuracy, reporting, writing, and communication. Giles's system has become a model that many newspapers follow. But, it also became a sticking point in union negotiations when he announced that the company planned to give merit raises only to those employees who were graded in the top two (outstanding and commendable) of the five performance categories.

Newsroom managers grade workers' performance on a scorecard

team system. Some teams, she says, were asked by *News Tribune* management to set productivity goals and were evaluated on how well they achieved them. Although Epler's team wasn't asked to set specific goals, she was nonetheless criticized in her annual evaluation for producing too many long, in-depth stories and not enough shorter, community news pieces.

"I kid you not," Epler says. "They would count your bylines and your stories. Not once did they talk about the quality of your stories. They just wanted you to do the run-and-gun, daily thing. It was a sweatshop culture."

David Zeeck, *News Tribune* executive editor, says the paper's performance evaluation system is part of an effort to change the attitude of a newsroom that hasn't been accountable enough to readers or to the business needs of the newspaper. He expects that a good newspaper will have reporters producing a mix of in-depth articles, as well as many shorter, local stories. But he believes that is no reason not to try to encourage improved productivity in the newsroom—which he says has happened at the *News Tribune*.

"Some reporters say, 'Oh, my God, these are quotas,'" Zeeck acknowledges. "Sure, it freaks some people out. But I fail to see how productivity is an inappropriate measure of how you're doing your job."

A common technique to tighten up on employee accountability is for newsroom managers to grade employee performance on a scorecard, and to link those scores to annual raises—as happens at the Gannett-owned *Des Moines Register*. Journalists report great unhappiness with the system, which ranks newsroom employees, and then bases their raises on a scale of one (at the bottom) through five—a number that is determined at an employee's annual evaluation. Employees who receive a

player" who has met all "quantitative objectives" and has an "understanding of company goals."

Reporter Kirsten Scharnberg, who recently left the *Register* for the Baltimore *Sun*, complains that many *Register* journalists, including a number of the paper's nationally recognized reporters, have not only received low ratings, but have also felt insulted by the company's terminology in characterizing their work. She blames the low ratings on the company's attempt to save money. "It's pretty obvious that the worse you do on your evaluation, the smaller the raise they have to give you." She adds that the company can't understand why the passion in the newsroom has dwindled. "You can't have it be more corporate and bottomline and then wonder why people aren't giving their soul to a place that isn't giving it back."

Jason Bobst, the *Register* human resources manager, denies that employees are fit into preordained categories in order to save money. People, he says, are graded fairly (with about 23 percent of the newsroom staff rated as a "four or five"). A measurable performance system can work well, Bobst contends, if expectations have been well laid out in advance—as he says they are at the *Register*.

At *The Detroit News*, efforts to move to a quantified employee evaluation system—and then to link the numbers to pay—played a key role in the 1995 strike. The *News*'s system was put in by Robert Giles, then its editor/publisher, now the executive director of the Freedom Forum's Media Studies Center. In his 1987 book, *Newsroom Management: A Guide to Theory and Practice*, Giles recommended that newspapers adopt thirty-eight performance appraisal stan-

A number of employees at the Gannett-owned *News* complain that Giles's system—despite its appearance of objectivity—was used by the middle managers to mark down troublesome employees so they wouldn't get raises. Says Norm Sinclair, a veteran investigative reporter at the newspaper: "It wasn't a fair system." That system has been set aside by Giles's successor at the *News,* Mark Silverman. He has set up teams of reporters, copy editors, and newsroom managers to advise him on developing a new performance evaluation system that will then be negotiated with The Newspaper Guild.

Giles, like most executives at newspapers that have adopted quantified performance evaluations systems, maintains that such systems aim at more than just managing people by the numbers. "The spirit" of his system, he says, is to let an employee know "where he or she stands, get each to understand the organization's ground rules and goals, and help each to make improvements."

Journalists have come to make many adjustments to a corporate management structure increasingly focused on profits, management efficiencies, and higher productivity. But newsroom managers who believe they can treat professionals as just an extension of the corporate spreadsheet may find themselves facing an alienated workforce. Having their work reduced to scores or grades or statistical measurements can be "traumatic" for journalists, as Christopher Quinn, a veteran at the *Winston-Salem Journal*, describes his experience with the paper's grid system. Or, as Quinn's new boss, Carl Crothers, puts it: "If you overlay some factory model onto the newsroom, you begin to detract from the thing that makes for a good newsroom—creative freedom. You can put a quantified system into any newsroom, but good journalists won't work there."

TALES FROM THE TRAIL

Journalists recall unforgettable moments of high drama and low comedy in presidential campaign coverage.

THE YEAR WAS 1956, AND PRESIDENT EISENHOWER WAS WHISTLE-stopping in the Upper Midwest in his campaign for reelection. In those days photographers on the campaign train had a workroom that was zestfully decorated in the true spirit of photographers of that era: with photos of naked young women.

Among the passengers accompanying Eisenhower on the train, however, were Sherman Adams, the straightlaced White House chief of staff, and Adams' wife, Rachel, who fancied herself something of an artist.

As recalled by Phil Goulding, who was aboard as a reporter for Cleveland's Plain Dealer, a time came when Eisenhower and the campaign entourage debarked for a motorcade and a presidential speech, to be gone for a couple of hours.

While the crowd was absent, Goulding recalls, Rachel Adams seized a grease pencil, crept into the photographic workroom and drew bras and panties on all of the photographs of the women.

The incident is only one of hundreds that live in the memories of reporters who have covered presidential election campaigns—stories of fun and frolic, pathos and bathos, drama and melodrama.

Reporters have embarrassed candidates, dramatically influenced elections, experienced personal trauma, witnessed riveting moments in the nation's political history—and have had many a roaring good time. It's often observed that somehow it doesn't seem to be nearly as much fun today as it used to be. Yet almost any reporter involved in campaign coverage has a tale or two to spin from Eisenhower right on up to Bill Clinton. Among them:

▶ David Broder may well have changed the nation's history with a story he wrote about Edmund Muskie

By James McCartney

Reprinted with permission from *American Journalism Review*, October 1996, pp. 28-31. © 1996 by the College of Journalism of the University of Maryland at College Park.

for the Washington Post in 1972.

▶ Gary Schuster, then Washington bureau chief for the Detroit News, parlayed a brief chat with Ronald Reagan on a campaign flight in 1980 into a job with CBS.

▶ James Naughton, then of the New York Times, confronted President Gerald Ford at a 1976 press conference dressed as a chicken. His chicken costume is on display today in the Ford Presidential Library in Grand Rapids, Michigan.

▶ Clark Hoyt, then with Knight Newspapers, realized in a flash of insight in 1972, when a doctor's face went pale, that Democratic vice presidential nominee Thomas Eagleton might be dumped.

▶ Patricia O'Brien, then with Knight-Ridder, recalls feeling aghast when during the 1988 campaign Gary Hart answered the door of his hotel room for a scheduled interview clad only in a bathrobe.

PHIL GOULDING HIMSELF BECAME A KEY figure in a memorable drama on Barry Goldwater's campaign plane in 1964.

Goldwater, the Republican nominee, was an airplane buff and was enchanted with the capabilities of a spanking new Boeing 727 hired for his campaign. After a speech in Kentucky, Goldwater had the plane's pilot "buzz" the airport—roaring 30 feet over the runway at 400 or 500 miles an hour.

Reporters on the plane had not been alerted in advance. Some were praying, fearing for their lives. Goulding wrote a memorable story, the lede of which went something like this:

"I was in combat in World War II, but I was never so frightened as I was in Barry Goldwater's campaign plane over Kentucky." On the campaign trail ever after Phil Goulding was known as "Frightened Phil." But, in fact, some of the other reporters were even more frightened. One told William J. Eaton, then with United Press, he thought he was about to die.

The Goldwater campaign remains a favorite of many reporters for its jocularity from beginning to end. It is certainly mine.

In those days many organizations

'I *WAS IN combat in World War II," wrote Phil Goulding, "but I was never so frightened as I was in Barry Goldwater's campaign plane over Kentucky."*

kept reporters with one candidate or another from beginning to end, which led to deep friendships and shared hilarity.

One of the major practical problems for national reporters on that 727 lay in efforts to preserve the middle seat of the three seats on each side of the aisle for work space as local and regional reporters came aboard the plane for brief stints.

At the time I was with the late Chicago Daily News and held the aisle seat. My seat mate, by the window, was the late John Averill of the Los Angeles Times. As the campaign wore on we contrived a fictional character to occupy the middle seat and gave him the name "Murgatroid Backfire." His paper: the Pocatello Post.

To preserve assigned seats we pasted the masthead of our paper on the back of the seat in front of us. We invented a masthead for Murgatroid.

How could a small paper like the Pocatello Post afford to cover a national campaign? Well, Murgatroid was a publisher. A publisher, obviously, is rich. He can afford anything.

As the campaign progressed, questions arose about what Murgatroid was filing. Other reporters in nearby seats—Marjorie Hunter of the New York Times, Jack Steele of Scripps Howard, Bill Eaton and Goulding—began asking what Murgatroid was using for a lede.

Soon a competition developed to write Murgatroid's lede. Marjorie Hunter suggested an all-purpose lede that could be used in emergencies in case Murgatroid wanted an early dinner: "Republican presidential nominee Barry Goldwater lied again today."

The Washington Post's David Broder remembers the wild airplane ride back to Washington in the closing days of the campaign, when many drinks were poured and many songs were sung. Goldwater came back to the press section wearing a Mexican serape and a giant sombrero and regaled reporters with tales of his courtship of his wife, Peggy.

One song, quoted word-for-word in Theodore White's classic, "The Making of the President 1964," drew its inspiration from the name Goldwater had chosen for his campaign plane—"Yai-Bi-Kin," Navajo for "House in the Sky."

"The man of our dreams has lost his hair,
His glasses are blank and black,
He hates to mess with the Eastern press,
His knife is in Lyndon's back.
The man of our dreams is free from care,
He's certain he's going to win.
The polls say he's not, but he's sure that's a plot—
He's the sweetheart of Yai-Bi-Kin."

When the campaign was over, with Goldwater losing by a historic margin, a question arose on the proper Murgatroid lede for Goldwater's swan song. It was noted that Goldwater seemed proud of his performance, despite the dimensions of his loss, because he had polled more than 27 million votes—more than any other Republican except Eisenhower. Lyndon Johnson, of course, polled more than 43 million.

The decision, a consensus, was: "Barry Goldwater proudly opined that he had won a moral victory in Tuesday's election."

DAVID BRODER'S CONTRIBUTION TO HISTory has become known in press corps legend as "The Great Ed Muskie Crying Incident."

It was New Hampshire primary time in 1972 and Sen. Edmund Muskie of Maine was the unquestioned Democratic front-runner. He had become enraged at editorials attacking him and impugning his wife's character in the archconservative Manchester Union Leader and had decided to confront the paper's publisher from a flatbed truck positioned in front of the paper's building.

Broder's story on page one of the Washington Post's Sunday paper began:

"With tears streaming down his face and his voice choked with emotion, Sen. Edmund S. Muskie (D-Maine) stood in the snow outside the Manchester Union Leader this morning and accused its publisher of making vicious attacks on him and his wife, Jane."

In defending his wife, Broder said in his lede, Muskie "broke down three times in as many minutes."

James Naughton was the New York Times reporter on the scene. His story ran on page 54 and mentioned tears and broken speech only once, in the sixth paragraph. The UPI story, which ran on page 2 of the Washington Star, said in the eighth paragraph that Muskie was "visibly shaken," but went no further.

To the time of his death last year Muskie insisted he did not cry. He acknowledged being upset, but insisted that the alleged tears were melting snowflakes. And Broder has publicly brooded that this one story has caused him more second thoughts than any other in his long and distinguished career. He has suggested in retrospect that he may have gone too far, drawn too many unwarranted conclusions from his own preconceptions and may well have taken the event out of context. Recalling the Muskie affair years later in his book, "Behind the Front Page," Broder wrote, "Even when we are fairly sophisticated in putting the event in context, the news we deliver can fall short of the truth." Today, Broder says he's more sure of that principle than ever.

One thing is certain. The incident killed Muskie's campaign for the presidency, and Broder's story almost certainly played a key role.

THEN THERE IS THE GARY SCHUSTER story—how a reporter's inspirational whim, teasing a candidate, dramatically changed his career.

Gary Schuster was the Washington bureau chief of the Detroit News when Republicans decided to hold their 1980 national convention in Detroit. He attached himself to Ronald Reagan and began his reporting in June 1979, covering him, on and off, for more than a year until election night.

Like other reporters, Schuster found that Reagan kept his distance from the press corps, preferring staged events. There was no such thing as intimacy.

Thus Schuster was more than a little annoyed on the final day of the campaign to find Reagan coming down the aisle of the campaign plane, profusely thanking reporters for their coverage, acting as though all were pals.

Schuster was seated in an aisle seat and noted that Reagan would glance at a reporter's credentials to pick up the name, then say things like: "Thanks so much, Joe"—or Pete, or Charlie—"for the wonderful job you've done."

So Gary Schuster hid his credentials in his shirt pocket.

Schuster recalls saying to Reagan when the candidate got to him: "You know, Mr. Reagan, I've been covering you for more than a year, but I don't think you know my name." And he continued: "How many of the reporters on this plane do you know by name?"

Reagan was visibly flustered, and acknowledged that he had trouble remembering names, and that he realized that wasn't a very good thing for a politician.

Schuster didn't want to embarrass

Reagan further and produced his credentials. Reagan quickly said: "Of course I remember you Gary. You've been with us all along."

Reagan staged his first press conference after the election in the Century Plaza hotel in Los Angeles and the room, of course, was packed with reporters from around the world. Schuster was far back in the crowd trying to get in a question.

Reagan took several questions, then raised an arm to point directly at Schuster in the back of the room and shouted out: "Gary, do you have a question?"

In subsequent press conferences, says Schuster, "he always recognized me—and always by name."

Those little dramas on television clearly made a deep impression on executives of CBS. The network had had a hard time dealing with the Reagan White House. Executives concluded that Gary Schuster must have developed a special relationship with the president.

By 1985 CBS had seen enough of Schuster's cozy relationship with the Gipper. The network offered Schuster a job, covering the White House. "That was a factor in CBS coming to me," Schuster says, "the fact that Reagan knew me by name."

Schuster's luck, however, did not last. Fifteen months later CBS fired about 300 people—Schuster among them. Today he is in public relations with Union Pacific.

J AMES Naughton, then with the New York Times, covered a Gerald Ford press conference clad in a chicken head.

THEN THERE ARE STORIES OF SHEER whimsy—like when the New York Times' James Naughton bought a chicken costume and wore it at a Gerald Ford press conference in 1976.

Naughton, now president of the Poynter Institute for Media Studies

in St. Petersburg, Florida, says it all started at a Ford rally at a San Diego shopping center when Ford spotted a man dressed in a chicken costume in the crowd. It was part of a publicity stunt for a local radio station. Ford exclaimed: "The chicken—I love it!" The chicken man, sensing an opportunity, pranced up to the platform, approached the president and embraced him with his wings.

"I said to myself, 'I have to have that chicken head,' " Naughton recalls.

After the rally Naughton tracked down the chicken man and asked if he could buy the costume. The man said no, he needed it to make his living, but he had an old chicken head that he would sell to Naughton for $100.

Sold. Naughton placed his acquisition in the overhead rack of the campaign plane. The following night in Portland, Oregon, after a no-news day, Ford agreed to hold a news conference at the airport. Naughton donned his chicken head and strolled down the airplane steps onto the tarmac.

"Suddenly flash bulbs are going off and people are saying: 'You have to ask a question or you're chicken,' " recalls Naughton. "…Some of the reporters hoisted me up on their shoulders and carried me into the press conference…. And if you were watching television you would have seen reporters asking Ford questions when suddenly, in their midst, this giant chicken emerges, being identified on TV as a representative of the New York Times. The chicken did not have the nerve to ask a question, but he did meet with the president afterward, and I told Ford: 'Your campaign put me in a fowl mood.' You could say this is the closest I've come to the Pullet-zer Prize."

There was a sequel. Naughton listed the $100 it cost to buy the chicken head on his expense account and an assistant managing editor agreed to pay half. But Arthur O. Sulzberger Sr., the paper's publisher, told Naughton privately that he should send the expense account directly to him and he'd pay it.

For personal drama, however, few memories rival those of Clark Hoyt, now a vice president of Knight-Ridder. In 1972 Hoyt, then a reporter, was assigned to investigate a tip that Democratic vice presidential nominee Sen. Thomas Eagleton had received electric shock treatments for a mental disorder.

Hoyt had been dispatched to St. Louis after the Democratic National Convention in Miami to prepare a profile piece on Eagleton, a senator from Missouri. An anonymous tipster had phoned the Detroit Free Press, a Knight newspaper, suggesting that the paper investigate Eagleton's medical history, including shock treatments.

The call from the tipster was received by John S. Knight III, grandson of the Knight group's founder, John S. Knight, who had the presence of mind to ask the tipster for some kind of confirmation—when and where, for example, were electric shock treatments administered, and who was the doctor?

The tipster called back a second time with the name of a doctor in St. Louis, the name of the psychiatric hospital and a date when treatments were administered. Hoyt was asked to track down the doctor. He learned his home address, screwed up his courage and knocked on the door.

"The door opened narrowly," says Hoyt, "and I saw this face and I just blurted out: 'My name is Clark Hoyt and I'm from the Knight Newspapers in Washington and I need to ask you about the time you were present at the...hospital when Senator Eagleton had electric shock treatments.' The face turned white. 'I can't talk to you about that,' the doctor said, and slammed the door in my face. I was completely shaken. I knew there could have been other responses like, 'I don't know what you're talking about,' or 'I never heard of such a thing.' I knew it wasn't enough for a story, but as I walked away I think I knew that Tom Eagleton might be through—that our tipster had it right." After the visit Hoyt and Knight Washington Bureau Chief Robert Boyd flew to South Dakota and confronted Frank Mankiewicz, McGovern's campaign manager, with the information they had. They said the paper didn't want to write about it until the McGovern campaign had a chance to respond. Soon afterward the campaign announced the treatments and Eagleton stepped down. Hoyt and Boyd went on to win the Pulitzer Prize for their coverage.

For many veteran political reporters the most vivid memories of all are of the Democratic National Convention in Chicago in 1968, when police rioted, according to an official investigation, in beating up antiwar demonstrators in front of the Conrad Hilton hotel. Haynes Johnson, who was then with the Washington Star, was on the street. "Violence

was in the air," he recalls. "You could feel the emotion—the lights, the masses of cops, the chanting. The taunting of the cops.... The cops went in and clubbed the hell out of them. Legend would have it that these were young, peace-loving kids. Not so. It was proactive. Deliberate taunting. Jeering. You knew what was going to happen when the cops took their badges off so they couldn't be identified. It was not a nice scene. You felt angry and ashamed and horrified and disgusted all at once."

David Broder has a different memory. He recalls coming into the hotel lobby from the park where demonstrations were underway and spotting a woman he had first met during the Eugene McCarthy campaign in New Hampshire. "Her name was Cindy Samuels," Broder still remembers. "She was seated on a bench crying. She had been gassed. I went over and I put my arm around her and I said: 'Cindy. What can I do for you?' She looked up at me with tears on her face and said: 'Change things.'"

QUITE ANOTHER KIND OF MEMORY REmains with Patricia O'Brien from the campaign of 1988, when Colorado Sen. Gary Hart was the Democratic frontrunner—but well before the Miami Herald destroyed Hart's presidential ambitions by reporting he had spent the night with a woman who was not his wife in his Washington townhouse. O'Brien was with the Knight-Ridder Washington bureau and was covering her first presidential election campaign. She was anxious to establish her professional credentials, she says, and had been trying for weeks to obtain a personal interview with the candidate. "I wanted that interview desperately." Finally, Kathy Bushkin, Hart's press secretary, told her Hart had agreed and she was given a time to meet with him in his hotel room. "I was really nervous covering him," she says, "because he had this incredible reputation as a womanizer."

O'Brien took the precaution of telling her desk that she was going to meet with Hart and proceeded to his room. "I knocked on the door, and Hart said, 'Oh Pat, come on in.' And he's wearing a bathrobe—with no pants.... My feet propel me into the room. He sits down and crosses his legs, bare legs, and I know he didn't have any pants on. And I'm thinking, 'I'm letting him define this.' Then I say: 'This is bullshit, senator. I can't con-

tinue this interview unless you go and put some pants on.'" O'Brien says that Hart reacted indignantly, got up and left the room, and she could hear the zipper going up on his pants in the other room. "He comes back, and it's clear to me he's not going to give me anything. Then the phone rings and it's his friend Warren Beatty. And he's talking on the phone. He ignores me and keeps talking. And I simply got up and walked out."

Angry and embarrassed, O'Brien did not write about the incident, but it was later reported in Richard Ben Cramer's book about the campaign, "What It Takes."

I was telling the story about Gary Hart to longtime Washington correspondent Bill Eaton. He said he could do one better. He had a story about a president in a campaign who was stark naked.

It happened in 1964. Eaton was a member of a pool covering President Lyndon Johnson on Air Force One. "The pool, four of us, were summoned from the back of the plane to meet with the president. We were ushered into the presidential bedroom on the plane and the president was stretched out on a massage table—wearing nothing.

"Suddenly he stood up to towel himself off, facing us. He proceeded to lecture us on why we should do more reporting on the state of the economy and his success in budget cutting."

I asked Eaton, now curator of the Hubert H. Humphrey Fellowship Program at the University of Maryland College of Journalism, "Did anyone write about it?"

"Oh, no," he said. "In those days you didn't write about such things. Today it would be around the world in a half an hour. But come to think of it, we didn't write about the budget either. I guess we were in a state of shock."

James McCartney retired from Knight-Ridder earlier this year after 34 years as a Washington reporter and columnist. He teaches courses about the media at Georgetown University and wrote about how the press has often been hoodwinked during election campaigns in AJR's March issue.

Myths of the Global Information Village

by Claude Moisy

The question seems as old as the world: Does progress make humankind better? Applied to the field of international relations, the question of the day is whether global electronic connections make citizens more aware of world problems and more able to contribute to their solution.

We should not delude ourselves. The Internet is a fantastic tool that makes life easier for a lot of professionals. It is certainly great for global stocks and for global smut. But it represents in no way the miraculous advent of the much heralded "global village." For decades now, hazy-eyed apostles of the communications revolution have prophesied about the coming of a world without boundaries where everybody will know everything about everybody else. Since knowing is understanding, we were all going to share our worries and unite in alleviating them.

This dream world would of course be of particular interest to practitioners of international relations, whose craft would change in an environment where most citizens were generally aware of and concerned about foreign affairs. The universal flow of information, bringing people closer together, would necessarily make the conduct of foreign policy more open and more responsive to the desires of the common man.

CLAUDE MOISY, *former chairman and general manager of Agence France-Presse, has spent almost 20 years as an international correspondent. This article is adapted from a paper he wrote as a visiting fellow at the Joan Shorenstein Center on the Press, Politics, and Public Policy at the John F. Kennedy School of Government, Harvard University.*

INFORMATION: MORE SUPPLY, LESS DEMAND

So much for the dream. A careful analysis of the current exchange of foreign news around the world reveals an inescapable paradox. The amazing increase in the capacity to produce and distribute news from distant lands has been met by an obvious decrease in its consumption. This is certainly true for the United States, but it appears that the same phenomenon exists, to some degree, in most developed societies.

On the supply side, an unending series of technical advances has transformed the production and distribution of news. Through the extensive use of computers and satellites, multiplexing and fiber optics, and digitalization and data compression, information providers can offer more news today—in text, sound, and pictures—than ever before. It can be done quickly and cheaply and delivered to more users. An irresistible policy of telecommunications deregulation keeps accelerating the process by doing away with inefficient state monopolies.

This is, alas, no reason to fall for the big claim of the self-styled "global television networks" that they can broadcast instantly *to* everywhere the news *from* everywhere. In fact, the largest global television network, CNN International, retains only 35 foreign correspondents in 23 foreign bureaus, compared with the nearly 500 correspondents and 100 bureaus supported by each of the major wire services—the Associated Press (AP), Reuters, and Agence France-Presse (AFP) (see table on following page). Nor should one believe that all humankind is about to share knowledge through a "global network" of communication. That capability does not exist any more

Reprinted with permission from *Foreign Policy*, Summer 1997, pp. 78-87. © 1997 by the Carnegie Endowment for International Peace.

than does the global village, and it probably never will. CNN International reaches only 3 per cent of the world's population, four-fifths of whom do not even have access to a television set. The number of people with access to the World Wide Web through their individual computers may grow exponentially, but it is certain to remain for a long time only a fraction of the 6 billion human beings who will inhabit the planet at the turn of the century.

Vast realms of our world either cannot or will not be covered by the news collectors because of the high costs involved in news gathering and because many repressive regimes will not let them in. There are large areas, particularly in Africa, Asia, and the Middle East, where news within countries is severely controlled, and news from the outside hardly penetrates at all. Even a well-informed citizen

sight of the scope of this phenomenon. From 1960 to 1995, the total circulation of American daily newspapers remained stagnant at around 59 million copies, while the population of the United States grew from 180 million to 260 million inhabitants. That translates into a one-third drop in per capita readership. This attrition is likely to accelerate since the rate of newspaper readership is twice as weak among those under 30 as among those over 65.

As far as news content is concerned, the shift from the printed word to the moving picture has turned out to be much more than a change of medium. We all know that television has progressively induced a radical change in our way of reacting to events. Politicians and diplomats have learned quickly that television is an emotional medium and that popular sentiment whipped up by tele-

RELATIVE DIMENSION OF THE THREE GLOBAL NEWS WIRES AND CNN (1997)

	AP	Reuters	AFP	CNN
Employees	3,420	15,500	3,100	3,500
Total bureaus	237	161	182	31
Foreign bureaus	93	139	176	23
Total journalists	1,312	1,960	1,100	156
Journalists abroad	520	1,040	1,040	50

Source: Annual Reports and other company documents

in an open country like the United States is largely unaware of living conditions in many other countries. The fact is that, contrary to the myth of global communication, the world is not fully wired, and our knowledge of it is spotty at best.

Is this situation likely to change? The public's capacity to pay attention to the outside world is normally enhanced by changes in the techniques of mass communication. But other factors have also come into play, some political, some social, and some psychological. And, for the time being, they all seem to contribute to a decrease in the demand for foreign news.

FEELING VERSUS THINKING: TV OR PRINT?

The decline of the print media and the simultaneous ascendancy of television as the masses' favorite source of information is almost 40 years old now—part of the history of communications technology. Most people lose

vision images can be an inescapable element of foreign policy. After Vietnam, military interventions abroad became highly vulnerable to the American public's low tolerance for casualties in foreign lands. A bloody terrorist attack on a U.S. troop cantonment in Lebanon proved this vulnerability in 1983, and President George Bush may have stopped short of total victory in Iraq in 1991 because he feared that the public would tire of the Persian Gulf war if it dragged on much longer.

Decisions taken vis-à-vis the U.S. intervention in Somalia provide the clearest example to date of the impact on policy of popular reactions to television pictures. The unbearable images of starving infants suckling at the empty breasts of their dying mothers quickly built a popular consensus for the dispatch of U.S. forces to "restore hope" in a desperate country. But a few months later, the equally unbearable spectacle of the twisted and bloodied body of a dead soldier being dragged through the dust of a Mogadishu street by a frenzied mob precipitated the withdrawal of the American troops. The unwritten law that U.S. military interventions abroad must now be swift and bloodless, at least for the GIs, is in part the result of the predominance of the television news show as a means of conveying information.

THE END OF USER-FRIENDLY MANICHAEISM

The end of the Cold War was a turning point in the consumption of foreign news in the United States. Both the media and the public could comprehend the bipolar, Cold War world: There was the good side—the American side—which was dedicated to freedom, democracy, and wealth creation, and it was threatened by the bad side—the Soviet side—

ered between 1970 and 1995, the share of foreign stories fell from 35 per cent to 23 per cent, and the average length of those stories dropped from 1.7 minutes to 1.2 minutes. Worse, while the networks devoted on average more than 40 per cent of total news time to foreign items in the 1970s, that share had been cut to 13.5 per cent of news time by 1995. (See table below.)

Whatever their other failings, the three oldest American television networks—ABC, CBS, and NBC—are at least retaining traces of their common tradition of international journalism. A fourth network, CNN, is struggling to make live global coverage its trademark. The legacy of the Cronkites and the Chancellors of old encourages a semblance of fidelity. But the trend in television consumption is far less comforting. Among the enormous offerings of

CONTINUING DECLINE OF FOREIGN NEWS ON NETWORK TELEVISION				
	1970s	1990–91	1993	1995
Per cent of foreign stories	35	41	24	23
Per cent of time	45	n/a	20	13.5
Average length of foreign story (min.)	1.7	2.2	1.6	1.2

Source: Pippa Norris, Television News Index from the Vanderbilt Archive, author.

which thrived on oppression and deprivation. Anybody who befriended the communists was bad, and anybody who opposed the communists was good. Virtually all world events had to fit that frame of reference to be of interest to the American public. The disappearance of the Soviet Union brought that Manichean framework to an end. As the threat of a nuclear strike faded, so too did the outside world in the American consciousness.

Scholars and professional organizations have studied the effect that the end of the Cold War has had on network television. Since network news shows are by far the main source of foreign news for the American people, they can be regarded as a good gauge of the public's attitude toward the outside world. Now a new trend is clear. Following an exceptional surge in 1990 and 1991, due to America's leading role in the Gulf War more than to the breakup of the Soviet Union, the number and length of foreign topics in the evening news have declined far below Cold War levels. As a percentage of all topics cov-

cable and satellite television, news programs in general—and foreign news in particular—are disappearing in a flood of entertainment and niche-oriented channels.

THE FOUNTAIN AND THE HORSE

It is fashionable among journalists to blame commercial television for the diminishing status of foreign news on the screen. But that is only partially true. The most internationally oriented of the print media—a handful of quality metropolitan dailies—have themselves been led to curtail their foreign coverage in recent years, and their executive editors excuse themselves by pointing to a reduced demand on the part of their readers. In the mid-1990s, when skyrocketing prices for newsprint and a weakened advertising market forced cost-control measures on most newspapers, the foreign news departments were nearly always the first to feel the pinch. Editors meekly recalled *New York Times* pub-

CNN retains only 35 foreign correspondents in 23 foreign bureaus, compared with the nearly 500 correspondents and 100 bureaus supported by each of the major wire services.

lisher A. H. Sulzberger's cute formula: "Along with responsible newspapers we must have responsible readers," because "the fountain serves no useful purpose if the horse refuses to drink."

The Times-Mirror Center for the People & the Press has been measuring the declining interest of the American public in foreign news for years now. Its surveys show that the only international events that still meet with a relatively high level of attention are those in which American forces or major American economic interests are involved. Without speaking of isolationism, it is obvious that the end of the Cold War has turned Americans inward. Surveys conducted every four years by the Chicago Council on Foreign Relations show that the percentage of respondents who perceive "foreign policy problems" to be a high U.S. government priority has dropped from almost 26 per cent in 1986 to 11.5 per cent in 1994. "Protecting the jobs of American workers" now tops "protecting weaker nations against foreign aggression" as a goal of foreign policy by 83 per cent to 24 per cent. Foreign policy issues were widely seen to be irrelevant in the 1996 presidential campaign.

Americans also seem to be feeling a weariness toward a world that is increasingly difficult to decipher. Twenty years ago it was easy to sympathize with peoples struggling to free themselves from dictatorial regimes, particularly if those regimes were communist. Today an endless litany of catastrophes and desperate situations in faraway countries, many of which seem to defy rational explanation, is all the more taxing on the Western world's compassion. Whatever their government's position, people find it difficult to feel any sense of responsibility toward the starv-

ing refugees caught between fighting groups in the jungles of Zaire while the leader of that country basks in the comfort of a palatial home on the French Riviera. Similarly, indifference marks the West's response toward events in Albania, where insurgents reject their government and the opposition alike and appear to be playing into the hands of criminal Mafias.

The globalization of the world economy is reinforcing this tendency to turn inward. An international marketplace where jobs go to the cheapest laborers has replaced nuclear confrontation between the two superpowers as the leading popular nightmare. This fear is especially strong in many developed countries outside the United States where high levels of unemployment threaten national cohesion.

In the United States, as in many other countries, the news horizon is tending to draw closer—from the international to the national and from the national to the local. This is perhaps one reason for the growing acceptance in American news organizations of the "public" journalism concept, which is not much more than the rediscovery of the local community by professionals who had hitherto taken pride in covering wider horizons. There would be a certain irony in seeing our world turn local just as it was about to become global.

INTERACTIVITY AND VIRTUALITY

The paradox of having more information to offer and less demand is nowhere more obvious than on the developing electronic network. In my view, two if its main characteristics—interactivity and virtuality—can have strongly negative effects on an individual's knowledge of and concern for the rest of the world. Radio talk shows, the first and crudest form of interactive communication, are not any worse than the Internet's so-called "news groups," where serious views on the news are seldom exchanged. Such activities generally cater to the primal yearning to be heard and to reinforce one's biases by sharing them with like-minded folks. They are rarely credited with opening anyone's mind and tend to promote simplistic answers to complex issues. The Internet has become the haven for a myriad of one-issue chapels estranged from the rest of the world.

Online customized newspapers are another novelty that does not hold much promise for the circulation of international news and the

Television in the Global Village

AP/Wide World Photos

building of a global village. In the prevailing climate of declining attentiveness to the outside world, there is no reason to believe that their electronic readers will select more foreign news for their self-made journals than they have been reading in the printed versions. To a certain extent, the traditional radio, television, newspaper, or magazine forcefeeds its more-or-less captive audience with an information menu that has been prepared by professional journalists according to their own sense of relevance. In the new interactive forms of information acquisition, the final judgment on the news value of events is instead made by the individual consumer. Since an automatic tally can be kept of what the electronic consumer selects from the news menu, publishers will be ever more inclined to allocate their editorial resources according to the customers' demands. And the foreign news budget is usually the first to lose.

Virtuality—the ability to create a fictitious world using one's computer and to conceal one's identity in dealings with others—is a more diffuse danger against which many commentators have already warned. The recreational function of the computer is usually what most attracts young people to it, and they soon relish the ease with which they can escape into endless galactic wargames. Psychosociologists have conflicting opinions on the influence that this activity may have on children's intellectual formation. But, in the long run, the too frequent immersion into fabricated worlds of make-believe is bound to al-

ienate cybernauts from the all too real world around us.

BOTTOM-UP OR TOP-DOWN DIPLOMACY?

Does it really matter for the United States's foreign relations if the mass media and the general public become less interested in international affairs? We assume that, in a true democracy, the people have a say in how their country's relations with the rest of the world are conducted and that an uninformed public is more likely to pressure its leaders into making inappropriate decisions. But are these proper assumptions?

The "establishment" approach envisions only a small group of specialized journalists, academic researchers, and educated readers taking part in the foreign policy debate with politicians and high officials. In the United States it can be argued that the attentive public for international affairs does not exceed 4 or 5 million people, which happens to coincide with the circulation of the four or five

The Internet has become the haven for a myriad of one-issue chapels estranged from the rest of the world.

most internationally oriented daily newspapers and with the maximum audience of PBS's *NewsHour with Jim Lehrer*. Though an élitist concept, the "establishment" approach has always had some validity and is not likely to be overturned by the new information technologies.

That reality does not necessarily discredit Alexis de Tocqueville's perception that public opinion is the "mistress of the world." As the experiences in Lebanon and Somalia indicate, wide swings in public opinion have led the U.S. government into momentous foreign policy decisions. Other governments may be equally vulnerable to the sway of public opinion.

The élitist and populist views of the foreign policy process are not mutually exclusive, and neither one is threatened with extinction in the Information Age. The interface between public opinion and the management of international relations will probably continue to happen at two levels, as it has for some time now. On the one hand, the day-to-day conduct of most of a country's international relations will remain the preserve of a small, informed establishment with the tacit consent of a relatively indifferent public. On the other hand, circumstances will arise in which the public at large stirs and makes itself heard on foreign policy matters out of a perception, right or wrong, that the very raison d'être of the nation is at stake. In these cases the public will not necessarily react on the basis of knowledge and pertinent information but more likely on the basis of collective emotions aroused by the mass media.

Whether the decisions made at either the élite or the popular level will be wise is another story.

WANT TO KNOW MORE?

There is a large body of work that addresses the media's impact on foreign affairs, the classic text being Walter Lippmann's *Public Opinion* (New York: Penguin, 1922). More recently, Johanna Neuman's *Lights, Camera, War* (New York: St. Martin's Press, 1996) analyzes the effect that television news has on foreign policy.

For an insightful analysis of the progress being made toward global television, read Richard Parker's *Mixed Signals: The Prospects for Global Television News* (New York: The Twentieth Century Fund, 1995). Pippa Norris's *The Restless Searchlight: Network News Framing of the Post Cold War World*, (Cambridge, Mass.: John F. Kennedy School of Government, February 1995) offers a look at the effect that the end of the Cold War had on television foreign news content. And Lawrence Grossman's *Electronic Republic* (New York: Viking, 1995) explores the impact of electronic media on the public policy debate.

The best sources revealing the public's interest in foreign news are periodic surveys released by the Pew Center for the People & the Press in Washington, D.C.

For contrary views on the wired man and the global village, a good starting point is Nicholas Negroponte's *Being Digital* (New York: Knopf, 1995).

To obtain a copy of Claude Moisy's original report, *The Foreign News Flow in the Information Age* (Discussion Paper D-23, Joan Shorenstein Center on the Press, Politics, and Public Policy, John F. Kennedy School of Government, Harvard University, November 1996), write to the Center or call (617) 495-8269.

Unit Selections

Key Points to Consider

❖ To whom do media practitioners owe allegiance in making ethical judgments? Who, besides the subject of a story, is affected by such judgments?

❖ What is your view on the use of deception in investigative journalism? On the use of hidden cameras? On the use of unnamed sources? On the paparazzi? On public service reporting practices as described in "Consumer Alert"? If television ratings and newspaper circulation figures indicate that the public is attracted to stories resulting from these practices, should the press give—or not give—media consumers what they want? Why or why not?

❖ How would you define the rules of "ethical practice"? To what degree do your rules provide guidance for making decisions in the various situations described in this unit's articles?

 **Links**

www.dushkin.com/online/

These sites are annotated on pages 4 and 5.

The freedoms of speech and of the press are regarded as fundamental American rights, protected under the U.S. Constitution. These freedoms, however, are not without some restrictions; the media are held accountable to legal and regulatory authorities, whose involvement reflects a belief that the public sometimes requires protection from irresponsibility.

Regulatory agencies, such as the Federal Communications Commission (FCC), exert influence over media access and content through their power to revoke or limit licenses to operate. They are primarily, though not exclusively, concerned with electronic media because of spectrum scarcity, the limited number of broadcast bands available in any community. In addition, the courts exert influence over media practice through hearing cases of alleged violation of legal principles, such as protection of privacy or protection from libel. Shield laws, which vary from state to state, grant reporters the right to promise informants confidentiality, although they are regularly challenged.

There is, however, a wide grey zone between an actionable offense and an error in judgment. For example, while legal precedence makes it particularly difficult for public figures (those in a position that attracts public attention) to prevail in either libel or invasion-of-privacy cases, it is not necessarily right to print information that might be hurtful to them. Nor is it necessarily wrong to do so. Sometimes being "fair" compromises telling the whole story. Sometimes being "truthful" is insensitive. Sometimes being "interesting" means being exploitive. Media sources are constantly aware that their reporting of an event has the potential of affecting the lives of those involved in it.

The articles in this unit present examples of situations that raise questions of ethical practice. Some media organizations seem to have a greater concern for ethical policy than do others and have attempted to articulate guidelines for practice. However, rules rarely can be applied without considering specific aspects of a particular case. Outright fabrication of facts is considered unethical, but what about the "selective distortion" practiced in times of war, with a goal of maintaining home front morale? This issue is addressed in "Missing on the Home Front." Lying, cheating, and stealing are usually considered unethical (see "Secrets and Lies"), but impersonating a sympathetic lawyer to get inside a criminal operation sometimes wins journalistic commendations. ABC was recently taken to court by the Food Lion grocery chain over a *PrimeTime Live* hidden-camera exposé of unsafe food-handling practices. Interestingly, Food Lion did not pursue this as a libel case and made no claim that the *PrimeTime Live* story was false; rather, they sued based on the fact that the reporters who got hidden camera footage did so by posing as job applicants and being hired and trained by Food Lion without revealing their true motives. This, argued Food Lion's attorneys, was fraud. Food Lion won the case.

When Pennsylvania state treasurer R. Budd Dwyer ended a 1987 press conference by putting a gun in his mouth and killing himself, news crews from stations around the state were left with extremely dramatic film footage—and a question of whether or not the probability of offending viewers' sensitivities and causing pain to Dwyer's family was too great to justify its use. When Ted Bundy murdered Caryn Campbell in Colorado in 1975, her family did not realize that they would have to reexperience their pain for almost 14 years, until Bundy's execution in 1989, as broadcasters reminded their viewers of the local angle in almost every story on the Bundy case. Many news stories deal with tragedy. What are the appropriate rules regarding sensitivity to subjects and those who love them?

Related issues of sensitivity to a story's subjects have been raised regarding the practice of "outing" homosexuals, particularly those in prominent positions, in the interest of gay and lesbian rights. When, if ever, is it appropriate for an advocacy agenda to come into play in making decisions about what constitutes news? What responsibility does a news organization have when the subject of a story threatens to kill him- or herself if the story runs? What should news organizations do when the police request that a story not run in order to avoid compromising an ongoing investigation? Writers struggle with the public's right to know, their sense of responsibility in informing readers/viewers, and their culpability if someone is hurt because of a news story.

Is it ethical for journalists to cover stories on issues about which they have strong personal views, or does such practice compromise objectivity? What about their relationship with sources? Is it fair to become a "friend" to win trust? What kind of favors promised are defensible as reasonable reimbursement for information? Is it fair to break through an interviewee's guard with nine innocent questions and go for the jugular with the tenth? If so, what kind of setup is demanded when editing the comments, since surely the tenth response will be central to the story? What standards apply for communicating the essence of what several people said by creating composite quotes? What standards apply in going public with information from sources who demand anonymity or in deciding whether to honor a subject's request, after the fact, that a piece of information not be used or that it appear without attribution? How much fact-checking is "reasonable" before breaking a story? The article "Consumer Alert" directly or indirectly poses these questions.

Where some sources wish to remain anonymous, others demand to be paid. Does the exchange of money undermine the credibility of a story and of the press? Can mainstream newspapers compete with the tabloids if they do not pay? Were the paparazzi responsible for Princess Diana's death? Should they be held legally responsible for causing harm to those they stalk, or should that responsibility be borne by consumers who buy their products? And what of the well-intentioned story that attempts to right a social wrong but hurts people in the process?

These are not easy questions, and they do not have pat answers. The practice of journalism in the United States is grounded in a legacy of fiercely protected First Amendment rights and shaped by a code of conducting business with a strong sense of moral obligation to society. However, as media writer William Henry has observed, "Whether it is staking out [presidential candidate] Gary Hart's bedroom, probing the background of an alleged rape victim, or pondering the number of months that passed between marriage and childbirth for the wives of Ronald Reagan and televangelist Pat Robertson, the press almost always strikes some people as having gone too far." In the final analysis, no code of conduct can prescribe behavior in every possible situation (see "Starr Turn").

Defining the Rules

George H. Roeder, Jr.

Missing on the Home Front

Wartime Censorship and Postwar Ignorance

World War II played a pivotal role in the education of Americans. In the armed services, in addition to receiving basic military training, many Americans learned how to speak a new language or wire a complex electrical apparatus, to cook for hundreds or break codes, to maintain an airplane engine or an operating room. Trainees viewed films such as Frank Capra's Why We Fight *series that explained important events in world history, albeit doing little to encourage critical thinking.*

Civilians on the home front saw some of these same films, and many learned to identify hundreds of different aircraft or master a new war-generated job. As they followed accounts of the war with keen interest, they learned about the geography of the Soviet Union or the natural resources of Indonesia. Millions of Americans who had never traveled more than a few miles from their birthplace found themselves in distant lands or worked in a war plant far from home. The 1944 Servicemen's Readjustment Act (the "G.I. Bill") extended the impetus to mass education into the postwar period, contributing to a more than doubling of the number of Americans graduating from college between 1940 and 1950.

Wartime policies and circumstances also left a legacy of ignorance. Even as governmental and private organizations provided the public with the massive amounts of information necessary for productive involvement in the war effort, they withheld information deemed detrimental to that effort. This article examines the censorship of visual materials.

Because of the immense popularity of *Life* magazine, other illustrated publications, and newsreels and films, visual imagery played a major role in educating Americans as to the nature of the war. Military personnel reviewed all pictures taken in American war zones and censored many, most for reasons of operational security, but some because they might raise disturbing questions. Hollywood studios, newspaper editors, and others involved in presenting images of the war occasionally disagreed with official policies (as did some in government), but usually made similar choices as to what the public should and should not see of the war. Thousands of recently declassified photographs in the National Archives reveal that censors suppressed images that blurred the distinction between friend and foe, suggested that the war might bring about disruptive social changes, or undermined confidence in the ability of Americans to maintain control over their institutions and their individual lives.

The Images We Did Not See

Photographs published during the war created the impression that American bombs, bullets, and artillery shells killed only enemy soldiers. Pictures of young, elderly, and female victims always ended up in the files of censored images. So did photographs of the residents in allied and occupied countries killed in traffic accidents involving military vehicles. Wartime necessities often required weary soldiers to rush these vehicles through unfamiliar terrain. Investigators visually recorded the numerous casualties that resulted. Authorities censored all the documents they produced, such as a poignant photograph showing a little Italian girl killed by an army truck after American troops occupied the southern part of her country.

"At a time when home front posters impressed on citizens the need to conserve on behalf of the war effort, officials censored images of waste within the military, such as one showing damaged cans of evaporated milk scattered about in an army warehouse in Australia." From *The Censored War: American Visusal Experience During World War Two* by George H. Roeder, Jr. Courtesy of Yale University Press.

Atrocities

The enemy committed all visible atrocities. Officials suppressed photographs of G.I.'s taking Japanese body parts as trophies. On rare occasions visual evidence of this practice slipped through holes in the censorship net, such as when *Life* published in its May 22, 1944, issue a photograph of a prim woman from Arizona looking at a Japanese skull that her Navy boyfriend had managed to get smuggled home to her. He and thirteen friends had signed it and added an inscription: "This is a good jap — a dead one picked up on the New Guinea beach." But officials censored all such photographs under their control, such as a 1945 image of a Japanese soldier's decapitated head hung on a tree branch, probably by American soldiers. This was mainly a phenomenon of the Pacific War; in reviewing thousands of censored photographs and tens of thousands of uncensored ones, I never have encountered one documenting that American soldiers took as trophies body parts of European soldiers.

The wish to maintain clear visual distinctions between friends and enemies was one reason for the decision to remove Americans of Japanese ancestry from coastal areas and place them in guarded camps in sparsely inhabited areas of the West. Although political expediency and unfounded fears of espionage were the main reasons for this action, an Office of War Information bulletin sent to the motion picture industry noted that Japanese-Americans were sent to relocation centers partly because they "*look like* our Japanese enemies." The "censorship" of living human beings accomplished by relocation was reinforced by actions that kept out of view photographs that revealed ironies of the process, such as those taken in 1942 by Dorothea Lange during her brief stint with the War Relocation Authority. One showed a Japanese-American, apparently a retired veteran, reporting to the Santa Anita Park assembly center, a first stage in the relocation process, dressed in his military uniform. The uniform markings and ribbons indicated that he had served in the United States Navy for a period of at least twenty years, stretching back to World War I.

Officials also suppressed evidence of disunity within the Allied camp, such as postwar photographs of the bloody interior of the apartment of an English officer whom two Americans had beaten. The government censored all of the numerous photographs, often gory, of victims of G.I. rapes and murders. G.I. criminals as well as G.I. crimes remained largely out of sight, although *Life* and others published photographs that recorded crimes committed in areas not subject to military censorship. Censorship of G.I. crimes helped minimize attention to potential disruptions within American society related to the war effort.

Race

Race was the touchiest issue. Wartime imagery urged blacks and whites to work harmoniously together in the common cause, but reassured the white majority that this did not require violations of widely accepted social norms. Propaganda took care of the first task, censorship the second. In 1943, after several newspapers ran pictures of African American G.I.s dancing with English women, the Army hastily ordered censors to stop all photographs showing blacks mixing socially with white women. In the war's final year, black troops' "vigorous protest" of this practice led General Dwight David Eisenhower to call for a slight modification of the restrictive policy. He agreed that publication of such photographs would "unduly flame racial prejudice in the United States," but suggested that army censors allow blacks to mail home the photographs after censors stamped them "For personal use only — not for publication." For part of the war the army also refused to release pictures showing wounded members of the black 92nd Division or burials of soldiers from that unit because of the "tendency on part of negro press to unduly emphasize" its achievements.

Not all censors worked for the government. Local newspapers refused a Maryland post commander's request to run a photograph showing an African American G.I. (Dempsey Travis, now a successful Chicago realtor) who had won a prize for the best-managed PX. Such images threatened a racial status quo based on the assumption of black subordination. The activities of Milton Stark show how intertwined government and private

efforts became. Stark, a white who owned several movie theaters with a largely black clientele, also worked as a "racial liaison" for the Office of Emergency Management. During the 1943 Detroit riots he ex-

"Carefully selected images of blacks and whites working together and of black achievements became a more familiar part of the American visual landscape during the war years." From *The Censored War: American Visual Experience During World War Two* by George H. Roeder, Jr. Courtesy of Yale University Press.

pressed concern because All-American News, a company that made newsreels for theaters with predominantly black clientele, had sent cameramen to Detroit. He hoped the company would not show their footage because that "would serve only to spread further disunity and racial prejudice throughout the entire country." Stark reported that he had talked to the company head, who assured him "that all material in the reels will be *favorable* rather than inflammatory." Stark added, "I feel I can control this to a large de-

gree, since contracts for the newsreel service to theaters which I control personally will represent a large percentage of the total income possibilities of the project." He exaggerated his own economic power, but Stark's position was consistent with that of others in government and business on whose support All-American depended. The company never ran a story on the Detroit riots.

Images of Death

The government initially censored all photographs of Americans who had died in battle, then began releasing such photographs when Allied successes caused officials to be more concerned that the public would take victory for granted than that they would become demoralized. Throughout the war officials censored photographs of the American dead that showed decapitation, dismemberment, and limbs twisted or frozen into unnatural positions. The government censored disturbing images of war's mayhem as it affected Americans for many reasons: out of respect for the feelings of family members, because of a widely shared sense of propriety, and because horrific pictures of the American dead seemed unlikely to help the government's ongoing recruiting efforts. But the army also censored such images because they did not fit seamlessly into a master narrative emphasizing the "we have everything under control" quality of the American war effort. This led the army not only to censor photographs of a field littered with bits of human flesh after the explosion of an ammunition truck, but also photographs of a soldier who fell to his death from a window, and numerous others documenting G. I. suicides.

Newspapers did run stories that described government mismanagement. However, photographs and film footage from combat areas almost always were presented in a way that reassured readers and viewers that the American war effort was rational not only in its overall goals, but in all of its details, including the mission assigned every soldier. In September of 1943, *Life* accompanied its first photograph of Americans killed in the war — George Strock's powerful, elegantly composed picture of three American soldiers lying dead on Buna Beach in New Guinea — with a full-page editorial. The editors drew on familiar sports imagery to guide viewers' responses: "we are still aware of the relaxed self-confidence with which the leading boy ran into the sudden burst of fire — almost like a halfback carrying the ball down a football field." Such presentations, combined with censorship of photographs showing American corpses piled on top of one another or being tossed onto trucks, placed each American death into a context that made it consistent with a well-ordered life and world.

Maintaining this impression of order required the suppression of photographs that revealed incompetence, irrationality, or loss of control in the United States war effort. Photographs censored at least in part for these reasons ranged from ones that showed Americans and others killed or wounded by allied "friendly fire" or other military blunders to those that showed turkeys intended for soldiers' Thanksgiving meals strewn over the floor of an army warehouse because of careless handling. In addition to suppressing evidence of disorder on the organizational level, the army censored photographs that might raise doubts about how completely individual American soldiers had control of their own behavior. Without such control, how could they consistently resist sliding into undisciplined modes of behavior attributed

only to the enemy? Thus censors kept soldiers visibly suffering from severe mental stress out of sight throughout the war and after, despite their large numbers. None of the censored pictures I have encountered in my research illustrate more vividly the human inability to keep complete control over war's chaos than those of "shell shocked" soldiers screaming and flailing out at their fellow soldiers and at the horror of their situation.

Throughout the war officials censored photographs of the American dead that showed decapitation, dismemberment, and limbs twisted or frozen into unnatural positions.

The Consequences of Ignorance

I agree with decisions that kept out of view those photographs of soldiers in the midst of mental breakdowns in cases where publication would have violated the privacy of individuals. However, censors suppressed many pictures not to protect individuals, but to conceal unpalatable truths. The images which Americans encountered during World War II sustained a less complex understanding of the nature and meaning of that war than Americans might have achieved had they also seen the censored images. Visual expurgation of black achievements, unpalatable to many because they undermined belief in white supremacy, hindered postwar struggles against racial bigotry. Visual denial that American soldiers sometimes lost control of themselves left citizens ill-prepared to evaluate their country's policies in Vietnam, or understand the experiences of the young men who fought there.

These shortcomings in the edu-

cation of the American public took on special significance when the United States emerged from World War II with more economic, technological, and military power than any country had ever possessed. Visual acknowledgment during the war of the uncertainties, injustices, and potential miseries attendant upon the exercise of such power, even on behalf of good causes, might have encouraged more circumspect use of it in the following decades, whether

for interventions abroad, or for environmentally and socially consequential projects at home.

Censorship decisions made fifty years ago continue to have consequences. The Smithsonian Institution, under intense pressure from Congress and veterans' organizations, recently canceled plans to include photographs of the victims of the atomic bombing of Hiroshima in its exhibition of the plane that dropped the bomb, the *Enola Gay*. This is consistent with wartime censorship policies and with official practices since then. The site of the exhibition, the Smithsonian's National Air and Space Museum, never has displayed pictures of the victims of Allied bombing. Although debates over the decision to drop the bomb will continue throughout the lifetime of all readers of this article, there can be no doubt that it caused great suffering. Documenting this suffering in an exhibition on the bombing does not imply criticism of the decision to use the bomb, but commitment to historical truth. This truth includes commitment to the proposition that actions have consequences and acknowledgment that in actual historical situations, good and evil are seldom delineated as clearly as they are in most of the war movies made between 1941 and 1945.

Such acknowledgment would help visitors comprehend two clashing ideas about World War II. The first is that American involvement in that war helped bring about the defeat of repugnant and dangerous authoritarian regimes. Allied victory greatly improved the prospect of a dignified life for hundreds of millions of people in the postwar world. Those who contributed to this victory deserve the respect and gratitude of future generations. The second idea is that the nature of this most costly of all wars ensured

that one consequence of American involvement would be infliction of terrible pain on people of all ages in many different countries. The suffering that occurred under the mushroom clouds in Hiroshima and Nagasaki in August of 1945 was unique in some ways, in that it included radiation sickness and other new horrors, but it also was representative of what war had become by that date, when all countries involved abandoned distinctions between military and civilian targets. Whatever the obstacles, American educational institutions such as the Smithsonian Institution must do everything they can to encourage this simultaneous comprehension of difficult-to-mesh realities. As the

destructive power at humanity's disposal increases, so does the cost of ignorance.

George H. Roeder, Jr. is the chair of the Undergraduate Division in the School of the Art Institute of Chicago and a lecturer in history at Northwestern University. His recent publications include "The Visual Arts" in Stanley Kutler, ed., *Encyclopedia of the United States in the Twentieth Century* (MacMillan, 1995) and *The Censored War: American Visual Experience During World War II* (Yale University Press, 1993; paperback edition, 1995).

Three shows. Twenty stories.* They report. You decide.

CONSUMER ALERT

IF YOU SCARE THEM, THEY WILL WATCH. WHEN IT COMES TO CONSUMER reporting, that could be a slogan for the television newsmagazine shows. NBC News's *Dateline NBC,* and ABC News's *20/20* and *PrimeTime Live* regularly run alarming stories about bad products and shady businesses that seem designed to worry viewers into paying attention, and sometimes viewers should be concerned. In fact, we found that, for the most part, these shows *do* provide a public service: in-depth reporting,

BY ELIZABETH JENSEN, D.M. OSBORNE, ABIGAIL POGREBIN, AND TED ROSE

varied viewpoints, and helpful tips. But we also found that the bad products in question were not always quite so bad, the shady businesses not always quite so shady, and viewers were not always getting the information they need to make reasoned decisions on their own.

We decided to focus on two years—1995 and 1996—to give us a slice of the consumer reporting by the major newsmagazines. We went back that far intentionally. The passage of time allows perspective. We looked at 20 stories—an arbitrary sampling of roughly 100 consumer reports aired by the three programs. (We did not look at CBS News's *60 Minutes*, the grandfather of investigative broadcast journalism, because the show had no segments of this type during the years we examined. Executive producer Don Hewitt says, "The people who work for me haven't come up with any stories in the category you're asking about, and if they did, we would do them.")

In every case, we checked the facts presented, attempted to talk to the main subjects, and gauged the overall fairness of the reports. Though ambiguity stalked our inquiry, we forced ourselves to make decisions about whether each story was basically "fair" or "unfair," and then to explain why in detail.

After much debate, we found 12 of 20 to be fair overall, despite a tendency—even in these segments—toward overplaying danger or heart-wrenching footage, the kind of viewer-grabbing hype that can obscure whatever caveats may be offered.

We judged eight of the 20—40 percent—unfair, because in these segments the hype went too far.

The unfair reports shared common flaws. When re-reported by us, stories that seemed solid on their face proved to have distorted or omitted facts or interviews. Had those facts or competing opinions been included, the resulting stories would have been different—not necessarily less compelling but certainly more balanced and thus more accurate. Dissecting these 20 segments gave us new insight into the type of reporting these shows like to trumpet as public-service journalism at its best. For a primer on how to watch these programs—indeed, on how to appreciate the tricks of the trade—see page 133.

Without having scrutinized every segment from these years, we can't draw conclusions about the quality of consumer reporting offered by any one show. In our sample, we determined that three of six *20/20* segments were fair, five of six *PrimeTime Live* pieces were fair, and four of eight *Dateline* segments were fair.

Unlike many—if not most—of the traditional daily national newscasts, these magazine shows generate huge profits. According to ad rates compiled by *Advertising Age*, the average one-hour newsmagazine can expect to gross roughly $2.7 million. That's for a program that costs up to $700,000 to produce—compared to $1 to $2 million in production costs for a standard hour-long drama, according to Tom Wolzien, a media analyst at Sanford C. Bernstein & Co. Inc. It is this economic reality that accounts, in large part, for the recent, phenomenal proliferation of these programs. (As of this writing, there are 12 hours of newsmagazines each week.) NewsTV Corporation, a news monitoring service, reported in August that "the major networks have increased the number of one-hour newsmagazines by 142 percent over the last three years...NBC led the pack with a 129 percent increase."

There's a cynical saying in newsrooms: "Never let the facts get in the way of a good story." There is always a temptation to simplify in order to capture and hold an audience. Toward this goal, news magazines strive to present clear heroes and villains, as well as a clear moral to every tale. Too often, what's lost in the process is the kind of even-handed presentation that the subjects of such investigations deserve.

All forms of media risk unfairness and hype in the cause of fashioning simple, catchy story lines. Our own cover headline, ("These TV Magazine Shows May Scare You About Products You Shouldn't Fear,") would be guilty of this if, for example, we ended up reporting inside that only one or two stories were suspect—rather than what we are reporting in detail: that 40 percent of those we examined were unfair, and that even the "fair" segments often presented a too-scary picture.

Some of those responsible for these shows say time and format prevent them from including every opinion and detail. We recognize those constraints, but they cannot and should not excuse burying relevant facts, offering incomplete or exaggerated statistics, or excluding a voice that may challenge preconceptions or change viewers' minds. Too often, when we peeled away the neat conclusions, we found stories that had misled more than they informed; too often, the public service that might have been performed was negated by misinformation. And, if a picture paints a thousand words, the well-produced pictures on these programs tended to obscure the words. It's hard to focus on caveats and provisos when viewing a picture of an eight-year-old who was ejected from the family minivan and killed. In fact, it's hard to remember anything but the victims—one tragic tale after another, usually filled with teary survivors, poignant home video, and accident photos that can overwhelm even the most balanced reporting.

We are not suggesting that the makers of this kind of television intend to dupe their audiences. Rather, in the drive to produce gripping television, facts and fair comment too frequently yield to hype and spin. This happens gradually, with compromise after compromise eroding a fair representation of the facts.

Both ABC News and NBC News maintain that their news-magazine consumer reports are fair. "Sometimes in telling a story, we personalize it by telling it from an individual point of view," says Cory Shields, an NBC News spokesman. "We tell the story and let our viewers come to their own conclusions. The human side of the story makes it much more relevant to viewers, but it's never our intention to overhype."

Says ABC News spokeswoman Eileen Murphy: "We have a strict procedure in place to ensure that the drama and power of a story does not overwhelm the facts." Often, she notes, "We conclude that including the real effects on real people is the only way to tell the story completely and to tell it fairly. All of our pieces should be judged in their context and their totality, the way our viewers receive them." Both news organizations say their reports are subject to strict reviews, including those conducted by network attorneys, before they go on the air. "We are confident in the review process and believe it helps us produce high-quality journalism," says Murphy.

Some corporate press representatives say they have become wary of these shows and often decline to be interviewed. Says one corporate spokesman: "It's like, 'Ready, aim, fire! And, oh by the way, do you have any last words?'" Producers say that that's too bad: If a company believes it has the truth on its side, it should make its best case. These companies say no—cooperating has burned them once too often.

ABC's Murphy says, "It should come as no surprise that some of the companies on whose products we report are not always happy with the attention....We treat all interview subjects fairly, but ultimately it is up to the company to decide what is in their own best interest." NBC's Shields says company response can ensure that *Dateline* gets correct information. "There are numerous instances of, after having done our homework and research, we concluded there was no story there and we just walked away."

Senior writer Elizabeth Jensen was a media reporter for The Wall Street Journal. *Senior writer D.M. Osborne was a senior reporter at* The American Lawyer *magazine. Senior writer Abigail Pogrebin was a producer for Mike Wallace at CBS News' 60 Minutes. Staff writer Ted Rose was an associate producer at* Dateline NBC.

THE FOOT DOCTORS 20/20: APRIL 14, 1995
PRODUCER: DONALD THRASHER   CORRESPONDENT: TOM JARRIEL

IN OCTOBER 1992, PODIATRIST EDWARD FISCHMAN RECEIVED a letter from ABC's 20/20 inviting him to go undercover as part of an investigation of "doctors with questionable qualifications." A founder and past president of two boards of podiatric surgery accredited by the American Podiatric Medical Association, Fischman had recently called for a crackdown on "bogus" medical boards, and he leapt at the chance. He ventured to Las Vegas wearing a hidden camera and easily obtained a phony certificate as a "podiatric plastic surgeon."

"I was so excited, because I thought, finally, we're going to get some national attention for this problem," remembers Fischman. But when the 20/20 segment finally aired, he says he was "shocked." Correspondent Tom Jarriel reported that "critics" claimed the nearly 14,000-member podiatric profession was "riddled with doctors who operate storefront clinics, use unsafe medical practices, and make money through insurance claims for unnecessary surgery."

Fischman, who says he was quoted out of context, appeared to vouch for 20/20's sweeping claims. "They made it look like I was trashing all boards, including my own," he says.

Officials at the American Podiatric Medical Association say they provided 20/20 with ample information proving that the podiatric field is not full of quacks. The APMA documented the increasing role played by podiatrists in veterans hospitals and in salvaging limbs among diabetics. The group also told producer Donald Thrasher that regulators in 42 states require podiatrists to complete one-year post-doctoral hospital residencies.

But in the March 21 interview at the APMA's Bethesda, Maryland, headquarters, Jarriel had "no interest in showing anything positive about podiatry," says the APMA's executive director, Glenn Gastwirth. "In just about every question he asked, there was a distortion of the facts."

Two days after that interview, APMA's public relations director, Geoge Tzamaras, asked 20/20 for a follow-up meeting to clarify what the APMA perceived as inaccuracies in Jarriel's questioning. According to an APMA April 28, 1995 letter to 20/20 executive producer Victor Neufeld, Tzamaras "made no fewer than 20 telephone calls to Mr. Thrasher's office over the next three weeks and got not the courtesy of a single return call until shortly after 12 noon on April 14, the air date," at which time Tzamaras was told it was too late to make any changes.

Watching the program, Tzamaras says he was horrified. Four scenes featured the same hawker, handing out leaflets and hollering "Free foot exam!" Jarriel pointed to a podiatrist who had relocated to the Chicago area from Nashville after losing two malpractice suits and settling 13 others. The out-of-context comments by podiatrist Fischman compounded the negative image of podiatry and seemed to support claims made by a New York state Medicaid-fraud prosecutor, who estimated that 75 to 90 percent of all billings by podiatrists and orthopedics were fraudulent.

In his interview with Jarriel, the APMA's Gastwirth disputed the prosecutor's figures as grossly inaccurate. Hiram Shirel, executive director of the New York State Podiatric Medical Association, concurs with Gastwirth. But 20/20 presented the prosecutor's claims without an APMA response.

Indeed, although Gastwirth says Jarriel "asked me about everything in the segment," 20/20 used only two of his comments, which is the main reason this segment fails to meet the fairness test. Both of the APMA's comments were reserved for the very end of the segment—one of them in response to

Jarriel's question, "Are you developing a tent of sleaze here with the podiatry business?"

In a cursory exchange with anchor Barbara Walters at the segment's conclusion, Jarriel did describe the APMA as "a good organization." At that point, positive comments carried no resonance. "Of course there are many very good podiatrists," Walters said, contradicting almost everything else in the show.

20/20 offered no response to questions concerning this piece. When pressed on the specific issue of fairness however, a spokesperson says, "We wouldn't have put the piece on the air if we didn't think it was fair."   —*DMO*

THE FOOT DOCTORS

A tawdry picture of podiatry, this report could have performed a consumer service by alerting people to the dangers of unaccredited foot doctors. Instead, *20/20* presented an overwhelmingly one-sided and negative story that tarred an entire profession.

RATING ☹ UNFAIR

● Out-of-context quotes created misleading impression
● Industry response limited to two comments at end

TRICKS OF THE TRADE

The consumer reports we viewed often followed a fairly predictable script—and presented an equally predictable cast of characters. Here are nine tips to keep in mind when viewing such reports:

1. Watch for opening bias. Opening statements can establish a false prism through which the rest of the piece is viewed. Often, openers take the form of a provocative question, such as this one from a *20/20* story: "Tonight, a traveler's advisory: is the cabin air you breathe hazardous to your health?" By the end of the program, the answer was still unclear—but the fear had been instilled.

2. Compare the hype to what is actually reported. Even the fairest reports can be over-hyped to attract viewers. Consider *PrimeTime Live*'s piece on the potential dangers of mixing alcohol and Tylenol. The grabby opener states that when Tylenol is "taken by people who drink alcohol regularly, there can be disastrous results." In fact, the potential problem only applies to people who consume more than three drinks daily.

3. Don't let pictures overwhelm the facts. The shows' common injunction: keep viewers hooked. They fear you'll switch the channel if their reports are slowed down by dry testimony from experts. Yet the interviews with teary family members, heart-wrenching home videos, and footage of victims—such as the child disfigured by burns in *20/20*'s piece on flammable plastic—can skew your impression of how safe a product actually is.

4. Beware of critics with an agenda. *Dateline*'s reporter didn't challenge toy cop Ed Swartz on whether he profits from finding faulty toys. Swartz is a plaintiffs attorney specializing in suing companies for their allegedly defective products.

5. Listen carefully for the buried truth. If the problem has been fixed, the story isn't as strong. *PrimeTime Live* dramatized the dangers of sightseeing helicopters in Hawaii before noting that the government had already taken steps to correct the problems there.

6. Beware white hats or black hats. The clearest stories have a victim and a villain—so shows sometimes try to find them, even when they don't exist. *Dateline*'s otherwise worthwhile report about improperly secured child car safety seats pinned most of the blame on car dealers alone, when there were other guilty parties.

Similarly, stories are more compelling if they are black and white, but the truth is often gray. MET-Rx, a protein supplement, had its critics, but it also had a credible supporter with arguably better credentials. *Dateline* ignored him.

7. Listen for questions that have a predictable but dramatic answer. *PrimeTime*'s Chris Wallace is a master at eliciting the kind of dramatic quotes that make segments more compelling, but that are not surprising given the person being asked. A report on the risks of combining Tylenol and alcohol included this exchange: Wallace: "Mr. Benedi, what destroyed your liver?" Benedi: "Tylenol destroyed my liver." Just six weeks later, in a piece on the debate over the safety of the bug repellent DEET, Wallace asked: "Ms. Christensen, what killed your husband?" "The chemical DEET that is used in bug repellents," she answered.

8. Remember that numbers can lie. Or at least they can be made to say anything. *Dateline*'s report about escalators overstated the problem. *20/20*'s report on Chrysler minivans' rear latches was accurate on its face, but didn't mention that Chrysler minivans were safer overall than others.

9. Look for the disclaimer at the end. It is often crucial to watch to the very end, where important balance and perspective lands, as if to absolve the telecast from its previous overstatements. An example: *20/20*'s caveat that not all podiatrists are as shady as those in its preceding report.

MOVING VIOLATIONS DATELINE: NOVEMBER 29, 1995
PRODUCER: JOHN GRASSIE   CORRESPONDENT: CHRIS HANSEN

PICTURES OF A MONASTERY'S STAINED GLASS AND THE SOUND OF organ music opened *Dateline*'s piece about injuries to children caused by aging escalators, seen partly through the eyes of a nun who became an activist on the issue after an escalator injured her nephew.

Dateline focused on serious entrapment injuries, those caused when clothing and body parts get caught in the gap between an escalator's steps and its side wall. The piece, punctuated by the account of a young victim, also looked at a remedy and explored why it had not been universally adopted.

The piece stated that the nun "found out that, according to the federal government, currently more than 16,000 people a year are sent to emergency rooms because of escalator accidents." In fact, the U.S. Consumer Product Safety Commission estimates that the number of emergency room-treated escalator injuries is about 5,500 annually, based on an average of incidents reported over a 24-year period. (For 1994, the year before the *Dateline* segment aired, the figure was 7,300 injuries.) Moreover, the vast majority of those injuries are falls, not entrapments, according to the CPSC: of 6,500 accidents in 1997, about 800 were entrapment-related. "The statistics that they used on escalator injuries were exaggerated and misleading," says CPSC spokesman Russ Rader. (It should be noted that the commission doesn't have actual figures; it derives its numbers using a sample of hospital emergency rooms.)

Producer John Grassie says NBC's figure was obtained from and verified with three different sources: the CPSC itself, the Elevator Escalator Safety Foundation, and a speech given by an executive with the Otis Elevator Co., a leading escalator manufacturer. But Ray Lapierre, executive director of the Elevator Escalator Safety Foundation, says his organization doesn't track accident statistics. And Otis spokesman Peter Kowalchuk says that when the *Date-*line piece aired "we at Otis were surprised and frustrated because we did not believe that that was an accurate number. It was much too high." *Dateline* stands by its report.

Grassie says that many of the injuries that do happen are "horrific, rather than cursory incidents," and adds, "Any parent, or anyone riding an escalator, should at least have some knowledge" of what can happen under certain circumstances.

Indeed, the issue, if less of a danger than *Dateline* indicated, is real, and had been the subject of an earlier *Boston Globe* investigation. The *Globe* piece, which also looked at elevator accidents, "certainly influenced our thinking," says Grassie, although he notes that the two reports took different tacks. CPSC spokesman Rader says the agency has "been prodding the industry for some time" to voluntarily address the entrapment issue, "and they have not done so." In 1996, the commission's staff began looking closely at the problem, and is expected to make a recommendation to the commissioners this fall about whether to create a mandatory standard to deal with escalator hazards. —*EJ*

MOVING VIOLATIONS

A nun who became an escalator-safety advocate after her nephew was hurt in an accident made a compelling storyteller, but, as *Dateline* noted, her story was 19 years old. There was a bigger problem with this piece, which focused on accidents where children's feet or clothing became entrapped in a gap between an escalator's steps and its side wall: *Dateline* overstated the number of escalator accidents, according to the U.S. Consumer Product Safety Commission.

RATING ☹ UNFAIR

● Entrapment issue is serious, and federal government has been pushing industry to address it voluntarily

● Vastly overstated number of accidents, creating misleading impression

---

BAD APPLES DATELINE: NOVEMBER 12, 1996
PRODUCER: SANDRA DENNISON   CORRESPONDENT: ROB STAFFORD

BAD APPLES

This report jumped on a serious outbreak of E. coli poisoning caused by unpasteurized apple juice, a previously unknown source of the bacteria. In measured tones, it laid out the problem and told consumers what to do to protect themselves.

RATING ☺ FAIR

● Straightforward reporting about potential new consumer risk

DATELINE TOOK THIS REPORT STRAIGHT FROM HEADLINES REPORTING ON a rash of E. coli-related illnesses connected to a previously unsuspected source: unpasteurized apple juice. Billed as a "consumer alert," this short report did just that: In a serious, non-hyped manner, it quickly disseminated to consumers important information about a potential new health risk, highlighting the case of one young boy who was sickened by tainted juice but had recovered.

The threat was later proven to be a serious one; the manufacturer of the juice in question paid a record fine in late July because of the outbreak. That same month, the FDA issued new rules requiring warning labels on unpasteurized juice. —*EJ*

THE SHELL GAME/A RAW DEAL? DATELINE: MAY 15, SEPTEMBER 17, 1996
PRODUCER: JOSEPH RHEE   CORRESPONDENT: LEA THOMPSON

THE SHELL GAME/A RAW DEAL?

The two-part report exposed the risks of eating raw shellfish. Report limited the gut-wrenching tales of sick people, emphasizing instead the alarming ease with which poachers harvest and sell contaminated oysters and clams. *Dateline* accompanied shellfish police on two night missions, both times catching poachers in sewage-infested waters. While shellfish supporters now decry a misleading spin on successful law enforcement efforts, other evidence is harder to dispute: Posing as poachers, *Dateline* peddled nine bags of unmarked clams to seafood buyers apparently unconcerned with labeling laws designed to protect consumers.

RATING ☺ FAIR

- May have exaggerated extent of poaching problem
- Rich variety of sources attested to problem
- Industry spokesman fairly and accurately presented

MICHAEL VOISIN OF MOTIVATIT SEAFOODS, INC., SERVED AS AN INDUSTRY spokesman for *Dateline*'s shellfish series, and claims the show exaggerated the magnitude of the problem. Three poachers caught red-handed in the segments "weren't major commercial operations," he says, arguing that *Dateline* could have suggested that the arrests it captured on tape prove that anti-poaching efforts work.

Ken Moore, executive director of the Interstate Shellfish Sanitation Conference in Columbia, South Carolina, concurs with Voisin, emphasizing that clams imported from England—not illegally harvested in the U.S.—account for the high rate of illness that *Dateline* reported in New York state.

Still, correspondent Lea Thompson interviewed a variety of sources who attested to the problem, including a poacher-turned-government informant and a professional fisherman who explained that poachers "bring a lot of hardship on the industry."

Thompson and producer Joseph Rhee did take some cheap shots: In-your-face camera confrontations with managers at three seafood processing plants undercut the overall integrity of the segments. —*DMO*

THE REAL McCOY? PRIMETIME LIVE: MAY 29, 1996
PRODUCERS: ANN SORKOWITZ, ELAINE PAPPAS-GRABER   CORRESPONDENT: CHRIS WALLACE

NO ONE QUIBBLES WITH THE SCAM BROUGHT TO LIGHT BY THIS piece—the fakes that are increasingly making their way into the fast-growing antiques business and fooling even some dealers, not to mention less-experienced collectors. But the examples used in this report—obtained via dramatic undercover video of dealers misrepresenting what they were selling—were so easy to spot that it was like shooting "fish in a barrel," wrote Samuel Pennington, editor of the well-respected *Maine Antique Digest*, in an editorial following the show. For example, he wrote, "the '1820 chest' was way too narrow, had wrong ball feet and screamed stylistic mishmash."

"They oversimplified things," Pennington recalls. "TV never does anything complicated. Everything is simplified so the lowest viewer can get it." Still, he concedes, the truly sophisticated frauds that are showing up and that the *Digest* points out to its readers, "are probably of interest to less than one percent of the viewers."

THE REAL McCOY?

The problem of fakes in the burgeoning antique business was highlighted with undercover footage of *PrimeTime* employees buying fraudulent goods. *PrimeTime* concentrated on the easy-to-spot fakes, however, ignoring the highly sophisticated frauds on the market. Also ignored: the majority of dealers who are reputable.

RATING ☺ FAIR

- Fake antiques are a growing problem in an unregulated business
- Report could have delved deeper and made clear that most dealers are reputable

ABC spokeswoman Eileen Murphy says the network disagrees with Pennington and believes the report "provided important information to consumers of antiques." —*EJ*

TOYING WITH DANGER DATELINE: NOVEMBER 15, 1995
PRODUCER: JOHN GRASSIE   CORRESPONDENT: LEA THOMPSON

THE TITLE CLUES YOU IN: THIS REPORT WON'T GIVE PARENTS PEACE of mind. It's a high-profile platform for Massachusetts attorney Edward Swartz, plaintiffs lawyer and self-appointed toy cop. Swartz has been making his annual list of dangerous toys for three decades; it's a roster tailor-made for the media at Christmastime. *Dateline* did not approach Swartz's list with any discernible skepticism. Correspondent Lea Thompson went on an undercover shopping spree as Swartz led the way; she never challenged his assertions about what made a toy unsafe.

While Swartz is obviously entitled to his opinions, the U.S. Consumer Product Safety Commission's findings undermine his record in identifying dangerous toys: ninety-five percent of the toys on his annual hit list actually comply with federal laws. "We don't judge our success by the toys that are banned," counters Swartz, who insists federal standards are inadequate.

Producer John Grassie says the show didn't report on how rarely the Swartz-targeted toys actually violate federal law because that isn't what is important to consumers. "To the parent of a child who purchases a toy," says Grassie, "whether it's ninety-five percent or five percent, the issue is the same: safety for the child. . . . These percentages don't do you any good if your kid is choking to death."

To the Toy Manufacturers of America, Swartz is Darth Vader, a doomsayer who sees a disaster in every toy box. "If you took every household product that was firm or hard, you would have nothing but deadly weapons," says TMA president David Miller, who was interviewed in the *Dateline* segment. He says toy companies would be stupid to knowingly market dangerous toys. "Ed Swartz has made a business out of crying wolf for the last thirty years," says Miller. "He's essentially an ambulance chaser; he is in business to sue toy companies."

Although Miller made this point about Swartz's potential self-interest on camera, there was no follow-up by Thompson. Grassie points out that Swartz was identified as an attorney and says viewers know what that means: "If I introduce F. Lee Bailey on camera, do I have to go through a list of his clients?"

Thompson also described Swartz as a "toy-safety crusader," whose "books, lawsuits, and the release of his worst-toy list each holiday season have led to dozens of recalls." (She neglected to mention that many more dozens of the toys he's targeted *haven't* been recalled.)

Swartz says, "Of course I'm a plaintiffs lawyer. If I was a doctor treating cancer, does that mean that I wouldn't want to find a cure for cancer? I'm using my expertise to try to put myself out of business." He suggests the toy companies hate him because "they know damn well I know what I'm doing."

TOYING WITH DANGER

Dateline presented Edward Swartz's list of terrible toys too uncritically. The show did not explore whether Swartz's profession—he's a plaintiff's attorney who specializes in suing companies over their illegally defective products—might prejudice his findings, nor was there any mention of the fact that most of the toys on his list comply with federal standards. The toy trade association representative was given air time but was arguably not the right person to respond to specific charges about each toy. As for the toy companies, one claims it was given little time to respond; another says it was never offered the chance to rebut Swartz's charges on camera. The producer admits he did not offer any of the companies that opportunity.

RATING ☹ UNFAIR

- Swartz was presented without discernable skepticism. Thompson never challenged his assertions on camera.
- *Dateline* did not tell viewers that government says 95 percent of toys on Swartz's list every year meet federal standards
- *Dateline* did not pursue Swartz's potential financial interest in finding bad toys

Swartz and the government do agree some of the time; two of the toys singled out in this 1995 *Dateline* segment were ultimately recalled. But other toys he flagged were not so obviously dangerous—the Grand Slam Bubble Bat from Cadaco, for instance. Shaped like a baseball bat, Swartz said "this is a weapon. Running around chasing bubbles with his heavy bat? It's a toy that's just going to cause misery for somebody."

"Any kid can pick up any product and hit another kid with it, no matter what it is," says Cadaco director of marketing Mark Abramson. "It was a sensationalist report." Cadaco felt sandbagged, Abramson says, because Grassie gave the company virtually no time to prepare a written response before the segment aired: "He called the night or the day before." Replies Grassie: "All the [inquiries] went out as per recommendation by NBC's attorneys," an explanation that suggests NBC was more interested in protecting a legal position than in balanced reporting.

Grassie acknowledges that none of the toy companies mentioned were invited to respond on camera.

Last November, ABC News's *20/20* killed a similar segment on Swartz's list of shame. ABC spokesman Chris Alexander explained the cancellation this way to *The Boston Globe*: "After conducting our own tests on the toys, we made an editorial decision not to go forward." —*AP*

JUST SAY NO DATELINE: FEBRUARY 14, 1996
PRODUCER: JOHN REISS   CORRESPONDENT: LEA THOMPSON

DATELINE DID NOT BASE ITS REPORT SOLELY ON THE CLAIMS OF A federal prosecutor pressing fraud charges against the Quadro Corporation. Correspondent Lea Thompson conducted two tests of the tracking device in Florida with a school security coordinator who had purchased a Tracker to use on the job. "With the help of a police officer," Thompson noted, *Dateline* hid a bag of marijuana—first in a student's locker, then in Thompson's pocket. Guided by the Tracker's free-floating, antenna-like pointer, the coordinator walked right past the contraband both times.

After a Quadro vice-president blamed the poor results on the searcher's training, Thompson conducted another round of tests. This time the hunter had been trained by Quadro. In four out of five cases, the Tracker again failed.

In every instance that someone challenged the Tracker, Thompson and producer John Reiss cut back to the Quadro vice-president, who was clearly responding to specific, direct questions. For example, after a scientist hired by the Justice Department to examine the Tracker explained that his laboratories had found no circuits, no conductors, and no electrical connections, *Dateline* presented a complete response from the company representative: "We're able to read the frequency of a particular substance and recreate that frequency in carbon crystals," he explained. "Then we use our bodies' magnetic field, and our bodies' static current to oscillate this frequency to make it communicate with a substance."

JUST SAY NO

When a federal judge in Beaumont, Texas, temporarily halted sales of the Quadro Tracker 250G in January 1996, NBC's *Dateline* was among the first national television news outfits on the scene, and in short order had assembled a thoroughly documented "consumer alert." The report explained how police and school security officers eager to wipe out drugs in their communities apparently had been seduced by a company peddling a high-priced, low-tech divining rod. Ample responses from the manufacturer bolstered the story, allowing viewers to weigh the evidence themselves.

RATING ☺ FAIR

- Assertions of magician not verified
- Company commented in direct response to each attack on its product
- After company representatives challenged results of two dismal product tests, *Dateline* re-tested, using someone trained by the company

---

"They managed to get in both sides of the story," observes Daryl Fields, a spokesman for the Beaumont, Texas, federal prosecutor at the time of *Dateline*'s report. "It was very fair, so that the individual sitting at home watching the TV set would have all the information necessary to make an appropriate decision."

To be sure, not everyone was convinced the Tracker was a *deliberate* hoax. Although the prosecutor obtained a permanent injunction barring sales of the device in April 1996, he failed to convince a jury that the manufacturer was guilty of fraud. —*DMO*

HOW SAFE A RIDE? PRIMETIME LIVE: JANUARY 18, 1995
PRODUCERS: ABBY HIRSCH, LEO MEIDLINGER, PAUL MASON   CORRESPONDENT: SAM DONALDSON

THE SEGMENT BEGAN WITH VIDEO OF MELISSA AND PETER BLAKE on their wedding day in July 1994. By the time the pair rushed past flying popcorn on their way to a Hawaiian honeymoon, viewers could guess that the trip had not gone as planned. In fact, the tourist helicopter carrying the Blakes crashed into the Pacific Ocean, and Melissa Blake seriously damaged her back. It was an accident that did not have to happen, Sam Donaldson said. A *PrimeTime* investigation, he reported, "uncovered [safety] problems" in the tourist-helicopter industry and "raise[d] disturbing questions about the federal government's supervision of sightseeing helicopter companies."

The segment accurately reported the government's conclusion that the injuries suffered by those involved in the Blakes' July 14 accident (and in a second, unrelated accident the same day) resulted partially from the absence of pontoon devices and accessible life vests on the helicopters, as well as from inadequate passenger safety-briefings on land.

What *PrimeTime* did not report was that the Federal Aviation Administration reacted quickly to the two July 14 accidents, implementing an emergency safety rule for Hawaiian operators. The rule took effect in October 1994—three months after the accidents—and three months before *PrimeTime*'s segment aired.

Donaldson's only mention of the new regulations was this cryptic comment: "Until [the second] crash, passengers on such flights didn't have to wear life vests, and the helicopters didn't have to have pontoons. The FAA now says it must be one or the other, a new rule that applies only in Hawaii."

Instead of giving credit where credit—or at least the benefit of the doubt—was due, Donaldson grilled the FAA's Daniel Beaudette about safety deficiencies connected to the July 14 accidents. When Beaudette noted that one of the helicopters landed just short of a beach, Donaldson interjected sanctimoniously, "Well, just short, Mr. Beaudette, cost three lives." You'd never guess that when Beaudette responded, "We have corrected that situation," you actually should believe him.

In a statement, ABC News defends its portrayal of the aviation agency: "The FAA was not responsive, that's why we did the story." Although *Prime Time* may not have known it when the piece aired, the new rule had an enormously positive impact on the industry, according to Thomas Rea, the FAA's pacific representative. After the Hawaiian rule took effect, there were no major accidents involving tourist helicopters until this June.

After its brief mention of important FAA changes, *Prime Time* left Hawaii as Donaldson made this sweeping statement: "All across the country, problems with sightseeing helicopters have arisen." One piece of evidence offered to back this up: a 1993 accident in the Grand Canyon that injured 12 people. *Prime Time* didn't report that this was the only accident to have occurred in the Grand Canyon region since 1986. Two years after that crash, the FAA responded by instituting emergency safety regulations for the area. The Grand Canyon rules were so successful that even the National Transportation Safety Board, the agency responsible for recommending safety improvements, credited them with creating "a safe operating environment over the Grand Canyon." The *Prime Time* piece made no mention of this finding. Instead, it shifted viewers' attention to New York and its tourist helicopters. "The piece was about unregulated helicopters," ABC News says in its statement. "That's why we mentioned the Grand Canyon incident."

Many of the issues the show raised about New York's helicopter industry were valid. The segment cited concern over inadequate rescue equipment and briefing standards, issues that have long troubled the NTSB, issues the FAA plans to address with new national regulations later this year. The piece also criticized the absence of an instrument-rating requirement for pilots, mentioning the 1994 New Jersey crash of a New York-based charter helicopter that killed three people.

HOW SAFE A RIDE?

PrimeTime Live flew over the topic of leisure-helicopter safety, dedicating plenty of air time to dramatic video of crashes but hardly any to the safety initiatives designed to correct the problems. Government responses to safety issues were virtually ignored. Anecdotes describing dangerous crashes overemphasized dangers to public.

RATING ☹ UNFAIR

- FAA official forced to defend practices already corrected
- Anecdotes suggested dangerous crashes more common than they were

But by focusing on an emotional profile of a young boy killed in a sightseeing accident in New York, the show implied that safety was a major concern in the city. On the contrary, helicopter accidents were rare. Between 1990 and 1994, New York's helicopter accident-rate was eight times below the national average, according to a 1998 draft study prepared by the New York City Economic Development Corporation. In fact, according to the same study, that 1990 case was the most recent fatality in New York at the time the *Prime Time* report aired in 1995. Time Forte, the NTSB director of aviation safety when the segment aired, calls New York's accident rate "statistically insignificant." In its statement, ABC News responds: "The New York accident rate is not statistically insignificant to the people involved in those accidents."

Forte says *PrimeTime* may not have presented the most balanced picture. "Alerting the public [about helicopter safety issues] was good," says Forte, "but I am not sure [the show] left the public with the impression that the Grand Canyon was safe." —*TR*

PLUGGED INTO DANGER? 20/20: NOVEMBER 22, 1996
PRODUCER: BONNIE VANGILDER   CORRESPONDENT: ARNOLD DIAZ

"THE PROBLEM," ANCHOR BARBARA WALTERS BEGAN, "IS PLASTIC, the kind of plastic found in most household appliances." Following this introduction, Arnold Diaz reported on how cheap plastic fuels fires in defective home appliances. Most of the piece centered on problems involving baby monitors made by Gerry Baby Products, and on the emotional story of the Mercer family of Davenport, Iowa. The Mercers blamed Gerry for a fire that killed one young son and left another horribly disfigured. *20/20* began its piece with video of the severely burned boy playing outside his home. A few moments later, viewers watched video of his brother's funeral.

Fire-science expert Patrick Kennedy provided the most graphic demonstration of the problem. With the ABC cameras taping, Kennedy set fire to two Gerry baby monitors, one encased in a flame-retardant plastic no longer used by the company, the other with the cheaper plastic that encased the

Mercers' baby monitor. "This is pretty horrendous, dangerous stuff," said Kennedy, as the cheaper plastic melted under heat while the flame-retardant model remained intact.

But plastic is not the main concern, according to Julie Ayres, an electrical engineer in the Consumer Product Safety Commission's Office of Hazard Identification and Reduction. Ayres worries that the story's premise—captured in Walters's introductory claim that "the problem is plastic"—sent the wrong message. The crucial problem, Ayres says, is defective products. Watching the *20/20* segment, she "got the impression that anything in plastic could catch on fire." A fire can only occur if there is a flaw in a product's heating element. Diaz did note that a manufacturing defect caused the Mercer fire, and also said that safety devices had been disabled in a space heater and a coffee maker before they burst into flames during the segment. But some viewers may have missed these disclaimers when they watched the dramatic images. In a statement, ABC News says it stands by its story.

Near the end of the piece, Diaz reported that the "government is so concerned" about flammable plastic that the CSPC asked the Underwriters Laboratory Inc., a group that sets product-safety standards, to upgrade its requirements. That's true, says the CSPC's Kathleen Begala, but identifying and recalling defective products is a higher priority for the commission. While plastics guidelines are still being hammered out between the CSPC and the UL, the defective Gerry baby monitors were recalled and improved. "If you have to look at one or another, the defects are more important," Begala says. "[They are] more important, because that's the problem." —TR

PLUGGED INTO DANGER

Viewers learned about the dangers of cheap plastic in defective home appliances. When a product was defective, cheap plastic could add fuel to fires. Graphic demonstration drove this point home, but at the same time may have left viewers with a distorted impression that plastic was the only problem.

RATING ☺ FAIR

- Identified plastic as safety issue
- Industry representative got his say; post-segment chat noted no real opposition to safer plastic
- Left wrong impression about core problem

A DEADLY MIX PRIMETIME LIVE: APRIL 12, 1995
PRODUCER: RICK NELSON   CORRESPONDENT: CHRIS WALLACE

PRIMETIME TOLD THE COMPELLING TALE OF ANTONIO BENEDI, WHO almost died after taking Tylenol. But Benedi also drank several glasses of wine per day, and doctors linked his liver failure to the combination of alcohol and acetaminophen, Tylenol's active ingredient, as a jury had found several months before the show aired. (Tylenol still maintains that his illness was caused by a herpes virus.)

PrimeTime highlighted two other cases involving Tylenol users who drank three to six alcoholic beverages daily. That was far less than the 16 drinks per day that Tylenol contended was the average amount of alcohol consumed by those acetaminophen-users who became ill (Tylenol also argued that most of those heavy drinkers had exceeded its recommended doses). Despite the conflicting opinions, *PrimeTime* viewers came away with an understanding of the potential for deadly interaction between the two products.

The report was arguably misleading in one respect. Only at the end was it made clear that the Food and Drug Administration was already on the case; the agency had begun recommending labels warning consumers who regularly consume at least three alcoholic drinks daily to see their doctors before using Tylenol. McNeil Consumer Products Co., Tylenol's maker, had already started using the new labels on its products, as *PrimeTime*'s report eventually pointed out.

Instead, *PrimeTime*'s hype could have led viewers to believe it had uncovered the link between alcohol and Tylenol. In his introduction, anchor Sam Donaldson said: "As chief correspondent Chris Wallace found out, when acetaminophen is taken by people who drink alcohol regularly, there can be disastrous results." Moreover, with its reference to consumers who "drink alcohol regularly," the introduction could well have led viewers to believe that even those who consume a single drink daily were at risk.

McNeil spokesman Ron Schmid takes issue with the tone and balance of the report and says it "scared a lot of

people about alcohol and Tylenol" unnecessarily.

ABC News spokeswoman Eileen Murphy says "we're comfortable [that] the introduction accurately reflects what's in the piece." —EJ

A DEADLY MIX

When taken by someone who drinks heavily on a regular basis, Tylenol (or more properly, its main ingredient, acetaminophen) can cause deadly liver damage. Tylenol contends that those most at risk are alcoholics who exceed its recommended doses, but this report focused on users who drink far less and still develop serious problems. On the whole, the piece highlighted for the public what seem to be the risks of mixing even moderate levels of alcohol with Tylenol, and in the process illustrated the hesitance of McNeil Consumer Products Co., Tylenol's parent, to put warnings on its products. While bringing the issue to light for a segment of the population that may not have realized they are potentially at risk, *PrimeTime* also made it seem as though it had discovered the link itself. In fact, the government was aware of the issue, and just before the piece aired, Tylenol had begun carrying a warning about its use by those who consume three or more alcoholic drinks daily.

RATING ☺ FAIR

- Opened with clear scare tactic: when Tylenol is "taken by people who drink alcohol regularly, there can be disastrous results," which could apply to someone who has just a single beer per day, not heavier drinkers most at risk
- Overall, correct impression was conveyed: If you drink at level warned against on package, you should be cautious about using Tylenol

*[**Editor's note**: Ten of the twenty stories analyzed by *Brill's Content* are included in this *Annual Editions* article. See *Brill's Content*, October 1998 for all twenty articles.]

SECRETS AND LIES

Strong indications that Boston Globe columnist Patricia Smith was making up material had surfaced before the fabrications that led to her downfall, but the paper decided not to confront her.

BY SINÉAD O'BRIEN

H ER WORDS SANG TO READERS. THEY WERE HEARTFELT AND they were proud and they were read. Patricia Smith's columns, landing on the doorsteps of a city that wears racial awareness on its sleeve, brought to the Boston Globe a black female voice so eloquent that it demanded to be heard. But in the end, that proved her downfall; many of the words people heard were not true.

She was raised a wordsmith; she said so in an apology to her readers on June 19, the day after resigning from the Globe for fabricating people and quotes in her columns. "The terse blocked type below the headlines became living, breathing stories," Smith wrote, detailing her father's ritual of reading her the newspaper each night before bed. "My daddy gave the newspaper a pulse," she wrote in her final column.

Smith's journalism career began in Chicago, where she grew up. Her father, who was murdered when she was 20, loved newspapers. A consummate self-starter, Smith began at the Chicago Daily News as a typist. Later she went to the Chicago Sun-Times as an editorial assistant.

As a columnist, she spoke for everyone. A glance at her body of work shows the connections she made with Bostonians in general, and her farewell to them underscores it. "So to the welders, the B-boys, the preachers, and the surgeons, to the grocery clerks and bartenders and single mothers, to the politicians, PR flacks, spokespersons and secretaries.... I am sorry for betraying your trust," she wrote.

The public response confirmed Smith's value in the community. While journalism critics hung their heads, readers rallied behind her. "We should not fail to acknowledge talent and contributions made, even in a time of sorrow," one reader wrote. Another condemned the extensive coverage of Smith's fall by writing, "Is there nothing left that the Globe's sanctimonious editor can do to pillory Patricia Smith? Maybe tar and feather her? Sue her for every cent paid to her?"

These, and the dozens of pro-Smith calls to the newspaper's ombudsman, prompted Globe columnist Eileen McNamara to write, "Sadly, a lot of readers apparently think she didn't do anything the rest of us don't do routinely."

Smith, 43, who declined to be interviewed for this article, is an accomplished poet. She writes plays and stars in them; she's a member of a jazz band. She had a child at 21 and now raises her granddaughter. In her apology, Smith talked about the overwhelming pressure she placed on herself: "To make up for the fact that I didn't get the 'correct' start in journalism, I set out to be 10 times as good by doing 10 times as much." Overextending herself left little time for friend-making in the newsroom. Her column appeared twice a week; so did she.

"There was a void at that desk," says Greg Moore, the Globe's managing editor and the person who edited Smith's columns since October 1996. "She was so busy doing so many things, one casualty was face time here."

If Patricia Smith was driven to embellish her work at the Globe because she was pulled in too

Award-winning columnist **PATRICIA SMITH**'s *use of fictitious characters brought her career to an abrupt end.*

many directions, as she said, maybe now she will devote more time to just one thing. As one reader wrote, "Journalism is the incorrect medium for her passions."

WHEN SMITH'S PREDILECTION FOR fabrication came to light in June, it came as a shock to her readers and to the journalism community at large. But a small circle of top Globe editors knew there was reason to suspect that the paper's premier black columnist had a penchant for inventing people who might, as she later put it, "slam home a salient point."

In the Smith saga's unhappy aftermath, Globe Editor Matthew V. Storin is apt to remind

critics of the adage, "hindsight is 20/20." But there were warning signs well before the end-game that seemingly went ignored.

As far back as 1995, some of the quotes in Smith's columns, succinct and dead on, provoked quiet conversations among senior editors about their veracity. Were they in fact too good to be true? Globe editors investigated, and while they identified 28 people in her columns who couldn't be tracked down, the paper's leadership decided not to ask her flat out if she had lied.

Instead, Storin presented the "rules of the road" to Smith. All characters in her columns had to be real. And she had to give her editor fact-checking information. The columns were to be spot-checked after they ran to make sure they were true.

This was not the first newspaper where questions had been raised about the integrity of Smith's work.

In 1986, while an editorial assistant at the Chicago Sun-Times, Smith covered an Elton John concert. Her negative review attracted the attention of John's representative. Smith's piece had the performer wearing an outfit he hadn't worn and singing two songs he hadn't sung. And it said that the audience hadn't been pleased by John's performance, although promoters claimed he was well-received. The representative also said Smith hadn't picked up her press tickets.

Globe Arts Editor Scott Powers was at the Sun-Times at the time, as assistant managing editor for features. He says when Smith was asked about the discrepancies, she insisted she had attended the concert but said she had been on a date and had paid more attention to her date than to the show. "There were some on staff who felt she never attended the show, but she did produce notes for me and I never heard any real proof that she was not at the show," Powers says. Smith said she watched from lawn seats purchased by her date.

Weeks after the incident, Storin became editor of the Sun-Times. The paper had run a correction about the concert, but Storin was approached with the question of how to punish Smith for her negligence.

Storin assumed Smith was a college-aged intern, given her youthful looks. "She got distracted. She came with her boyfriend and that's how she fouled up some of what she said," he says. "She was not covering the legislature or anything like that. I gave her a lecture." Smith, who actually was 30 at the time, was not allowed to write for several months.

Powers was not at the Globe when Smith was hired to join the Living Arts section in 1990, but he says her mistake at the Sun-Times seems common enough among young critics—combining work and play. Storin was editing the New York Daily News at the time. When he was called by the Globe for a reference check, he mentioned the concert incident, "because it was the only thing I knew about her."

After four years on the arts beat, Smith became a Metro columnist. The concert fiasco was long forgotten. "Since more than eight years had passed, I did not mention this incident to anyone at the Globe when Smith was made a columnist," Powers says. "And I was not asked about her."

IN THE YEAR THAT FOLLOWED, SMITH'S WRITing championed all people, not just those of her race. As Globe Ombudsman Jack Thomas put it in a July 20 column: "Although she wrote aggressively from the African-American perspective, Smith cannot be accused of a pattern of fabricating racist white characters." Ultimately, it might have been that reaching out to all classes of people that tipped off newsroom colleagues. When that lyrical, clear voice cropped up in too many characters with too many different backgrounds, the buzz began.

Suspicions might have gone unnoticed were it not for Walter Robinson, then the Globe's assistant managing editor for local news. Robinson, who had championed the idea of making Smith a columnist, was told in late 1995 that someone on the copy desk had raised questions about the level of truth in Smith's work. About the same time he received a call from a reader expressing doubt in the existence of the central figure in a November 13, 1995, column.

The column focused on a man named Ernie Keane of Somerville, Massachusetts, who supposedly had called Smith in the newsroom on a Sunday morning to talk about President Clinton's upcoming visit to Boston. Keane purportedly wanted Smith to relay a message to the president for him. Smith wrote that she promised the man she would include his message for the president in one of her columns.

Keane, now listed among the characters in Smith's work the Globe considers nonexistent, is quoted as saying: "I ain't real smart and I don't have no fancy words to make folks sit up and take notice. I'm just ordinary, but there are a lot of ordinary folks here getting sick of screaming and no one hearing. Our country's supposed to take care of us when we get old, that's our reward for working all these years and living here in this so-called democratic place. Just tell him that. When you see him, tell him that for Ernie Keane."

Now Smith's work was suspect in and out of the newsroom. For Robinson, it was time to take action.

The editor, who declined to comment for this article, went to Executive Editor Helen W. Donovan and Storin in late 1995 or early 1996—no one is sure exactly when—with his suspicions. They decided he should follow up on them. Unfortunately, Robinson's fears seemed on target; attempts to contact numerous people quoted in Smith's work were futile. He went to the paper's top editors with the bad news.

Editor Storin moved cautiously, not eager to

fire one of his stars over what might be an unfortunate misunderstanding. As for the call from the reader who was positive there was no Ernie Keane, Storin says, it's "a vague complaint. You can't call and say, 'That person's not true.'"

Storin was acutely aware of the latitude given in the past to such legendary columnists as Mike Royko and Jimmy Breslin, who made extensive use of clearly fictional characters to drive their points home. Royko's Slats Grobnik and Breslin's Fat Thomas were Everyman characters, symbols representing an entire stratum of people. And so the editor was reluctant to take harsh action against Smith.

And there was another factor. Columnist Mike Barnicle, a 25-year fixture on the Metro page affectionately known throughout the city as "Boston Mike," a Globe franchise player, had been accused of fabrications sporadically over the years.

It began in 1973, when a gas station owner denied making a racial slur Barnicle quoted him as using. Barnicle was sued, and although parts of the quotation were in his notebook, a judge ordered the columnist to pay $40,000 to the gas station owner because the entire quote couldn't be verified.

Boston Magazine for a time published a regular feature called "Unbelievably Barnicle," which raised questions about Barnicle's veracity but never proved any improprieties.

A quote Barnicle attributed to lawyer Alan Dershowitz in a 1990 column drew even more fire. Focusing on the high-profile lawyer's publicity seeking, the "Open Mouth, Get in Paper" column ended with Dershowitz saying, "I love Asian women, don't you? They're...they're so submissive."

In a letter to the Globe and in columns in the Boston Herald, Dershowitz denied making the comment. He claims the columnist admitted to him and to mutual friends that he had fabricated the quotation. Barnicle stands by the quote.

In the wake of the Smith contretemps, the Globe this summer reviewed 364 columns by Barnicle, finding no improprieties. But two months after Smith resigned, Barnicle followed suit, quitting after serious doubts were raised about the veracity of a column he had written in 1995.

Says Storin, "Columnists of the Breslin/Royko nature have always been a kind of gray area." When concerns were raised in late 1995, he hoped Smith was merely emulating them, using what were clearly fictional characters, rather than passing off fictional characters as real people.

"I had to manage the situation as I thought would be fair and honest for the paper," Storin says. "If we confronted Patricia Smith and she admitted it, we would have fired her on the spot. But then there would have been questions about Mike Barnicle, and we would have had to deal with those."

Boston Globe Editor **Matthew V. Storin** *says that in the case of apparent fabrication, it's difficult to prove a negative.*

Assistant Managing Editor **Walter Robinson** *triggered the investigation that led to Smith's downfall.*

The editor feared that Smith was aware of the allegations about Barnicle and may have gotten the impression that a little fiction was OK. "It could have been the noise about Mike, unfair though it may be, gave her the wrong impression," he says.

Storin consulted Donovan, the executive editor. They decided not to ask Smith if she had lied in any columns. Either by chance or craft, no questionable figure in the 28 columns that Robinson studied could be proved nonexistent. Every suspiciously pat quote was attributed to a person with no defining characteristic, such as a traceable occupation.

Storin is quick to note that it's difficult to prove a negative. "The fact that these people didn't have telephone numbers one by one wouldn't be a story," he says.

So why didn't the Globe's top leadership simply ask Smith point-blank why no one could be found? One reason, Storin says, is that they anticipated her reaction. "She'd say, 'They're out on the street, they move around a lot, they don't have phones,'" he says.

ROBINSON DID TALK TO SMITH TWICE IN early 1996 with what he had found—or what he hadn't found. Smith simply didn't respond; she didn't have to. Following orders, no one asked her the question that could have ended it all: Why can't these people be located?

And so rather than question Smith about the elusive characters in her columns, Storin decided to give Smith and Barnicle a refresher course in Journalism 101. The editors devised "rules of the road," now an empty phrase whose very mention can cause Globe staffers to cringe. The columnists were to be told exactly what was expected from them—namely, everything in their columns had to be real.

Donovan says the guidelines weren't aimed at McNamara, a columnist with an impeccable record. Storin says no questions had been raised about McNamara's work, and he didn't present the rules to her.

But the Globe editors did try to send Smith a message. "It was put to her in a sense that would let her know we had a good bit of evidence she's fabricating," Donovan says. "Essentially, the decision was to put her on notice: She had to cut it out."

Editors met with Smith and Barnicle separately in the editor's office soon after Robinson confirmed the suspicions about Smith's work. "It was proposed we talk to Mike and Pat and tell them we're implementing a documentation system on unnamed or unidentified people in their columns," Storin says. "Then I knew that everyone would be truly advised."

Storin has said Smith seemed "shaken" by the meeting, and afterwards the quality of her work went down. She began writing mostly commentary, reacting to news events.

The paper now has confirmed 52 suspicious columns since 1995. Of those, only two occurred in 1996, the year following the "rules of the road" meeting.

While Smith was given a second chance, Storin says there was no way she could survive a similar problem in the future. Once the rules had been presented to her, there was simply no margin for error.

HERE'S HOW THE MONITORING SYSTEM was supposed to work: The editor overseeing each columnist would be responsible for making sure his or her work was truthful.

The pairings, chosen by Storin, ultimately followed racial lines. McNamara and her editor, Donovan, are white women. Managing Editor/News Operations Thomas F. Mulvoy Jr. edits Barnicle; both are white men. After Robinson stopped overseeing local news in October 1996 (he remains an assistant managing editor at the paper), Managing Editor Greg Moore took over the responsibility for editing Smith. Moore and Smith are black. "It's an unfortunate coincidence," Storin says.

The columnists were instructed to give the editors details about the identity of significant figures in their columns. "We were going to require [Smith] give passport-level ID," Storin says. Columnists were told that periodically the information might be checked, but not all the time.

(Asked if the paper has a similar process for checking the veracity of its reporters' work, Moore scoffs, "We have about 275 reporters here. If we did that, we wouldn't be able to put out a paper." If a reporter required such monitoring, he adds, "that's someone we can't trust.")

The editors admit the system didn't work. Mulvoy was quoted in a Globe article as saying that he asked Barnicle for names and phone numbers about a dozen times, then eased off. Donovan says she didn't have to check McNamara's work; her columns had easily identifiable people that no one would question.

When Moore began editing Smith in late 1996, he asked her for notes about people in the columns but didn't try to track them down. By that time, he says, the process had been in effect for months. He assumed that by then she'd gotten the picture, and he accepted the notes as sufficient proof that the characters she wrote about were real.

But even had he fact-checked her work, the system had a major loophole. Smith's columns appeared on Monday and Friday. Moore doesn't work on Sunday, the day Smith's Monday column was edited. This means half of Smith's columns were edited by other senior editors. Moore, like the Globe's readers, first saw Smith's Monday columns when he picked up the newspaper.

And because the suspicions about Smith were kept secret among top editors, those handling

Executive Editor HELEN W. DONOVAN *says that while editors didn't directly confront Smith with their initial findings, they did try to "put her on notice."*

Questions about the veracity of MIKE BARNICLE*'s columns complicated the Globe's efforts to deal with the Smith situation.*

her columns each Sunday had no idea that they shouldn't take too much for granted.

In fact, the column that attracted Robinson's attention the second time ran on a Monday, May 11 of this year. It focused on a cancer victim named Claire, who had just learned about cancer therapies tested in mice. She was quoted as saying, "I'm not proud. Right away, I said, 'Rub it on my skin, pop it to me in a pill, shoot me up with it.' If I could find a way to steal it, I would. Hell, if I could get my hands on it, I'd swallow the whole…mouse."

Moore says, "Clearly some columns, in retrospect, like [the one quoting] 'Claire'…were quite cute, a little too formulated." He says it's unfair to ask if he would have flagged that particular column had he been its editor, but "my hope is that she wouldn't have submitted that to me." It wasn't questioned by that day's editor, Deputy Managing Editor/Features Mary Jane Wilkinson. She had no reason to second-guess Smith's work, not knowing about past red flags.

Once the column appeared, Robinson's suspicions were aroused again. And again it was Robinson who made a move.

This time he approached Donovan alone. "We had a conversation earlyish in May and he told me about his concerns," Donovan says. "We agreed he would do preliminary checking."

Robinson, this time turning to voter registration, telephone and Registry of Motor Vehicles databases, had the same experience he had before: People could not be found. But now there was a difference: This time he could prove they were bogus. Smith had cited people with occupations that require licensing and therefore should be able to be tracked down, like the fictitious cosmetologist Janine Byrne. When they couldn't be located, the game was over.

But it was three weeks before the paper's editor was notified that Smith, once again, was under scrutiny, and that, once again, the findings were bleak. "That's the result of people being busy," Donovan says, noting that from May 11, the day the column about "Claire" appeared, to Smith's resignation on June 18, many key players weren't around.

Donovan didn't tell Storin about the situation until early June. For one thing, she waited until Robinson's investigation made it clear there was a problem. "It takes time to do that research. Other things are going on," Storin says. "They just decided to see if something was there before they told me." After that, Donovan, Storin and Robinson were all out of the office at various times, making it difficult for the three of them to get together. Meanwhile, Smith was away for 10 days attending a poetry slam and the editors didn't want to discuss the matter with her over the phone, Donovan says.

Eight more of Smith's columns ran between the time the suspicions surfaced and Moore confronted her on June 17. Unaware that her bosses were on to her, Smith wrote three columns with people the paper can't find and believes to be fictitious.

Why didn't the paper take some interim action as it investigated the situation? Donovan says her main concern was columns that already had appeared.

Once the paper determined in June that a star columnist had made up some of her colorful characters, Storin delivered the bad news to the staff. Meanwhile, Moore took Smith to lunch. The meeting ended when, after Moore asked her to verify the existence of six questionable people in her columns, Smith admitted four were figments of her imagination.

"Anytime you put your trust in someone and it's abused and violated, you feel personally bad,"

The Beginning of the End

Suspicions about the veracity of the May 11 column excerpted below started the investigation that led to Patricia Smith's resignation:

Claire has heard the media furor about the "cure" for the killer, about the mice who had what she has and now they don't. "I'm not proud," she says. "Right away I said, 'Rub it on my skin, pop it to me in a pill, shoot me up with it.' If I could find a way to steal it, I would. Hell, if I could get my hands on it, I'd swallow the whole…mouse." Claire laughs, an ugly sound. She uses harsh language, new language for her. It's the only language she feels the ogre understands.

Nobody knows she has it yet. She's still a chubby 142 pounds, she still has her hair, and her eyes haven't sunk back into her head like the eyes of the people in those pictures she sees, those pictures that look like death no matter how perky the silk scarf, determined the smile, or well-crafted the makeup. Nobody but she and her doctor and her mother know the diagnosis. None of her friends know that there is something false and foreign growing inside her, an ogre she imagines chomping away slowly at her heartbeat. No one has recoiled at those two syllables before drowning her in their damnable pity. Right now nobody knows that Claire has cancer.

Claire is her middle name. And she's glad nobody knows that either, especially if she's finally going to talk out loud about the ogre.

Moore says. By admitting the fabrications—Smith later alluded to more in her farewell column—she had sealed her fate. Storin asked for her resignation rather than firing her because her contract provided more benefits that way. "It was the humane thing to do," he says.

Did the paper deal aggressively enough with strong indications that one of its columnists was making things up? "I would suggest that the blame really falls on Patricia Smith," Globe Publisher Benjamin B. Taylor says. "She's the one who violated readers' trust and the newspaper's trust placed in her." He learned about the decision to ask for Smith's resignation the day before she quit. Says Taylor, "I think Matt's handled the thing well."

ONCE THE PAPER DECIDED IT HAD TO let one of its leading writers go, it had to explain why. "We have great responsibility to our reading public," Storin says. "We owe it to our readers to come clean."

But did it in fact come entirely clean in its early coverage? "In a way this was a test of whether we could be as grueling on ourselves in print as we are on companies like Raytheon or Blue Cross and Blue Shield when those companies have suffered some embarrassments," says Sarah Snyder, an assistant Metro editor. "I don't know if we were as tough. A reader would have to judge that."

Globe media writer Mark Jurkowitz wrote the first-day story, which focused on Smith's resignation, citing the four 1998 columns that she had admitted fabricating.

The Friday, June 19, piece said, "The paper began monitoring Metro columns for accuracy several years ago in response to concerns about veracity." Storin is quoted as saying, "People would bring up Barnicle, a couple of people brought her [Smith] up. I just decided we didn't have a system" for checking the columns. The article also said that each columnist was informed about the "rules of the road" they would have to follow. As for Smith, it says, "Several weeks ago, top editors became concerned about of number of 'troubling' quotations" in her work.

A press release issued by Globe spokesman Richard P. Gulla said, "The fabrications were discovered two weeks ago by Globe editors in the normal course of monitoring by senior editors of columns." It goes on to describe the process that had been set up and says, "This problem was discovered as part of that process."

Of course, the phony columns weren't uncovered by the long-discontinued system; they were flagged by Robinson. But Robinson was noticeably absent from the first article. He was out of the country at the time, which might account for why he wasn't interviewed. But his role in the saga was not just downplayed, it was eliminated.

That the press release, which Gulla says was reviewed by the publisher and editor, misrepresents how the fabrications were discovered, and by whom, is nit-picking, according to Storin. "You could split hairs that monitoring or Greg [Moore] didn't turn it up and it took Walter's [Robinson] surveillance to detect it," Storin says. "But it was an internal thing by editors at one time responsible."

Jurkowitz says he was told to cover the story like any other and received no special instructions, but adds, "I can only report what I'm told." He says in the course of reporting that first day, no one mentioned the previous suspicions about Smith and Robinson's subsequent investigation.

Jurkowitz's second story, on June 21, had a fuller account. But sandwiched in between was Kate Zernike's story on the 20th, which detailed lawyer Dershowitz's charge that the paper hadn't been fair to Smith. He charged the Globe with practicing a double standard "based on race, gender and ethnicity" because it ousted Smith but hadn't gotten rid of Barnicle.

Storin says that Jurkowitz's more complete June 21 story was not prompted by Dershowitz's claims. He also says the 1995 events weren't left out of the initial story by design. "In all honesty, I had not thought about '95 at the time. We did say we set up this monitoring system," Storin says. "The important thing is, even if it took until Sunday, that we did it."

Moore, who co-edited the first story and edited the Sunday piece, says, "I think we realized Friday's story was incomplete, and we had to go much deeper."

It did go deeper. The second story, contradicting the first, revealed that it was Robinson, not the system, who caught Smith. Robinson was also quoted extensively in the follow-up.

Globe staffers learned about the saga just before Globe readers did. When Storin called an emergency staff meeting on June 18 to announce the news, "Nobody was even close to suspecting what it was," says statehouse reporter Adrian Walker.

Many staffers are reluctant to discuss on the record their feelings about the affair. But dissatisfaction with the way the Globe first reported the story and the fact that it had kept previous concerns about Smith quiet is palpable.

"I know nothing more than any other reporter or editor watching the thing unfold," Snyder says. "All I can describe are the questions newsroom people were asking each other at the time, which included, 'If some possible fabrication concerns were a concern two years ago, why wasn't she hyper-edited, by whoever was her line editor, after that?'

"At the risk of sounding Pollyanna-ish, I don't think a newspaper, or any other business for that matter, risks having problems as long as they're willing to admit screw-ups and then plow on," she adds. "The more questions answered by Globe brass, the faster staffers are willing to put it behind them."

In the wake of the revelations, at a regular meeting of top editors and managers, Storin urged the staff to move on. Someone at the meeting said it seemed as if the editors considered the issue a "dead horse"—in effect, they wanted people to stop flogging it.

In addition to questions about how it dealt with Smith from the start, editors faced questions about their decision to nominate the columnist for a Pulitzer Prize and an American Society of Newspaper Editors writing award despite past suspicions about the veracity of her work.

Smith won the ASNE award in 1998. When the news of her fabrications broke, ASNE rescinded the award. As for the nomination for a 1998 Pulitzer, no one's memory about how it came about is clear. One thing everybody is sure about, though: The final decision was Storin's.

Donovan says a group of senior editors met several times to discuss Pulitzer nominations, but

Smith admitted to Managing Editor **GREG MOORE** *that she had made up four characters. She resigned soon afterward.*

Globe columnist **EILEEN MCNAMARA** *says race had everything to do with Smith's rise and nothing to do with her fall.*

"we didn't have a group discussion" about Smith. Early in the process, she says, some people did talk in a general way about past doubts about the columnist. "But after it was decided [to nominate Smith], we didn't talk about it," she says. The editors assumed the situation had been cleared up, Donovan says, and if there had been any lingering concerns, "she wouldn't have been nominated."

Storin says Donovan and Moore were the only other editors involved in the Pulitzer discussions who knew about the past questions.

When the editors decided to submit Smith's work, columnist McNamara, a 1997 Pulitzer winner, approached Donovan to express her concern that Smith had made up elements of her work, according to the executive editor. Although she says McNamara's concern was "completely legitimate," Donovan didn't go to Storin on behalf of the columnist.

On June 25, Storin wrote a contrite letter to the members of the Pulitzer board. He opened with the obvious question: "Why, given her history, was Patricia Smith submitted for the Pulitzer Prize and ASNE Writing Award?" He admitted speaking with her in early 1996— when he delivered the famous "rules of the road" speech. He added, "Though we had evidence, I felt it was possible that she did not understand that even in columns of this type, that was absolutely verboten. I made that clear in my January 1996 conversation."

He went on to plead guilty "to the charge of unjustified ignorance or naivete" for thinking "she was clean after January 1996."

"I have my faults," he wrote, "but I am not so stupid as to submit for a Pulitzer someone who I think could be exposed as a cheat."

IN ACCUSING THE GLOBE OF EMPLOYING A double standard by ousting Smith after it had failed to take strong action against Barnicle, celebrity lawyer and Harvard law professor Dershowitz injected the unmentionable into the Smith saga: race. Despite an obvious reluctance by many to broach the subject on the record, the question of race has never been far beneath the surface.

Some inside and outside the Globe feel Smith's race played a role in her rapid ascent at the paper and what they consider management's failure to deal more sternly with the first wave of evidence of fabrication. Others feel equally strongly that the paper's decision to make her resign and its voluminous coverage of the tumultuous aftermath were overly harsh. Some, like Dershowitz, see racism as a factor.

In a letter to the Globe in July, a group of 20 black women complained about the extensive coverage of the Smith affair. They assailed it as an "ugly, vindictive campaign...to obliterate the columnist's otherwise stellar record of achievement as a journalist." Smith's lawyer, John T. Williams, objected to the notion that Smith had risen because of her race.

McNamara tackled the issue head-on in a column. Rejecting Dershowitz's charge that Smith was the victim of a double standard, she wrote, "To the contrary, she was the beneficiary of one. Her fall had nothing to do with her race; her rise had everything to do with it…. It was the worst sort of racism that kept us from confronting the fraud we long suspected. If we did ask, and she did tell, we might lose her, and where would we be then? Where would we find an *honest* black woman columnist who wrote with such power and grace?"

Tom Rosenstiel, director of the Project for Excellence in Journalism, praises the Globe for its extensive coverage since June. "I think the Globe is distinguished from some others,

A Columnist's Farewell

atricia Smith's final Globe column on June 19 was an apology which is excerpted below:

My daddy gave the newspaper a pulse. He taught me to love its changing canvas, its omnipotent eye, its infinite throat. And since one long-ago tabloid featured his obituary, it's much too late to apologize to him for compromising that love.

But it's not too late to apologize to you.

From time to time in my Metro column, to create the desired impact or to slam home a salient point, I attributed quotes to people who didn't exist. I could give them names, I could give them occupations, but I couldn't give them what they needed most—a heartbeat. As anyone who's ever touched a newspaper knows, that's one of the cardinal sins of journalism: Thou shall not fabricate. No exceptions. No excuses.

And yet there are always excuses. Usually they point to the cursed fallibility of human beings, our tendency to spit in the face of common sense, zigging when the world says zag. Sometimes excuses reveal real or imagined inadequacies, or the belief that the world, if it is to be conquered, must be conquered singlehandedly….

In Boston, my face was my column. I wanted the pieces to jolt, to be talked about, to leave the reader indelibly impressed. And sometimes, as a result of doing too much at once and cutting corners, they didn't. So I tweaked them to make sure they did. It didn't happen often, but it did happen. And if it had only happened once, that was one time too many.

because it represents stricter standards than the press has had in the past," he says.

The coverage, he adds, touched off an essential disscussion in the community. "It was about trust with a capital T," he says. "It was also about race, feminism, class, Irish vs. everyone else."

As for those who claim the Globe's response smacks of racism, Rosenstiel says, "Talk about shooting the messenger. The Globe's not wrecking a reputation; making things up wrecks a reputation."

Sinéad O'Brien, a frequent contributor to AJR, wrote about covering the Monica Lewinsky story in the March issue.

TOO MUCH INFORMATION?

BY SHARYN WIZDA

JULIO GRANADOS AGREED IN JANUARY TO ALLOW RALEIGH INTO HIS LIFE.

He let News & Observer reporter Gigi Anders come to the bodega where he worked, to the home he shared with other Mexican immigrants—even to the shrine he'd built in a nearby thicket of trees. He told her all about sending money home to his family in Mexico and his lonely life in America.

On March 8, readers of the North Carolina daily opened their Sunday papers to find "Heart without a home," two full pages on Julio's life. And two weeks later, they learned of the postscript: Granados, 21, and five other illegal aliens at the El Mandado market had been arrested by the Immigration and Naturalization Service. Agents in Charlotte had seen the N&O's article—which mentioned Granados' undocumented status and included details about where he lived and worked—and decided to arrest him.

Incensed, the Hispanic community blamed the N&O. And some of the paper's own reporters and editors were asking whether the newspaper had acted responsibly and whether it had weighed the ramifications of its actions before publishing the story.

In the weeks after the story ran and Granados was arrested, Anders received dozens of calls—including death threats—at home and at work. The paper published letters decrying the story as "irresponsible journalism" that "destroyed this young man's life." Anders and her editors met with the staff as well as with members of the Latino community to talk about what the paper did and why it did it. Executive Editor Anders Gyllenhaal wrote a Sunday column praising the piece but acknowledging there were things editors might do differently next time.

Central to the story of Julio Granados and its aftermath is the paper's role. How much responsibility do journalists have in ensuring that their sources— particularly those who aren't media savvy—fully understand the potential consequences of a page one story?

"Our goal here was not to do anything but try and explain this person's life,"

A profile of an illegal alien in Raleigh's News & Observer led to the man's arrest. Should the paper have revealed his name, workplace and immigration status?

Gyllenhaal says. "We certainly didn't mean for this to happen."

Executive Editor ANDERS GYLLENHAAL *wrote a column praising the story but saying editors would do some things differently next time.*

Projects editor ROB WATERS *wondered aloud at a news meeting how much illegal alien Julio Granados had been told about the story's possible ramifications.*

NEWS & OBSERVER FEATURES EDITOR Felicia Gressette had noted an increase in the numbers of immigrants working in and around the city. This was a new phenomenon for white-bread Raleigh; Gressette thought it made sense to humanize these faceless workers.

"If you live here in the Triangle, it's increasingly clear that there's a growing Hispanic population. You see Hispanic people more and more," Gressette says. "And for an awful lot of people, middle-class whites, it's outside of their frame of reference. We wanted to do a story that would get inside the life and world of someone who had come to the Triangle."

She assigned the story to Anders, a Cuban-born features reporter fluent in Spanish who had profiled other Hispanics in the community. Anders knew exactly where to look: the El Mandado bodega in north Raleigh, a sort of crossroads for the area's growing Hispanic population. Over lunch, she explained to proprietress Ana Roldan what she was looking for and asked Roldan if she knew anyone who might fit that description.

"She didn't hesitate," Anders recalls. "She said, 'Julio. He's perfect. He's exceptional.' "

And he *was* exceptional, Anders would find out. Though a bit bemused as to why the News & Observer would be interested in him, he gamely let Anders and photographer Robert Miller join him at work at El Mandado as he unpacked crates of mangoes and stocked shelves with stacks of tortillas, at home as he strummed his acoustic guitar and hummed "Ave Maria," and in the woods behind his house as he struggled through the brambles to a makeshift altar with a statue of the Virgin of Guadelupe. A former seminary student, he was articulate and thoughtful in their Spanish-language interviews, detailing memories of Mexico made painful by their distance from his current life.

Anders was excited. She knew she had the makings of a great profile on her hands. But she admits to being worried when she asked Granados about his U.S. work status and he told her he had no papers.

"I felt my heart sinking because I thought, 'He's going to pull out,' " Anders remembers. "But he didn't. I said, 'OK, do you understand that your name is going in this story? And your picture? Do you understand what this means?' And he asked, 'Do they read the N&O in Charlotte?' Charlotte is a synonym for the INS. And I said, 'Yes.'

"He said, 'Might I get deported?' I said, 'You might.' And he said, 'Well, if that's what happens, then I guess it's my destiny.' That's the word he used—destiny."

Granados says he doesn't remember it that

way: He told the N&O in April that he gave Anders permission to use his name but not his status. "My name, yes," he said. "But not the fact that I'm here without papers."

Still, Anders feels she gave Granados fair warning. "This is, to my mind, a full-grown person making his own decision," she says.

She continued reporting, keeping Gressette up to date on her progress. Eventually the story became a contender for Sunday front page play. Projects editor Rob Waters wondered aloud at a news meeting exactly what Granados had been told.

"I remember thinking that this would be at least an implicit invitation to the INS to come get this guy," Waters says. "I just made a very simple comment asking if this had been considered and whether Julio himself had been told of this. It wasn't really explored; I was simply raising one question, and I think I remember being told that those questions were being raised."

The story went to press.

"I think that there was some naiveté on our part about what the reaction would be," Executive Editor Gyllenhaal says. "Part of what happened was that a lot of people in the community are divided on the whole question of undocumented workers, and some of them who are opposed called the INS and said, 'You look at this, you've gotta do something about this.' I don't think we thought that was going to happen.... We just didn't think the thing through."

Sixteen days after the story ran, INS agents arrived mid-morning at El Mandado, loading Granados and five others into a van for the trip to jail. Anders got a hysterical call at home from Roldan and promptly called Gressette to let her know what had happened. Word began filtering through the newsroom, and Gyllenhaal and Managing Editor Melanie Sill called a meeting. Some 50 to 60 staffers showed up for the hour-long session.

"It was not a relaxed meeting," Anders says, describing pointed queries on how much Granados really understood about what might happen to him after the story ran. Had a trusting 21-year-old immigrant been exploited? How much had she talked with Granados about the INS? And what had she told the Roldans?

"It was quite a healthy crowd," says state government editor Linda Williams. "A lot of people asked questions. I think people were concerned, and they expressed those concerns."

Williams was one of those people. She says that when she read Anders' story that Sunday morning, she instantly thought, "Oh my God, he's going to be deported." While Anders may have talked with Granados about the potential repercussions of the profile, Williams says, she also should have talked with Roldan and her husband, Marco, about the story's implications for them.

"The people who own the store—why were they not quoted in the story about why they were hiring people illegally? How do they justify hiring him?" Williams asks. "Maybe you can just think in the absence of any knowledge about what happened that the reporter sat down and went through and gave them all the opportunity to comment, but it appears that these people didn't know what was going on.... It looks like we didn't give them the full opportunity to comment."

Williams also says the minute detail in the story was a road map for government agents. "We're telling the public we're neutral, we can't take sides. I think we erred by including all that information. We actually look like an arm of the INS," she says.

If the newsroom was concerned, Raleigh readers were downright angry. They barraged the paper with letters, and they weren't fan letters. "Irresponsible journalism resulted in the arrest of Julio Granados, the hard-working Mexican featured in your March 8 article," fumed Eunice Brock and Charles Tanquary of Chapel Hill. "This feature story could have been written equally forcefully without showing Granados' face or revealing his name and place of employment."

"I am sure he will enjoy being back in his homeland, courtesy of the N&O," wrote Charlie Ramirez of Apex. "Whatever happened to journalistic integrity?"

The Roldans say Anders misled them about how much detail she would include in her story. "She said, 'I will not write something like that. I will not write something to put Julio or your business in any trouble,'" Marco Roldan insists. Anders says she made no such pronouncements to the couple.

INS agents say they received copies of the Granados article from two sources. But Charlotte-based agent Scott Sherrill says it was more than just the front page play that triggered action. "There were some things in there that made us feel like it was important that we do this," Sherrill says. "The fact that he claims he was smuggled across the border.... It implies in there that he eluded arrest by the Border Patrol by running after he was smuggled across the border. That makes it a little more of a serious violation."

GYLLENHAAL TACKLED THE CONTROVERSY in a column on March 29, "Lessons in a story gone wrong." He defended the piece as a "powerful package." But he acknowledged that the fact that the story was so detailed led INS agents to Granados at El Mandado. And he said that the N&O didn't think hard enough about the impact of such a story on "one largely powerless, fairly ordinary young Mexican."

He says that the paper could have left out the name of the market, one crucial detail that might have kept the INS from acting.

Others aren't so sure. Anders points out that because the story was indeed so acutely detailed,

leaving out the name of the market would have made the N&O look like it was deliberately trying to hide Granados from the INS—something the paper wouldn't do for other lawbreakers.

"I think a lot of people felt this way because the story was sympathetic.... If Julio was a wifebeater or a gang-banger, we wouldn't shield him," Anders says.

That's a view shared by Roberto Suro, a deputy national editor at the Washington Post and author of "Strangers Among Us: How Latino Immigration is Transforming America."

"One thing that makes me uncomfortable is this idea that someone who is just a straightforward illegal alien, basically for economic reasons, somehow deserves some kind of protection," Suro says. "How much do you get in the business of making judgments? What if you're writing about people who use and sell drugs— you won't ID a user, but you would ID a seller? You're making a judgment that one violation of the law is somehow less serious than another."

Suro also questions whether someone like Granados was truly ignorant of the backlash potential of such a story: "He was certainly conversant with the law as it applies to be here illegally. To have gotten as far as he did—to go across the border all the way to North Carolina, he had to have had a fair knowledge of the law as it applies to the foreign-born and what's required to avoid getting caught. I mean, he may not have understood the U.S. tax code, but where it mattered, he knew."

What he may not have understood was how likely the INS was to come after him, says Leonel Sanchez, who covers immigration and Latino issues for the San Diego Union-Tribune. In an area like Raleigh where immigration is still relatively new, it's likely that someone like Granados would stand out as a target more than in areas where Hispanic faces are quite common, Sanchez says.

"It's a very sensitive matter, and you really have to take into account the demographics of the place," he says. "San Diego is conservative, but it is a border town and Hispanics have a bigger political role. They're likely to make noise if something like [the Granados arrest] happened."

Even so, Sanchez says, Union-Tribune editors have decided to withhold information about undocumented workers in some stories. He used only first names in a piece about throngs turning themselves in to the INS office, after extensive discussion with editors, because of concerns that using full names might alert employers. In another piece, about a family of 10 seeking citizenship, editors decided to use full names but describe where they worked as "a laundromat" or "a factory."

Gressette says the paper's responsibility is simply to deal honestly with subjects about their potential risks. "If they consent, it's our obligation to tell it," she says. "I think where the process went awry was in not discussing what

"I THINK that there was some naiveté on our part about what the reaction would be...," Executive Editor Anders Gyllenhaal says. "I don't think we thought that was going to happen.... We just didn't think the thing through."

ROGER WINSTEAD

PAUL MAGANN

Managing Editor **MELANIE SILL** *says the Granados episode is a vivid reminder of the importance of carefully considering a story's consequences.*

State government editor **LINDA WILLIAMS** *says the story's minute detail was a road map for government agents.*

the ripple effects could be.... As part of our process we should have discussed whether we should not name the place."

GRANADOS IS NOW FREE ON BOND posted by the city's Hispanic community as he awaits a deportation hearing in Atlanta in July. He told the N&O in April that he wants to stay in the United States to work. There has been no resolution to the questions posed by his arrest, and the debate his story sparked is far from over.

"There is still a difference of opinion in the newsroom," Gressette says. "There's no consensus about what we did wrong or about what we should have done."

Within a week of the N&O's newsroom meeting, editors and Anders gathered again to discuss the ramifications of what happened to Granados—this time with about 25 area Latinos. "There's a level of trust that you want with all your readers," Gyllenhaal says. "That level has been hurt by this as far as some of the Hispanic community is concerned."

The two-hour session generated a fair amount of finger-pointing as well as discussion of how the newspaper could better cover the Hispanic community. Though no promises were made, Sill, the managing editor, is well aware that those community leaders will be watching—and reading—to see what the N&O does. A follow-up meeting is planned for July.

"I don't feel that that's a subject that's closed," Sill says. "It's still something to be cognizant of.... It's clear that there are several things still to talk about, not just this story but how we do our coverage and our relationship to their lives."

As editors weigh how they'll cover the news, the N&O has extended a financial olive branch. On April 30, Publisher Fred Crisp said the newspaper would give $5,000 to the Latino Fund, set up by a Durham church to help the six arrested at El Mandado. Crisp described the donation as "the right thing to do" but did ask that it only be used for living expenses. "It would be inappropriate for us to contribute to the legal defense that our coverage helped to provoke," Crisp wrote in a letter accompanying the donation.

And it's clear that Granados' legacy to the N&O lies in the area of internal communication. Although the newsroom still doesn't agree on how much information about him should have been revealed to readers, top editors all say that subject should have been much more fully aired in the newsroom.

"It's a reminder for me of taking care over big stories that are going to have an impact," Sill says. Editors are more apt to carefully consider the consequences of pieces that cast suspicion on a person or a program, she points out.

"But this was a sympathetic story that ended up having an impact."

Sharyn Wizda, the Palm Beach Post's southern Palm Beach County bureau chief, wrote about Aspen's newspaper war in AJR's April issue.

THE INTERVENTION DILEMMA

A powerful Los Angeles Times series on the mistreatment of children by their drug-addicted parents spotlights an ethical quandary: When should journalists shed their observer status and go for help?

By Susan Paterno

THE OBSERVATIONS AND PHOTOGRAPHS TWO LOS ANGELES TIMES JOURNALISTS brought back from the front lines of American poverty are as frightening as images from war.

Throughout last summer, reporter Sonia Nazario and photographer Clarence Williams watched as children were endangered and neglected time and time again by their drug-addicted parents.

In one family, a three-year-old girl lived an itinerant life in deplorable conditions, moving from garage to crack house to addict's apartment, going 24 hours without eating. Her weight dropped 10 percent in one week. Her teeth were brushed "with a toothbrush she is sharing with [her mother], who is HIV positive" and has bleeding gums, read the cutline of a photo showing a man with bloody sores brushing the little girl's teeth. While her mother scores drugs, the toddler "passes the time alone...in the kitchen, where she steps on shards from a broken jar," Nazario wrote, observing while the toddler "hobbles to the sofa, sits down and digs two pieces of glass from her bleeding feet."

Nazario witnessed the drug-chasing mother "smack [her three-year-old] hard, then tell her to stop crying and wash her face." She observed the mother so "intent on smoking the last crumbs of crack, she gently lowers [her daughter] onto a mattress moist with urine and semen. As mom inhales, [the toddler] sleeps, her pink and white sundress absorbing the fluids of unknown grownups."

Titled "Orphans of Addiction," the two-part series ran in November and included a second-day profile of a drug treatment program for addicts and their children. The first day focused primarily on two families and three children, with snapshots of a few others, illuminating a dark and shameful part of America.

In another family, Nazario watched while a drug-addicted father "hauls back and lets his hand fly" to discipline eight-year-old Kevin's "destructive hijinks," she wrote, behavior that in the past had included poking a pencil in a girl's eye and biting a teacher's ankle. Kevin told Nazario his dad beats him regularly, and has deliberately kept him and his 10-year-old sister Ashley out of school during the previous four months. The children often eat one meal of rice a day and go for weeks without bathing, since their tub, Nazario observed, "brims with dirty clothes alive with fleas."

After months of 10- and 14-hour days spent observing the chaos and suffering in these children's lives, Nazario interjected herself into the published story only once: "As a reporter rises to leave," she wrote, three-year-old Tamika stands. "Looking up, she asks simply: 'Are you taking me with you?' "

The toddler's question highlights a dilemma for journalists: Should reporters and photographers intervene when they witness a child being harmed over a period of time? Should they notify authorities, or look the other way for the greater good of the story?

Nazario, Williams and editor Joel Sappell stand by the long-held journalistic tenet that reporters and photographers must remain "a fly on the wall," say Nazario and Sappell. "We wanted to tell a story that was real, that held up this big, giant mirror to society and said, 'Take a look at this! This is real serious stuff. And it's a world you've never been in before, and we're not going to tamper with the world,' " Sappell says. "There's no characterization in those stories of right and wrong, good and bad. It's just what it is."

That paradigm may work most of the time in journalism, say media ethicists and legal and social welfare experts who reviewed the Times' series, but not when it comes to watching powerless children suffer, especially over a period of months. While the story graphically portrays the horror of the children's lives it chronicled, it also raises questions about the Times' ethical judgments and about the paper's decision to reveal nothing to readers about how editors dealt with the moral dilemmas the story presented.

As soon as reporters search for mistreatment, as long as they know ahead of time they will find suffering, they become obligated to confront the question of how much abuse a few children have to endure to serve the story's purpose, many experts say. To simply "hold up a mirror to society" is "outrageous," says Elizabeth Bartholet, a Harvard law professor who specializes in child welfare, abuse and neglect. "The only moral defense possible for not calling social services is that they felt they were accomplishing some greater social purpose

with these articles. If they're just trying to hold up a mirror to society, then how do they escape their responsibility as members of the public to help helpless children?"

Around the country, ethicists, child welfare experts and journalists on the social issues beat had complicated reactions to the Times' series. Some were outraged, arguing the paper's attitude extends the notion of objectivity to a dangerous extreme, not only harming children but eroding readers' faith in the media.

Editors should "draw the line at common sense. How many times do you have to see a kid being beaten?" asks Jane Daugherty, a projects editor at the Detroit News who was a 1994 Pulitzer Prize finalist for her columns on abused children. "If you sit there for three months and watch, what you're saying is that what you have to document at length is more important than those individual children."

Others had mixed emotions and no clear answers about when, where and how to draw the line. "I believe I would have done what the Times did," says Jerry Ceppos, executive editor of the San Jose Mercury News. "I can see not calling authorities. I can see the thinking that writing about these children in a moving way would yield longer lasting results."

At least four months elapsed from the time the Times found the children to the day after the series began, when the Los Angeles County Department of Children and Family Services quickly located three-year-old Tamika, put her in foster care and notified police, who arrested her mother and had her jailed. The other two children had moved with their father to central California before the Times published its exposé.

"What is the obligation of the journalists in this situation? Why can't you write the story and still protect the kids? The public would still be informed," says Michael Nash, presiding judge of the Los Angeles County juvenile court. "The journalists clearly knew [Tamika] was in significant danger. Why let this situation ride for months, print your story and then take credit for children's services locating the kid—which is basically what the Times has done in subsequent articles. That's despicable. By the time the story came out, that kid could have been dead."

After the "Orphans" series ran, the photographer and reporter were featured on television news shows, talked about in living rooms and offices, in hundreds of phone calls the Times received on a special hotline and in nearly 200 responses on an Internet site created for the series. Times Publisher Mark H. Willes says the series was "spectacular" and "compelling. This is one of the kinds of stories we want to do and have done and will continue to do."

While some readers writing on the Web site predicted a Pulitzer Prize for the Times, about one in five demanded an explanation. "How could you two look yourselves in the mirror every night as you slept safely and cleanly?" wrote Joe Soriano. "We know why, because if you had helped and gotten these children the help they desperately needed, there would have been no story."

The ethical questions raised by the Times' stories "are enormously useful," says Steven M. Gorelick, a journalism professor at the City University of New York, whose expertise is press coverage of crimes against children. When journalists cover a story of such magnitude, he says, they are obliged to confront the repercussions ahead of time, to remember "the moral obligations we have as human beings. Journalists have to—they must—ask the question: Can I do something to alleviate the suffering that's put in front of me? Otherwise, what's the point of being there? What's the point of being a human being?"

Social workers considered Tamika's plight serious enough to immediately remove her from her mother. But Times editors concluded the children profiled weren't in imminent danger, says Leo Wolinsky, the paper's managing editor for news. "If you decide to go to authorities when you witness abuse, you'd have to call off the story before getting started," he says. "The result is there'd be no investigation, the kids would still be in danger and the public wouldn't know about it."

The idea for "Orphans of Addiction" came from Senior Metro Projects Editor Joel Sappell, 44. As a reporter, Sappell exposed the underside of Scientology and won a George Polk Award for his investigation of illegal intelligence gathering by the Los Angeles Police Department. As an editor, he helped preside over coverage of the '92 Los Angeles riots and the '94 earthquake, both earning the paper Pulitzers for spot news. He also directed coverage of the O.J. Simpson trial and the story that helped discredit the San Jose Mercury News' controversial "Dark Alliance" story.

On the "Orphans" series, Sappell's vision was clear from the beginning: He wanted to "find out what it's like for children living in an alcoholic or drug-addicted family." He tapped urban affairs writer Sonia Nazario, 37, a Wall Street Journal veteran and '94 Polk Award winner for a series on hunger; and photographer Clarence Williams, 31, in his first year as a full time Times staff member. Sappell, Nazario and Williams focused their search for children in Long Beach, a port city of 425,000 about 20 miles south of downtown Los Angeles. "We didn't choose South L.A. because then the kids would be all black. We didn't choose East L.A. because then it would be all Latino. In Long Beach, it's mixed. We don't want to further the belief that there's this born pathology within people of color to use drugs," Williams says.

For more than a month late last spring, Williams and Nazario talked to social welfare experts, getting a sense of what to expect. It took several days of sitting in the social services office of a local university, approaching about 50 parents, before Nazario settled on Theodora Triggs, a 34-year-old heroin addict, and her three-year-old daughter Tamika. Triggs introduced Nazario to a drug-addicted father named Calvin Holloman and his two children, eight-year-old Kevin and 10-year-old Ashley. Both families became the story's focus; both parents are white.

"My only instruction was: Don't tamper with reality," Sappell says. "That was the only thing I think I was very clear about. We're making a documentary here, in some ways. Don't intrude into it. Because that changes it."

The three had informal meetings whenever necessary to discuss obstacles, mostly related to gaining and maintaining access to the families. They rarely felt the need to bring higher ranking editors into discussions, though Sappell says he did make "the higher ups here aware of what was going on, that it could be potentially a very good, important story."

Throughout the summer, Nazario and Williams saw scenes out of a modern day Dickens novel: "Children as young as two or three wander the streets alone. Kindergartners sometimes panhandle for food money outside grocery stores. Mother-daughter prostitute teams walk on nearby Pacific Coast Highway," Nazario wrote. She heard the same prayer nightly from Ashley, who had been beaten and punched in the face by her father in the past: "Just once give me something good. Please, make life get better." In another scene, Nazario watched Tamika, dressed in a filthy nightgown, jumping up and down on a bed, her exuberance melting into cries for "Mommy! Mommy!" as she realizes her mother has left her alone in the apartment again "without so much as good-bye."

The first-day story, told in six pages of text and photographs, was "emotional, unvarnished, about the little moments. Not the grotesque abuse, which exists, for sure," Sappell says. "If you know what the universe of abuse is—and if abuse is the toddler being raped by the drug dealer—if that's abuse, then what is this? I don't know. I guess you kind of have to figure that out yourself. I don't want to put labels on it, in a way, because I think it's for everybody to kind of decide for themselves what it is."

Unlike medical professionals, social workers and teachers, journalists have no legal obligation to report child abuse to authorities. Nazario was never "conflicted about our purpose," she says: "To show a portrait to society of what kids go through when they grow up in homes where there's substance abuse. I think you would not be a human being if you didn't go into these situations, seeing some of these things, and not coming home with a knot in your stomach.

"On most days, I just dealt with it as this is part of getting to this goal, which I think is a very good goal, explaining to society that this is where a lot of our problems begin," Nazario says. "I thought it would not only help in terms of that, but also might help these particular kids. And so on most days, I felt very strongly that I wore my journalist's hat, and that if I intervened in any way, I would change that situation, and I would not paint a portrait of reality."

Though neither Nazario nor Williams has children, Sappell does. "And believe me," he says,

"I BELIEVE I would have done what the Times did," says Jerry Ceppos, executive editor of the San Jose Mercury News. "I can see not calling authorities. I can see the thinking that writing about these children in a moving way would yield longer lasting results."

"when I got home at night after hearing some of these stories and seeing the pictures, I'd give my kids an extra hug."

To help cope with the suffering he was witnessing, Williams says he talked to his editor, coworkers and friends. He has no clear recollection of what advice they gave him, but he remembers that "they listened. It helped a lot. I always tried to remember the greater good that will come of it. Sonia and I would have these talks—but we never came up with specifics—about how much we were willing to watch and how far we were willing to go to do this."

They decided they could "handle watching parents do drugs in front of their kids. And I remembered getting spankings for some of the silly things I did. So I had no qualms with—I'm not into sparing the rod. But at the same time, I'm not into abuse. I'm not going to watch a kid getting beat to death or beat down."

At one point Williams did intervene, when he saw that a baby, left alone in a room, was about to bite down on an electrical cord. "I made one frame, but at that point, it's crazy. I just ended up holding the baby that afternoon," he says. "At some point you've got to be human."

Nazario, too, intervened, in an experience she chose not to share with her readers. In the story, she refers obliquely to "a trip earlier that week to a medical clinic for several infected spider bites" where she discovered Tamika "had lost 10 percent of her weight in a week."

There was more to it than that.

Before the little girl fell ill, Nazario had established the ground rules, she says. She told the families: "I'm not driving you anywhere; I'm not giving you money. I can't do any of these things, and I will not do any of these things for you." On one or two occasions, when the children said they were hungry, she took them to McDonald's for an interview, as she would any other source, she says. One early morning, Nazario arrived to find Tamika screaming in pain. She said she "didn't think twice" when the girl's mother asked her for a ride to the hospital. "I got into the car and drove her."

The photographer remained behind. "Sonia asked me if I was going to come along," Williams remembers. "And I'm like, 'Well, no, I'm not.' For me, photojournalistically, I can't really photograph a reporter driving her to the hospital. Now, she's part of the story. If she doesn't drive her, she would have to walk. Now, if she was going to walk to the hospital, which wasn't that far away, I would photograph her carrying her daughter, or however she's going to get this girl who couldn't walk to the hospital. Then that's her dealing with that situation of getting her daughter to the hospital. Now I can understand that she wanted to take the woman and her sick child to the hospital. Like I said, I'm glad she [Tamika's mother] didn't ask me. I don't know what I would have done at that point. But what I do know is that if I would have driven her to the hospital, I'm not going to drive to the hospital and then photograph her.

Is Anybody There?

AS IT DOES WITH MOST SPECIAL REPORTS, THE LOS ANGELES TIMES PUT "Orphans of Addiction" on its Web site. "Let's discuss your thoughts and questions" it urged readers as it launched a bulletin board debate. Despite nearly 200 postings, there were only two responses from the Times, both from electronic editors.

The site is "more geared for users to raise questions and talk to each other," explains Rob Cioe, an electronic editor with *latimes.com*. "We can't force reporters and editors to come onto the Web site."

Why not? asks media critic and author Jon Katz. If newspapers really want to engage readers and win new audiences, they must move beyond a token presence on the Web, Katz argues.

Newspapers "have to get off their arrogant perch," he says. "Having a Web site doesn't make you interactive. What makes you interactive is an ongoing dialogue between editors and readers." (See The World of Online Journalism, page 52.)

About an hour after the Times opened the forum, dozens of questions poured in. "Isn't there some way for families like mine to 'babysit' these kids for extended periods of time?" asked Susan Breidenbach.

"Did these children have to remain in these horrific conditions until the article came out?" asked Susan Medart.

"Why couldn't [the Times] have notified child protective services back in the summer when the article was being researched?" asked Cathie Gentile.

"I need to know if there has been a response by social services for these kids. Will someone from the Times staff e-mail me back to discuss this?" asked Connie Nelson.

At about 4:30 p.m., a Times electronic editor sent one of the two official responses posted. He reprinted a list that ran in the paper under the headline: "Where to get help." Electronic editor Cioe also sent a message to reporter Sonia Nazario and editor Joel Sappell, "letting them know we had an active discussion going, that it was attracting a lot of attention. We invited them to look at it.

"That's where we left it," he adds. "They're free to respond or not." As of early February, the Web site had no messages from the Times newsroom.

"If you don't respond, it's very insulting to readers," argues Katz. "Interactivity has been the toughest pill for journalists to swallow. They're taught to be disconnected from readers. It's almost a virtue not to care what people think, that if you listen to your readers, you're pandering. That's a big mistake."

Newspapers have to realize interacting with readers is an opportunity to do better journalism, not an invitation to fraternize with the enemy, adds the longtime newspaper editor. "How many readers would understand why you need to leave kids in peril? Most editors know ahead of time that's something tough for readers to swallow, but maybe there is a reason. I'd have the reporter and editors online, explaining what they did and why."

—Susan Paterno

That's a big fat no. You don't do that. Because now you're part of the story. It's the Golden Rule."

As much as possible, in reporting the story, the reporter and photographer say they stuck to their rules. In the writing, Nazario and Sappell broke a few. "We decided to write it in the present tense. We [wrote] it using first names, which is very unusual," Sappell says. "It's done to personalize it. We were moving into people's lives and that takes a great measure of care. Not to be disruptive. Not to change what transpires in front of you. Not to interfere with it at all." The biggest challenge for Nazario and Williams, he says, "was not asking questions."

Nazario, for instance, says she never asked the emergency room physician about Tamika's chronic neglect or tipped health care workers to the girl's predicament. The story cites neighbors unwilling to alert authorities to the three-year-old's suffering, "fearful that she might end up in an abusive foster home," and quotes Tamika's 70-year-old babysitter calling social welfare workers "baby snatchers."

But the stories never explored the neighbors' disdain for child protective services; and Nazario never questioned authorities about their alleged neglect of the children chronicled because, Sappell explains, "it was not a system story in its conception or its execution. The problem of children's services is not new." The Times had already done "stuff on the problems of foster care, group homes, blah, blah, blah. There's been a lot of stuff on that. It was more of an issue of just wanting to let the public know about the living conditions of these children."

Maintaining access to the families was such a great concern, Sappell and Nazario say, they didn't call child welfare officials to verify claims, published in the story, that "social workers questioned [Kevin's father] after noticing bruises and scratches on the boy. They later visited the house at least three times, neighbors and others say, but allowed the children to remain." Instead, Nazario says, she spent time with the families "sitting and being a fly on the wall, which is different from what reporters normally do, which is, continually ask a lot of questions."

The series' two stories took about two months to write and edit, Nazario says. When the first one appeared on November 16 "it was like a bomb went off," Sappell recalls, "people wanting to help, saying, 'Where can I adopt these kids?' 'How do I become a foster parent?'" Within 24 hours, child abuse reports had increased 20 percent, and social workers had found Tamika Triggs and placed her in a foster home, the Times reported in a front page story. Because Calvin Holloman had moved his two children several months earlier to central California, Los Angeles County social services had no jurisdiction over the family. The Los Angeles County Board of Supervisors "directed the children's services department to report back next week on ways to better identify children of substance abusing families." Nazario quoted the director of the

Department of Children and Family Services, who said the series "will forever alter the landscape of how people see children who are abused and neglected."

" 'Orphans of Addiction' are the Children of Us All," a Times editorial announced on November 18. "The first step," the paper said, "is finding and protecting these children."

BY NOW THE TIMES HAD RESUMED REFERRING TO the drug-addicted parents by their last names. "Triggs initially was charged with one felony count of willful cruelty to a child but pleaded no contest to a misdemeanor count of child endangerment," the paper reported three days after the series ran.

"A couple hundred calls" came in from the public, says Times Director of Communications Laura Morgan. "The vast majority of callers wanted to help; a few didn't understand how [the journalists] could have continued reporting without notifying authorities. We explained that while it did pose a certain ethical dilemma, the purpose of the story was to help all of the children."

Amid the praise, some readers raised angry questions: "If I'm reading the paper correctly," wrote Betty Ann Downing of Long Beach, "apparently nothing was done to assist these children until the social workers learned about it at the same time as the rest of us. Is this the Times' contribution to 'finding and protecting these children' that it editorializes about?" From Carol A. Richardson of Los Angeles: "The article proved…that the reporter and photographer would go to any length for a story, including allowing innocent children to go hungry and to remain at risk of severe neglect and physical and sexual abuse without contacting proper authorities."

In a November 21 article in the Long Beach Press-Telegram, the Department of Children and Family Services and the police said they planned to do nothing differently as a result of the series; police and social workers blamed the Times for failing to alert them sooner. "Our agency is only as effective as the referrals it gets," says children and family services spokesman Schuyler Sprowles. "We're not omnipresent."

Sappell explained in an interview why no one felt compelled to intervene. "Sometimes you don't know where the line is until you reach it," he says. "If we had seen something that was over the line—the line which you don't know [you've crossed] until you see it, till your gut tells you—then we would have called somebody." Witnessing child sexual abuse, for example, or knowing a pregnant woman was abusing drugs, would constitute crossing the line, he says. "But," he adds, "that's not really our role…. What we're really about is exposing things, then letting the appropriate authorities fix them."

On January 11, nearly two months after "Orphans of Addiction" ran, the Times published a front page follow-up, a much more traditional

"JOURNALISTS really do wrestle with these issues," says ethicist Michael Josephson, "but since the public only sees what's published, they never know what went into the struggle. When they don't see [the struggle], the public can only assume journalists don't care."

report on troubles within the Department of Children and Family Services. Though the follow-up's lead included allegations that Tamika Triggs had been reported to authorities numerous times, it focused primarily on chronic problems endemic to the department long before the Times discovered Tamika, Kevin and Ashley. The January 11 account had little of the pathos of the original series, but it pushed the Board of Supervisors into substantive action for the first time. It voted to hire 300 social workers and ordered a management audit of the Department of Children and Family Services. Ironically, the most significant change in the system "was not as a result of the original 'Orphans' story," says Sprowles, "but as a consequence" of the more conventional follow-up article.

By early February, the Times reported Kevin and Ashley were in central California, living with their father, who only a few days before had begun drug treatment. Tamika was still in foster care, occasionally visiting her mother at a residential drug rehabilitation clinic. And the Board of Supervisors had yet to act on task force recommendations to examine the problem of drug-addicted parents.

The Times' failure to examine the child welfare system in depth until two months after the original series ran strains the paper's credibility with readers, says Arlene Morgan, the Philadelphia Inquirer's assistant managing editor for readership. "When you talk about ethics, that includes completeness. This story wasn't complete. You don't do a voyeuristic story, drop it in the paper and wait for the reaction," then expose the system's flaws two months later, she says. "It doesn't take two months to do a turnaround on a story like this."

LIKE MORGAN, MANY JOURNALISTS WHO READ "Orphans of Addiction" found it graphic and powerful, but they also questioned how editors handled the ethical dilemmas they encountered. Do you simply observe the suffering of children and eventually report on it? Is there a point when you should take direct action?

The Times called what it found "neglect." Marc Parent, child abuse investigator turned journalist and author of the book "Turning Stones: My Days and Nights with Children at Risk," wonders how anyone could call it anything but abuse. "That's a no-brainer. If they're smart enough to be reporters, they're smart enough to know abuse when they see it," he says. "We need to have different [journalistic] standards when it comes to kids. Because they're totally helpless, cut off from people who can help them."

When editor Jane Daugherty, then at the Detroit Free Press, found one of her reporters had witnessed incidents similar to what was reported in the Times series, she called authorities "myself, that day, the minute I found out about it," she says. "Then we did stories about how long it took social services to respond." Journalists can do both: Write a compelling story and immediately remove the children from danger, she says. "You don't have to take three months of watching someone being abused."

The dilemma is not new, says Daugherty, who has been covering social welfare issues for 22 years. In the early '80s, before Washington Post editors discovered the eight-year-old drug addict profiled in "Jimmy's World" was fiction, they refused to cooperate with authorities who wanted to find the child. Then in 1989, in an acclaimed Post series, reporter Michele Norris and photographer Dudley M. Brooks spent more than two months virtually living with Dooney Waters, the six-year-old son of a drug addict.

Though Norris never witnessed suffering as severe as what was chronicled by the Times, dur-

· ·

Explaining to Readers

COVERAGE OF DISADVANTAGED CHILDREN HAS GROWN CONSIDERABLY IN the last five years, and so too has the number of ethical questions related to the beat, says Cathy Trost, a former Wall Street Journal reporter who directs the Casey Journalism Center for Children and Families at the University of Maryland College of Journalism.

When faced with ethical dilemmas, Trost and others emphasize the need for news organizations to explain the rationale for their actions in a sidebar or editor's note.

It's important to take that step, says Bob Steele, ethics director at the Poynter Institute for Media Studies, "so readers understand that due caution was taken in dealing with potential ethical land mines."

He adds, "Every day newspapers hold other powerful institutions accountable by writing about what they do—banks, major corporations, churches. Newspapers should hold themselves and each other accountable by asking hard questions of news organizations and publishing the answers to those questions."

When reporters feel compelled to drop their cloaks of detachment and take action, they must tell readers, says Pulitzer Prize-winning reporter Leon Dash, who chronicled underclass life for four years for the Washington Post. "When a toddler is clearly in danger, I've crossed the line and written that I dropped the reporter's hat and intervened. If you get involved, you're obligated to tell readers you felt the need to intervene. You have to let the reader know. That's just being honest."

Crossing lines can cause journalists unwarranted anxiety, says Alex Kotlowitz, a former Wall Street Journal reporter and author of "There Are No Children Here," a critically acclaimed book about a poor, urban family. In his book, Kotlowitz acknowledges providing small amounts of financial assistance to the boys he wrote about, of using $2,000 in prize money he had won for a newspaper story on the family to bail one of them out of jail, of setting up a trust fund for the children, of sending them to private school.

"I know there are people who will say I broke my pact as a journalist to remain detached and objective. But in the end, I had to remind myself that I was dealing with children," he wrote in the book's afterword.

"I thought I'd come into criticism for getting too close to the kids, for crossing the line that I thought, in my earlier days, was much more rigid than I found it to be," he said recently. The opposite, he found, was true. "The line we draw as reporters is not rigid. There are other ways to tell the story that would not compromise ethics."

—S.P.

ing the course of covering Dooney, she says she had "lots of soul searching conversations with my editors. We wanted to maintain journalistic integrity, but we bent the rules in other ways. We kept him out of harm's way, and we gave him food so he wouldn't get hungry." The story also questioned teachers and social workers, examining their involvement in the boy's life and explored the failures of the system designed to protect children like Dooney.

"No mother ever gave birth to a journalist. You're a human first. You bring your humanity to your story," says Norris, now an ABC News correspondent. But, she adds, "there are no set rules, no clear cut lines."

Not so, say media ethicists. "Morality is about drawing lines. If you refuse to draw any lines, that perhaps is the most immoral position to take," says Michael Josephson, an ethicist used as a consultant by various newspapers, including the Orange County Register, where he helped editors and reporters wend their way through a thicket of ethical problems that arose from a 1996 Pulitzer Prize-winning story about fertility doctors secretly stealing women's eggs.

To avoid appearing arrogant, he says, journalists need to explain the ground rules to readers. "It's morally defensible to say, 'This is who we are and why we did it.' But the ground rules should be provided, so that the L.A. Times acknowledges that they thought about it ahead of time. State it, and let the public decide whether the rules are acceptable."

Withholding information can break faith with readers, Josephson adds. "Journalists really do wrestle with these issues, but since the public only sees what's published, they never know what went into the struggle. When they don't see [the struggle], the public can only assume journalists don't care. That sort of arrogant trust will not cut it anymore with the public, or with many journalists who I find are becoming increasingly more cynical with the decisions made by their news organizations, because they know how business-driven these decisions have become."

If the public were asked what it wanted the Times to do, "my opinion is the public would say,

'Don't let the children get hurt,' " he says. "If I'm right, then the variance between what the public says is right and moral and what the newspaper says is right and moral leaves the media with a huge credibility gap. The only way the media can justify that gap is to say: 'We know what's best.' Where does the media come off developing a different standard of decency?"

At the very least, he says, the news organization should explain its rationale to readers. "You can write what you want, but at least you're accountable, you've made a choice. As long as journalists get to stand by unwritten, informal standards, no one has to be formally accountable. That's irresponsible."

Editors at the Times decided against publishing an explanation of how the story was reported or why journalists didn't intervene to help the children, Sappell says. "I felt very committed to keeping ourselves out of [the story] as much as we could," says Sappell. "I didn't want anything to detract in any way from the power of the pieces we were trying to present to the public. The whole concept from the beginning was: Don't intervene. Let life unfold."

Nazario agrees. "The story was not about us or about ethical questions. The story was about these kids and what they face when they're growing up in homes with substance abuse. Journalists should not focus stories on themselves. They should focus on the story."

The paper will submit the series and photographs for Pulitzer Prize consideration, says Publisher Willes. Willes, Wolinsky and Sappell say they have no regrets about how the story was handled. There is one thing Willes says he would contemplate doing differently in the future: He would explain to readers how journalists struggle with ethical questions they encounter while reporting. "I think doing something to allow readers to better understand the very real issues that we face and have to work through—I think readers would find that fascinating."

Contributing writer Susan Paterno explored whether it's ever acceptable for journalists to lie to get a story in AJR's May 1997 issue.

STARR TURN

*T*HE SPLIT-SCREEN IMAGE ON ABC NEWS WAS SURREAL. On the left was a live shot of President Clinton behind the podium at the United Nations delivering a speech about global terrorism. On the right was the videotape of the president delivering his testimony to Independent Counsel Kenneth Starr's grand jury.

ABC—like other broadcast and cable networks—was struggling to make judgments on September 21 about which news event was more important: the president's speech to world leaders and U.N. delegates, or the release of his videotaped statements about his relationship with former White House intern Monica Lewinsky.

A graphic on the screen read, "Clinton addressing UN," but the audio was from the president's testimony, as he confronted probing questions about his relationship with Lewinsky.

The twin images were a metaphor for deep divisions among the public and the press about congressional decisions to release the Starr report and Clinton testimony, and about the way the news media handled them.

The "data dumps" led to an intense national debate about the news media's roles and responsibilities in an age when information is instantly available to the public and the press. Among the questions: How should graphic sexual material be handled? Were the news media in danger of becoming arms of law enforcement? And when the public at large has instant access to information online, what is the role of the journalist?

Millions of Americans read the unexpurgated Starr report on

Coverage of the Starr report and President Clinton's videotaped testimony raised provocative questions about journalism ethics.

BY JACQUELINE SHARKEY

congressional or news media Web sites, then got verbatim reprints in their hometown newspapers. An estimated 22.5 million Americans watched the president's testimony on the seven U.S. networks that provided live coverage the morning the videotapes were released. That night, ABC, NBC and CBS expanded their nightly newscasts to an hour for the first time since the Persian Gulf War.

CBS News President Andrew Heyward told news directors gathered in San Antonio for their annual convention that television handled the situation "very responsibly," and had a duty to show the testimony. But New York Times columnist Anthony Lewis wrote that the videotapes "should never have been shown," and 78 percent of Americans agreed with him, according to a New York Times/CBS News poll conducted September 22 and 23.

Many newspapers around the country printed the Starr report in special sections, insisting, as did Arizona Daily Star Editor Stephen Auslander, that readers should have access to the entire document because it involved "a serious political issue" that called for informed judgments.

Many readers agreed, but others resented the relentless coverage of the independent counsel's investigation, have become participants in the nation's political and legal systems rather than observers. Journalists have acted like "adjuncts to the special prosecutor's investigation," says Bill Kovach, curator of the Nieman Foundation at Harvard University and chairman of the Committee of Concerned Journalists.

Others wonder about the extent to which news values are eroding democratic values, such as the right to privacy. "There are no secrets anymore," NBC News anchor Tom Brokaw acknowledged moments before the network began airing Clinton's testimony.

The debate about coverage also has international ramifications in an age when information technology has transformed U.S.-based news organizations into global media. CNN senior international correspondent Christiane Amanpour reported that some foreign leaders thought televising the president's testimony was an "electronic lynching" that undermined American leadership.

U.S. news media have received calls, e-mails, faxes and letters from people all over the world criticizing the coverage. "Posting the independent counsel's report on the Internet was disrespectful, unnecessary and aimed at damaging

"Posting the independent counsel's report on the Internet was disrespectful, unnecessary and aimed at damaging Clinton," wrote Heidelberg University student Andreas Volk in USA Today: "Broadcasting his testimony proved to many Germans that political and social life in the U.S. has dropped to a 'Baywatch' level."

probe. "After reading only the table of contents, the Starr report went into the recycle bin," wrote Star reader Priscilla Walker. "I guess the media doesn't even pay attention to the polls that indicate most of us are fed up with Starr's behavior."

Some readers also were fed up with the report's explicit language and detailed depictions of sex. Some canceled subscriptions at newspapers such as the Chicago Tribune, Kansas City Star and Arizona Republic. These reactions helped renew discussion about whether the press should reflect or challenge cultural values about sex and language. New York Times columnist Russell Baker decried the fact that "sober commentators...were writing like pornographers." But the Baltimore Sun's Rosemary Armao, a former executive director of Investigative Reporters & Editors, supported publishing the graphic language, saying that news media censorship of explicit words and details sometimes distorts information.

Some members of the public and journalists think coverage of the independent counsel's report and Clinton's testimony symbolize the extent to which the news media, during the Starr

Clinton," wrote Heidelberg University student Andreas Volk in USA Today. "Broadcasting his testimony proved to many Germans that political and social life in the U.S. has dropped to a 'Baywatch' level."

Despite the criticism at home and abroad, many news media reported spikes in sales and ratings. The Los Angeles Times sold more than 60,000 additional papers the day it published extensive excerpts of the Starr report. The Chicago Tribune sold more than 80,000 extra copies. Tom Johnson, chairman and CEO of CNN News Group, said ratings for the president's testimony were among the highest ever for the time slot.

WHEN CONGRESS RELEASED THE Starr report September 11, the strengths and weaknesses of various news media were readily apparent.

Television correspondents, on the air moments after they had the document, struggled to deal with its explicit language and detail. CBS chief Washington correspondent Bob Schieffer commented on the report while flipping through it. CNN's Bob Franken summarized one part of the material by saying, "According to Miss Lewinsky, she and the president kissed, she unbuttoned his jacket, et cetera, et cetera."

Although there were no disasters on the Internet, some users faced long waits, as millions of people jostled electronically for access to Web sites. "[O]ne advantage television has over the Internet is you'll never see the words 'Site Unavailable,'" quipped CBS anchor Dan Rather.

Newspapers had their own advantages. The longer news cycle gave editors and reporters time to read the report and plan coverage. On the other hand, the cycle was shorter than for news magazines, whose printed product did not reach readers for days. This provided "a rare chance" to demonstrate why "we bring something to the table that other media don't," including nuanced stories and a range of opinions "instead of sound bites from talking heads," says Sandra Mims Rowe, editor of Portland's Oregonian.

During the weekend, many papers—among them the New York Times, Washington Post, Chicago Tribune, Kansas City Star and Oregonian—published the entire report as a special section. Others, such as the Baltimore Sun, published lengthy excerpts.

Many newspapers dealt with the Starr report's frank detail by printing warnings on their front pages and special sections. Editors said the graphic descriptions were not a deterrent to printing the report because the political issues were so grave.

"This is a document which has the potential to cause the president of the United States to leave office," says Chicago Tribune Editor Howard A. Tyner. "I don't think that if you have any sense of responsibility that you can say, 'Well, it's just too yucky.'"

Editors worked hard to provide careful coverage of the report's explicit sexual accounts in news stories. "There's no way of talking about the perjury charge without talking about oral sex, breasts and genital areas," says New York Times Executive Editor Joseph Lelyveld. "But we've tried to be generic...in describing particular sexual acts and encounters."

The report evoked intense public interest. Papers across the country sold thousands of additional copies, and some reported unprecedented reader response.

The Kansas City Star "got considerable praise" for printing the report, says Doug Weaver, the paper's editor for readership and new initiatives. "We would've gotten a ton of criticism if we had not run it."

At first, Arizona Daily Star readers reacted with "an unbelievable outcry of 'shoot the messenger,'" says Editor Auslander. Once people learned about this negative response, he adds, "there was a second wave of support."

The newspaper's decision to sell the special section at Circle K convenience stores in southern Arizona created some spirited civic discussion. A middle-aged woman at one Tucson store pointed out that Penthouse and Playboy were kept behind the cash register, but the Starr report was out on the counter, "where any kid can buy it." A clerk spent several minutes earnestly trying to explain the difference between news and pornography.

In newsrooms, reporters and editors talked about whether the Starr report is a signal that guidelines for using sexually explicit language in news stories should be revised.

The Sun's Armao thinks it's time for an update. Concerns about language are "causing us to self-censor important elements of the news that the public needs to know to make judgments about political and social issues," she says.

Armao finds it ironic that shortly before the Sun printed unedited sections of the Starr report, the paper would only paraphrase sexually explicit passages from a Maya Angelou book that some parents wanted removed from a high school reading list. Armao suggested running some passages verbatim, but editors thought this would take the graphic language out of context.

Armao doesn't disagree with that decision, but believes that newspapers are too apt to take the "we don't lead, we follow" approach to cultural standards. She recalls having to fight to get the words "anal intercourse" into stories about the emerging AIDS epidemic in the early 1980s. Using such language—distasteful as it was to many readers—saved lives, she says.

If the Starr report "does nothing more than force us to look at the words we use in a paper and the way we write, then it's done something good," Armao says.

The report compelled newspaper editors to look at other issues as well. One is fairness. Some journalists are troubled that many newspapers, because of time constraints, only included the White House "pre-rebuttal" to the Starr report, written before the president or his lawyers had a chance to examine the document. By the time the White House issued a more detailed response on Saturday, some papers already had printed their special sections.

The Chicago Tribune included the second rebuttal in its final edition. The Oregonian printed the text in its commentary section on Sunday. But many newspapers simply summarized the White House document.

Another issue raised by the Starr report involves the changing role of the journalist in an age in which the public can independently access information as quickly as the media. Some analysts believe the news media's attempts to deal with the report—which the public received over the Internet as journalists pored over their printed copies and computer screens—show that they should put more emphasis on analyzing facts.

"With the advent of the Internet, anybody can be an information collector," says University of Missouri journalism professor Lee Wilkins. What people need now "is the analysis and the synthesis and the context" to put information

Chicago Tribune Editor **HOWARD A. TYNER** *says it was important to publish the entire Starr report, "yucky" details and all.*

The Baltimore Sun's **ROSEMARY ARMAO** *thinks newspapers are too prissy in dealing with explicit language about sex.*

into perspective and make judgments about it.

This, in turn, raises questions about the traditional definition of objectivity, which calls for giving equal space or weight to competing sides of an issue.

Wilkins thinks this definition presents a false impression of journalists and their role. The minute reporters ask, "Where did those documents come from? What questions did they ask? What questions did they perhaps not ask?" they are moving from objectivity to analysis, Wilkins says.

Oregonian Editor Rowe, immediate past president of the American Society of Newspaper Editors, says journalists should no longer tell the public, " 'We just bring you the news. We're objective. You know, just the facts, ma'am.' The fact that we have tried to pretend that is true has hurt us in terms of the range of things we do, and I think it has hurt our image with the public.

"There is an increasing awareness that we put a framework on almost every story," Rowe says, and "making sure that you have the best possible framework for a story" is one of a journalist's most important responsibilities.

Reporters and editors covering the Starr report soon faced another challenge to that responsibility, when the Republican-led House Judiciary Committee announced it was releasing Clinton's videotaped testimony on September 21.

T HAT MORNING, MILLIONS OF AMERIcans from Times Square to Texarkana watched on television as Judiciary Committee staffers delivered the videotapes to technicians in Room B365 of the Rayburn Building.

TV viewers included many dedicated Internet users, who didn't want to endure the long download times that video requires on the World Wide Web.

As seven U.S. broadcast and cable networks struggled to present live coverage of the four hours of videotaped testimony, occasional technical glitches caused what NBC's Tom Brokaw called "electronic meltdown."

Media critics were more concerned about what the New York Times' Baker called "the Great Media Meltdown," citing actions that he said "were variously foolish, shameful, dangerous to American democracy and destructive for the reputation of the news industry."

One embarrassing misstep involved the prevalent speculation that the videotapes would show an angry president losing control. These reports, based on anonymous sources, "proved false," says CBS' Schieffer, who earlier told viewers that Clinton had used profanity and had "stormed out of the room."

These errors show that "sources have gained the upper hand, and journalists have become more easily manipulated by all sides," said Tom Rosenstiel, director of the Project for Excellence in Journalism, on CNN's "Inside Politics."

Barbara Cochran, president of the Radio-Television News Directors Association, says competitive pressure helped create the "urban myth" about the president's behavior. Twenty-four hour news cycles and increasing numbers of information sources sometimes make journalists seem "a little out of control," she says.

Fox News Chairman and CEO Roger Ailes said at RTNDA's September convention that one reason the networks decided to run the president's testimony live was "so that we wouldn't spin it, and [would] just give the president every opportunity to speak for himself as opposed to have us interpret it."

Showing the videotapes rekindled debate over how to handle sexual details, this time in the independent counsel's questions. All the networks provided viewers with verbal warnings and graphics; most showed the entire tape. But NBC deleted two brief passages it deemed too explicit to air, and MSNBC deleted one.

Showing the entire four hours of grand jury testimony also raised questions about fairness and balance. Anchors tried to provide perspective, reminding viewers that this was a one-sided proceeding. "It is prosecutorial in nature. There's no opportunity for the president to defend himself," ABC's Peter Jennings said. Some journalists did not think these comments were sufficient. New York Times columnist Lewis said televising the tape "degraded this country" and turned TV journalists into "the prosecutor's chorus."

Jon Katz, a Freedom Forum First Amendment Center scholar and online columnist, agrees. "Journalists aren't just covering the Starr inquiry, they're coproducing it," he says.

Network news chiefs defend their decision. The videotapes marked "a historic moment in this nation's history that relates to the possible impeachment of a twice-elected president," CNN's Johnson said. "For us not to carry it is almost censoring information from people of all ages, and that isn't what democracy is all about."

Bill Wheatley, NBC News vice president, says the tape "was an important piece of evidence." Because "there was already a national debate going about it," he says, "we felt it a reasonable thing to do to air it and let people decide for themselves."

What many members of the public decided is that they did not like the way the news media were responding to the situation. A CNN/Time magazine poll taken after the videotapes aired found that 71 percent of respondents disapproved of the media's coverage of impeachment issues.

An ongoing stream of calls and correspondence to news media echoed that finding. During a C-SPAN call-in show after the videotapes were shown, a 16-year-old schoolgirl from Alamo, California, explained that she was reading Arthur Miller's "The Crucible" for English class. The play, she said, helped her understand that "this thing going on with President Bill Clinton is a modern-day witch hunt."

RTNDA's **BARBARA COCHRAN** *says competitive pressures helped create erroneous stories about President Clinton's grand jury appearance.*

CBS News President **ANDREW HEYWARD** *says television networks had a duty to air the president's testimony.*

Another concern is whether major stories have been ignored as the Starr report and the president's testimony dominated the news agenda. Rep. Vince Snowbarger (R-Kan.) told MSNBC he feared that Americans were not receiving information about crucial legislation.

His concerns are reinforced by data from the Tyndall Weekly, which monitors broadcast news programs. The week after the Starr report's release, the major broadcast networks produced 54 stories about the Clinton-Lewinsky affair and four about public policy, the newsletter reported.

"I think it's fair to say that some other important stories have gotten less coverage than they would have," says NBC's Wheatley. "On the other hand, I'm not sure that we've missed any major story."

CBS' Heyward told his RTNDA audience that issues such as education routinely are "woefully undercovered" on television "because it's difficult to find a headline and, frankly, because education stories aren't as sexy as Monica Lewinsky or…a breaking story, like a crime story."

Television is "a medium that has to be so entertaining even when we do the news, because you're scared of boring people and losing the audience," he said.

CNN Chairman Johnson said ratings for his is what people are talking about," he said, "but personally, I'm troubled that we've gone this far with it."

Some members of the public also were troubled. "If any…one group has completely lost the faith of the citizens it is the media who have inflated this panty raid into what it is today," John Martin said in a message to CNN's Web site.

Analysts are concerned that these attitudes could have a profound effect on the news media. They warn that as public trust declines, so does support for the press' traditional protections and privileges. This sets up a climate in which judges, juries and legislatures believe they have the responsibility for placing controls on the press.

Media excesses during the O.J. Simpson trial led the California legislature to consider laws restricting press access to information about criminal cases. Public perceptions about the news media's role in Princess Diana's death led members of Congress to introduce legislation to protect people's privacy by deterring journalists' access. In September, California Gov. Pete Wilson signed a bill allowing people to collect damages if they can prove that a photo of a "personal or family activity" involved an unreasonable invasion of privacy.

"If any…one group has completely lost the faith of the citizens it is the media who have inflated this panty raid into what it is today," John Martin said in a message to CNN's Web site.

company's Headline News channel—which covered Clinton's U.N. speech live—were "very meager," while ratings for CNN—which was showing the Clinton videotape—were very high. "I just hope that we can resist the pressures to take our programming down for the sake of bringing audience levels up," Johnson said. "But it's one of the sad realities of the world we live in."

Another reality is that U.S. press coverage of the Starr report and Clinton testimony has had an impact around the world. A German newspaper, Hamburger Morgenpost, ran two blank pages under the headline, "Clinton's pornographic interrogation—Without us."

French 2 Television, in an attempt to understand "how U.S. politics and media came to this point," sent correspondent Philippe Gassot to visit CBS News the day the videotapes were released. C-SPAN ran his report.

Gassot said some CBS staffers were uncomfortable with the "relentless" coverage of the Clinton-Lewinsky affair but did not want to discuss their misgivings. "It's not easy to express your doubts when you're not supposed to have any," Gassot noted.

A man identified as a CBS production assistant did speak up. "I don't think there's any way that we can safely ignore this. This is news, this

Freedom Forum columnist Katz warns that if journalists ignore the way recent press coverage has compromised privacy and the criminal justice system, "It's hard to imagine how somebody is not going to start raising the specter of the British judicial system, which puts some limits on the press' coverage of these matters."

Nieman Curator Bill Kovach thinks there is "a real disconnect between the journalists who are producing the information" and the readers and viewers "who care about what kind of journalism they get." Kovach believes the news media must bridge the gulf separating them from the public if they hope to regain people's confidence and maintain support for First Amendment freedoms.

"We insist on transparency of every institution in America but our own," he says. "We have to become a hell of a lot more transparent to the people who consume our information, about who we are and what we do and why we do it the way we do."

University of Arizona journalism professor Jacqueline Sharkey has written for AJR about coverage of Princess Diana's death and the O.J. Simpson saga. David Schaenman and William Wing provided research assistance for this story.

SPOT NEWS
THE PRESS AND THE DRESS

BY LAWRENCE K. GROSSMAN

"Of all the stories we reported involving the president and Monica Lewinsky, ABC was most vilified for our reports about the semen-stained dress," says ABC News Washington correspondent Jackie Judd. "Critics kept asking, 'where's the proof?' Most people think it was the story's 'yuk' factor that made us so unpopular, but there was more to it than that."

Here is an account of how the press covered the bizarre story of the semen-stained dress, which was more accurately reported than most critics have been willing to admit, and what that coverage reveals about the journalism in today's high intensity, echo-chamber world of cyberspace.

Jackie Judd first reported the semen-stained dress story on ABC's *World News Tonight* on Friday, January 23: "Lewinsky says she saved, apparently as some kind of souvenir, a navy blue dress with the president's semen stain on it. If true, this could provide physical evidence of what really happened." Judd repeated her account later that night on *20/20*.

Surprisingly, in the first draft of her script, Judd had failed to mention anything about the dress, even though she had nailed down the basic facts from two trusted sources and had alerted her editors in New York to the story. Asked why she held back, Judd told me, "At that stage, only the third day into the Lewinsky scandal, I was still squeamish about putting a story like that on the air. It was all new territory for us."

Lawrence K. Grossman is a former president of NBC News and PBS.

But Judd's editors persuaded her to revise her script and report the facts she had learned about the dress with President Clinton's semen stain still on it. The dress, they argued, would be "the smoking gun" that could contradict the president's denials and take the scandal out of the "he-said, she-said" cul-de-sac in which it seemed to be stuck.

Judd was not the first to go public with the story. That distinction went to cyber gossip Matt Drudge, who had posted his attention-getting scoop on the Internet two days earlier. On Wednesday, January 21, his heavily trafficked *Drudge Report* broke the news that Linda Tripp had told investigators Lewinsky claimed she "kept the garment with Clinton's dried semen in it—a garment she allegedly said she would never wash." Drudge repeated the story the next morning in an interview on NBC's *Today* show.

However, it was Judd's January 23 report on ABC that was the first in the mainstream media to rely on the reporter's own sources, rather than on secondhand information from Drudge. Peter Jennings introduced Judd's report this way: "Today, someone with specific knowledge of what it is that Monica Lewinsky says really took place between her and the president has been talking to ABC's Jackie Judd."

Where Judd got the dress story has become a matter of tradecraft controversy. Last June, in the premiere issue of *Brill's Content*, media critic Steve Brill accused Judd of basing her report on an untrustworthy, biased single source, Lucianne Goldberg, the self-confessed Clinton-hater. He wrote, "Although Judd would not comment on her source, Lucianne Goldberg told me that she herself is the source for this Jackie Judd report and for others that would follow." While Goldberg, a New York book agent, claimed to have given Judd the story, she denied

to Brill that she had been the source for the Drudge scoop, even though in January she had bragged to the New York *Daily News*: "The dress story? I think I leaked that. . . . I had to do something to get [the media's] attention. I've done it. And I'm not unproud of it." Brill's article charged, "[W]hether it turns out that [the president] stained one dress or one hundred dresses, Judd's every utterance is infected with the clear assumption that the president is guilty at a time when no reporter can know that."

In her own defense, Judd insisted to me that she had adhered to ABC's two-source rule on the dress story. She got her information, she said, from two sources she knew well and considered to be reliable, a fact confirmed by ABC News senior vice president Richard C. Wald, who oversees the network's news standards. Judd says she had met Goldberg only once briefly, and "spoke to her only for thirty seconds or less." It was made clear that Brill was mistaken in his assertion that Goldberg was her source.

I asked Judd why, in her January 23 piece, both she and Jennings had referred to only a single source for the story, when now she says she had relied on two sources. "The first person who told me about the dress told it to me off the record on condition that I not use it," Judd replied. "Then I confirmed the story from another source who insisted on anonymity, but who did not say we couldn't run it. So, to be accurate, we cited only one source on *World News Tonight*."

Drudge, as was his custom, had cited no source for his story of January 21. But his revelation earned the former Hollywood gift shop clerk with no journalistic credentials an interview on *Today*, the number one network morning news show. Most mainstream journalists disdain *The Drudge Report*. They

Reprinted from *Columbia Journalism Review*, November/December 1998, pp. 34-36, 38. © 1998 by Columbia Journalism Review.

consider it not a legitimate news outlet but a gossip sheet posted on the Internet, where anybody can report or expose anything as fact whether true or not. Nevertheless, with many scoops about recent scandals to his credit, Drudge has become a hot media property. The Fox News Channel has given him his own news-gossip show.

Introducing Drudge on *Today*, co-anchor Matt Lauer described *The Drudge Report* as "a media gossip page known for below-the-Beltway reporting." Lauer then asked his guest about his semen-stained dress story that had appeared on the Internet the day before. Said Drudge: "I have reported that there's a potential DNA trail that would tie Clinton to this young woman." Lauer asked Drudge if he had any confirmation. Drudge answered, "Not outside of what I've just heard, but I don't think anybody does at this point."

Another *Today* guest that morning was *Newsweek*'s Michael Isikoff, whose reporting on the president's sex scandals had earned him a consulting contract with NBC. Appearances by *Newsweek* staffers on television's rapidly expanding schedule of talk shows generate valuable publicity for the magazine, part of the high decibel ricochet effect of today's nonstop multimedia environment. *Time* has even installed a small TV studio in its New York offices so its editors and reporters can appear on screen at the drop of a newsbreak.

Lauer asked Isikoff if he heard anything about the dress. An experienced journalist, Isikoff knew better than to speculate on network television: "I have not reported that, and I am not going to report that until I have evidence that it is, in fact, true," he said. "I've heard lots of wild things, as I am sure you have. But you don't go on the air and blab them."

Still, simply by appearing on NBC News's highly regarded *Today*, the stained-dress story immediately graduated from gossip to news, gaining a measure of credibility and legitimacy despite the fact that no mainstream journalist had yet verified it. At that point, NBC News had done none of its own reporting on the story or gotten any independent verification. Landing a guest who makes a bombshell revelation on an established show like *Today* is a ploy guaranteed to gain instant worldwide attention, as Drudge's interview certainly did.

The beauty of getting the guest to deliver the sensational news is that the network itself doesn't have to hold back and risk being scooped on the story until its own reporters and editors are satisfied that it is accurate. No one at the network has to spend time and money digging for facts. Even better, if the story turns out to be wrong, the network has an out: "Matt Drudge said it; we didn't. We were only doing our job trying to find out from him whether it was true." This can be a dubious practice, and lately it has become all too commonplace, especially on cable talk shows.

A story of that magnitude appearing on *Today* also creates a king-sized dilemma for the rest of the press. Editors ask themselves, "Now that it's been on *Today*, shouldn't we carry it? True, we have no verification ourselves, but neither does anybody else. The fact that *Today* carried the story is itself news. Besides, if we don't run it, you can bet other guys will." And so, before any reporter for the mainstream press had even checked the story out (Judd's piece on ABC did not appear until January 23, the day after Drudge's *Today* interview), the unsubstantiated gossip posted by Matt Drudge on the Internet had risen to the level of apparently credible news. NBC's Tom Brokaw calls this multimedia, echo-chamber effect, "the Big Bang theory of journalism." But is it journalism, or gossip-mongering on a worldwide scale?

On Thursday, January 22, while

stained model.) "How do we know" about the gift? *Good Morning America* co-anchor Lisa McRee asked Donaldson. "Well," he replied, "I guess we don't know. We're talking about leaks." Donaldson's revelation on *GMA* is a textbook example of an unsourced, unsubstantiated, pseudo-fact, disseminated by a reporter playing catch up, that simply feeds the public's distrust of the news media.

Donaldson was repeating a story that had been posted on Newsweek-on-Line the previous day. It said Lewinsky had been heard, on a tape in *Newsweek*'s exclusive possession, claiming that Clinton had given her a dress as a present. *Newsweek*'s Washington bureau chief Ann McDaniel repudiated this report two weeks later, explaining that the magazine's reporters had misinterpreted what they heard on the tape.

Other outlets would make a similar mistake. On Monday, January 26, for example, *The New York Times* reported, "People who have heard the tapes said Monica Lewinsky had reportedly claimed that Mr. Clinton gave her a dress and that it was later stained with semen." In fact, the claim was not on the tape and the dress that Lewinsky said had the stain was not the one the president allegedly gave her. The *Times*, *The Washington Post*, and the Baltimore *Sun*, among others, repeated that error on succeeding days. Did that story really come from "people who have heard the tapes," or did the reporters get it secondhand from Newsweek-on-Line,

The press got some things wrong, but the major facts right.

Drudge was dropping his bombshell on NBC's *Today*, Sam Donaldson was breaking an entirely different dress story on ABC's *Good Morning America*. Donaldson talked about a dress that, he said, the president had allegedly given Lewinsky as a gift. (Later on, *The New York Times* and many others were to confuse the gift dress with the semen-

GMA, Drudge, or elsewhere and, as in the children's game Telephone, garble the information?

By Saturday morning, January 24, news of the *real* semen-stained dress hit the world and splattered in all directions. The garment, in print, on-air, and on cable, was the blockbuster story of the week. The New York *Daily News* blared on page one, SHE KEPT SEX DRESS. The *New York Post* bannered, MONICA'S LOVE DRESS. Many newspaper and broadcast accounts picked up a UPI story that reported as fact that Lewinsky had kept a dress with Clinton's semen, eliminating the detail that Lewinsky had only *claimed* to have such a dress.

Time and *Newsweek*, released on Sunday, January 25, carried almost identical reports about the dress, adding a few marginally different details of their own. *Time*: In an untaped conversation with Tripp, Lewinsky "allegedly held up a dress she claimed was stained with the president's semen and said, 'I'll never wash it again.'" *Newsweek*: "Lewinsky told Tripp that she was keeping, as a kind of grotesque memento, a navy blue dress stained with Clinton's semen. Holding it up as a trophy to Tripp, she declared, 'I'll never wash it again.'"

Neither of the newsmagazines, which appear to have gotten their quotes from the same anonymous leaker, gave any indication of the nature of the source. A month later *Time* wrote, its "source was someone close to Tripp that *Time* believes credible." *Newsweek*'s piece that week reported Lewinsky was given a dress by Clinton, although later the magazine said it was no longer sure there ever was a dress given to her by the president. *Newsweek*, however, did stand by its account that Lewinsky claimed she had the dress with Clinton's semen.

On Monday, January 26, *The New York Times* quoted Lewinsky's lawyer William Ginsburg dismissing press reports about the semen-stained dress: "I would assume that if Monica Lewinsky had a dress that was sullied or dirtied, she would have had it cleaned. I know of no such dress."

On Thursday, January 29, CBS News's Scott Pelley broke the story that the FBI had found no evidence on any of the clothes taken from Lewinsky's apartment. The next night on ABC, Judd, citing "law enforcement sources," said, "Starr so far has come up empty in a search for forensic evidence," explaining that the Lewinsky clothes the FBI tested had been dry cleaned. As it later turned out, dry cleaning had nothing to do with the absence of the semen stain; the FBI had tested the wrong garments. *The Washington Post* reported that President Clinton assured associates there was no such dress.

In the spring, the tale of the semen-stained dress fast lost credibility. Critics came forward in force. *The Toronto Star* wrote, "Take the notorious blue dress, the one said to have been stained with the president's 'residue.' Can anyone blame the public for not trusting wild and sometimes truly unbelievable daily news reports, no matter what medium?" A Cox News Service piece by Scott Shepard began, "The dress? It has vanished into the misty realm of yesterday's newspaper and last night's TV news broadcast." Shepard blamed "the well-traveled route of hearsay in today's brave new information world, where a few established 'facts' are repeated and mixed with speculation and allegations from unidentified sources." Kathleen Hall Jamieson, dean of the Annenberg School for Communications at the University of Pennsylvania, complained on PBS's *NewsHour with Jim Lehrer* about the press's lack of careful sourcing and confirmation, citing allegations about the semen-stained dress. "It turns out now that there may be no dress."

Longtime TV news producer Ed Fouhy, now at the Pew Center in Washington, D.C., deplored the apparent fact that, "so many good journalists [were] spending so much time analyzing so little." *Los Angeles Times* contributing editor Robert Scheer wrote of the press performance, "It's sick. There was no blue dress and no semen stain, but America's mass media fell for the lurid tales." *The New York Times* columnist Frank Rich blasted the reports of "phantom semen stains."

Then, at the end of July, Lewinsky and special prosecutor Kenneth Starr finally agreed on an immunity deal. On *World News Tonight*, July 29, Judd, citing legal sources (plural this time), revealed that "as part of the immunity deal with prosecutors, Monica Lewinsky agreed to turn over evidence she claimed would back up her story that she had a sexual relationship with the president. The sources confirm that one piece of evidence is, in fact, the dress Lewinsky said she saved after an encounter with Mr. Clinton because it had a semen stain on it. Lewinsky's claim of the dress's existence was first reported by ABC News six months ago. The dress may provide Starr with forensic evidence of a relationship."

As Judd's script made clear, the beleaguered ABC News correspondent felt vindicated at last.

The next day, July 30, on CNN's *Inside Politics*, CNN White House correspondent Wolf Blitzer revealed the astonishing news that Lewinsky had given the stained dress to her mother, who, he said, hid it in her New York apartment for six months. According to Blitzer, when the president agreed to testify to the grand jury, he was unaware that Lewinsky would be turning over the dress with its physical evidence of their sexual relationship.

The blue dress with the president's semen stain existed after all. It was real. And it had returned to center stage.

That same day, like a recurring nightmare, an improbable connection was made between the dress and the O.J. Simpson murder case. Former Los Angeles police detective Mark Fuhrman, a key witness in the Simpson trial, appeared on MSNBC, the cable news channel that gained the dubious reputation of programming "All Monica, All the Time." Fuhrman revealed that he had been contacted the previous October by his one-time book agent Goldberg, who asked him how DNA could be extracted from a dress.

In their August 10 editions, both *Time* and *Newsweek* reported that Goldberg and Tripp had plotted to get their hands on Lewinsky's dress, take a swab of the stain if they could, and have it tested for semen themselves. Goldberg described their scheme, which sounded like a dark soap opera mystery: Tripp allegedly called Lewinsky and told her she was so broke she would like to come over to Lewinsky's apartment while Lewinsky was away to check out her wardrobe and borrow a dress. Would Lewinsky tell her doorman to let her in? Tripp's plan to get at the blue dress with the semen stain did not succeed. Lewinsky failed to respond, according to Goldberg. *Time* reported the Goldberg tale and concluded, "Tripp's associates say that story is not true." *Newsweek* credited "sources familiar with the investigation" for its account.

On August 4, the *New York Post* reported that Goldberg claimed to have declined an offer of $500,000 from the *National Enquirer* for a photo of Lewinsky wearing the infamous blue dress. Goldberg said the photo exists but since it was not in her possession, she had to turn down the offer. According to the

New York Post, Goldberg said: "'This is not about money. This is about right and wrong,' . . . adding with a wicked chortle, 'Besides, I don't have it [the photo].'"

In hindsight, it is easy to be critical of those who beat up on the press for its "phantom dress" reports before the full story came out. It is also somewhat unfair. It is now clear that Matt Drudge's scoop on the dress turned out to be essentially accurate. So did the reports by Jackie Judd, Wolf Blitzer, and most other reporters. The issue here is not about how the press spread misinformation; when it came to the dress, the press got some things wrong, but the major facts right. Still, too many news organization paid too little attention to basic rules of the trade in their hot pursuit of the story. In today's nonstop news environment, the real issue is: How can the press overcome the public's growing distrust, even when it gets the story right?

Many critics have complained that the press has been promiscuous in its use of anonymous sources. But those who urge the press to "Stop using anonymous sources," as former Poynter Institute president Robert J. Haiman did recently, are unrealistic. It was virtually impossible to find a firsthand source in the special prosecutor's office, the White House, or anywhere else willing to be quoted on the record. Reporters had no choice but to rely largely on anonymous leakers and spinners. The dress story could never have been reported by any news medium that held to the ideal journalistic standard of full disclosure.

Certainly, reporters try to persuade their sources to go on the record. But failing that, they should at least indicate the level of the sources' direct knowledge and the nature of their vested interest. People recognize that it is all too easy for anonymous sources with axes to grind to avoid accountability and therefore, to lie, mislead, or exaggerate.

A study commissioned by the Committee of Concerned Journalists examined the reporting of the first six days of the scandal, in which the dress played a central role. It concluded that: "Nearly one in three statements (30 per cent of what was reported) was effectively based on no sourcing at all by the news outlet publishing it." Also: "Four in ten statements (41 per cent of the reportage), out of "the 1,565 statements and allegations contained in the reporting [of the scandal] by major television programs, newspapers, and magazines . . . were not factual reporting at all . . . but were instead journalists offering analysis, opinion, speculation, or judgment."

Those who practice journalism in the volatile new media age could do worse than abide by a few of the old fashioned rules from a more leisurely time, before the arrival of the endless news cycle: When sources insist on anonymity, disclose enough about their connection with the story so the audience can judge both their trustworthiness and the story's. Take care to separate fact from speculation and reporting from commentary. In covering personal and private matters that go public, restraint and dignity are more credible than excessive and unseemly enthusiasm. Resist the rush to judgment; it's better for the audience to reach its own conclusions based on the facts. Above all, before going with anyone's gossip, no matter how explosive, check it out.

Recently, in a special message to journalists, Pope John Paul II stressed the need for still greater responsibility in the age of the Internet and other speedy information systems. The pope called on journalists to "transmit information while respecting truth, fundamental ethical principles, and personal dignity." It's advice from a credible source, and it's worth heeding.

Unit 4

Key Points to Consider

❖ After reading "Sex, Lies, and Advertising," why did *Ms.* magazine decide to drop advertising? Why did it have problems attracting enough advertising revenue to break even? Gloria Steinem is highly critical of advertisers' relationships with *Ms.* and with women's magazines in general. What is defensible, from a business standpoint, in advertising policies as both Steinem and Russ Baker (see Article 31) describe them?

❖ What is the difference between television programming that will appeal to older versus younger audiences? Do you see evidence of age bias in network television programming? Defend your answer.

❖ Is it worth it to you to pay more for television, magazines, newspapers, movies, and/or Internet access with fewer advertising messages? Why or why not?

 **Links** | **www.dushkin.com/online/**

These sites are annotated on pages 4 and 5.

Advertising is the major source of profit for newspapers, magazines, radio, and television, and advertising tie-ins are a common element in motion picture deals. While media writers may have the potential of reflecting their own agendas and social/political viewpoints as they produce media messages, they depend largely upon financial backing from advertisers, who have their own interests to protect. Advertisers use media as a means of presenting goods and services in a positive light. They are willing to pay generously for the opportunity to reach mass audiences. In 1997, technology companies such as America Online, Lotus, and Packard Bell NEC Inc. spent $492 million on television commercials, more than double the $208 million spent in 1995; automobile companies spent over $5 billion. However, advertisers are unwilling to support media that do not deliver the right kind of audience for their advertisements or that do not provide an appropriate frame within which to view them.

Mass advertising developed along with mass media (see "Inventing the Commercial"); in fact, commercial media have been described by some as a system existing primarily for the purpose of delivering audiences to advertisers. While this may be an overly simplistic indictment, it reflects the marketplace orientation of the American media system, which depends on advertising revenue to offset enormous production costs and turn a profit. In 1998, the most expensive 30-second advertisement slots by network were: *ER* (NBC) $551,000; *Monday Night Football* (ABC) $380,000; *Touched by an Angel* (CBS) $277,000; and *The Simpsons* (Fox) $248,000. In its final season, *Seinfeld* was able to command more than $500,000 for 30 seconds of commercial time.

The dependent relationship between those who make decisions regarding media content and those who underwrite the production and distribution of that content has been an issue of some concern among media critics. Protecting advertising accounts can contribute to editorial decisions. Some advertising account executives admit, and others deny, that they consider a publication's overall trend in supporting their product category and that they also look at whether their brands or companies are featured favorably when they are mentioned in news or editorial copy. The reports "Sex, Lies, and Advertising" and "The Squeeze: Some Major Advertisers Step Up the Pressure on Magazines to Alter Their Content. Will Editors Bend?" provide examples of "insertion orders" that both stipulate placement of advertisements and dictate topics considered unacceptable for discussion anywhere within magazines in which particular companies will buy advertising space. Newspaper publishers report pressure to print favorable reviews of restaurants that buy advertising space and to downplay negative mention of brand names in news articles associated with an advertiser's product. Advertising and editorial staffs of newspapers have traditionally been regarded as independent entities; however, as reported in "Blowing Up the Wall," the separation of their respective influence on content decisions is narrowing and in some cases disappearing.

Sometimes news or feature stories are developed specifically to attract or placate advertisers. Former editor of *Vanity Fair* Tina Brown reversed a 1984 advertising slump by running a series of feature stories about fashion designers Bill Blass, Giorgio Armani, Ralph Lauren, Calvin Klein, and Yves Saint Laurent, who subsequently became loyal advertisers. Sometimes product pitches creep into entertainment media, often striking below the level of consumer awareness. In fall of 1998, *Chaos! Comics* began offering to weave commercial products into its comic book story lines, charging advertisers up to $100,000 for the service. Mercedes-Benz paid $5 million to replace the Ford Explorer in *Jurassic Park* with its M-Class jeep-style car in *The Lost World* sequel (Ford paid $500,000 to appear in the original). For $3 million, Matsushita Electric's new video camera got a close-up. Burger King paid $20 million for the right to distribute *Lost World* trinkets at its restaurants and for a brief glimpse of a Burger King ad on a bus in the movie. The 1995 television movie *Derby*, sponsored by Wendy's and cowritten by the fast-food chain's executive vice president for marketing, cast Wendy's founder, Dave Thomas, in a small role in its climactic scene. Asked for a comment on the ethics of this casting, ABC spokesperson Judd Parkin noted, "The guy is paying for the movie; he can do what he wants." Nine 30-second Wendy's spots aired during the broadcast.

Advertisers are sensitive to controversy and are prone to avoid supporting controversial media content. When consumer groups threatened to boycott companies advertising on television's *Married . . . with Children* because they objected to the show's content, the companies looked carefully at whether it was in their best interest to remain associated with the program. Several advertisers withdrew; others refused to commit to further advertising unless they could screen and approve individual episodes. As a result, Fox asked the producers to tone down the scripts. For the same reason, ABC canceled reruns of episodes from *thirtysomething* (showing two gay men in bed discussing friends who had died from AIDS) and *Roseanne* (focusing on teenage drinking) because advertisers' boycotts of the first showings cost the network over $1.5 million in lost revenue.

Circulation data (for print media) and ratings data such as that provided by the A. C. Nielsen and Arbitron organizations (for television and radio) are instrumental in determining rate scales for advertising sales. The traditional model has been straightforward: the more viewers or listeners or readers we attract, the more we can charge for an advertisement. The current focus of many ad agencies is niche advertising, with particular interest in ratings data split out by age, gender, ethnic background, and income factors that determine how a given consumer might respond to a product pitch. Target marketing puts a premium on reaching certain advertiser-desirable groups by supporting media most likely to reach those groups. Media targeted to the interests of the advertiser-desirable audience proliferate and those attractive to other audiences—even large audiences—becomes scarce (see "Television Is Losing Its Largest Viewing Audience"). Cable targets niche audiences; in one week of August 1998, its share of viewers surpassed that of network TV for the first time ever. In the fall of 1998, "upfront" ad sales—advertisers' commitment to buying commercial time before the season begins—for the four major networks went down for the first time in 6 years. In light of such trends, Joshua Levine ("The Last Gasp of Mass Media?") contends that we are moving toward a future in which true "mass" media will be obsolete.

TELEVISION GROWS UP

Inventing the Commercial

THE IMPERIUM OF MODERN TELEVISION
advertising was born in desperate improvisation

BY HARRY MATTHEI

IT WAS 1945, AND EVERYBODY NEEDED EVERYTHING. IF YOU KNEW HOW to build a car, a house, or a washing machine, you could sell it faster than you could make it. Car dealers, including fine old names that soon would be history—Hudson, Nash, Packard, and Studebaker—all had long waiting lists. Many dealers bluntly quoted not the price of the car but the price of getting on their waiting lists.

In 1945 I had barely heard of either television or the advertising business, and I had no idea what a boom was, even though I was smack in the middle of one. I was thirteen years old, just out of grade school, and my goal was to become an engineer. Instead I spent forty-six years in advertising, mostly as a TV copywriter, later as a writer-producer and agency owner. While it wasn't always fun, it certainly was never dull.

In 1945 on New York's Madison Avenue—Main Street for America's advertising agencies—business had never been better. Freed of wartime paper restrictions, the big general-interest magazines—*Life, Look, The Saturday Evening Post,* and *Collier's*—swelled with advertisements. So did the major women's magazines: *Good Housekeeping, McCall's,* and *Ladies' Home Journal.* Fifteen percent of the placement cost of every ad went straight into the advertising agencies' pockets.

Of course, every city of any size in 1945 had at least two newspapers: morning and evening. Big cities had three or four of each, plus the foreign language press, and every one of them was stuffed with advertising. Americans once again could buy cigarettes, film, shoes, steaks, nylon stockings, tires, and everything else missing from their lives since December 7, 1941.

Into this giddy, superheated economy, commercial television was born. Again.

Television broadcasting had been launched in the United States in 1928 by the General Electric Company, in Schenectady, New York. The station—today's WRGB, Channel 6—had been licensed to broadcast "experimental" television only. Commercials were expressly forbidden.

According to *Advertising Age,* the industry's trade weekly, the first "legal" television commercial was aired on WNBT, the NBC station in New York, on July 1, 1941, during a Dodgers-Phillies game at Brooklyn's Ebbets Field. The camera focused on a Bulova watch with the second hand ticking as the announcer read the correct time. Bulova time checks ("It's three o'clock,

Bulova watch time") were already fixtures in radio advertising; Bulova simply adapted them to TV. For the first time in all of advertising, Bulova was able to combine the stimuli of sight, sound, and motion via television.

Bulova's agency, the Biow Company, billed its client nine dollars: five for airtime and four more for "station charges." Fifteen percent of this ($1.35), we can assume, was profit to the Biow Company as its standard advertising-agency commission. There were then about four thousand TV sets in the New York City area, roughly half of all the sets in the country.

"Illegal" commercials, *Advertising Age* noted, had appeared as early as 1930, when all TV licenses were strictly "experimental"—i.e., noncommercial. On July 1, 1939, General Mills, Procter & Gamble, and Socony Oil (now Mobil), all sponsors of Brooklyn Dodgers' radio coverage, were given free plugs by Red Barber, the Dodgers' announcer, during the first televised major-league baseball game. Red sliced bananas into a bowl of Wheaties, held up a bar of soap, and donned a gas-station attendant's cap. He thereby became the father of the demonstration commercial. The Federal Communications Commission (FCC) apparently missed this debut. Earlier violators of the noncommercial rule had drawn fines and threats of license suspension, but Red got off scot-free.

During the war years commercial television went on hold. The government halted the manufacture of new sets and transmission equipment and stopped issuing station licenses. Established stations provided regular programming, but only a handful of people were equipped to watch it.

In October 1945, less than two months after the war ended, commercial television got two major shots in the arm: The FCC lifted the wartime bans on licensing TV stations and making sets, and RCA demonstrated an improved TV camera that delivered a

The well-groomed Sharpie spent decades asking viewers how they were fixed for Gillette blades.

In 1946 Gillette and NBC staged the first TV sports spectacular: the Louis-Conn fight. Louis won. So did Gillette.

far crisper, clearer picture. So, after years of sluggish progress, a depression, and a war, television at last was ready to roll.

The major advertising agencies—the "hucksters" that had turned network radio into a money machine—saw the new medium as a natural outgrowth of the older, better-established one. The admen ruled radio as they never could newspapers or magazines, controlling the editorial content. Companies like Procter & Gamble, Ford, and General Foods paid advertising agencies to create and produce—or buy from independent producers—hours of network radio programs every day. The broadcasters functioned only as an electronic pipeline. They generally accepted whatever programming the advertisers chose.

Filling the pipe usually began with an independent producer or talent agent proposing a program to an agency. This might be anything from a soap opera to a quiz show. The agency would then sell the idea to one of its clients and negotiate a time slot with a network. The network in turn would offer the show to local affiliate stations, which simply took the network feed via AT&T lines and broadcast it within their areas. The only locally produced radio programming usually was local news, farm and market reports, and fillers for dead times like Sunday mornings, when the audiences were too tiny to attract big advertisers.

With the coming of television the agencies and their clients assumed that the new medium simply would be radio with pictures, commercials included. The agencies would develop the programs, the TV stations would air them, advertising dollars would pay the bills, and everyone would make money. What could be simpler?

Still, from a 1940s advertising viewpoint, television was a feeble medium. It had neither the scope nor the prestige of the big national magazines. It lacked the stars of radio—Jack Benny, Fibber McGee, Bob Hope. It was just radio's baby brother. In 1946 the four radio networks—"webs," they were called—reached more than 90 percent of the homes in the forty-eight states plus about half the cars. By contrast the only television network linked just three cities: Philadelphia, New York, and Schenectady. Period.

As Fred Allen, one of radio's most popular wits—and one of TV's bitterest critics—put it, "In television, coast-to-coast means from here to Passaic." He was in Manhattan at the time; Passaic is barely ten miles away on the opposite side of the Hudson River. All through the forties television continued to be a local medium. As with today's Internet and on-line services, nobody could be sure how fast it would grow, what it could offer, or how advertising agencies could make money from it. In fact, it would be 1948 before a million homes had TV sets and 1951 before coast-to-coast television networks existed. Except for a few major cities, most of the U.S. heartland would have no TV at all until the mid-fifties or later.

George Pryde, a Connecticut advertising man born in Wyoming, remembers his grandparents taking him to visit friends in the little town of Ranchester, a few miles from Sheridan, in 1949. He was ten years old. At one especially nice house, he recalls, "the people seemed pretty well-off. In their living room was a new wooden cabinet like a big radio, with an opaque glass window in the front of it. I asked what it was, because I had no idea. Our host said, 'That's a television set.' And he seemed really pleased with himself. It didn't impress me much because I'd never even heard of television, and the screen was blank." It would be at least five more years before television reached Ranchester, Wyoming.

In the middle of 1946 there were fewer than ten thousand sets in the entire country, half of them still in New York City. This was the age of vacuum tubes and hand-soldered wiring, not printed circuits and transistors, so the sets were not easy to mass-produce. Neither were they cheap. Prices ranged from $350 to $2,000, at a time when a typical family could live nicely on $10,000 a year.

MOST MAJOR ADVERTISING agencies weren't eager to shift dollars out of high-profit, measurable network radio and mass magazines into this highly questionable and uncharted frontier. So the new medium grew slowly through the forties. Even during the early fifties you'd be more likely to find a TV set in a neighborhood bar than in a living room.

Saloonkeepers loved the tube. A televised baseball game or boxing match would pack in the customers and hold them spellbound for hours. In fact, until the sixties, most men probably saw their first TV program in a bar. For advertisers of cigarettes, beer, cars, and the Gillette Safety Razor Company, this was the medium of their dreams. Their best customers were males over eighteen, and saloons and sports were more purely male territory in the fifties than today.

IN JUNE 1946 GILLETTE AND NBC staged the first televised sports spectacular: the Joe Louis–Billy Conn heavyweight championship bout at Yankee Stadium in New York. Louis won. So did Gillette. For the first time the blade maker was able to demonstrate its products to a TV audience estimated at 150,000 fans in New York City, plus bonus viewers in Schenectady and Philadelphia. The next year Gillette joined with Ford to televise the first game of the 1947 World Series. Over the following decades, Gillette's "Look Sharp, Be Sharp" march music, its jingle, "How're you fixed for blades? (Do you have plenty?)," and "Sharpie," its animated parrot, became three of television's best-known and longest-lived commercial properties.

By the late forties television sets were beginning to appear in more and more American living rooms. And during commercial television's first postwar decade, no matter what was televised, people watched. Roller derbies. Wrestling. Harness racing. Vaudeville. Amateur shows. The very worst B movies. Like it or not, the new medium seemed to mesmerize people—both sexes and all ages, urban, suburban, and eventually rural. Indeed, viewers couldn't tear themselves away even to eat. Housewives were torn between watching television and cooking dinner. Then along came frozen TV dinners. In many households dinnertime—the nightly ritual with everyone gathered at the table—simply faded away. America preferred to watch TV.

Some advertisers and their agencies dismissed our compulsive viewing habit as little more than a fad. TV equaled free movies. Once the novelty wore off, the whole medium might just dry up and blow away. But more thoughtful and prescient advertising people recognized television as the natural successor to radio. Far more attention-getting and involving and harder-selling, it was radio with teeth.

Radio didn't demand the listener's undivided attention; kids did homework, moms sewed, and dads painted the kitchen to its background babble

and steady throb of commercials. Television, by contrast, caught the eye as well as the ear. It seemed to insist, "Look here! Pay attention! Watch this!" Advertisers and their agencies soon realized that TV audiences did pay attention. Products hawked on the tube seemed to sell faster than non-TV brands.

Some of these sales reflected the makeup of the audience. Viewers tended to be more sophisticated and prosperous than average. They all lived in major cities. They were more likely to experiment with new, untried products. What's more—and this is still true—retailers were favorably impressed by the brands advertised on television. With buyers and sellers alike so willing to be wooed, television advertising began flexing its muscles.

LIVE TELEVISION TODAY USUALLY means news, sports, and special events. But from 1945 to 1950 *all* television was "live," including most commercials. There were no other options, except for showing motion pictures or kinescopes—poor-quality films made by shooting specially synchronized movies of television images.

Local sponsors and stations usually couldn't afford film, and videotape wasn't available until 1956. So for a few years every night was amateur night. (Daytime TV was almost nonexistent until the 1950s.) Live television was a grab bag of minor-league talent mingled with promising unknowns and recycled radio announcers. The latter were there to open and close the programs and deliver commercials in a suitably dignified manner.

Each performance was, for better or worse, unique and then gone. This ephemeral, spontaneous quality made live television both challenging to produce and fun to watch. For viewers it seemed personal, almost participatory. Audience and performers, together, were partners in an intriguing experiment. And neither was sure what would happen next. For those of us who wrote, directed, and produced live television, it's fair to

say we made it up as we went along. We really did. Without quite realizing it, we virtually invented an advertising, news, entertainment, and information medium.

ONE OF THE EARLIEST OF television's trailblazers was Sy Frolick. Discharged from the U.S. Coast Guard in 1946 and just married, Frolick set out to become an advertising copywriter. In March 1946 he took a job on trial for thirty days writing radio commercials at the Campbell-Ewald Company, in New York. This later became the Fletcher D. Richards agency, then Richards, Calkins & Holden. Frolick's thirty-day trial lasted nearly twenty years, during which he rose to the head of television production and earned awards for his commercials almost every year. In the sixties he joined the William Esty advertising agency. He retired almost twenty years later.

"Every Tuesday night," Sy remembers, "my boss, a senior copywriter

FROLICK WAS STUNNED. "Here we were on television, with moving pictures, and we were doing radio commercials!"

named Scotty Kosting, would go down to the old John Wanamaker department store on lower Broadway to produce a TV show with live commercials for our client, the U.S. Rubber Company. We got a free half-hour every week from WABD, Channel 13, New York [then, as no longer, a commercial channel], just to help fill empty airtime. That would be prime time today. In '46 they were giving it away."

The agency had created a science program using *Encyclopaedia Britannica* films, called "Serving Through Science," which was U.S. Rubber's corporate slogan. The company's U.S. Royal tires and Keds sneakers were promoted on the show. Sy's boss, Scotty, hated this weekly TV assignment. It wiped out every Tuesday night for him. Like most senior copywriters in 1946, Scotty yearned to write big full-color spreads for *Life, Look,* and *The Saturday Evening Post.* That was where the money was.

Frolick was younger and frankly curious about television. So one Tuesday night he asked Scotty if he could tag along to Wanamaker's to see TV in the making. As he recalls it, "The studio was behind Wanamaker's music department, in a tiny area rented by WABD, Alan B. DuMont's flagship station in New York City. When it came time for the commercials, an announcer stepped up to the camera and read a typewritten script."

Frolick was stunned. "Here we were on television, with moving pictures, and we were doing radio commercials!" The copy chief at the agency sensed Sy's interest in TV and assigned him to relieve Scotty of the Tuesday-night follies at Wanamaker's. Three weeks later Scotty quit his job and moved to another agency to work exclusively on print ads. That left Sy Frolick as Mr. Television at the Richards agency: writer, producer, casting, wardrobe, everything. Mr. Television proceeded to teach himself the business.

One day the U.S. Rubber people said, "Be sure to mention that Keds are washable." Immediately Sy thought, "We should *demonstrate* that." So he asked the WABD production crew, "Why don't we get a washing machine in here and show how clean the Keds come out?"

"Aw, come on, Sy," they all moaned. "We don't have any running water."

"Well," said Sy, "there's a men's room down the hall. We can hook up a hose in there and wash the sneakers while the show's going on. Then at the end we'll show them nice and clean." That's what they did. And it worked.

Soon Keds had a Friday-night show for teenagers broadcast live on WNBT, NBC's New York station. The set design was a simple forties soda shop. Frolick named the show "Campus Hoopla," and the following year it was broadcast on the "network" that now linked Schenectady, New York City, Philadelphia, and Washington.

To give the commercials more pizzazz, Frolick created the Keds Cheerleaders and wrote them a cheer—possibly the only commercial cheer ever written:

Keds are keen. Keds are neat.
Keds are best for your family's feet.
Wear 'em! Keds! Keds! Keds!

Then Frolick canvassed model agencies for teens who looked like cheerleader material. He met one pretty blonde girl who had just come to New York to become an actress. He had her in for an audition and instantly hired the young Eva Marie Saint.

Thirty years later Frolick happened to see Eva Marie Saint appearing on the Johnny Carson show. Carson asked her how she got her start in show business. "I was a Keds Cheerleader," she told him.

"Do you remember the cheers?" Johnny asked. According to Frolick, "She not only remembered the Keds cheer, she remembered every move that went with it. She popped up and did her Keds routine for thirty million Johnny Carson fans and got a huge round of applause."

TELEVISION COMMERCIALS became an important first step for more than one aspiring talent. They paid better than off-Broadway or summer stock, as much as ten dollars a day in preunion days. They combined the close-up intimacy of the movies with the real-time, real-life spontaneity of the stage. In some ways they were more demanding than either medium.

As always actors had to learn their lines and hit their marks. But they also had to keep one eye peeled for the red light on the cameras—there might be three on the set—that told them which one was live, while staying aware of the countless wires and cables that littered the studio floor, waiting to trip the unwary.

Most important, they had to deliver all their lines "to time." The commercials were almost all exactly sixty seconds long. Not fifty-two. Not sixty-seven. Noncommercial segments were just as rigidly timed. So performers learned to speed up or slow down their speeches. This implacable time discipline was unknown in films and theater. Only radio actors learned to pace themselves so precisely.

A live TV show usually shared its studio with the sets and cast of the sponsor's commercials. During commercial breaks the noncommercial performers were expected to freeze in place and remain absolutely silent for the minute when the commercial players did their turn. This usually took place in a quiet corner of the studio, away from the main action, but even so, an audible background sneeze, squeaky shoes, or a fit of giggles could throw the client into a tantrum. Commercials, lest anyone forget, paid the wages of everyone in the studio.

JULIA MEADE, A YOUNG ACTRESS fresh from the Yale University Drama School, remembers working in the tiny, cramped Wanamaker's studio that Sy Frolick used, though the two never met. She would later become the spokesperson for Lincoln and Mercury cars on "The Ed Sullivan Show," as well as for the American Gas Association on "Playhouse 90" and for other sponsors on other shows. She began her television career, which spanned more than thirty years, as a model on a local New York show called "Fashion Parade." Recently she recalled, "The lights in that studio were so hot I was always wringing wet within minutes. My makeup was always running off my face. On one occasion I had my hair pinned up with plastic combs. When I came out of the studio, the lights had melted the combs into my hair. When I finally disentangled them, they'd shriveled into hairy, weird-looking plastic claws. I guess I was lucky I wasn't bald."

TV cameras in the 1940s needed a great deal of light, but TV lighting didn't yet include cool-burning fluorescent tubes, so studio heat was a constant problem. It not only baked the actors but exploded beer bottles, liquefied candles, blistered paint, and made some props too hot to touch, as scorched actors learned firsthand. One producer remembers that his lights once melted the glue bonding the wood veneer to a grand piano. The veneer buckled and peeled off in huge, sticky sheets. The owners of the piano were not amused.

Of course, faster, more sensitive cameras and cooler, brighter lights were on the way, along with more efficient air conditioning. And in 1947 Dr. Frank G. Back invented the revolutionary Zoomar lens. This was the first lens that allowed zooming in for a close-up and zooming out for a long shot without moving the camera or losing the focus. Cameramen and directors wondered how they had ever lived without it. A frenzy of in-and-out zoom shots followed until Dr. Back's Zoomar became just another lens in the cameraman's bag.

D URING THE FALL OF 1948 Milton Berle burst into television with the "Texaco Star Theater." By November he had achieved a record rating, reaching nearly 90 percent of all the TV homes in the country. That same autumn "The Ed Sullivan Show" made its debut, sponsored by Ford's Lincoln-Mercury Division.

George Burns and Gracie Allen, sponsored by B. F. Goodrich, abandoned radio in 1948 to be among these first stars of the new medium. By this time, *Advertising Age* reported, more than a hundred new TV licenses had been issued by the FCC, and at least as many more were being processed. Nearly a thousand advertisers bought television time in 1948, five times as many as the year before. For the men who ran the major advertising agencies—there were no women—it was time to take television seriously.

In 1950, coming through the back door as a messenger, I joined the biggest, most buttoned-up agency of all, the J. Walter Thompson Company. WASP-ish, decorous, Ivy League (Yale)–oriented, Thompson had been founded in 1864. At J. Walter Thompson a key to the executive washroom carried almost as much cachet then as a personal limousine would today.

Between 1946 and 1956, according to *Advertising Age*'s estimates, Thompson's billings grew from $78 million to $220 million, and they topped

The pioneer spokesperson Betty Furness expertly demonstrates the many virtues of a Westinghouse.

I N 1959, IN DAYTON, Ohio, I nearly electrocuted a lady named Betty Rogge while she was doing a live Frigidaire demo.

$300 million before 1960. Most of this growth was based on the television boom. With few exceptions Thompson's major competitors grew as fast or faster.

JWT, as it was called, was the very model of a modern advertising firm. At its New York headquarters in the Graybar Building, an appendage of Grand Central Terminal, waves of secretaries arrived each morning in their ladylike hats, fresh white gloves, and stockings in both winter and un-air-conditioned summer. JWT men were uniformly tailored by Brooks Brothers, J. Press, Chipp, or at the very least Rogers Peet.

Thompson's tall, patrician president, Stanley Resor, set the tone at the agency from 1917, when he bought it, well into the fifties. With his striking, icy-eyed wife, Helen—a gifted copy-

writer—Resor devoted his life to making the business responsible, professional, and dignified. In the early 1940s, the legend goes, one of Resor's vice presidents set out to win the Camel cigarette account for JWT. It looked like a sure thing. All the agency had to do to close the deal was submit some speculative advertising. Camel was the biggest cigarette in the business—the best seller and biggest spender. Most agencies would have killed for the account. Stanley Resor felt otherwise.

JWT policy forbade doing speculative work for any prospect. The vice president, Bill Esty, urged Resor to make an exception for Camel. Resor haughtily refused, and Esty departed JWT in what *Fortune* magazine later described as a "shower of sparks." He opened the William Esty Company a block away. Overnight the William Esty Company was a major agency. Esty launched R. J. Reynolds's Winston and Salem brands in the mid-fifties, and both became gold mines for his agency.

Resor pioneered consumer research with the JWT Consumer Panel, a national list of householders recruited to keep diaries of their everyday purchases. They regularly mailed the diaries to JWT, New York, in exchange for modest rewards, such as coupons for products the agency handled. If a new soap, toothpaste, or food product ignited the sales charts, the JWT Consumer Panel would sound the alarm, so when television arrived, Thompson was quick to sense its selling power. JWT urged its clients to take the lead in sponsoring quality TV programs the agency would create, just as it had for radio.

In 1947 Thompson launched "The Kraft Television Theater," bringing original live drama and star talent to television for the first time. Schlitz beer, Armstrong floors, Philco appliances, Goodyear, and others all launched television theaters of their own. But "Kraft Theater" was the opening curtain. It survived for more than twenty years.

"KRAFT THEATER" ALSO TOOK Red Barber's naive demo commercials to new heights for Kraft foods. During intermissions Ed Herlihy, the voice of Kraft for the next forty years, described the action as viewers saw Miracle Whip, Velveeta, and Cheez Whiz transformed live into an endless menu of culinary delights.

What viewers did not see were the harried "home economists"—they're called "food stylists" today—who heated and stirred, sliced and poured, just out of camera range. Endless rehearsals, truckloads of food, and real human tears went into these live how-to commercials. If the cheese sauce spilled or the lady poked her finger through an egg, well, that was live television. No matter how many rehearsals, nobody's perfect. But JWT became masters of the demo for Kraft, Scott Paper, Lever Brothers, and a long list of others.

The most ingenious demos were usually those promoting consumer goods in highly competitive product categories. This was where a demonstrable difference—even a tiny one—could make a product soar off the sales graph. Only television could turn tiny differences into compelling theater, sixty seconds at a time.

Classic early demos included the egg test (1956), in which a Band-Aid plastic strip with "Super Stick" clung fast to an egg even in boiling water; the Remington shaver peach test of 1954 ("shaves close enough to shave a peach"); the Timex watch torture tests, with John Cameron Swayze ("Timex takes a licking and keeps on ticking"), from 1948 to 1968; RCA's "Impac Case," a plastic portable radio that survived a drop from a twelve-foot ladder (1954); and of course Betty Furness's Westinghouse appliance demos, each of which proved "You can be *sure* . . . if it's Westinghouse"(1949–1960).

Betty Furness was the undisputed queen of the live demo, first gaining national attention during the 1952 and 1956 Republican and Democratic conventions. Day and night, product after product, in the heat of high summer, Betty coolly sold appliances as nobody has before or since. But one of the most perversely memorable Westinghouse demos—for which Betty has been incorrectly credited—was handled by a bright, unflappable young actress named June Graham.

June was demonstrating an "easy open" Westinghouse "frost-free" refrigerator, the door of which stubbornly refused to yield. She pressed, tapped, and then thumped the "easy open" button. But no luck. So, barely missing a beat, she shifted emphasis to the "frost-free" feature as the camera moved in close on her face, squeezing the fridge out of the picture while someone in the studio crew overcame the traitorous easy-open mechanism. As the camera moved back out again, it revealed a smiling June Graham beside the now open door. Millions who saw the spot never forgot it, and it was reported in newspapers nationwide.

In 1959, in Dayton, Ohio, I nearly electrocuted a lady named Betty Rogge while she was doing a live demo with a Frigidaire electric range. Frigidaire was a client of Dancer-Fitzgerald-Sample, Inc., and I, in my mid-twenties, was the creative director of the DFS Dayton office. When Frigidaire asked me to produce four live commercials at WLW-D, Dayton, on election night, I was delighted. This would be my first solo production. I had written dozens of TV commercials, but in this case I was required to write, direct, and produce the commercials entirely on my own. I never imagined I might threaten somebody's life in the process.

Frigidaire had a new campaign created at DFS, New York: "You'll feel like a queen with Frigidaire." I was told to find a "queen" in Dayton and have her deliver the commercials while balancing a brass coronet on her head. No easy job for live television.

I booked Betty Rogge, a talented local spokesperson, as our queen and had her rehearse with the crown until she could do cartwheels while wearing it. On election night Betty donned her crown and clipped the microphone to her bra beneath her soft, high-necked dress. She was ready: regal, cool, and lovely. When I cued her, she stepped up to the range, draped her hand on it, and delivered her lines flawlessly. But as soon as she heard, "Cut," Betty screamed, "Help! I can't move!" The microphone had somehow short-circuited to her skin when she touched the range. She could not let go. Some quick-witted person disconnected the microphone wire and possibly saved Betty's life.

Until the networks, under agency pressure, began selling thirty-second commercials in 1971, advertisers had sixty seconds to make their demos work. To minimize risk, most demos were filmed or taped. Today's commercials are almost all thirty seconds long. Result: More commercials but fewer demos. Reason: Performing a credible demonstration in thirty seconds is not easy at all.

IN 1949 THE RULES OF TV BEGAN to change when Sylvester ("Pat") Weaver left the highly respected Young & Rubicam agency to join NBC-TV as its president. Weaver believed that the networks, not the advertisers, should decide what shows to air and at what times to air them. When he took the job with NBC, he made it clear that he would devote himself to programming, not just to selling minutes of commercial time. This was heresy.

Since the days of radio's "A&P Gypsies," "The Ford Sunday Evening Hour," and "The Voice of Firestone," advertisers had owned not only their shows but their time slots too. Pat Weaver rewrote the book. First he launched his "Magazine Concept": Advertisers could participate in shows that NBC would produce just as advertisers participated in magazines. But NBC would own and control the programs' content. A tectonic power shift was at hand.

If Weaver succeeded, NBC would

earn a profit from producing shows as well as from the commercials that ran within them. Also, by selling one-minute participations, NBC could bring network TV within the reach of smaller advertisers, companies that couldn't afford to sponsor entire programs on their own.

CBS had taken this tack in radio in 1948 and succeeded, gambling on launching a number of untried shows on its own, unsponsored. Within a year advertisers were lining up to buy participations in them. Two of the shows—"Our Miss Brooks," with Eve Arden, and "My Favorite Husband," with Lucille Ball —became TV hits as well, the latter as "I Love Lucy," which is still running. In 1950 Weaver launched "Today," with Dave Garroway, and "The Home Show," with Arlene Francis. In 1954 he added "The Tonight Show," with Steve Allen. All three were hits with viewers and advertisers. Forty-three years later "Today" and "The Tonight Show" still run.

The shows ran in "fringe" time—early morning, midday, and late night—time that network advertisers normally shunned. But all three offered participations rather than full sponsorships, so an advertiser could buy commercials a minute at a time. NBC also offered "Today"/"Home"/ "Tonight" combination buys, giving smaller advertisers a way to pitch their goods to three different audiences at a relatively low cost. Weaver's new concept turned a healthy profit. So he next planted his flag in prime time, 8:00 to 11:00 P.M. NBC launched "Your Show of Shows," starring Sid Caesar and Imogene Coca, on Saturday nights, again selling only participations. And again with success.

Across town at CBS, its president, Frank Stanton, was happy to align his network with Weaver's in the spot-not-sponsorship shift. Stanton had seen it work for CBS radio. So NBC and CBS, independently but in

There was tension before any live demo started; this one is on "The Kraft Television Theater."

ENDLESS REHEARSALS, truckloads of food, and real human tears went into these live how-to commercials.

parallel, edged the agencies out of programming. In exchange the networks assumed the risk for buying and creating new shows and for paying for those that flopped.

THE AGENCIES RESISTED SUR-rendering control over programming—and the profits that went with it—but they soon saw the benefits in picking and choosing their spot participations. This gave them new flexibility in how and where to spend their clients' money, and it excused them from facing irate clients when an expensive agency-created show turned out to be a turkey. A few advertisers continued to sponsor shows of their own, regardless of rising costs and network pressure. "Hallmark Hall of Fame" is still a valiant holdout after nearly fifty years, but as a special event, not a weekly regular.

What this change meant for the viewer was that original quality drama and experimental or exploratory television, such as "Omnibus" and "See It Now," disappeared to make room for mass entertainment—Westerns, cop shows, sitcoms, and games. These were hardly all bad, but excellence became rare, greatness even rarer.

Most major agencies and their clients had exited show business entirely by the sixties. Instead they focused their creative energies on building more distinctive commercials. By then the agencies were scattering one-minute spots here, there, and yonder, so it became more important than ever that these messages be noticed and remembered, no matter where viewers might find them. This dictated filmed, not live, commercials. Some advertisers, especially of autos and cigarettes, had been able to afford filmed commercials even during television's barroom epoch in the forties. And when color TV arrived in 1953, they were among the first to switch over to it, swallowing production costs that grew by a third or more.

Chevrolet and Ford filmed their gleaming new beauties swooping about the landscape from coast to coast. The Utah salt flats, surf-washed beaches, and the Pacific Coast Highway came to symbolize emancipated driving, TV-style. Chrysler—pre-Iacocca— used much the same imagery but usually with lower budgets and less panache. And Volkswagen led the way for imports in the early sixties with its memorable commercials from the new agency on the block, Doyle Dane Bernbach.

Such early VW Beetle commercials as "How does the man who drives the snowplow get to the snowplow?" set a new standard for auto advertising. And Doyle Dane Bernbach—non-WASP, informal, and brilliantly creative—began its meteoric ascent.

CIGARETTE MAKERS—ALWAYS lavish spenders until banned from the air in 1971—tended toward lighthearted image advertising, most of it on film when film cost too much for most advertisers. Among the first cigarette commercials were square-dancing cigarettes (Lucky Strike, 1948), dancing packs with women inside (Old Gold, 1950), and an animated penguin (Kool, 1954).

As the filter-versus-regular cigarette war sputtered through the fifties, Viceroy thundered about its "filter traps," Parliament introduced its recessed filter, Kent created the Micronite filter (made of asbestos), and Marlboro offered the slinky, seductive Julie London crooning, "You get a lot to like with a Marlboro—filter . . . flavor . . . flip-top box." The Marlboro cowboy and Marlboro Country, created by Chicago's Leo Burnett agency, came later, around 1959. Perhaps the most successful cigarette advertising campaign in history, it still runs worldwide.

Very late in the TV cigarette era, around 1968, when Salem advertising was my responsibility at the William Esty Company, we launched "You can take Salem out of the country *but* . . . you can't take the country out of Salem." It was a relatively expensive campaign to film, using city and country locations from coast to coast.

One of my commercials called for a white gazebo with a Dixieland band and singers set among flowering trees. A search for just the right location turned up a slightly run-down gazebo in a grove of apple trees at a convent in New York's Hudson River valley. The setting was ideal, and in exchange for a substantial contribution, the mother superior agreed to allow the use of the property for the filming. The gazebo was given a fresh coat of white paint with accents of gold and Salem green,

and buses and vans were poised to whisk cast and crew there just as soon as the apple trees reached full flower.

Then, the night before the big day, a lashing rainstorm moved in and stripped the apple trees of their blossoms. But the location still looked fresh and springlike, and that was Salem's trademark. As I drove to the convent, dawn broke sunny and warm.

At six that morning a van filled with thousands of plastic apple blossoms rolled up to the convent, and by eight-thirty the trees were beautifully abloom with polyethylene flowers. The mother superior—a tiny sixtyish lady with a saintly smile—watched as a swarm of workers redecorated her denuded apple trees. Then she turned to the film's director, the late Peter Miranda, and said, "Oh, my! I thought only God

The once-ubiquitous Ajax pixies. Don't mourn them; they may very well be back.

could make a tree." Miranda—one of the quickest wits in a witty business—clasped his hands, smiled, and replied, "Sister, this is what God would do—if he had our budget."

AS THE LIVE TELEVISION ERA wound down—as Pat Weaver launched his magazine concept and as coast-to-coast networks were born, thanks to the laying of coaxial cable in 1951—Rosser Reeves emerged as the creative maestro of the Ted Bates Agency. For the next twenty years Reeves was

Madison Avenue's leading advocate of "hard sell" advertising.

In his 1961 book, *Reality in Advertising*, he claimed that his commercials for Anacin pain reliever had tripled annual sales in less than two years. Trumpeting "Fast . . . FAST . . . FAST RELIEF" from "tension headache" and replete with lightning bolts and sledgehammers, Anacin's one-minute spots were generally despised by viewers and derided by competitors. But Reeves and Anacin seemed to prove that people needn't like a commercial to be influenced by it. They needed only to understand the message, find its promise appealing, and be willing to believe it. "Fast relief" is, after all, what a painkiller is supposed to deliver. Anacin made "tension headache" its own private ailment, and the spots ran everywhere, ad nauseam.

Rosser Reeves, Southern-born, was a shrewd thinker and marketer and an unabashed salesman. He was indifferent to style, taste, and artistry in advertising. He cared only about clarity, persuasion, and uniqueness. These he refined and distilled into his personal advertising formula—the "Unique Selling Proposition," or U.S.P. —which he considered a virtual reinvention of salesmanship.

The U.S.P. meant describing a product and its benefits so that consumers would feel they had never heard of such a thing before and had to have it, yet no competitor could duplicate it without appearing to be a craven imitator. Once this was accomplished, the advertiser had only to keep hammering away at the same message as often and loudly as possible. On television, of course.

By scattering his spots far and wide, with little regard for what programs they were in, Reeves spent his clients' money efficiently, and he never (well, almost never) changed the commercials, which also saved a few dollars. He insisted, correctly, that even a weak commercial, run again and again, will outperform individually stronger commercials that keep changing.

Under Reeves's guidance the Ted Bates Agency launched TV campaigns for Colgate toothpaste ("Cleans your breath while it cleans your teeth"), M&M's candy ("Melts in your mouth, not in your hand"), Wonder bread ("Builds strong bodies 12 ways"), and a flock of others. In 1952 Reeves wrote, produced, and directed the first TV spots ever used in a presidential election. They were titled "The Man From Abilene." He gave Dwight Eisenhower very few lines to speak on camera, relying on Ike's folksy image rather than his painfully self-conscious acting. By election day "The Man From Abilene" was almost as omnipresent on the tube as Ivory soap or Listerine. Some people were shocked to see Eisenhower peddled like toothpaste, but Adlai Stevenson became the last presidential candidate not to use television.

ROSSER REEVES'S POLAR OPPOsite was probably Leo Burnett, of Chicago's Leo Burnett agency. Burnett made commercials that were distinctive and direct but also fun to watch. His agency probably created more animated commercial characters than anyone else in the business: the Jolly Green Giant, Tony the Tiger, the Keebler Elves, Charlie the Tuna, and dozens of others. Many are still performing.

Animated characters make superb salespeople. They never grow old. They never get in trouble with the law or spouses not their own. And they can do anything people can do and more —like baking cookies in hollow trees.

Among television's very first animated characters were the pixies created in 1948 by the Sherman & Marquette agency for Colgate's Ajax cleanser. Its singing commercial made Ajax— the first scouring powder to contain detergent—the number one brand. Its ditty was unforgettable:

Try Ajax (Bum Bum),
*   the foaming cleanser,*
(Ba, Ba, Ba, Ba, Ba, Bum, Bum),
Floats the dirt . . .
*   right down the drain!*
(Ba, Ba, Ba, Ba, Ba, Ba, Bum!)

The pixies were *too* unforgettable, it turned out. When Procter & Gamble's Comet cleanser with chlorine bleach arrived some years later, nobody seemed able to write a television spot for Ajax that could effectively introduce new Ajax with bleach. According to Colgate's consumer-recall tests, housewives remembered nothing about Ajax except (Bum, Bum) *pixies*! It wasn't until around 1960s when I wrote a "slice of life" commercial using Bess Myerson—a former Miss America and a popular game-show panelist—that the pixies disappeared. But don't be shocked if they reappear one day. It wouldn't be the first time an old commercial idea was resurrected. Speedy Alka-Seltzer came back from the dead after twenty years to replace some very clever Alka-Seltzer advertising: the famous "Bellies" commercial and "Some spicy meatball," both award winners. Trade gossip says Speedy simply sold more Alka-Seltzer.

In 1954, television became the dominant medium for national advertising. At the same time, network radio imploded as the major stars and their audiences abandoned it in favor of TV. Even general magazines grew thinner and thinner as advertisers moved their dollars to television scatter plans, shotgunning one-minute spots throughout prime time.

By the early sixties the ad-lib, ad hoc quality of live television had almost totally disappeared. Fewer live shows and live commercials went on the air. Live hosts—Arthur Godfrey, Garry Moore, Dave Garroway, and Jack Paar—cut their involvement with advertising to live lead-ins to filmed spots: "Here's good news from the folks who make Glass Wax!" or "Don't go 'way, we'll be back in one minute . . ."

Television had matured, become formalized. Shows, time slots, commercials, and even personalities acquired ratings. Each measurement was crucial. The financial stakes had become so enormous that live television was nearly dead. It simply didn't fit the formula.

To paraphrase Winston Churchill, this was not the end or even the beginning of the end. But it was certainly the end of the beginning.

Harry Matthei retired from advertising [in 1996] and became a freelance writer. He died in February of [1997].

BLOWING UP THE WALL

The Los Angeles Times embarks on a ground-breaking plan in which the editorial and business sides will work closely together, section by section. Is this a threat to the integrity of the paper or an exciting attempt to foster dynamism and growth?

BY ALICIA C. SHEPARD

A
BOUT 50 REPORTERS AND EDITORS FROM THE LOS ANGELES Times features sections trooped upstairs at five o'clock on a Tuesday in September for a "meet and greet" with Mark H. Willes. Only four days earlier, Willes had named himself publisher of the Times, a job he'd been itching to do since joining parent Times Mirror in June 1995 as chairman and CEO.

Many of the Life & Style staffers entered the sixth-floor conference room with great trepidation. The day before, Willes had introduced himself to the business section staff. As soon as the meeting ended, word spread that the boss wasn't too impressed with Life & Style. Everyone at the paper already knew Willes wanted to create a women's section, possibly to replace Life & Style, and even had a prototype in the works. Yet many writers walked into the room hoping for some upbeat words or reassurance about their jobs.

Instead they got pure Willes: candid, direct, unwilling to talk around a subject. And not afraid to hurt feelings.

Willes says he knew rumors were flying, and he wanted to clarify his position. And so the 56-year-old former cereal executive from General Mills, hands in pockets, came right to the point: "Life & Style doesn't work."

Yes, he said, he did like some elements of the section. But, he continued, it lacked focus. "Business covers business. Sports covers sports. What do you cover?" he asked.

One writer spoke up weakly: "The human condition."

Then, to the delight of his staff, Life & Style Editor Terry

"THE people with experience, for the most part, have been running America's newspapers into the ground," says book review editor Steve Wasserman. "I like Willes' approach, which is passionate and intelligent and free of prejudice, not tied to the old ways of doing things."

Schwadron rose to defend his section. "I said that we detail those activities that distinguish us from apes," Schwadron says. "That we cover our values, how we behave, how we dress, making the ordinary appear to be extraordinary. The rest of the paper is what the world does to us."

After an hour, one reporter gingerly asked what everyone in Life & Style really wanted to know. "If we don't get the section fixed," she inquired, "would you close it?"

"I wouldn't rule it out," Willes replied. End of conversation.

"It was the worst meeting of my professional life," says one feature writer who has worked at the paper for nearly two decades.

"The point is Willes said it in a very blunt manner," says Schwadron, who has left the paper and is looking for a job. "I came downstairs after the meeting, and it was like a wake. People were very upset. It's his style I have an issue with. It's easier to build on risk-taking by being positive than it is to be dismissive."

The next day, Schwadron's staff sent him flowers. Three weeks later, as part of a massive reorganization, Schwadron was told his services were no longer needed on the news side.

Willes says he has no regrets about how he handled the encounter. "If we pride ourselves in being honest with our readers, how can we pride ourselves in not being honest with each other?" Willes told AJR when asked about the meeting. "How can I be reassuring when it does lack focus, and it needs to be fixed? We either need to find a way to fix it, or we need to do something else. I think if I had said anything other than that, I would have undermined my own credibility. I also think what I said was probably shared by 80 percent of the people in the newsroom."

It isn't that readers ignore Life & Style. According to Narda Zacchino, who until recently oversaw the paper's features sections, it is one of the best read parts of the paper, a section research shows that people read all the way through.

But it doesn't work for the publisher. Not only does Willes have problems with its content, he doesn't like the fact that it attracts little advertising. It is a surprisingly thin section, sometimes only six pages. And since it's not aimed at a specific audience, Willes believes, advertisers don't want to appear there.

Advertisers, unbeknownst to them, are changing the ways of the Los Angeles Times, big time. In mid-October, Willes shook up the newspaper world by announcing his plans to radically change the model on which newspapers are based. No longer would the once-sacrosanct wall stand between business and editorial. The two sides would work closely together in an effort to strengthen the paper.

"I've got no problem taking advertising salesmen to lunch," says David Shaw, the paper's media critic. "But I don't want them dictating what goes into the paper."

And that is the critical question: What are the ramifications of the demolition of the wall? Willes insists that he simply wants the business side and editorial to join forces to make the newspaper flourish. Allowing advertisers to call the shots about what goes in the paper would not only be wrong, it would be bad for business, he says.

But one thing is clear: Both his anxious staff and the world of journalism will be watching Willes' bold experiment very closely. If Willes' reassuring words aren't matched by reality, everyone will know.

H AVING JOURNALISTS TALK TO ADVERtising salesmen is only part of Willes' radical revamping of the nation's fourth largest newspaper. Business managers are being assigned to each section to "partner" with the section's editor and work closely on strategic planning. And, unlike the way things function at other newspapers, many sections must account for profit and loss. Focus groups will play a large role in determining the direction of each of the sections.

"I think the A section—and every section—will need to have a strategic plan," Willes says. "But I think the strategic plan for the A section will probably have more to do with readership than it will with revenues and profit and loss." Other sections that can be more easily targeted, such as business, sports, travel, the Sunday magazine and Life & Style, he says, "will have both readership objectives and revenue objectives. It does not mean they will all have to be profitable. It does mean that they will need to be measured on that. Doing better is better than doing worse."

In a sense, Willes' initiative is simply an extension, albeit a dramatic one, of an existing trend in the newspaper business. These days editors and publishers often work closely together on marketing initiatives, and editorial and business side personnel routinely join forces in creating new sections. What's new in Los Angeles is viewing each section as, in effect, an individual business, and having news and business personnel work as partners on an ongoing basis.

Rather than succumbing to the view that newspapers are in decline, Willes is certain the Times' circulation can grow. In fact, he's put out the word that he wants it to jump from 1 million to 1.5 million, an astonishingly ambitious goal.

Willes believes the best way to achieve that objective is to systematically increase circulation section by section. He wants to shake up the industry and put to rest assumptions that an "outsider" can't maintain strong journalistic standards, all the while using the brand-management techniques he learned at General Mills to boost circulation and attract advertisers.

Willes named himself publisher September 12 and moved into the job October 1 (see Bylines, October). He succeeded Richard T. Schlosberg III, 53, who, it is widely believed, had been nudged aside (Willes says he tried to convince him to stay).

It didn't take long for Willes, an economist who once headed the Federal Reserve Bank in Minneapolis (see "General Mills' Gift to Journalism," July/August 1995), to turn the place inside out. On October 9, after eight years as editor, Shelby Coffey III abruptly resigned, unwilling to work under a fourth publisher. Michael Parks, 54, a longtime Times foreign correspondent who became managing editor in 1996, replaced Coffey (see Bylines, November). And in an unusual move for a big-city daily, the paper implemented a structure with four managing editors.

But all of that could have taken place quietly—especially since Coffey had been rumored to be on his way out for quite some time—if Willes hadn't declared a revolution in the newspaper industry.

The question for many journalists at the Times now is how to view their paper. Is a particular section a vehicle for good journalism or a marketing tool? Or both? Instead of producing exemplary journalism and hoping advertisers will follow, is the paper going to create journalistic products specifically aimed at attracting advertisers? No, says Willes, who sees it rather simply. If a section is clearly targeted, well-executed and relevant, readers will come; circulation will grow, advertisers will follow and revenue will increase.

Willes embarked on a controversial series of cost-cutting measures when he took over Times Mirror in 1995 (see Bylines, September 1995). And while he encountered a great deal of criticism for such actions as killing New York Newsday, he has dramatically improved the financial picture at Times Mirror, previously known as an underachiever on Wall Street. The company's stock has nearly tripled in price since 1995, and for his efforts Willes received a $1.35 million bonus in addition to his $798,000-a-year salary last year.

Some at the paper are delighted to have a successful businessman at the helm. "As for his lack of experience running a newspaper, I welcome that," says Steve Wasserman, who rejoined the paper a year ago as editor of its book review. "The people with experience, for the most part, have been running America's newspapers into the ground. They are largely people without vision, and they lack confidence about the future. I like Willes' approach, which is passionate and intelligent and free of prejudice, not tied to the old ways of doing things."

Others are more fearful about Willes' grand experiment. "When I was a kid growing up here in the 1950s, the Los Angeles Times was a really crummy, biased newspaper," says Henry Weinstein, a metro reporter for 19 years. "Then Otis Chandler started turning the paper around and transformed it into one of the best newspapers in the nation. I think we are all hoping that no one will tamper with that."

And some are more outspoken. "Willes has decided he's a great newspaperman," says Noel Greenwood, a former top Times editor. "If he can

Timeline

■ **1881** ■
The Los Angeles Times is founded by Nathan Cole Jr. and Thomas Gardiner. The next year their interests are sold to Harrison Gray Otis, who becomes the Times' first publisher.

■ **1884** ■
Times Mirror is incorporated.

■ **1960** ■
Otis Chandler becomes publisher, and the Times' ascent to the top tier of American newspapers begins.

CHANDLER

■ **1980** ■
Chandler steps down.

■ **1987** ■
The Los Angeles Herald Examiner folds.

COFFEY

■ **1989** ■
Shelby Coffey III becomes editor of the Times.

■ **EARLY 1990s** ■
Recession hits Southern California; the Times' advertising revenue and profits plummet.

■ **1993** ■
The Times wins a Pulitzer for coverage of L.A. riots the year before.

■ **1994** ■
Richard T. Schlosberg III becomes the Times' publisher.

SCHLOSBERG

■ **APRIL 1995** ■
The Times wins a Pulitzer for coverage of the 1994 Northridge earthquake.

■ **JUNE 1995** ■
General Mills executive Mark H. Willes, a newspaper neophyte, takes over as chairman, president and CEO of Times Mirror. Major cuts are implemented at the Times and elsewhere in the company. Times Mirror's stock price begins a dramatic upswing.

COTLIAR

■ **1996** ■
Managing Editor George Cotliar retires and is succeeded by longtime foreign correspondent Michael Parks.

■ **SEPTEMBER 1997** ■
Times Mirror announces Willes will become the Times' publisher after Schlosberg retires at age 53.

■ **OCTOBER 1997** ■
Coffey resigns and is succeeded by Managing Editor Parks. Willes launches a bold restructuring of the business side, stressing a much closer relationship with editorial.

make cereal, he can make great newspapers. The boundless ego of this man is awesome to behold. I feel pissed off because I put 25 years into that paper and was there when we thought we had a real purpose. Now it's all unraveling."

TO UNDERSTAND THE SEISMIC SHAKEUP at the Times and its lingering aftershocks, one has to study the eight-year reign of Editor Shelby Coffey III, or SC3 as he's known around the office. While Willes dramatically changed the Times' landscape in weeks, Coffey's tenure was marked by what many call an indecisive management style.

Coffey, 50, became editor in 1989, presiding over coverage of the Los Angeles riots, the Northridge earthquake and the O.J. Simpson saga. Under his direction, the paper won four Pulitzer Prizes and was a finalist 22 times. It was in the forefront in uncovering the Asia money scandal, for which it won a number of prestigious awards this year. In 1995, Coffey was named editor of the year by the National Press Foundation.

That said, he did not have a huge base of support in his own newsroom. Many praise him for his creativity in inventing new sections and renovating the old. They note his ability to quote Cicero, his Southern charm, his gentlemanly qualities (he's a descendant of a U.S. senator from Tennessee).

"But mostly he is the quintessential guilty white male: insular, kindhearted, cluelessly patronizing, endlessly infuriating," wrote Catherine Seipp in the L.A. Weekly, an alternative paper. "And so, during his eight-year tenure, was the Los Angeles Times." For five years, Seipp chronicled the goings on at the Times in a wickedly bitchy but often dead-on column in the old Buzz magazine, where she relied on Times sources sharing off-the-record secrets.

Others rate Coffey much more highly. For example, Glenn Bunting of the Times' Washington bureau says Coffey was instrumental in creating investigative teams in Los Angeles, Sacramento and Washington.

"Shelby has been a terrific editor on several levels," says Doyle McManus, the Times' Washington bureau chief. "He's brought a whole list of terrific, talented reporters into the paper. He's vastly improved the quality of editorial. People forget how undisciplined and sprawling the L.A. Times was in the late 1970s. It was edited by a shovel. Shelby has maintained the L.A. Times' tradition of long, literary stories, but has also brought much more discipline to the paper."

But Coffey was cruelly cut down by the recession Southern California endured in the early 1990s. He used to jokingly blame Mikhail Gorbachev for his woes. The end of the Cold War slowed down the robust aerospace industry that helped keep the area's economy booming. The paper's profits tumbled. Enter Mark Willes.

"One of the things that was more difficult during the recession is that when you are in it, you don't know how long it's going to last," Coffey says. "The first year and a half I was here, we hired an extra 150 people. We were adding the World Report section, the Ventura County edition. Then comes the recession, and you have to start making other kinds of choices. You work with attrition."

Coffey was forced to shutter the San Diego edition in 1992. Later he folded some of the zoned editions he had expanded and shut down City Times, launched to cover the inner city after the riots, and World Report—two sections Coffey had initiated.

But his critics focus on what they consider his lack of strong leadership. "Shelby likes to put off decisions...," says Greenwood, who worked with Coffey and unsuccessfully competed with him for the paper's top job. "You'd say, 'Shelby, should we do this or shouldn't we?' and he'd say: 'Let's talk it through.' And we'd get exasperated: 'Shelby, we've been talking about it for three weeks.' "

Some say what comes off as an inability to make a decision stems from Coffey's reluctance to hurt anyone's feelings. When he and former Publisher Schlosberg were trying to choose a managing editor after the popular George Cotliar retired, Coffey wanted to create a managing editor's job shared by editors Narda Zacchino and Carol Stogsdill. Instead Parks, who had spent most of his career overseas, won the coveted slot in the summer of 1996, largely, say many, because Schlosberg pushed for him. (New Editor Parks, it should be noted, ended up with *four* managing editors.)

"Shelby never settled on a choice," says one insider. "He liked Narda. He liked Carol. Michael Parks was clearly Schlosberg's favorite. He was Shelby's consensus choice. It's inaccurate to say that Schlosberg put him in over Shelby's dissent. Shelby's endearing quality is that he never wants to hurt anyone's feelings. He loves all his children equally."

Coffey's journey to Los Angeles began in 1984, when he met former Times Publisher Otis Chandler, then a member of the Times Mirror board, lifting weights at an athletic club in Washington, D.C. The two men developed an immediate rapport. At the time Coffey was working at the Washington Post, where he ultimately spent 17 years in a career that took him from sportswriter to major editing posts. While he served briefly at the end of his tenure as assistant managing editor for national news, for much of his time there Coffey was closely associated with the Post's groundbreaking Style section.

Coffey left in March 1985, spending a year in what was then the revolving door position of editor of U.S. News & World Report. He then joined Times Mirror as editor of the now-defunct Dallas Times Herald. Less than a year later, the paper was sold, and Coffey moved to Los Angeles as deputy associate editor.

"At the time Shelby took over the paper, I

A Conversation with Mark Willes

Excerpts from Alicia C. Shepard's interview with Los Angeles Times Publisher Mark H. Willes:

AJR: So have you ever worked with such a recalcitrant work force?

MHW: Yeah, when I was a professor. The honest truth is our people aren't that recalcitrant. Our people have lots of questions, which they should have. They are very concerned that we stay sensitive to things which they hold near and dear, and I don't fault them for that. Those things are important. This whole issue that everybody is preoccupied with at the moment having to do with editorial independence is an important issue. If I weren't sensitive to it, they'd have every right to jump up and down. So for them to raise a little yellow flag and say: "Hey, are you sensitive to this?" I think is absolutely appropriate. I've had far less difficulty with our own people than I have had with some people in other newspapers who kind of think we've somehow broken the tablets here.

AJR: Tell me about that. Where are you getting this sense that you've broken the tablets?

MHW: Well, I read everybody else's newspaper. You'd think we'd just done something terrible. As I've thought about it, there are two things about it I find curious. The first is for a profession that prides itself on objectivity, this immediate rush to judgment is a little surprising. If people want to say: "There's a real issue here, we hope you are sensitive to it; we'll wait and see," I can understand that. But to kind of automatically assume that we are going to do all these terrible things, that we are going to let advertisers dictate the content of the paper, which we absolutely are not going to do, and would be silly to do, I find perplexing.

The second thing I also find perplexing is if you read the words and some of the quotes by people in the profession, it comes across that the only people who know how to make good moral judgments are journalists. The kind of "nobody else is capable of understanding those issues and able to make those judgments"—not only do our own editors find that offensive, because they're perfectly capable of it, but I find that offensive because I'm capable of making them. This notion that you have to be in journalism 30 years in order to understand what's important, I find rather quaint.

AJR: Quaint? Or obnoxious or too sanctimonious?

MHW: It's certainly sanctimonious.

AJR: This whole thing of being called the cereal killer. Do you think you made a mistake comparing newspapers to cereal products? Do you wish you hadn't done that?

MHW: It clearly became a lightning rod. In that sense I wish I hadn't done it so early because people thought I was equating a newspaper with a box of cereal or detergent and, obviously, I was not. On the other hand, again for an industry that prides itself in looking out on the world, to kind of assume that there isn't anything to be learned by what others do strikes me as a rather strange conclusion....

For any successful business, the product has to be perceived as special by the buyer or user. Special in the case of a newspaper has everything to do now with not just readability but with this important element of trust. Can I believe what I see in the newspaper? Do they hype the truth? Do they tell me the truth? Do they tell me all the truth? Any time we do anything to damage that relationship with the reader, we basically damage our own franchise. Strictly from a business point of view, it is imperative that we not ever, ever lose sight of what journalists hold near and dear. So even if I didn't believe it personally, which I do, as a businessman I'd say, "We can't do it."

AJR: So if it became known that advertisers were running the Los Angeles Times, your credibility would be shot and you would lose the value of your product?

MHW: Exactly. We would lose the whole thing.

AJR: I read that you said a newspaper ought to be a more crusading force. Talk about that.

MHW: I think newspapers do have an enormous opportunity to be a constructive force in their community. In many respects most newspapers are. But I think we can move to another level. What we do and most newspapers do is focus on a problem and bring a lot of attention to it, and then go on to the next problem. In the meantime, we don't have it on this one anymore. So if we can find those issues and those problems that are so central that if progress could be made it would make a significant difference in their lives in a significant, sustained way.... We are not talking about getting involved in politics. We are not talking about running things. But we are talking about using the platform and spotlight of a great newspaper to help others who have the desire and focus to make change.

AJR: How much are you going to be involved in editorial content?

MHW: In terms of reading it before it goes in the paper? Zero.

AJR: So are you having fun?

MHW: Some days [laughs]. Most days.

AJR: Does all of this attention surprise you?

MHW: I don't like the attention. I'd rather just do our own thing and show that it works.... The questions of journalists are getting more thoughtful, much less knee jerk. What really is it you are trying to get? What are you doing to protect the paper?

What I'm encouraged about is people are now thinking about it instead of reacting against it. That's an important thing from our point of view. I mean we don't know that we've got it right. I mean all we're going to do is try. And if it works, we'll continue to do it. And exactly like the Washington edition [which Willes eliminated and later reinstated], if we're finding it doesn't work, we'll say we made a mistake and we're going to fix it.

AJR: There does seem to be something with newspapers where you don't try something new unless you are sure you are going to succeed.

MHW: It's amazing. It's amazing. It's not the way the world is. ●

> **"THIS** *notion that you have to be in journalism 30 years in order to understand what's important, I find rather quaint."*

think this was the most profitable paper in the country," recalls media critic Shaw. "Shelby was young, smart. We thought we would see a lot of creative things taking place. And then the recession hit. I'm not sure he ever fully psychologically recovered from firing all the people he had to fire [see 'The Shrinking L.A. Times,' October 1995]. He was ashen in the days leading up to and right after laying off 147 people. He's always been somebody who, despite his formal, stiff, cool demeanor, is very open to problems at a personal, family level."

Willes and Coffey couldn't be more different. Willes is quick to make decisions. He throws out ideas and expects instant response. He wants goals set, things done. "Willes' attitude is you try things and if they don't work, you move on," says an editor who has spent more than a decade at the Times. "If they don't work, you learned something by trying, and you try something else." Coffey likes to ponder situations, put together committees to study problems, and in a collegial, democratic way, reach consensus decisions. Many joke that he's a hologram, and they need a translator after a meeting with him.

ANOTHER WIDELY VOICED CRITICISM OF the Coffey era is that the paper didn't do a very good job of covering the sprawling Los Angeles area, that it wallowed in complacency after the death of the Los Angeles Herald Examiner in 1989. It's often said that the farther a story is from Los Angeles, the better the Times covers it.

"In some respects the Times does an excellent job, certainly with some of the coverage," says Edwin Guthman, a journalism professor at the University of Southern California and the Times' national editor from 1965 to 1977. "But they've given up the tradition of having someone in an area long enough to make sources that make a difference in a story."

"The fundamental problem that needs to be addressed is they're just completely out of touch with their own community," says David Cay Johnston, who quit in disgust after 12 years at the paper and is now a reporter at the New York Times (another paper not known for its local coverage). "They are masterful at covering a big disaster and deserved their Pulitzer for the riots coverage [see 'City of Anger,' July/August 1992]. But they are just blind to the important issues that affect the lives of their readers, and they are timid, preferring big investigations about small fry to serious coverage of big fish."

(Guthman, however, points to a powerful investigative piece, "And Justice for Some: Solving Murders in L.A. County," a Pulitzer finalist this year.)

"Willes could well sell a half million more copies a day," says Johnston, "but only by publishing a paper that is vital to people's lives instead of one that you don't have to read to know what is going on in Southern California."

And many don't read the Times. The paper's penetration in its home market is just 23 percent, compared to 43 percent for the San Jose Mercury News and 45 percent for the San Diego Union-Tribune. "The Los Angeles Times is somewhat analogous to the New York Times [9 percent penetration] in that its appeal has been to the upper income range," says media analyst John Morton. "The only way to expand it is to go after a lower demographic profile."

One way or another, Willes is determined to attract more readers. And the paper already has forward momentum. Thanks in part to dropping the price from 50 cents to a quarter in June 1996 and to a multimillion dollar "brand" marketing campaign begun in April 1996, the paper's daily circulation has shown year over year gains for three consecutive reporting periods. For the six-month period ending September 30, daily circulation was up by about 21,000 (to just over 1,050,000) and Sunday by nearly 12,000 (to almost 1,362,000) over the past year, the Times' first Sunday circulation gain in six years.

But despite the rising numbers, the staff's disappointment in the paper is palpable, illustrated by the steady exodus over the last few years of top Times reporters to the New York Times. Each of the at least 20 defections can be explained individually, but collectively they amount to a no-confidence vote, say many.

New York Times Editor Joseph Lelyveld gloated about the phenomenon in his paper's October in-house newsletter: "I think we are going through a great period at the Times. No one else in American journalism sustains the level of writing we do, puts as much good stuff on the newsstands day by day, week by week. It's recognized. We're the place really ambitious reporters want to be. Ask Shelby Coffey."

Such a talent drain—even to the New York Times—would have been unthinkable in the past, particularly in the Otis Chandler era. Then the Los Angeles Times, dubbed the "velvet coffin," was the place to be. Reporters flew first class to farflung locales to write seemingly endless take-outs.

New York Times White House correspondent John Broder worked at the Los Angeles Times for 12 years, starting out as a young business reporter. Within two years, the Washington bureau beckoned and Broder was covering the Pentagon, politics and eventually the White House. Then the call came from the New York Times.

"And like every journalist, I wondered if I could play at the very highest level," says Broder, 45. "I didn't know, and I was a little afraid to try. But that challenge and the broader unease about the Los Angeles Times' future made the decision for me." He left in November 1996.

"I've got 20 years left in my career," Broder says. "Do I want to spend it at the Los Angeles Times with the uncertainty that hovered over it a year ago and certainly today? Or do I want to put my stock in the New York Times? I made that decision, and I have no regrets. And the events of the past weeks made me feel I've made the right decision."

'I'S THIS THE COOLEST THING YOU HAVE ever heard of?" asked Kelly Ann Sole, then the Times' wildly enthusiastic national sales manager for financial advertising, when I called to ask for an interview about Willes' bold venture. While some appear mystified by the new publisher, Sole, 31, "gets" what he wants to do. She radiates excitement for the new publisher's plans to organize the business side around editorial sections.

"It baffles me that no one thought of this before," says Sole, who was promoted in November to general manager of the business section. "I can't think of a better way to build a business. What Mark Willes is doing is just formalizing what a few of us have been doing for a year. Mark has the vision and the guts to make it happen faster. I believe if Mark carries that off, he will revolutionize the newspaper industry."

The Times' business pages, in effect, blew up the wall between advertising and editorial a year ago. Sole, who joined the Times 18 months ago, may have single-handedly and, she says, naively, provided the dynamite. "I didn't know you never call someone in editorial," she says.

After a couple of road trips, she learned mutual funds didn't advertise in the business section because there was no vehicle geared to individual investors. So one night she called the section's editor, Bill Sing. "We don't get any mutual fund advertising," she told him. "Why don't we create an editorial vehicle to demystify investing? It would be a logical home for financial advertisers. This marketplace is starved for investment education."

" 'It's funny you called,' " Sole says Sing told her. " 'We get 100 calls a week asking our reporters how to pick a stock, what mutual fund to buy.' " Out of their conversations and the pairing of editorial and marketing staffers grew Wall Street, California, a section targeted at small investors, which debuted a year ago and appears each Tuesday.

Wall Street, California, says Sole, has increased ad revenue 40 percent over previous Tuesday business sections. "It means we have a whole heck of a lot more advertising, and it's been instrumental in driving circulation," she says. Sole sees the possibilities, and has already proven, according to Sing, that business staffers can come up with great ideas that don't threaten editorial integrity.

"The business side is probably best situated to do what Willes wants to do," says Sing, who became business editor in June 1996. "A lot of the coverage talks about the business side of the paper in the newsroom telling us what to write. The reality is the opposite. What's happened with us is we have a number of ideas for editorial products that would serve our read-

"THE fundamental problem that needs to be addressed is they're just completely out of touch with their own community," says David Cay Johnston, who quit in disgust after 12 years at the paper and is now a reporter at the New York Times.

Blocks of Times

The year-old Wall Street, California section, aimed at small investors, appears each Tuesday.

The Calendar section, which appeals to the movie industry, is packed with advertising.

Publisher Mark H. Willes says the Life & Style section lacks focus and "needs to be fixed."

ers. But we need the business side to create new products."

Market research, for example, indicates some 100,000 small business owners in the Times' market don't get the paper. "That's a big number," says Willes. And so a small business-oriented section was launched in September. Says Willes, "Having a feature in the paper that is directly helpful to them gives us a basis now to market to them: to say, 'Here, we have this. This is going to be helpful to you. Why don't you try it and see if you like it?' That's very different than running a general campaign on TV saying, 'Get the story. Get the Times.'"

Sing is adamant that his section won't create a vehicle just for advertisers. "If the ad side says, 'We can sell ads on widgets, let's create a widget section,' we will say no," he says. "But as journalists we should be open to ideas regardless of who they are from. That's different than an ad guy saying, 'I'm trying to sell an ad to Bank of America, why don't you do a story?'"

But the slope, as they say, is a slippery one. Only days after Sing made those comments, one of his reporters received something that dramatically raised her anxiety level. One morning in mid-October Debora Vrana, who covers mergers and acquisitions, picked up her faxes. One from the Times' advertising department caught her attention. The cover letter said something like: "Here's this press release from an advertiser. Could this run in the paper on page two or three?"

Deeply concerned, Vrana took the fax straight to Sing's office. The editor was outraged and called higher-ups. News of Vrana's "nightmare" fax ricocheted around the newsroom. To many, it confirmed their worst fears.

Soon afterward, Sing wrote a memo to reassure the troops: "Some of you have heard about an incident yesterday where an ad department executive passed along an advertiser's press release to Debora Vrana. This is not to be tolerated and has been taken up with Janis Heaphy [senior vice president of advertising and marketing], who we expect to take action. Mark Willes also has been notified and I hope he acts quickly to put a stop to this by issuing a statement to the ad department and others stating the rules and that this type of behavior is not to be tolerated, particularly in these sensitive times."

Later Vrana said, "I was really upset when I got it, but I was very encouraged by the response…. Maybe it was good this happened so early in the whole changeover, because it made it clear that this kind of thing is not acceptable to the Los Angeles Times."

Says Willes, "If journalists can come to understand this, they'll worry less about thinking about journalism as a business," he says. "What 'this' is is the following: Any time we do anything to damage that relationship with the reader, we basically damage our own franchise."

If it became known advertisers were calling the shots at the Los Angeles Times, the paper would lose its credibility, and the value of its

product would diminish. "We would lose the whole thing," Willes says. "And, of course, if we lose our readers, then we lose our advertisers."

Newly crowned Editor Parks says he isn't worried. "If Mark's logic fails to get through, take a look at the people leading the editorial side," he says. "We're kind of known entities. If we thought this was bad, we wouldn't be doing it. On the contrary, I'm confident we are doing something great."

WHAT WILLES THINKS HAS BEEN missing from some sections of the paper is a clear sense of precisely what their roles are and who reads them. He is determined to change that. For example, it's likely individual investors will read Wall Street, California, since it offers investment advice. In fact, each business section is now clearly targeted. Sunday's focus is personal finance and careers, for example, while Monday's is technology.

"Pardon me if I talk about it as a business, but that's how I see things," Willes says. "What marketers have found out is that you're more likely to have a sustainable competitive advantage if you are very clear about what you are and, then, what you have is better than anything else out there."

The Times' Calendar section, which is thick with movie ads and appeals to the entertainment industry, is an example Willes likes to cite. "Calendar is very clear about what it is, and our readers are very clear about what it is," he says. "So it's become this fabulously successful section."

Calendar is roughly 70 percent ads and 30 percent copy, according to Associate Editor Narda Zacchino.

In September, the paper launched a weekly Health section. There's serious talk of a section aimed at Hispanic readers, which prompted a letter signed by 110 staffers urging Willes to drop the idea because, in their view, it's offensive to create a section based solely on ethnicity.

The prospect of a Hispanic section illustrates a dilemma the paper encounters in implementing its new strategy. Yes, there is a large Latino population that doesn't read the Times. Many inside the paper argue that the best way to attract those potential readers is by covering them well throughout the paper. But if wooing new advertisers is also your goal, it's much easier to do so in a specific section targeted at Latinos.

Meanwhile, Lennie LaGuire, the paper's city editor, is working on a prototype of a women's section. "Willes called me up and invited me to lunch several months ago," LaGuire said in October. "He started asking me about ways of making the paper more attractive to women. My first feeling was, my heart sunk. A women's section sounds so retro."

But LaGuire began to see the possibilities. She and assistant city editor Stephanie Chavez came up with a prototype they saw more as a

"The best case scenario is through creative approaches we get more readers, more advertisers and pour some of those profits back into making the paper better journalistically," says media critic David Shaw.

"consumer/quality of life" section. "A daily effort to do something magaziney," is the way LaGuire describes it.

The initial prototype, put together in two weeks, included a huge, much-ridiculed graphic on how to fold fitted sheets. Folding techniques have vanished in the third prototype, which has evolved into an 18-page daily magazine with the working title "The Source: A Guide to Outfitting Your Life." Its best feature may be a 10-minute meal recipe incorporating prepared foods that can be picked up on the way home.

Having a city editor work on the prototype is pure Willes. He wants to break up dukedoms and get people all over the paper brainstorming on new ideas. "One of the things that's been a problem here is this is a very territorial, turf-driven paper...," LaGuire says. "I firmly think going through this exercise of inventing something new is important. It shakes us out of our fiefdoms. It's made me a much better journalist."

Willes says he hasn't decided yet if Life & Style will get the ax, and at press time the folks there were running scared. Some were sending out resumés. Others were waiting, watching. Rumors were flying.

The uncertainty about where the Times is heading has created palpable paranoia at the paper. While I interviewed more than 30 current staffers for this piece, very few would talk on the record. Off, no problem. "I can't be quoted by name," pleaded more than one person. "Don't even call me a business editor. Just an editor is fine," one staffer said. When I wanted to get past security to roam the newsroom after Coffey's resignation on October 9, a reporter agreed to let me in but insisted I walk behind her and we not be seen together.

Shaw says the anxiety is understandable. The paper is no longer the "velvet coffin," and the future seems uncertain. He sees two potential storylines: "The best case scenario is through creative approaches we get more readers, more advertisers and pour some of those profits back into making the paper better journalistically." The worst case? "Regardless of what happens to revenues, there are further cuts which diminish the quality. There's a business side incursion which diminishes credibility."

Ironically, Shaw began working on a takeout about the breakdown of the wall between business and editorial in the news media across the country before Willes announced he was eliminating it in Los Angeles.

"Whatever happens, the next six months around here will be extremely interesting," Shaw says. "They could be exciting and exhilarating, or they could be depressing. But they won't be dull."

Senior writer Alicia C. Shepard (lshepard @erols.com) interviewed New York Times Washington Bureau Chief Michael Oreskes in AJR's November issue. She has profiled many newspapers, most recently Baltimore's Sun, for AJR.

A Bureau's "Woman Problem"

OVERSHADOWED BY THE TURMOIL INSPIRED BY RECENT changes at the Los Angeles Times is a plea by the women in the paper's Washington bureau to change its white male-dominated ways. According to a recent memo, the bureau has a "woman problem."

"The memo reflects a long-standing situation that has festered over a great many years," says Melissa Healy, one of its authors. Only 12 of 42 editorial staffers are female. Only one of six editors is a woman. The two top positions are held by men.

"Women are a distinct and embarrassingly small minority—and often feel we are treated accordingly," said the memo, sent to management in October and signed by Healy, Geraldine Baum, Marlene Cimons, Nina Easton, Faye Fiore, Janet Hook, Vicki Kemper, Alissa Rubin, D.J. Salem, Elizabeth Shogren, Jodi Wilgoren and Robin Wright.

No one seems to dispute that for a prominent Washington bureau in 1997, the statistics are disappointing. "The numbers are a problem...," says Bureau Chief Doyle McManus. "It clearly has not been intentional. And it's our intention to do better."

In the past year, four women on the editorial staff have opted to leave. "In departing, some cited specific instances of poor treatment in which they believed gender played a role," the memo says. "Others cited a broader climate in which they believed their gender proved a disadvantage. Irrespective of how important it was in their decision to leave, all left believing the bureau has a 'woman problem.'"

FRITZ

The case of Sara Fritz, who left the bureau in July to become managing editor of Congressional Quarterly, is cited as an example of what's wrong. After turning down a job at the New York Times in 1994, Fritz was handed the plum job of heading a Washington-based investigative team. It turned out that she was in charge in name only. "I wanted a management position at the Times, and they clearly thought I was totally incapable of management," she says. "I want you to know I am doing very well here."

The memo says tension has eased since Jack Nelson turned over the reins to McManus in January 1996. "I have to plead guilty since I was the bureau chief for 22 years," says Nelson, now the paper's chief Washington correspondent. He cites an ongoing dispute over whether to hire the best qualified person or the best qualified woman or minority. Nelson says he often wanted to hire the best qualified minority. But, he adds, "the answer always was, 'You have to hire the best qualified, and if it's a minority, all the better.' But I still have to bear some responsibility."

Some men in the bureau say there may not be a gender problem so much as a situation in which some people get special deals, regardless of gender. Several women work almost exclusively from home. When her husband got a job in Hartford, Fritz was allowed to work out of the Connecticut city.

Regardless, it's clear the memo has gotten Times' management's attention. A group including all of the women and six men in the bureau is working to improve the climate. A heated debate is in progress over whether to bring in an outsider to "sensitize" people to the existence of a gender problem.

"The idea is that where things are broken, they should be fixed," McManus says. "It's up to all of us to fix them. The whole bureau." ●

—Alicia C. Shepard

Sex, Lies & Advertising

GLORIA STEINEM

Gloria Steinem was a founding editor of "Ms." in 1972 and is now its consulting editor. She is also at work on "The Bedside Book of Self-Esteem" for Little, Brown.

About three years ago, as *glasnost* was beginning and *Ms.* seemed to be ending, I was invited to a press lunch for a Soviet official. He entertained us with anecdotes about new problems of democracy in his country. Local Communist leaders were being criticized in their media for the first time, he explained, and they were angry.

"So I'll have to ask my American friends," he finished pointedly, "how more *subtly* to control the press." In the silence that followed, I said, "Advertising."

The reporters laughed, but later, one of them took me aside: How *dare* I suggest that freedom of the press was limited? How dare I imply that his newsweekly could be influenced by ads?

I explained that I was thinking of advertising's media-wide influence on most of what we read. Even newsmagazines use "soft" cover stories to sell ads, confuse readers with "advertorials," and occasionally self-censor on subjects known to be a problem with big advertisers.

But, I also explained, I was thinking especially of women's magazines. There, it isn't just a little content that's devoted to attracting ads, it's almost all of it. That's why advertisers—not readers—have always been the problem for *Ms.* As the only women's magazine that didn't supply what the ad world euphemistically describes as "supportive editorial atmosphere" or "complementary copy" (for instance, articles that praise food/fashion/beauty subjects to "support" and "comple-

ment" food/fashion/beauty ads), *Ms.* could never attract enough advertising to break even.

"Oh, *women's* magazines," the journalist said with contempt. "Everybody knows they're catalogs—but who cares? They have nothing to do with journalism."

■ Suppose archaeologists of the future dug up women's magazines and used them to judge American women. What would they think of us—and what can we do about it?

I can't tell you how many times I've had this argument in 25 years of working for many kinds of publications. Except as moneymaking machines—"cash cows" as they are so elegantly called in the trade—women's magazines are rarely taken seriously. Though changes being made by women have been called more far-reaching than the industrial revolution—and though many editors try hard to reflect some of them in the few pages left to them after all the ad-related subjects have been covered—the magazines serving the female half of this country are still far below the journalistic and ethical standards of news and general interest publications. Most depressing of all, this doesn't even rate an exposé.

If *Time* and *Newsweek* had to lavish praise on cars in general and credit General Motors in particular to get GM ads, there would be a scandal—maybe a criminal investigation. When women's magazines from *Seventeen* to *Lear's* praise beauty products in general and credit Revlon in particular to get ads, it's just business as usual.

I.

When *Ms.* began, we didn't consider *not* taking ads. The most important reason was keeping the price of a feminist magazine low enough for most women to afford. But the second and almost equal reason was providing a forum where women and advertisers could talk to each other and improve advertising itself. After all, it was (and still is) as potent a source of information in this country as news or TV and movie dramas.

We decided to proceed in two stages. First, we would convince makers of "people products" used by both men and women but advertised mostly to men—cars, credit cards, insurance, sound equipment, financial services, and the like—that their ads should be placed in a women's magazine. Since they were accustomed to the division between editorial and advertising in news and general interest magazines, this would allow our editorial content to be free and diverse. Second, we would add the best ads for whatever traditional "women's products" (clothes, shampoo, fragrance, food, and so on) that surveys showed *Ms.* readers used. But we would ask them to come in *without* the usual quid pro quo of "complementary copy."

We knew the second step might be harder. Food advertisers have always demanded that women's magazines publish recipes and articles on entertaining (preferably ones that name their products) in return for their ads; clothing advertisers expect to be surrounded by fashion spreads (especially ones that credit their designers); and shampoo, fragrance, and beauty products in general usually insist on positive editorial coverage of beauty subjects, plus photo credits besides. That's why women's magazines look the way they do. But if we could break this link between ads and editorial content, then we wanted good ads for "women's products," too.

By playing their part in this unprecedented mix of *all* the things our readers need and use, advertisers also would be rewarded: ads for products like cars and mutual funds would find a new growth market; the best ads for women's products would no longer be lost in oceans of ads for the same category; and both would have access to a laboratory of smart and caring readers whose response would help create effective ads for other media as well.

I thought then that our main problem would be the imagery in ads themselves. Carmakers were still draping blondes in evening gowns over the hoods like ornaments. Authority figures were almost always male, even in ads for products that only women used. Sadistic, he-man campaigns even won industry praise. (For instance, *Advertising Age* had hailed the infamous Silva Thin cigarette theme, "How to Get a Woman's Attention: Ignore Her," as "brilliant.") Even in medical journals, tranquilizer ads showed depressed housewives standing beside piles of dirty dishes and promised to get them back to work.

Obviously, *Ms.* would have to avoid such ads and seek out the best ones—but this didn't seem impossible. *The New Yorker* had been selecting ads for aesthetic reasons for years, a practice that only seemed to make advertisers more eager to be in its pages. *Ebony* and *Essence* were asking for ads with positive black images, and though their struggle was hard, they weren't being called unreasonable.

Clearly, what *Ms.* needed was a very special publisher and ad sales staff. I could think of only one woman with experience on the business side of magazines—Patricia Carbine, who recently had become a vice president of *McCall's* as well as its editor in chief—and the reason I knew her name was a good omen. She had been managing editor at *Look* (really *the* editor, but its owner refused to put a female name at the top of his masthead) when I was writing a column there. After I did an early interview with Cesar Chavez, then just emerging as a leader of migrant labor, and the publisher turned it down because he was worried about ads from Sunkist, Pat was the one who intervened. As I learned later, she had told the publisher she would resign if the interview wasn't published. Mainly because *Look* couldn't afford to lose Pat, it *was* published (and the ads from Sunkist never arrived).

Though I barely knew this woman, she had done two things I always remembered: put her job on the line in a way that editors often talk about but rarely do, and been so loyal to her colleagues that she never told me or anyone outside *Look* that she had done so.

Fortunately, Pat did agree to leave *McCall's* and take a huge cut in salary to become publisher of *Ms.* She became responsible for training and inspiring generations of young women who joined the *Ms.* ad sales force, many of whom went on to become "firsts" at the top of publishing. When *Ms.* first started, however, there were so few women with experience selling space that Pat and I made the rounds of ad agencies ourselves. Later, the fact that *Ms.* was asking companies to do business in a different way meant our saleswomen had to make many times the usual number of calls—first to convince agencies and then client companies besides—and to present endless amounts of research. I was often asked to do a final ad presentation, or see some higher decision-maker, or speak to women employees so executives could see the interest of women they worked with. That's why I spent more time persuading advertisers than editing or writing for *Ms.* and why I ended up with an unsentimental education in the seamy underside of publishing that few writers see (and even fewer magazines can publish).

Let me take you with us through some experiences, just as they happened:
■ Cheered on by early support from Volkswagen and one or two other car companies, we scrape together time and money to put on a major reception in Detroit. We know U.S. carmakers firmly believe that women choose the

upholstery, not the car, but we are armed with statistics and reader mail to prove the contrary: a car is an important purchase for women, one that symbolizes mobility and freedom.

But almost nobody comes. We are left with many pounds of shrimp on the table, and quite a lot of egg on our face. We blame ourselves for not guessing that there would be a baseball pennant play-off on the same day, but executives go out of their way to explain they wouldn't have come anyway. Thus begins ten years of knocking on hostile doors, presenting endless documentation, and hiring a full-time saleswoman in Detroit; all necessary before *Ms.* gets any real results.

This long saga has a semihappy ending: foreign and, later, domestic carmakers eventually provided *Ms.* with enough advertising to make cars one of our top sources of ad revenue. Slowly, Detroit began to take the women's market seriously enough to put car ads in other women's magazines, too, thus freeing a few pages from the hothouse of fashion-beauty-food ads.

But long after figures showed a third, even a half, of many car models being bought by women, U.S. makers continued to be uncomfortable addressing women. Unlike foreign carmakers, Detroit never quite learned the secret of creating intelligent ads that exclude no one, and then placing them in women's magazines to overcome past exclusion. (*Ms.* readers were so grateful for a routine Honda ad featuring rack and pinion steering, for instance, that they sent fan mail.) Even now, Detroit continues to ask, "Should we make special ads for women?" Perhaps that's why some foreign cars still have a disproportionate share of the U.S. women's market.

■ In the *Ms.* Gazette, we do a brief report on a congressional hearing into chemicals used in hair dyes that are absorbed through the skin and may be carcinogenic. Newspapers report this too, but Clairol, a Bristol-Myers subsidiary that makes dozens of products—a few of which have just begun to advertise in *Ms.*—is outraged. Not at newspapers or newsmagazines, just at us. It's bad enough that *Ms.* is the only women's magazine refusing to provide the usual "complementary" articles and beauty photos, but to criticize one of their categories—*that* is going too far.

We offer to publish a letter from Clairol telling its side of the story. In an excess of solicitousness, we even put this letter in the Gazette, not in Letters to the Editors where it belongs. Nonetheless—and in spite of surveys that show *Ms.* readers are active women who use more of almost everything Clairol makes than do the readers of any other women's magazine—*Ms.* gets almost none of these ads for the rest of its natural life.

Meanwhile, Clairol changes its hair coloring formula, apparently in response to the hearings we reported.

■ Our saleswomen set out early to attract ads for consumer electronics: sound equipment, calculators, computers, VCRs, and the like. We know that our readers are determined to be included in the technological revolu-

tion. We know from reader surveys that *Ms.* readers are buying this stuff in numbers as high as those of magazines like *Playboy;* or "men 18 to 34," the prime targets of the consumer electronics industry. Moreover, unlike traditional women's products that our readers buy but don't need to read articles about, these are subjects they want covered in our pages. There actually *is* a supportive editorial atmosphere.

"But women don't understand technology," say executives at the end of ad presentations. "Maybe not," we respond, "but neither do men—and we all buy it."

"If women *do* buy it," say the decision-makers, "they're asking their husbands and boyfriends what to buy first." We produce letters from *Ms.* readers saying how turned off they are when salesmen say things like "Let me know when your husband can come in."

After several years of this, we get a few ads for compact sound systems. Some of them come from JVC, whose vice president, Harry Elias, is trying to convince his Japanese bosses that there is something called a women's market. At his invitation, I find myself speaking at huge trade shows in Chicago and Las Vegas, trying to persuade JVC dealers that showrooms don't have to be locker rooms where women are made to feel unwelcome. But as it turns out, the shows themselves are part of the problem. In Las Vegas, the only women around the technology displays are seminude models serving champagne. In Chicago, the big attraction is Marilyn Chambers, who followed Linda Lovelace of *Deep Throat* fame as Chuck Traynor's captive and/or employee. VCRs are being demonstrated with her porn videos.

In the end, we get ads for a car stereo now and then, but no VCRs; some IBM personal computers, but no Apple or Japanese ones. We notice that office magazines like *Working Woman* and *Savvy* don't benefit as much as they should from office equipment ads either. In the electronics world, women and technology seem mutually exclusive. It remains a decade behind even Detroit.

■ Because we get letters from little girls who love toy trains, and who ask our help in changing ads and box-top photos that feature little boys only, we try to get toy-train ads from Lionel. It turns out that Lionel executives *have* been concerned about little girls. They made a pink train, and were surprised when it didn't sell.

Lionel bows to consumer pressure with a photograph of a boy *and* a girl—but only on some of their boxes. They fear that, if trains are associated with girls, they will be devalued in the minds of boys. Needless to say, *Ms.* gets no train ads, and little girls remain a mostly unexplored market. By 1986, Lionel is put up for sale.

But for different reasons, we haven't had much luck with other kinds of toys either. In spite of many articles on child-rearing; an annual listing of nonsexist, multi-racial toys by Letty Cottin Pogrebin; Stories for Free Children, a regular feature also edited by Letty; and other prizewinning features for or about children, we get virtually no toy ads. Generations of *Ms.* saleswomen explain to toy

You may be surprised to learn, as I was, that in the ratio of advertising to editorial pages in women's magazines, the ads average only about 5 percent more than in "Time," "Newsweek," and "U.S. News." That nothing-to-read feeling comes from editorial pages devoted to "complementary copy"; to text or photos that praise advertised categories, instruct in their use, or generally act as extensions of ads.

To find out what we're getting when we actually pay money for these catalogs, I picked random issues, counted the number of pages (even including letters to the editors, horoscopes, and so forth) that are not ads and/or copy complementary to ads, and then compared that number to the total pages. For instance:

Glamour, April 1990
339 pages total;
65 non-ad or ad-related

Vogue, May 1990
319 pages total;
38 non-ad or ad-related

Redbook, April 1990
173 pages total;
44 non-ad or ad-related

Family Circle, March 13, 1990
180 pages total;
33 non-ad or ad-related

manufacturers that a larger proportion of *Ms.* readers have preschool children than do the readers of other women's magazines, but this industry can't believe feminists have or care about children.

■ When *Ms.* begins, the staff decides not to accept ads for feminine hygiene sprays or cigarettes: they are damaging and carry no appropriate health warnings. Though we don't think we should tell our readers what to do, we do think we should provide facts so they can decide for themselves. Since the antismoking lobby has been pressing for health warnings on cigarette ads, we decide to take them only as they comply.

Philip Morris is among the first to do so. One of its brands, Virginia Slims, is also sponsoring women's tennis and the first national polls of women's opinions. On the other hand, the Virginia Slims theme, "You've come a long way, baby," has more than a "baby" problem. It makes smoking a symbol of progress for women.

We explain to Philip Morris that this slogan won't do well in our pages, but they are convinced its success with some women means it will work with *all* women. Finally, we agree to publish an ad for a Virginia Slims calendar as a test. The letters from readers are critical—and smart. For instance: Would you show a black man picking cotton, the same man in a Cardin suit, and symbolize the antislavery and civil rights movements by smoking? Of course not. But instead of honoring the test results, the Philip Morris people seem angry to be proven wrong. They take away ads for *all* their many brands.

This costs *Ms.* about $250,000 the first year. After five years, we can no longer keep track. Occasionally, a new set of executives listens to *Ms.* saleswomen, but because we won't take Virginia Slims, not one Philip Morris product returns to our pages for the next 16 years.

Gradually, we also realize our naiveté in thinking we *could* decide against taking cigarette ads. They became a disproportionate support of magazines the moment they were banned on television, and few magazines could compete and survive without them; certainly not *Ms.*, which lacks so many other categories. By the time statistics in the 1980s showed that women's rate of lung cancer was approaching men's, the necessity of taking cigarette ads has become a kind of prison.

■ General Mills, Pillsbury, Carnation, DelMonte, Dole, Kraft, Stouffer, Hormel, Nabisco: you name the food giant, we try it. But no matter how desirable the *Ms.* readership, our lack of recipes is lethal.

We explain to them that placing food ads *only* next to recipes associates food with work. For many women, it is a negative that works *against* the ads. Why not place food ads in diverse media without recipes (thus reaching more men, who are now a third of the shoppers in supermarkets anyway), and leave the recipes to specialty magazines like *Gourmet* (a third of whose readers are also men)?

These arguments elicit interest, but except for an occasional ad for a convenience food, instant coffee, diet drinks, yogurt, or such extras as avocados and almonds, this mainstay of the publishing industry stays closed to us. Period.

■ Traditionally, wines and liquors didn't advertise to women: men were thought to make the brand decisions, even if women did the buying. But after endless presentations, we begin to make a dent in this category. Thanks to the unconventional Michel Roux of Carillon Importers (distributors of Grand Marnier, Absolut Vodka, and others), who assumes that food and drink have no gender, some ads are leaving their men's club.

Beermakers are still selling masculinity. It takes *Ms.* fully eight years to get its first beer ad (Michelob). In general, however, liquor ads are less stereotyped in their imagery—and far less controlling of the editorial content around them—than are women's products. But given the underrepresentation of other categories, these very facts tend to create a disproportionate number of alcohol ads in the pages of *Ms.* This in turn dismays readers worried about women and alcoholism.

■ We hear in 1980 that women in the Soviet Union have been producing feminist *samizdat* (underground, self-published books) and circulating them throughout the country. As punishment, four of the leaders have been exiled. Though we are operating on our usual shoestring, we solicit individual contributions to send Robin Morgan to interview these women in Vienna.

The result is an exclusive cover story that includes the first news of a populist peace movement against the Afghanistan occupation, a prediction of *glasnost* to come, and a grass-roots, intimate view of Soviet women's lives. From the popular press to women's studies courses, the response is great. The story wins a Front Page award.

Nonetheless, this journalistic coup undoes years of efforts to get an ad schedule from Revlon. Why? Because the Soviet women on our cover *are not wearing makeup.*

■ Four years of research and presentations go into convincing airlines that women now make travel choices and business trips. United, the first airline to advertise in *Ms.,* is so impressed with the response from our readers that one of its executives appears in a film for our ad presentations. As usual, good ads get great results.

But we have problems unrelated to such results. For instance: because American Airlines flight attendants include among their labor demands the stipulation that they could choose to have their last names preceded by "Ms." on their name tags—in a long-delayed revolt against the standard, "I am your pilot, Captain Rothgart, and this is your flight attendant, Cindy Sue"—American officials seem to hold the magazine responsible. We get no ads.

There is still a different problem at Eastern. A vice president cancels subscriptions for thousands of copies on Eastern flights. Why? Because he is offended by ads for lesbian poetry journals in the *Ms.* Classified. A "family airline," as he explains to me coldly on the phone, has to "draw the line somewhere."

It's obvious that *Ms.* can't exclude lesbians and serve women. We've been trying to make that point ever since our first issue included an article by and about lesbians, and both Suzanne Levine, our managing editor, and I were lectured by such heavy hitters as Ed Kosner, then editor of *Newsweek* (and now of *New York Magazine*), who insisted that *Ms.* should "position" itself *against* lesbians. But our advertisers have paid to reach a. guaranteed number of readers, and soliciting new subscriptions to compensate for Eastern would cost $150,000, plus rebating money in the meantime.

Like almost everything ad-related, this presents an elaborate organizing problem. After days of searching for sympathetic members of the Eastern board, Frank Thomas, president of the Ford Foundation, kindly offers to call Roswell Gilpatrick, a director of Eastern. I talk with Mr. Gilpatrick, who calls Frank Borman, then the president of Eastern. Frank Borman calls me to say that his airline is not in the business of censoring magazines: *Ms.* will be returned to Eastern flights.

■ Women's access to insurance and credit is vital, but with the exception of Equitable and a few other ad pioneers, such financial services address men. For almost a decade after the Equal Credit Opportunity Act passes in 1974, we try to convince American Express that women are a growth market—but nothing works.

Finally, a former professor of Russian named Jerry Welsh becomes head of marketing. He assumes that women should be cardholders, and persuades his colleagues to feature women in a campaign. Thanks to this 1980s series, the growth rate for female cardholders surpasses that for men.

For this article, I asked Jerry Welsh if he would explain why American Express waited so long. "Sure," he said, "they were afraid of having a 'pink' card."

■ Women of color read *Ms.* in disproportionate numbers. This is a source of pride to *Ms.* staffers, who are also more racially representative than the editors of other women's magazines. But this reality is obscured by ads filled with enough white women to make a reader snowblind.

Pat Carbine remembers mostly "astonishment" when she requested African American, Hispanic, Asian, and other diverse images. Marcia Ann Gillespie, a *Ms.* editor who was previously the editor in chief of *Essence,* witnesses ad bias a second time: having tried for *Essence* to get white advertisers to use black images (Revlon did so eventually, but L'Oréal, Lauder, Chanel, and other companies never did), she sees similar problems getting integrated ads for an integrated magazine. Indeed, the ad world often creates black and Hispanic ads only for black and Hispanic media. In an exact parallel of the fear that marketing a product to women will endanger its appeal to men, the response is usually, "But your [white] readers won't identify."

In fact, those we are able to get—for instance, a Max Factor ad made for *Essence* that Linda Wachner gives us after she becomes president—are praised by white readers, too. But there are pathetically few such images.

■ By the end of 1986, production and mailing costs have risen astronomically, ad income is flat, and competition for ads is stiffer than ever. The 60/40 preponderance of edit over ads that we promised to readers becomes 50/50; children's stories, most poetry, and some fiction are casualties of less space; in order to get variety into limited pages, the length (and sometimes the depth) of articles suffers; and, though we do refuse most of the ads that would look like a parody in our pages, we get so worn down that some slip through. . . . Still, readers perform miracles. Though we haven't been able to afford a subscription mailing in two years, they maintain our guaranteed circulation of 450,000.

Nonetheless, media reports on *Ms.* often insist that our unprofitability must be due to reader disinterest. The myth that advertisers simply follow readers is very strong. Not one reporter notes that other comparable magazines our size (say, *Vanity Fair* or *The Atlantic*) have been losing more money in one year than *Ms.* has lost in 16 years. No matter how much never-to-be-recovered cash is poured into starting a magazine or keeping one going, appearances seem to be all that matter. (Which is why we haven't been able to explain our fragile state in public. Nothing causes ad-flight like the smell of nonsuccess.)

My healthy response is anger. My not-so-healthy response is constant worry. Also an obsession with finding one more rescue. There is hardly a night when I don't wake up with sweaty palms and pounding heart, scared that we won't be able to pay the printer or the post office; scared most of all that closing our doors will hurt the women's movement.

Out of chutzpah and desperation, I arrange a lunch with Leonard Lauder, president of Estée Lauder. With the exception of Clinique (the brainchild of Carol Phillips), none of Lauder's hundreds of products has been advertised in *Ms.* A year's schedule of ads for just three or four of them could save us. Indeed, as the scion of a family-owned company whose ad practices are followed by the beauty industry, he is one of the few men who could liberate many pages in all women's magazines just by changing his mind about "complementary copy."

Over a lunch that costs more than we can pay for some articles, I explain the need for his leadership. I also lay out the record of *Ms.:* more literary and journalistic prizes won, more new issues introduced into the mainstream, new writers discovered, and impact on society than any other magazine; more articles that became books, stories that became movies, ideas that became television series, and newly advertised products that became profitable; and, most important for him, a place for his ads to reach women who aren't reachable through any other women's magazine. Indeed, if there is one constant characteristic of the ever-changing *Ms.* readership, it is their impact as leaders. Whether it's waiting until later to have first babies, or pioneering PABA as sun protection in cosmetics, *whatever* they are doing today, a third to a half of American women will be doing three to five years from now. It's never failed.

But, he says, *Ms.* readers are not *our* women. They're not interested in things like fragrance and blush-on. If they were, *Ms.* would write articles about them.

On the contrary, I explain, surveys show they are more likely to buy such things than the readers of, say, *Cosmopolitan* or *Vogue.* They're good customers because they're out in the world enough to need several sets of everything: home, work, purse, travel, gym, and so on. They just don't need to read articles about these things. Would he ask a men's magazine to publish monthly columns on how to shave before he advertised Aramis products (his line for men)?

He concedes that beauty features are often concocted more for advertisers than readers. But *Ms.* isn't appropriate for his ads anyway, he explains. Why? Because Estée Lauder is selling "a kept-woman mentality."

I can't quite believe this. Sixty percent of the users of his products are salaried, and generally resemble *Ms.* readers. Besides, his company has the appeal of having been started by a creative and hardworking woman, his mother, Estée Lauder.

That doesn't matter, he says. He knows his customers, and they would *like* to be kept women. That's why he will never advertise in *Ms.*

In November 1987, by vote of the Ms. Foundation for Education and Communication (*Ms.*'s owner and publisher, the media subsidiary of the Ms. Foundation for Women), *Ms.* was sold to a company whose officers, Australian feminists Sandra Yates and Anne Summers, raised the investment money in their country that *Ms.* couldn't find in its own. They also started *Sassy* for teenage women.

In their two-year tenure, circulation was raised to 550,000 by investment in circulation mailings, and, to the dismay of some readers, editorial features on clothes and new products made a more traditional bid for ads. Nonetheless, ad pages fell below previous levels. In addition, *Sassy,* whose fresh voice and sexual frankness were an unprecedented success with young readers, was targeted by two mothers from Indiana who began, as one of them put it, "calling every Christian organization I could think of." In response to this controversy, several crucial advertisers pulled out.

Such links between ads and editorial content was a problem in Australia, too, but to a lesser degree. "Our readers pay two times more for their magazines," Anne explained, "so advertisers have less power to threaten a magazine's viability."

"I was shocked," said Sandra Yates with characteristic directness. "In Australia, we think you have freedom of the press—but you don't."

Since Anne and Sandra had not met their budget's projections for ad revenue, their investors forced a sale. In October 1989, *Ms.* and *Sassy* were bought by Dale Lang, owner of *Working Mother, Working Woman,* and one of the few independent publishing companies left among the conglomerates. In response to a request from the original *Ms.* staff—as well as to reader letters urging that *Ms.* continue, plus his own belief that *Ms.* would benefit his other magazines by blazing a trail—he agreed to try the ad-free, reader-supported *Ms.* you hold now and to give us complete editorial control.

II.

Do you think, as I once did, that advertisers make decisions based on solid research? Well, think again. "Broadly speaking," says Joseph Smith of Oxtoby-Smith, Inc., a consumer research firm, "there is no persuasive evidence that the editorial context of an ad matters."

Advertisers who demand such "complementary copy," even in the absence of respectable studies, clearly are operating under a double standard. The same food companies place ads in *People* with no recipes. Cosmetics companies support *The New Yorker* with no regular beauty columns. So where does this habit of controlling the content of women's magazines come from?

Tradition. Ever since *Ladies Magazine* debuted in Boston in 1828, editorial copy directed to women has been informed by something other than its readers' wishes. There were no ads then, but in an age when married women were legal minors with no right to their own money, there was another revenue source to be kept in mind: husbands. "Husbands may rest assured," wrote editor Sarah Josepha Hale, "that nothing found in these pages shall cause her [his wife] to be less assiduous in preparing for his reception or encourage her to 'usurp station' or encroach upon prerogatives of men."

Hale went on to become the editor of *Godey's Lady's Book,* a magazine featuring "fashion plates": engravings of dresses for readers to take to their seamstresses or copy themselves. Hale added "how to" articles, which set the tone for women's service magazines for years to come: how to write politely, avoid sunburn, and—in no fewer than 1,200 words—how to maintain a goose quill pen. She advocated education for women but avoided controversy. Just as most women's magazines now avoid politics, poll their readers on issues like abortion but rarely take a stand, and praise socially approved lifestyles, Hale saw to it that *Godey's* avoided the hot topics of its day: slavery, abolition, and women's suffrage.

What definitively turned women's magazines into catalogs, however, were two events: Ellen Butterick's invention of the clothing pattern in 1863 and the mass manufacture of patent medicines containing everything from colored water to cocaine. For the first time, readers could purchase what magazines encouraged them to want. As such magazines became more profitable, they also began to attract men as editors. (Most women's magazines continued to have men as top editors until the feminist 1970s.) Edward Bok, who became editor of *The Ladies' Home Journal* in 1889, discovered the power of

Elle, May 1990
326 pages total;
39 non-ad or ad-related

Lear's, November 1989
173 pages total;
65 non-ad or ad-related

advertisers when he rejected ads for patent medicines and found that other advertisers canceled in retribution. In the early 20th century, *Good Housekeeping* started its Institute to "test and approve" products. Its Seal of Approval became the grandfather of current "value added" programs that offer advertisers such bonuses as product sampling and department store promotions.

By the time suffragists finally won the vote in 1920, women's magazines had become too entrenched as catalogs to help women learn how to use it. The main function was to create a desire for products, teach how to use products, and make products a crucial part of gaining social approval, pleasing a husband, and performing as a homemaker. Some unrelated articles and short stories were included to persuade women to pay for these catalogs. But articles were neither consumerist nor rebellious. Even fiction was usually subject to formula: if a woman had any sexual life outside marriage, she was supposed to come to a bad end.

In 1965, Helen Gurley Brown began to change part of that formula by bringing "the sexual revolution" to women's magazines—but in an ad-oriented way. Attracting multiple men required even more consumerism, as the Cosmo Girl made clear, than finding one husband.

In response to the workplace revolution of the 1970s, traditional women's magazines—that is, "trade books" for women working at home—were joined by *Savvy, Working Woman,* and other trade books for women working in offices. But by keeping the fashion/beauty/entertaining articles necessary to get traditional ads and then adding career articles besides, they inadvertently produced the antifeminist stereotype of Super Woman. The male-imitative, dress-for-success woman carrying a briefcase became the media image of a woman worker, even though a blue-collar woman's salary was often higher than her glorified secretarial sister's, and though women at a real briefcase level are statistically rare. Needless to say, these dress-for-success women were also thin, white, and beautiful.

In recent years, advertisers' control over the editorial content of women's magazines has become so institutionalized that it is written into "insertion orders" or dictated to ad salespeople as official policy. The following are recent typical orders to women's magazines:

■ Dow's Cleaning Products stipulates that ads for its Vivid and Spray 'n Wash products should be adjacent to "children or fashion editorial"; ads for Bathroom Cleaner should be next to "home furnishing/family" features; and so on for other brands. "If a magazine fails for 1/2 the brands or more," the Dow order warns, "it will be omitted from further consideration."

■ Bristol-Myers, the parent of Clairol, Windex, Drano, Bufferin, and much more, stipulates that ads be placed next to "a full page of compatible editorial."

■ S.C. Johnson & Son, makers of Johnson Wax, lawn and laundry products, insect sprays, hair sprays, and so on, orders that its ads "*should not be opposite extremely controversial features or material antithetical to the nature/copy of the advertised product.*" (Italics theirs.)

■ Maidenform, manufacturer of bras and other apparel, leaves a blank for the particular product and states: "The creative concept of the ____ campaign, and the very nature of the product itself appeal to the positive emotions of the reader/consumer. Therefore, it is imperative that all editorial adjacencies reflect that same positive tone. The editorial must not be negative in content or lend itself contrary to the ____ product imagery/message (e.g. *editorial relating to illness, disillusionment, large size fashion, etc.*)." (Italics mine.)

■ The De Beers diamond company, a big seller of engagement rings, prohibits magazines from placing its ads with "adjacencies to hard news or anti/love-romance themed editorial."

■ Procter & Gamble, one of this country's most powerful and diversified advertisers, stands out in the memory of Anne Summers and Sandra Yates (no mean feat in this context): its products were not to be placed in *any* issue that included *any* material on gun control, abortion, the occult, cults, or the disparagement of religion. Caution was also demanded in any issue covering sex or drugs, even for educational purposes.

Those are the most obvious chains around women's magazines. There are also rules so clear they needn't be written down: for instance, an overall "look" compatible with beauty and fashion ads. Even "real" nonmodel women photographed for a woman's magazine are usually made up, dressed in credited clothes, and retouched out of all reality. When editors do include articles on less-than-cheerful subjects (for instance, domestic violence), they tend to keep them short and unillustrated. The point is to be "upbeat." Just as women in the street are asked, "Why don't you smile, honey?" women's magazines acquire an institutional smile.

Within the text itself, praise for advertisers' products has become so ritualized that fields like "beauty writing" have been invented. One of its frequent practitioners explained seriously that "It's a difficult art. How many new adjectives can you find? How much greater can you

make a lipstick sound? The FDA restricts what companies can say on labels, but we create illusion. And ad agencies are on the phone all the time pushing you to get their product in. A lot of them keep the business based on how many editorial clippings they produce every month. The worst are products," like Lauder's as the writer confirmed, "with their own name involved. It's all ego."

Often, editorial becomes one giant ad. Last November, for instance, *Lear's* featured an elegant woman executive on the cover. On the contents page, we learned she was wearing Guerlain makeup and Samsara, a new fragrance by Guerlain. Inside were full-page ads for Samsara and Guerlain antiwrinkle cream. In the cover profile, we learned that this executive was responsible for launching Samsara and is Guerlain's director of public relations. When the *Columbia Journalism Review* did one of the few articles to include women's magazines in coverage of the influence of ads, editor Frances Lear was quoted as defending her magazine because "this kind of thing is done all the time."

Often, advertisers also plunge odd-shaped ads into the text, no matter what the cost to the readers. At *Woman's Day,* a magazine originally founded by a supermarket chain, editor in chief Ellen Levine said, "The day the copy had to rag around a chicken leg was not a happy one."

Advertisers are also adamant about where in a magazine their ads appear. When Revlon was not placed as the first beauty ad in one Hearst magazine, for instance, Revlon pulled its ads from *all* Hearst magazines. Ruth Whitney, editor in chief of *Glamour,* attributes some of these demands to "ad agencies wanting to prove to a client that they've squeezed the last drop of blood out of a magazine." She also is, she says, "sick and tired of hearing that women's magazines are controlled by cigarette ads." Relatively speaking, she's right. To be as censoring as are many advertisers for women's products, tobacco companies would have to demand articles in praise of smoking and expect glamorous photos of beautiful women smoking their brands.

I don't mean to imply that the editors I quote here share my objections to ads: most assume that women's magazines have to be the way they are. But it's also true that only former editors can be completely honest. "Most of the pressure came in the form of direct product mentions," explains Sey Chassler, who was editor in chief of *Redbook* from the sixties to the eighties. "We got threats from the big guys, the Revlons, blackmail threats. They wouldn't run ads unless we credited them.

"But it's not fair to single out the beauty advertisers because these pressures came from everybody. Advertisers want to know two things: What are you going to charge me? What *else* are you going to do for me? It's a holdup. For instance, management felt that fiction took up too much space. They couldn't put any advertising in that. For the last ten years, the number of fiction entries into the National Magazine Awards has declined.

"And pressures are getting worse. More magazines are

more bottom-line oriented because they have been taken over by companies with no interest in publishing.

"I also think advertisers do this to women's magazines especially," he concluded, "because of the general disrespect they have for women."

Even media experts who don't give a damn about women's magazines are alarmed by the spread of this ad-edit linkage. In a climate *The Wall Street Journal* describes as an unacknowledged Depression for media, women's products are increasingly able to take their low standards wherever they go. For instance: newsweeklies publish uncritical stories on fashion and fitness. *The New York Times Magazine* recently ran an article on "firming creams," complete with mentions of advertisers. *Vanity Fair* published a profile of one major advertiser, Ralph Lauren, illustrated by the same photographer who does his ads, and turned the lifestyle of another, Calvin Klein, into a cover story. Even the outrageous *Spy* has toned down since it began to go after fashion ads.

And just to make us really worry, films and books, the last media that go directly to the public without having to attract ads first, are in danger, too. Producers are beginning to depend on payments for displaying products in movies, and books are now being commissioned by companies like Federal Express.

But the truth is that women's products—like women's magazines—have never been the subjects of much serious reporting anyway. News and general interest publications, including the "style" or "living" sections of newspapers, write about food and clothing as cooking and fashion, and almost never evaluate such products by brand name. Though chemical additives, pesticides, and animal fats are major health risks in the United States, and clothes, shoddy or not, absorb more consumer dollars than cars, this lack of information is serious. So is ignoring the contents of beauty products that are absorbed into our bodies through our skins, and that have profit margins so big they would make a loan shark blush.

III.

What could women's magazines be like if they were as free as books? as realistic as newspapers? as creative as films? as diverse as women's lives? We don't know.

But we'll only find out if we take women's magazines seriously. If readers were to act in a concerted way to change traditional practices of *all* women's magazines and the marketing of *all* women's products, we could do it. After all, they are operating on our consumer dollars; money that we now control. You and I could:

■ write to editors and publishers (with copies to advertisers) that we're willing to pay *more* for magazines with editorial independence, but will *not* continue to pay for those that are just editorial extensions of ads;

■ write to advertisers (with copies to editors and publishers) that we want fiction, political reporting, consumer reporting—whatever is, or is not, supported by their ads;

■ put as much energy into breaking advertising's control over content as into changing the images in ads, or protesting ads for harmful products like cigarettes;

■ support only those women's magazines and products that take *us* seriously as readers and consumers.

Those of us in the magazine world can also use the carrot-and-stick technique. For instance: pointing out that, if magazines were a regulated medium like television, the demands of advertisers would be against FCC rules. Payola and extortion could be punished. As it is, there are probably illegalities. A magazine's postal rates are determined by the ratio of ad to edit pages, and the former costs more than the latter. So much for the stick.

The carrot means appealing to enlightened self-interest. For instance: there are many studies showing that the greatest factor in determining an ad's effectiveness is the credibility of its surroundings. The "higher the rating of editorial believability," concluded a 1987 survey by the *Journal of Advertising Research,* "the higher the rating of the advertising." Thus, an impenetrable wall between edit and ads would also be in the best interest of advertisers.

Unfortunately, few agencies or clients hear such arguments. Editors often maintain the false purity of refusing to talk to them at all. Instead, they see ad salespeople who know little about editorial, are trained in business as usual, and are usually paid by commission. Editors might also band together to take on controversy. That happened once when all the major women's magazines did articles in the same month on the Equal Rights Amendment. It could happen again.

It's almost three years away from life between the grindstones of advertising pressures and readers' needs. I'm just beginning to realize how edges got smoothed down—in spite of all our resistance.

I remember feeling put upon when I changed "Porsche" to "car" in a piece about Nazi imagery in German pornography by Andrea Dworkin—feeling sure Andrea would understand that Volkswagen, the distributor of Porsche and one of our few supportive advertisers, asked only to be far away from Nazi subjects. It's taken me all this time to realize that Andrea was the one with a right to feel put upon.

Even as I write this, I get a call from a writer for *Elle*, who is doing a whole article on where women part their hair. Why, she wants to know, do I part mine in the middle?

It's all so familiar. A writer trying to make something of a nothing assignment; an editor laboring to think of new ways to attract ads; readers assuming that other women must want this ridiculous stuff; more women suffering for lack of information, insight, creativity, and laughter that could be on these same pages.

I ask you: Can't we do better than this?

THE SQUEEZE

by Russ Baker

SOME MAJOR ADVERTISERS STEP UP THE PRESSURE ON MAGAZINES TO ALTER THEIR CONTENT. WILL EDITORS BEND?

In an effort to avoid potential conflicts, it is required that Chrysler Corporation be alerted in advance of any and all editorial content that encompasses sexual, political, social issues or any editorial that might be construed as provocative or offensive. Each and every issue that carries Chrysler advertising requires a written summary outlining major theme/articles appearing in upcoming issues. These summaries are to be forwarded to PentaCom prior to closing in order to give Chrysler ample time to review and reschedule if desired . . . As acknowledgement of this letter we ask that you or a representative from the publication sign below and return to us no later than February 15.

— from a letter sent by Chrysler's ad agency, PentaCom, a division of BBDO North America, to at least fifty magazines

I s there any doubt that advertisers mumble and sometimes roar about reporting that can hurt them? That the auto giants don't like pieces that, say, point to auto safety problems? Or that Big Tobacco hates to see its glamorous, cheerful ads juxtaposed with articles mentioning their best customers' grim way of death? When advertisers disapprove of an editorial climate, they can — and sometimes do — take a hike.

Russ Baker is a free-lance writer who lives in New York. His last piece for CJR, *in the March/April issue, was about the Food Lion v. ABC trial.*

But for Chrysler to push beyond its parochial economic interests — by demanding summaries of upcoming articles while implicitly asking editors to think twice about running "sexual, political, social issues" — crosses a sharply defined line. "This is new," says Milton Glaser, the *New York* magazine co-founder and celebrated designer. "It will have a devastating effect on the idea of a free press and of free inquiry."

Glaser is among those in the press who are vocally urging editors and publishers to resist. "If Chrysler achieves this," he says, "there is no reason to hope that other advertisers won't ask for the same privilege. You will have thirty or forty advertisers checking through the pages. They will send notes to publishers. I don't see how any good citizen doesn't rise to this occasion and say this development is un-American and a threat to freedom."

Hyperbole? Maybe not. Just about any editor will tell you: the ad/edit chemistry is changing for the worse. Corporations and their ad agencies have clearly turned up the heat on editors and publishers, and some magazines are capitulating, unwilling to risk even a single ad. This makes it tougher for those who do fight to maintain the ad-edit wall and put the interests of their readers first. Consider:

◆ A major advertiser recently approached all three newsweeklies — *Time, Newsweek,* and *U.S. News* — and told them it would be closely monitoring editorial content. So says a high newsweekly executive who was given the warning (but who would not name the advertiser). For the next quarter, the advertiser warned the magazines' publishing sides, it would keep track of how the company's industry was portrayed in news columns. At the end of that period, the advertiser would select one — and only one — of the magazines and award all of its newsweekly advertising to it.

◆ An auto manufacturer — not Chrysler — decided recently to play art director at a major glossy, and the magazine played along. After the magazine scheduled a photo spread that would feature more bare skin than usual, it engaged in a back-and-forth negotiation with that advertiser over exactly how much skin would be shown. CJR's source says the feature had nothing to do with the advertiser's product.

◆ Kimberly-Clark makes Huggies diapers and advertises them in a number of magazines, including *Child*, *American Baby*, *Parenting*, *Parents*, *Baby Talk*, and *Sesame Street Parents*. Kimberly-Clark demands — in writing in its ad insertion orders — that these ads be placed only "adjacent to black and white happy baby editorial," which would definitely not include stories about, say, Sudden Infant Death Syndrome or Down's syndrome. "Sometimes we have to create editorial that is satisfactory to them," a top editor says. That, of course, means something else is likely lost, and the mix of the magazine is altered.

◆ Former Cosmo Girl Helen Gurley Brown disclosed to *Newsday* that a Detroit auto company representative (the paper didn't say which company) asked for—and received—an advance copy of the table of contents for her bon voyage issue, then threatened to pull a whole series of ads unless the representative was permitted to see an article titled "How to Be Very Good in Bed." Result? "A senior editor and the client's ad agency pulled a few things from the piece," a dispirited Brown recalled, "but enough was left" to salvage the article.

Cosmo is hardly the only magazine that has bowed to the new winds. Kurt Andersen, the former *New York* magazine editor—whose 1996 firing by parent company K-III was widely perceived to be a result of stories that angered associates of K-III's founder, Henry R. Kravis—nonetheless says that he always kept advertisers' sensibilities in mind when editing the magazine. "Because I worked closely and happily with the publisher at *New York*, I was aware who the big advertisers were," he says. "My antennae were turned on, and I read copy thinking, 'Is this going to cause Calvin Klein or Bergdorf big problems?' "

National Review put a reverse spin on the early-warning-for-advertisers discussion recently, as *The Washington Post* revealed, when its advertising director sent an advance copy of a piece about utilities deregulation to a an energy supplier mentioned in the story, as a way of luring it into buying space.

And Chrysler is hardly the only company that is aggressive about its editorial environment. Manufacturers of packaged goods, from toothpaste to toilet paper, aggressively declare their love for plain-vanilla. Colgate-Palmolive, for example, won't allow ads in a "media context" containing "offensive" sexual content or material it deems "antisocial or in bad taste" — which it leaves undefined in its policy statement sent to magazines. In the statement, the company says that it "charges its advertising agencies and their media buying services with the responsibility of pre-screening any questionable media content or context."

Procter & Gamble, the second-largest advertising spender last year ($1.5 billion), has a reputation as being very touchy. Two publishing executives told Gloria Steinem, for her book *Moving Beyond Words*, that the company doesn't want its ads near anything about "gun control, abortion, the occult, cults, or the disparagement of religion." Even nonsensational and sober pieces dealing with sex and drugs are no-go.

Kmart and Revlon are among those that editors list as the most demanding. "IBM is a stickler — they don't like any kind of controversial articles," says Robyn Mathews, formerly of *Entertainment Weekly* and now *Time*'s chief of makeup. She negotiates with advertisers about placement, making sure that their products are not put near material that is directly critical. AT&T, Mathews says, is another company that prefers a soft climate. She says she often has to tell advertisers, "We're a *news* magazine. I try to get them to be realistic."

Still, the auto companies apparently lead the pack in complaining about content. And the automakers are so powerful—the Big Three pumped $3.6 billion into U.S. advertising last year—that most major magazines have sales offices in Detroit.

After *The New Yorker*, in its issue of June 12, 1995, ran a Talk of the Town piece that quoted some violent, misogynist rap and rock lyrics—along with illustrative four-letter words—opposite a Mercury ad, Ford Motor Company withdrew from the magazine, reportedly for six months. The author, Ken Auletta, learned about it only this year. "I actually admire *The New Yorker* for not telling me about it," he says. Yet afterwards, according to *The*

Wall Street Journal, the magazine quietly adopted a system of warning about fifty companies on a "sensitive advertiser list" whenever potentially offensive articles are scheduled.

It is the Chrysler case, though, that has made the drums beat, partly because of Chrysler's heft and partly because the revelation about the automaker's practice came neatly packaged with a crystalline example of just what that practice can do to a magazine.

In the advertising jungle Chrysler is an 800-pound gorilla — the nation's fourth-largest advertiser and fifth-largest magazine advertiser (it spent some $270 million at more than 100 magazines last year, behind General Motors, Philip Morris, Procter & Gamble, and Ford). Where it leads, other advertisers may be tempted to follow.

The automaker's letter was mailed to magazines in January 1996, but did not come to light until G. Bruce Knecht of *The Wall Street Journal* unearthed it this April in the aftermath of an incident at *Esquire*. The *Journal* reported that *Esquire* had planned a sixteen-page layout for a 20,000-word fiction piece by accomplished author David Leavitt. Already in page proofs and scheduled for the April '97 issue, it was to be one of the longest short stories *Esquire* had ever run, and it had a gay theme and some raw language. But publisher Valerie Salembier, the *Journal* reported, met with then editor-in-chief Edward Kosner and other editors and voiced her concerns: she would have to notify Chrysler about the story, and she expected that when she did so Chrysler would pull its ads. The automaker had bought four pages, the *Journal* noted — just enough to enable the troubled magazine to show its first year-to-year ad-page improvement since the previous September.

Kosner then killed the piece, maintaining he had editorial reasons for doing so. Will Blythe, the magazine's literary editor, promptly quit. "I simply can't stomach the David Leavitt story being pulled," he said in his letter of resignation. "That act signals a terrible narrowing of the field available to strong, adventuresome, risk-taking work, fiction and nonfiction alike. I know that editorial and advertising staffs have battled — sometimes affably, other times savagely — for years to define and protect their respective turfs. But events of the last few weeks signal that the balance is out of whack now — that, in effect, we're taking marching orders (albeit, indirectly) from advertisers."

The Chrysler letter's public exposure is a rough reminder that sometimes the biggest problems are the most clichéd: as financial concerns become increasingly paramount it gets harder to assert editorial independence.

After the article about *Esquire* in the *Journal*, the American Society of Magazine Editors — the top cops of magazine standards, with 867 members from 370 magazines — issued a statement expressing "deep concern" over the trend to give "advertisers advance notice about upcoming stories." Some advertisers, ASME said, "may mistake an early warning as an open invitation to pressure the publisher to alter, or even kill, the article in question. We believe publishers should — and will — refuse to bow to such pressure. Furthermore, we believe editors should — and will — follow ASME's explicit principle of editorial independence, which at its core states: 'The chief editor of any magazine must have final authority over the editorial content, words, and pictures that appear in the publication.'"

On July 24, after meeting with the ASME board, the marketing committee of the Magazine Publishers of America — which has 200 member companies that print more than 800 magazines — gathered to discuss this issue, and agreed to work against prior review of story lists or summaries by advertisers. "The magazine industry is united in this," says ASME's president, Frank Lalli, managing editor of *Money*. "There is no debate within the industry."

How many magazines will reject Chrysler's new road map? Unclear. Lalli says he has not found any publisher or editor who signed and returned the Chrysler letter as demanded. "I've talked to a lot of publishers," he says, "and I don't know of any who will bow to it. The great weight of opinion among publishers and editors is that this is a road we can't go down."

Yet Mike Aberlich, Chrysler's manager of consumer media relations, claims that "Every single one has been signed." Aberlich says that in some cases, individual magazines agreed; in others a parent company signed for all its publications.

CJR did turn up several magazines, mostly in jam-packed demographic niches,

'I WAS AWARE WHO THE BIG ADVERTISERS WERE. I READ COPY THINKING, IS THIS GOING TO CAUSE CALVIN KLEIN BIG PROBLEMS?'

Kurt Andersen,
former editor of
New York magazine

whose executives concede they have no problem with the Chrysler letter. One is *Maxim*, a new book aimed at the young-men-with-bucks market put out by the British-based Dennis Publishing. "We're going to play ball," says *Maxim*'s sales manager, Jamie Hooper. The startup, which launched earlier this year, signed and returned the Chrysler letter. "We're complying. We definitely have to."

At *P.O.V.*, a two-and-a-half-year-old magazine backed largely by Freedom Communications Inc. (owners of *The Orange County Register*) and aimed at a similar audience, publisher Drew Massey says he remembers a Chrysler letter, can't remember signing it, but would have no problem providing advance notice. "We do provide PentaCom with a courtesy call, but we absolutely never change an article." Chrysler, alerted to *P.O.V.*'s August "Vice" issue, decided to stay in. Massey argues that the real issue is not about edgy magazines like *P.O.V.*, but about larger and tamer magazines that feel constrained by advertisers from being adventurous.

Hachette Filipacchi, French-owned publisher of twenty-nine U.S. titles, from *Elle* to *George*, offered Chrysler's plan for a safe editorial environment partial support. Says John Fennell, chief operating officer: "We did respond to the letter, saying we were aware of their concern about controversial material and that we would continue — as we have in the past — to monitor it very closely and to make sure that their advertising did not appear near controversial things. However, we refused to turn over or show or discuss the editorial direction of articles with them."

It has long been a widely accepted practice in the magazine industry to provide "heads-ups" — warnings to advertisers about copy that might embarrass them — say, to the friendly

skies folks about a scheduled article on an Everglades plane crash, or to Johnnie Walker about a feature on the death of a hard-drinking rock star. In some instances, advertisers are simply moved as far as possible from the potentially disconcerting material. In others, they are offered a chance to opt out of the issue altogether, ideally to be rescheduled for a later edition.

In the 1980s, Japanese car makers got bent out of shape about news articles they saw as Japan-bashing, says *Business Week*'s editor-in-chief, Stephen B. Shepard, a past ASME president. Anything about closed markets or the trade imbalance might be seen as requiring a polite switch to the next issue.

Chrysler, some magazine people argue, is simply formalizing this long-standing advertiser policy of getting magazine executives to consider their special sensitivities while assembling each issue. But Chrysler's letter clearly went beyond that. PentaCom's president and c.e.o., David Martin, was surprisingly blunt when he explained to *The Wall Street Journal* the automaker's rationale: "Our whole contention is that when you are looking at a product that costs $22,000, you want the product to be surrounded by positive things. There's nothing positive about an article about child pornography."

Chrysler spokesman Aberlich insists the brouhaha is no big deal: "Of the thousands of magazine ads we've placed in a year, we've moved an ad out of one issue into the next issue about ten times a year. We haven't stopped dealing with any magazine." He compares placing an ad to buying a house: "You decide the neighborhood you want to be in." That interesting metaphor, owning valuable real estate, leads to other metaphors—advertisers as editorial NIMBYs (Not In My Back Yard) trying to keep out anybody or anything they don't want around.

As for the current contretemps, Aberlich says it's nothing new, that Chrysler has been requesting advance notice since 1993. "We sent an initial letter to magazines asking them to notify us of upcoming controversial stuff — graphic sex, graphic violence, glorification of drug use." But what about the updated and especially chilling language in the 1996 letter, the one asking to look over editors' shoulders at future articles, particularly *political*, *social* material and *editorial that might be construed as provocative*? Aberlich declines to discuss it, bristling, "We didn't give you that letter."

How did we get to the point where a sophisticated advertiser dared send such a letter? In these corporate-friendly times, the sweep and powers of advertisers are frenetically expanded everywhere. Formerly pure public television and public radio now run almost-ads. Schools bombard children with cereal commercials in return for the monitors on which the ads appear. Parks blossom with yogurt- and sneaker-sponsored events.

Meanwhile, a growing number of publications compete for ad dollars — not just against each other but against the rest of the media, including new media. Those ads are bought by ever-larger companies and placed by a shrinking number of merger-minded ad agencies.

Are magazines in a position where they cannot afford to alienate any advertiser? No, as a group, magazines have done very well lately, thank you. With only minor dips, ad pages and total advertising dollars have grown impressively for a number of years. General-interest magazines sold $5.3 billion worth of advertising in 1987. By 1996 that figure had more than doubled, to $11.2 billion.

Prosperity can enhance independence. The magazines least susceptible to advertiser pressures are often the most ad-laden books. Under its new editor-in-chief, David Granger, the anemic *Esquire* seems to be getting a lift, but *GQ* had supplanted it in circulation and in the serious-article business, earning many National Magazine Awards. This is in part because it first used advertiser-safe service pieces and celebrity profiles to build ad pages, then had more space to experiment and take risks.

Catherine Viscardi Johnston, senior vice president for group sales and marketing at *GQ*'s parent company, the financially flush Condé Nast, says that in her career as a publisher she rarely was asked to reschedule an ad — perhaps once a year. Meddling has not been a problem, she says: "Never was a page lost, or an account lost. Never, never did an advertiser try to have a story changed or eliminated."

At the other extreme, *Maxim*, which signed the Chrysler letter, does face grueling ad-buck competition. The number

'I KNOW THAT EDITORIAL AND ADVERTISING STAFFS HAVE BATTLED FOR YEARS. BUT EVENTS SIGNAL THAT THE BALANCE IS OUT OF WHACK'

Former Esquire *literary editor Will Blythe, in his resignation letter*

of new magazine startups in 1997 may well exceed 1,000, says Samir Husni, the University of Mississippi journalism professor who tracks launches. And *Maxim*'s demographic — 21- to 34-year-old males — is jam-packed with titles.

This is not to say that prosperity and virtue go hand in hand. Witness Condé Nast's ad-fat *Architectural Digest*, where editor-in-chief Paige Rense freely admits that only advertisers are mentioned in picture captions. The range of standards among magazines is wide.

And that range can be confusing. "Some advertisers don't understand on a fundamental level the difference between magazines that have a serious set of rules and codes and serious ambitions, and those that don't," says Kurt Andersen. "The same guy at Chrysler is buying ads in *YM* and *The New Yorker*."

If it is up to editors to draw the line, they will have to buck the industry's impulse to draw them even deeper into their magazines' business issues. Hachette Filipacchi's U.S. president and c.e.o., David Pecker, is one who would lower the traditional ad-edit wall. "I actually know editors who met with advertisers and lived to tell about it," he said in a recent speech. Some editors at Hachette — and other news organizations — share in increased profits at their magazines. Thus, to offend an advertiser, it might be argued, would be like volunteering for a pay cut. So be it; intrepid editors must be prepared to take that.

Ironically, in fretting over public sensibilities, advertisers may not be catering to their consumers at all. In a recent study of public opinion regarding television — which is even more dogged by content controversies than magazines — 87 percent of respondents

said it is appropriate for network programs to deal with sensitive issues and social problems. (The poll was done for ABC, NBC, and CBS by the Roper Starch Worldwide market research firm.) Asked who should "have the most to say about what people see and hear on television," 82 percent replied that it ought to be "individual viewers themselves, by deciding what they will and will not watch." Almost no one — just 9 percent — thought advertisers should be able to shape content by granting or withholding sponsorship. Even PentaCom admitted to the *Journal* that its own focus groups show that Chrysler owners are not bothered by Chrysler ads near controversial articles.

So what's eating these folks? Partially, it may be a cultural phenomenon. Ever since magazines began to attract mass audiences and subsidize subscription rates with advertising, many magazines have chased readers — just as networks chase viewers now — with ever more salacious fare. But corporate executives have often remained among the most conservative of Americans. Nowhere is this truer than in heartland locations like Chrysler's Detroit or Procter & Gamble's Cincinnati.

Ad executives say one factor in the mix is sponsors' fear of activist groups, which campaign against graphic or gay or other kinds of editorial material perceived as "anti-family." Boycotts like the current Southern Baptist campaign against Disney for "anti-family values" may be on the rise, precisely because advertisers do take them seriously. This, despite a lack of evidence that such boycotts do much damage. "Boycotts have no discernible impact on sales. Usually, the public's awareness is so quickly dissipated that it has no impact at all," says Elliot Mincberg, vice-president and general counsel of People For the American Way, a liberal organization that tracks the impact of pressure groups. Why, then, would advertisers bother setting guidelines that satisfy these groups at all? "They're trying to minimize their risk to *zero*," says an incredulous Will Blythe, *Esquire*'s former literary editor.

Yet not every advertiser pines for the bland old days. The hotter the product, it seems, the cooler the heads. The "vice" peddlers (booze & cigarettes), along with some apparel and consumer electronics products, actually like being surrounded by edgy editorial copy — unless their own product is zapped. Party *on*!

Even Chrysler's sensitivities appear to be selective. *Maxim*'s premier issue featured six women chatting provocatively about their sex lives, plus several photos of women in scanty come-hither attire, but Chrysler had no grievances.

The real danger here is not censorship by advertisers. It is self-censorship by editors. On one level, self-censorship results in omissions, small and large, that delight big advertisers.

Cigarettes are a clear and familiar example. The tobacco companies' hefty advertising in many a magazine seems in inverse proportion to the publication's willingness to criticize it. Over at the American Cancer Society, media director Susan Islam says that women's magazines tend to cover some concerns adequately, but not lung cancer: "Many more women die of lung cancer, yet there have hardly been any articles on it."

To her credit, *Glamour*'s editor-in-chief, Ruth Whitney, is one who has run tobacco stories. She says that her magazine, which carries a lot of tobacco advertising, publishes the results of every major smoking study. But Whitney concedes they are mostly short pieces. "Part of the problem with cigarettes was— we did do features, but there's nobody in this country who doesn't know cigarettes kill." Still, everybody also knows that getting slimmer requires exercise and eating right, which has not prevented women's magazines from running that story in endless permutations. Tobacco is in the news, and magazines have the unique job of deepening and humanizing such stories.

Specific editorial omissions are easier to measure than how a magazine's world view is altered when advertisers' preferences and sensitivities seep into the editing. When editors act like publishers, and vice versa, the reader is out the door.

Can ASME, appreciated among editors for its intentions, fire up the troops? The organization has been effective on another front — against abuses of special advertising sections, when advertise-

'MORE ADVERTISERS WHO WEREN'T AWARE OF THIS SYSTEM HAVE GONE TO THEIR AGENCIES AND SAID, HEY, WHY NOT ME TOO?'

G. Bruce Knecht of
The Wall Street Journal

ments try to adapt the look and feel of editorial matter. ASME has distributed a set of guidelines about just what constitutes such abuse.

To enforce those guidelines, ASME executive director Marlene Kahan says the organization sends a couple of letters each month to violators. "Most magazines say they will comply," she reports. "If anybody is really egregiously violating the guidelines on a consistent basis, we'd probably sit down and have a meeting with them." ASME can ban a magazine from participating in the National Magazine Awards, but Kahan says the organization has not yet had to do that. In addition, ASME occasionally asks the organization that officially counts magazine ad pages, the Publishers Information Bureau, not to count advertising sections that break the rules as ad pages — a tactic that ASME president Lalli says tends to get publishers' attention.

Not everyone in the industry thinks ASME throws much of a shadow. "ASME can't bite the hand that feeds them," says John Masterton of *Media Industry Newsletter*, which covers the magazine business. During Robert Sam Anson's brief tenure as editor of *Los Angeles* magazine, the business side committed to a fifteen-page supplement, to be written by the editorial side and called "The Mercedes Golf Special." Mercedes didn't promise to take any ads, but it was hoped that the carmaker would

think kindly of the magazine for future issues. The section would appear as editorial, listed as such in the table of contents. Anson warned the business side that, in his opinion, the section would contravene ASME guidelines, since it was in effect an ad masquerading as edit. A senior executive told him not to worry — that at the most they'd get a "slap on the wrist." The section did not run in the end, Anson says, because of "deadline production problems."

The Chrysler model, however — with its demand for early warnings, and its insistence on playing editor — is tougher for ASME to police. Special advertising sections are visible. Killed or altered articles are not. And unless it surfaces, as in the *Esquire* case, self-censorship is invisible.

One well-known editor, who asks not to be identified, thinks the problem will eventually go away. "It's a self-regulating thing," he says. "At some point, the negative publicity to the advertisers will cause them to back off."

Of course, there is nothing particularly automatic about that. It takes an outspoken journalistic community to generate heat. And such attention could backfire. The *Journal*'s Knecht told the audience of public radio's *On the Media* that his reporting might actually have aggravated the problem: "One of the negative effects is that more advertisers who weren't aware of this system have gone to their advertising agencies and said, 'Hey, why not me too! This sounds like a pretty good deal!' "

Except, of course, that it really isn't. In the long run everybody involved is diminished when editors feel advertisers' breath on their necks. Hovering there, advertisers help create content that eventually bores the customers they seek. Then the editors of those magazines tend to join the ranks of the unemployed. That's just one of the many reasons that editors simply cannot bend to the new pressure. They have to draw the line — subtly or overtly, quietly or loudly, in meetings and in private, and in their own minds.

MASS MEDIA

Television Is Losing Its LARGEST VIEWING AUDIENCE

Americans over the age of 50 are beginning to tune out because programming is too violent, vulgar, boring, youth-oriented, and insulting to their intelligence.

by Frank Conaway

A study conducted by the Primelife Advisory Network (PLAN) concluded that today's television programming offers little to the segment of the population that watches, according to Nielsen Media Research, more TV per week than any other demographic group. This segment views a median of three hours of television a day, compared to 2.8 hours among all adults.

The study should be a wake-up call for those who control television programming, especially advertisers. Not only do these consumers watch the most television, they also control 77% of the nation's assets, have higher discretionary income than any other population segment, and will grow twice as fast as the total U.S. population in the next decade.

The population segment in question is the mature market, individuals age 50 or older. It is a group that grew up with the advent of television and the explosion of advertising, is extremely savvy and discerning, and will not be willing to continue investing time in poor or distasteful TV programming.

Mr. Conaway is president and CEO of Primelife, Orange, Calif., a marketing communications firm specializing in mature consumers.

The purpose of the PLAN survey was to identify program topics that would appeal to the mature market, as well as current programming that is of no interest or value to them. Obviously, not all network programming is intended for adults age 50 and older. In fact, *most* network programming is not aimed at that audience. That explains why more and more mature viewers are seeking alternatives such as cable television for quality programs and entertainment.

The survey was conducted by PLAN, a volunteer group of mature Americans with more than 1,300 members nationwide. Its primary goal is to affect positive change in the way mature adults are portrayed in the media and the advertising and entertainment industries. PLAN works with companies to provide input on their advertising and marketing efforts and materials, as well as to critique product design and packaging and assist in developing new marketing strategies.

The research study was conducted through a six-page mail survey, which solicited information and opinions from members in 31 states. More than 315 members participated. The average age was 61, and 71% were female.

Overwhelmingly, respondents expressed dissatisfaction with the amount of violence, sex, and vulgar language on television. Many felt today's programming was "boring" and "insults one's intelligence." Over 77% indicated they would watch a television station devoted to the active lifestyles of mature individuals. A few of the comments made by PLAN members included:

• "Most shows are aimed at youth. Television is boring for us. We need intellectual stimulation."
• "I get tired of ads and programs slanted toward youth. There are many more of us experienced (notice I didn't say old) people around, and we need our own programming."
• "So much stuff on television now is embarrassing and insults one's intelligence."
• "I'm tired of bad soaps and bad talk shows."
• "I loathe the talk shows featuring the problems of dysfunctional people."
• "I am bored and disgusted with the majority of talk shows and daytime serials. We have all the sensationalism we need."

Many of the respondents felt television programs were turning to sensationalistic tactics to try to create an audience, concentrating more on shocking viewers than entertaining them. Is this working, especially in a society that is aging; one that indicates, politically and socially, a swing back to conservatism?

Even more importantly, will this affect the purchase behaviors of the mature market? It seems so, according to one PLAN member, Betty Vickery, of Seattle, Wash. "Over my life, I've watched television programming deteriorate terribly, mostly because of the sex, violence, and lack of plot and story lines. In fact, I lost interest before most shows can even get to the first advertisement. I also don't buy products that are advertised on a show that makes me feel foolish just for watching it, even if I currently buy it. It's my way of getting even for the stupidity of the program and the advertisers."

Some of the most successful (and longest-running) shows of all time—including "The Golden Girls," "Murder, She Wrote," and "60 Minutes"—commanded a significant mature market viewership. In fact, the most popular older-skewing shows deliver more total adult viewers, and more affluent ones, than do younger-skewing shows. For example, "Murder, She Wrote" rated in the top 10 for nine of the 11 seasons it was on the air. Although it often drew higher ratings than ABC's "Lois and Clark: The New Adventures of Superman," the latter earned more ad revenue because its appeal to 18-49-year-olds means higher advertising rates, according to *The New York Times*.

From *USA Today Magazine*, May 1997, pp. 74-76. © 1997 by the Society for the Advancement of Education. Reprinted by permission.

"Murder, She Wrote," "Jeopardy!," "Wheel of Fortune," "60 Minutes," "20/20," "Dateline," "Oprah," and "Meet the Press" were the most often cited programs preferred by the PLAN group. The Discovery Channel, PBS, and The Learning Channel were the most often mentioned networks. These shows and channels offer entertainment without "trash" and information and intellectual stimulation without sensationalism.

PLAN respondents rated more than 25 topics of interest, ranging from health and fitness to dating and relationships. The survey concluded that news and information are most important to mature adults, especially subjects that can enhance their lifestyles. Medical and health information ranked first and second, with enhancing communications skills and legal advice rounding out the top four. Mature viewers' interest in maintaining their health, and subsequently their active lifestyles, was confirmed by the Roper Report, a study conducted by *Modern Maturity* magazine. Its findings place "the latest developments in medicine and health" at the top of the mature adult's interest list.

The audience is highly concerned with pertinent social issues and volunteerism, demonstrated by such statements as: "My interest is in anything that might enhance my life as a senior." "There is a world to be saved. Deal with meaningful issues—overpopulation, poverty, lack of education, domestic and child abuse, racism."

Mature adults are more attracted to real-life situations. "The only programs I now watch are clever, high quality shows with real people in real life situations who react in an intelligent way," indicates Diane Shattuck, a PLAN member in Orange, Calif. "I don't like the silly sitcoms which portray groups, no matter what the age, as stupid and not involved in real life."

PLAN members were surveyed about television personalities who appealed most to them. Walter Cronkite ranked number one, followed closely by Charles Kuralt, Hugh Downs, Betty White, and Alan Alda. These celebrities were perceived as having "integrity," "credibility," and "responsibility" and being "informed," "educated," and "of quality."

Advertisers and the mature market

Networks and advertising executives must realize that, if the mature audience can not find the entertainment or information they are seeking on network programming, they will turn to alternatives such as cable or satellite TV. In fact, cable television's total prime-time audience has increased by more than 24% since October, 1994, according to Nielsen figures, while the four broadcast networks' has declined by nearly seven percent.

Advertising revenue among cable networks is growing, an indication that some companies have identified the popularity of this broadcast alternative, as well as the opportunities that exist with the markets it serves. The expansion of cable programming over the past decade is due partly to the tremendous interest of the mature market. Networks such as CNN, Lifetime, Discovery, and TNT have attracted and retained a large mature audience. New cable networks are being established, some targeting the mature audience specifically, such as the Prime Life Network, headed by chairman and CEO Michael Eisenberg, a former CBS executive.

"The phrase we hear most frequently when we discuss the concept of the Prime Life Network is 'It's about time,'" Eisenberg explains. "Our programming will be exclusively for the active mature adult. We believe that this market is so large, so affluent, and so diverse that it now demands a quality television channel all of its own."

Advertising and media buying agencies, and the companies they work for, directly influence network programming. They demand programming that attracts the 18-to-49 age demographic, and are themselves professionals typically in that same age group. Yet, this younger age segment, which is perceived to hold the most opportunity by advertisers, is not the most powerful economic age demographic in the U.S. In reality, it is the mature market. In spite of the mature market's great financial strength, though, most advertising executives and network programmers hold false views of this age segment and promote ageism and negative stereotyping in both their advertising and in their shows.

Negative, false stereotyping includes such conceptions as mature consumers are too brand loyal, and no amount of advertising will make them switch or try new brands; mature consumers don't spend money; mature consumers only are concerned about health care; mature consumers are not active, enjoy few hobbies, and are overly conscious of price; mature adults are poor, in ill health, senile, cranky, and lonely; and mature adults dress funny.

Although advertising dollars have great influence over programming, there is another even more powerful entity—the audience. "Advertisers don't take responsibility for the end result; all they care about is their return on investment," maintains Kevin Carlisle, a director and producer who has seen television programming change over the past 25 years and is now a member of the mature market. "The most powerful influence on programming is the public. The mature market has a huge voice—over 65,000,000 strong—which still is just a whisper at this point. We have more power than anyone else because we have the money and we buy the products."

Advertising executives are sure to have seen the statistics on the mature market and understand the changing demographics. Maybe they feel programs should target youth because younger viewers are more prone to peer influence and impulse purchases.

The truth is, the mature market spends more than one trillion dollars annually on products and services. They are inclined to try new products or switch brands if they perceive it will enhance their lifestyles. "Advertisers who support shows that skew towards the 18-to-49-year-olds are thinking they are more apt to buy, being impulse purchasers. Reality is, I will try a new product if it gives me more than the product I currently use," Carlisle points out. Moreover, the types of products and services the mature adult purchases are extremely diverse, just like the market itself. For example, the mature market accounts for 25% of all toy purchases, and grandparents spend approximately $819 annually on each grandchild. Individuals over the age of 55 also account for 46% of all vacation and pleasure trips.

The market is diverse, but reachable. There has been a subtle change in the perceptions about aging and the mature market over the past year as the first of the baby boom generation began to turn 50. More and more companies are beginning to look at the mature market as a strong, economically powerful, and desirable age demographic. Advertisers can begin to attract these individuals by offering programming that deals with their issues, concerns, and needs; does not include excessive violence, sex, and vulgar language; and provides quality, intelligence, credibility, and responsibility. It is being discovered that this type of programming also will appeal to families and even the ever-sought-after 18-to-49-year-olds.

If these dominant trends and demographics had a voice, it would be that of the mature market. It would talk of values, conservative views, and the need and desire for programming that addresses the issues and concerns of more than 65,000,000 Americans. It would tell network programmers, and the advertisers who support them, they had better take a good look at the realities of the mature market instead of clinging to their negative misperceptions. It would say they should start catering to this market, or the future may not be so profitable, as this age segment grows in size by 60% over the next decade. Otherwise, they will lose millions who are beginning to tune out because programming is too violent, vulgar, boring, youth-oriented, and insulting to the experience and intelligence of the country's largest viewing audience.

The Last Gasp
of Mass Media?

by Joshua Levine

Editor's Note: While America's mass media have become global entertainers, the media are changing at home. To survive in the fast-changing American world, mass media are becoming less massive. Falling ratings, alternative media, and narrow-interest programming are eroding television's mass audience.

This article illustrates how broadcasting is becoming narrowcasting, how mass media are becoming specialized and even individualized. The future promises even more change in that direction. By the year 2000, experts predict that 40 percent of American homes will have interactive television, where individual viewers actually become part of the communication process, for example, by shifting camera angles at sporting events or by selecting various levels of skill and difficulty for aerobic exercises.

A major step toward individualizing media will be taken when the nation is wired with fiber optic cable sometime in the early twenty-first century. This, says James Ogilvy, president of the research firm Holen North America, "will completely destroy the very idea of mass media" because it will open so many possibilities for sending and receiving individualized messages.

Joshua Levine is the marketing editor of *Forbes* magazine, where this article appeared on September 17, 1990.

Mark Stahlman, 42, a securities analyst with Alex. Brown & Sons, is a prize catch for marketers. Along with his wife and two children, he lives in affluent Montclair, N.J., just outside New York City. With his high income, prestige address and growing family, he's in the market for lots of upscale goods and services. But Stahlman's not biting on the usual lures.

Instead of network television, Stahlman each night zips through 42 cable channels while thumbing through some of the 30 special interest magazines he subscribes to. Everything from the *Wine Spectator* to *Road & Track*. More often than not, Stahlman confesses, most end up half-read in a 4-foot pile. Because there's simply not enough time. Certainly not enough to allow much network televiewing.

Yet, while the most attractive part of its audience is drifting away, TV networks have been steadily raising their prices. In 1980 the average price for 30 seconds of prime time on the networks was $63,800. Thirty seconds of network prime time [in 1990] goes for an average of $112,600. That's a 76% jump in prices.

Faced with the decline in network televiewing and with rising prices for TV time and advertising space, people with goods and services to sell are looking for more efficient ways to reach potential customers. Thus the TV networks and mass circulation magazines are finding they can no longer prosper merely by delivering tons of undifferentiated audiences to advertisers.

"The way mass media work now, advertisers simply 'buy eyeballs,'" as one ad agency media director puts it—hoping that Stahlman's will be among them. But in the future, advertisers will demand that the media pinpoint not only the age and income of their prospects but also their psychology and buying patterns. Often this

won't be done program by program and page by page but in combinations of magazine, TV programs, books and videotapes. Knowing who it is he wants his message to reach, the marketer will demand a media package that promises to deliver his target audience—not just an audience. If Mark Stahlman is in a marketer's target group, he will look for advertising media that can deliver Mark Stahlman and not just any pair of eyes.

"That is clearly what is coming," says Rupert Murdoch, whose News Corp. is buying and building exactly these sorts of bundled media options on a global scale. Looking ahead to when homes will get 100 or more cable or satellite channels, Murdoch says there will be "a lot more fragmentation in the audience and a lot more targeted broadcasting."

Within ten years, maybe sooner, those mass media that can't subdivide their audiences like this to include the Stahlmans of this world will be crippled—or worse.

Back in 1978 ABC, NBC and CBS had a lock on viewers, with 90% of the television audience during prime time. By [1989] that had dropped to 64%, with independents (including Murdoch's new Fox network) up to 24% and cable channels at 22%. Worse for the networks, the viewers they have lost are often people like Mark Stahlman.

By [1989] roughly half of U.S. households could choose from among more than 30 TV channels. With so many choices, the audience becomes, as Rupert Murdoch says, "fragmented." Each fragment offers different viewer profiles and correspondingly different marketing opportunities. Only [a few] years ago less than a third had so many options. Viewing choices will only multiply in the decade ahead, according to a report issued by New York-based ad agency Ogilvy & Mather. That will further undermine network viewing.

The networks argue they've hit bottom. Not everyone agrees. "There's really no mass media left," says Eugene DeWitt, who runs his own media buying company. "The Emperor's got no clothes."

Mass-circulation magazines face the same dilemma the TV networks face. They offer a somewhat undifferentiated audience, and isn't what marketing people generally want.

Faced with an avalanche of new competition from specialized interest publications—nearly 3,000 new titles hit the newsstands in the last ten years—the general interest, mass-circulation magazine industry is currently suffering through a gruesome downturn. All this has disturbing echoes for the demise in the 1950s and 1960s of such powerhouse national magazines as *Collier's*, *Look* and the *Saturday Evening Post*.

Reader's Digest, the most widely read general interest magazine, is down to 16.3 million readers from a high of 18.4 million in 1977. Over the same period, *TV Guide's* circulation has dropped by more than 4 million—which is more than the combined circulations of *Travel & Leisure, Working Woman* and *House Beautiful.* "You probably won't see *Time* magazine grow," concedes Reginald Brack, president of the Time Inc. Magazine Co., a division of Time Warner. He's being optimistic. Actually, *Time* is shrinking. *Time,* the largest-circulation newsweekly, is down to 4 million readers from its peak of 4.8 million in 1986. Twice in the last two years it reduced the circulation it guarantees to advertisers, because it was becoming increasingly costly to maintain the old levels and because advertisers were less and less interested in sheer numbers.

Most disturbing to advertisers, the defectors from the mass media tend to be richer, better-educated people who can afford specialized material that fits their needs more snugly. Which leaves mass television and magazine audiences increasingly made up of a "media underclass" that will only become more impoverished over time.

Take women aged 25 to 54, a basic audience sector in TV advertising. On average, the poorest 40% of the audience sees 77% of the prime-time commercials, while the richest 40% sees only 8%. Instead of watching a network show, the more affluent women are probably spending their time reading *Architectural Digest*, the *National Review, Town & Country* or the *New Republic*. Or, if televiewing, they may be watching Bravo or the Arts & Entertainment Network.

"The networks are straining to maintain the institution, but the institution is dying like a tree—from the inside out," says David Braun, who runs the media services department for the merged Kraft General Foods. "Suddenly you notice there's no wood in the middle."

Some advertisers have already noticed, and are acting on it. Starting on Labor Day, for example, Buick began sponsoring a series of six syndicated television shows devoted to winners of the Medal of Honor. The programming is designed in response to the profile of Buick buyers, who are conservative, mature, decidedly not flashy and earn at least $35,000 a year.

The problem is, these people don't watch much television. So Buick and *U.S. News & World Report* devised a series of six special sections on these medal winners to run in the magazine the weeks the broadcasts air. Afterwards, the inserts will be bound in book form and sold in bookstores and newsstands. Buick, aware that its target audience does not watch much television, hopes the inserts are getting readers to watch the TV series. This is the kind of thing Rupert Murdoch is talking about when he says the future lies in bundled media: Here Buick is using a bundle comprising magazines, special-interest TV and books. "We're going to have to bend the mass media to our needs," says Phil Guarascio, who can do quite a bit of bending with the $1 billion ad budget he throws around as head of advertising at GM.

Kraft General Foods' David Braun agrees. Ten years ago Braun's job was relatively easy: To snare women aged 25 to 54, the basic target market for a product like Grape Nuts cereal, Braun used to call the three television networks, the seven big women's service magazines and *Reader's Digest*. Mission accomplished.

Today Braun considers about 100 magazines for Grape Nuts, and ends up placing ads in as many as 30, including *Backpacker, Prevention* and *Shape.* Braun still buys network television but supplements that with numerous cable channels and syndicated shows to reach his target audience.

Gordon Link, media director at McCann-Erickson Worldwide, the New York-based ad agency, says when the networks' share of viewers dips to 40%, their days as a mass medium will be over. When will that be? David Braun thinks it could happen within five years.

Not surprisingly, the networks say that will never happen. They've banded together to form the Network Television Association to mount the first-ever trade campaign to convince advertisers they're alive and well.

Mass magazines may have more flexibility than network television moving into an age of more specialized audiences. *Time* magazine is considered the leader among big publishers in slicing and dicing its circulation. Using a process called selective binding, Time recently began inserting specially targeted ads into 900,000 copies of *Time, Sports Illustrated* and *People* that go only to subscribers who have just moved. The ads, from makers of appliances, carpeting and other home improvement items, zero in on the likeliest prospects for these products.

Time says it's too early to say how this is working. But it's certainly not clear that a focus on demographics alone is going to placate advertisers. For many years now, *Time* has offered advertisers over 200 demographically and geographically targeted editions, ranging from business executives to college students. But more than 70% of *Time's* advertising still runs in the full edition, roughly the same percentage as ten years ago. Meanwhile, the cost of fragmenting press runs balloons the cost of producing the magazine—higher costs that get passed on to the advertisers.

In future, selective binding and a companion process, inkjet printing, will let mass magazines treat their circulations much like direct-mail lists—at a fraction of the cost. This way an advertiser can, in theory at least, reach only those *Time* readers it considers worth reaching, not the full subscription list. Says Time Warner's Reginald Brack: "Dozens of advertisers are already running their own databases against our subscription list."

Chevrolet is matching a list of owners of competing makes with *Time's* circulation. With inkjet printing, Chevy can address those readers by name in the ad, possibly steering them to their nearest Chevy dealer for a test drive. *Time* readers who don't own the make of car Chevy is targeting will never see the ad, which is supposed to run later this year.

Not surprisingly, that kind of customized service doesn't come cheap. A full bells-and-whistles *Time* magazine ad using both selective binding and inkjet printing costs about $45 per thousand readers, compared to *Time's* $30 average. By contrast, a comparable direct-mail campaign averages about $400 per thousand.

The next step: *Time* and other magazines will turn selective binding loose on their editorial copy, tailoring the mix of articles to the taste of individual readers—the ultimate response to specialized reader needs. Will it work? Skeptics say that people with specialized interests—which means all of us—are more likely to turn to a specialty magazine than to look at *Time* for what they want to know. Cat lovers will prefer cat magazines to articles about pets in *Time;* for fans of popular music, *Rolling Stone* will probably be more popular than an issue of *Time* with a few extra articles about pop music.

But TV broadcasters can't subdivide the airwaves the way magazines can cut and paste their pages. Publicly, at least, they say they don't have to. With deep-pocket budgets to spend on splashy programming, networks say a majority of viewers will always choose to watch them. But that may be wishful thinking. CBS figured it could pull in male viewers by shelling out $3.6 billion over four to seven years for the rights to a broad range of big-time sporting events like baseball's All-Star Game and auto racing's Daytona 500. So far, it's not working that way. Ratings for the Daytona 500 [in] February [1990], for instance, dropped to 7.3, from 8.1 in 1989, and CBS is whispering to Wall Street that it's facing big losses this year.

The networks' programming advantage will keep shrinking as cable operators and syndicators boost their spending on original programming, most notably sports. ESPN now carries about 160 major league baseball games each season and 8 National Football League games. Ted Turner's TNT cable network has a big chunk of NBA basketball, with 75 regular-season games. News junkies—an educated and affluent lot, by and large—will probably turn first to CNN rather than wait for the evening network television news.

Rupert Murdoch's Fox network has also proved there are alternatives to mass programming. Fox has corralled huge numbers of viewers aged 12 to 34 with brash, irreverent shows like *In Living Color* and *The Simpsons* that speak directly to youth in their own voice. Targeted TV.

That approach has obviously appealed to advertisers. Fox raked in $550 million in advance advertising commitments for the new season, up from $300 million [in 1989]. CBS took in only $900 million, and it airs seven nights a week to Fox' five. Says McCann-Erickson's Link: "The networks argue that they couldn't have done what Fox did. I say bull!"

At least one of the networks is hedging its bets. [In] February [1990], NBC joined forces with Murdoch's News Corp., Cablevision Systems and Hughes Communications to form Sky Cable, the first U.S. direct broadcast satellite (DBS) venture. Sky Cable will enter orbit and start beaming programming to the home via napkin-size satellite dishes in late 1993. It will also give niche TV programming a significant boost. Sky Cable will carry as many as 108 channels, many of which will resemble special interest magazines. "Programming of the future will have to be niche-oriented to succeed," says Marc Lustgarten, vice chairman of Cablevision Systems Corp. A channel carrying only westerns, or science fiction shows? Why not, says Lustgarten. But advertisers won't be buying piddling audiences of wrangler-lovers or sci-fi freaks. They'll buy demographic packages of viewers on a number of these niche channels.

Christopher Whittle, whose Whittle Communications is 50% owned by Time Warner, is gearing up to launch Special Reports TV this fall. This outfit will put video disc players in the waiting rooms of 20,000 pediatricians, obstetricians and family doctors. Whittle's pitch is simple: Here's a way to reach potential customers that your regular advertising somehow missed. Says Whittle: "Since there's less time to consume media today, we try to figure out places where people still have the time."

Future Whittle screens may appear in airports and even the workplace. More fragmentation of the mass markets, less money and time for the mass media.

"BUT FIRST, A WORD FROM OUR SPONSOR"

JAMES B. TWITCHELL

Mr. Twitchell is a professor of English at the University of Florida.

Whenever a member of my paunchy fiftysomething set pulls me aside and complains of the dumbing down of American culture, I tell him that if he doesn't like it, he should quit moaning and go buy a lot of Fast-Moving Consumer Goods. And every time he buys soap, toothpaste, beer, gasoline, bread, aspirin, and the like, he should make it a point to buy a different brand. He should implore his friends to do likewise. At the same time, he should quit giving so much money to his kids. That, I'm sorry to say, is his only hope.

Here's why. The culture we live in is carried on the back of advertising. Now I mean that literally. If you cannot find commercial support for what you have to say, it will not be transported. Much of what we share, and what we know, and even what we treasure, is carried to us each second in a plasma of electrons, pixels, and ink, underwritten by multinational advertising agencies dedicated to attracting our attention for entirely nonaltruistic reasons. These agencies, gathered up inside worldwide conglomerates with weird, sci-fi names like WPP, Omnicom, Saatchi & Saatchi, Dentsu, and Euro RSCG, are usually collections of established shops linked together to provide "full service" to their global clients. Their service is not moving information or creating entertainment, but buying space and inserting advertising. They essentially rent our concentration to other companies—sponsors—for the dubious purpose of informing us of something that we've longed for all our lives even though we've never heard of it before. Modern selling is not about trading information, as it was in the 19th century, as much as about creating an infotainment culture with sufficient allure to enable other messages—commercials—to get through. In the spirit of the enterprise, I call this new culture Adcult.

Adcult is there when we blink, it's there when we listen, it's there when we touch, it's even there to be smelled in scent strips when we open a magazine. There is barely a space in our culture not already carrying commercial messages. Look anywhere: in schools there is Channel One; in movies there is product placement; ads are in urinals, played on telephone hold, in alphanumeric displays in taxis, sent unannounced to fax machines, inside catalogs, on the video in front of the Stairmaster at the gym, on T-shirts, at the doctor's office, on grocery carts, on parking meters, on tees at golf holes, on inner-city basketball backboards, piped in along with Muzak . . . ad nauseam (and yes, even on airline vomit bags). We have to shake magazines like rag dolls to free up their pages from the "blow-in" inserts and then wrestle out the stapled- or glued-in ones before reading can begin. We now have to fast-forward through some five minutes of advertising that opens rental videotapes. President Bill Clinton's inaugural parade featured a Budweiser float. At the Smithsonian, the Orkin Pest Control Company sponsored an exhibit on exactly what it advertises it kills: insects. No venue is safe. Is there a blockbuster museum show not decorated with corporate logos? The Public Broadcasting Service is littered with "underwriting announcements" that look and sound almost exactly like what PBS claims they are not: commercials.

Okay, you get the point. Commercial speech is so powerful that it drowns out all other sounds. But sounds are always conveyed in a medium. The media of modern culture are these: print, sound, pictures, or some combination of each. Invariably, conversations about dumbing down focus on the supposed corruption of these media, as demonstrated by the sophomoric quality of most movies, the fall from the golden age of television, the mindlessness of most best-sellers, and the tarting-up of the news, be it in or on *USA Today, Time,* ABC, or *Inside Edition.* The media make especially convenient whipping boys because they are now all conglomerated into huge worldwide organizations such as Time Warner, General Electric, Viacom, Bertelsmann, and Sony. But, alas, as much fun as it is to blame the media, they have very little to do with the explanation for whatever dumbing down has occurred.

The explanation is, I think, more fundamental, more economic in nature. These media are delivered for a price. We have to pay for them, either by spending money or by spending time. Given a choice, we prefer to spend time. We spend our time paying attention to ads, and in exchange we are given infotainment. This trade is central to Adcult. Economists call this "cost externalization." If you want to see it at work, go to McDonald's. You order. You carry your food to the table. You clean up. You pay less. Want to see it elsewhere? Buy gas. Just as the "work" you do at the self-service gas station lowers the price of gas, so consuming ads is the "work" you do that lowers the price of delivering the infotainment. In Adcult, the trade is more complex. True, you are entertained at lower cost, but you are also encultured in the process.

INFOTAINMENT CULTURE

So far, so good. The quid pro quo of modern infotainment culture is that if you want it, you'll get it—no matter what it is—as long as there are enough of you who (1) are willing to spend some energy along the way hearing "a word from our sponsor" and (2) have sufficient disposable income possibly to buy some of the advertised goods. In Adcult you pay twice: once with the ad and once with the product. So let's look back a step to examine these products because—strange as it may seem—they are at the center of the dumbing down of American culture.

Before all else we must realize that modern advertising is tied primarily to things, and only secondarily to services. Manufacturing both things *and* their meanings is what American culture is all about. If Greece gave the world philosophy, Britain drama, Austria music, Germany politics, and Italy art, then America gave mass-produced objects. "We bring good things to life" is no offhand claim. Most of these "good things" are machine made and hence interchangeable. Such objects, called parity items, constitute most of the stuff that surrounds us, from bottled water to toothpaste to beer to cars. There is really no great difference between Evian and Mountain Spring, Colgate and Crest, Miller and Budweiser, Ford and Chevrolet. Often, the only difference is in the advertising. Advertising is how we talk about these fungible things, how we know their supposed differences, how we recognize them. We don't consume the products as much as we consume the advertising.

For some reason, we like it this way. Logically, we should all read *Consumer Reports* and then all buy the most sensible product. But we don't. So why do we waste our energy (and billions of dollars) entertaining fraudulent choice? I don't know. Perhaps just as we drink the advertising, not the beer, we prefer the illusion of choice to the reality of decision. How else to explain the appearance of so much superfluous choice? A decade ago, grocery stores carried about 9,000 items; they now stock about 24,000. Revlon makes 158 shades of lipstick. Crest toothpaste comes in 36 sizes and shapes and flavors. We are even eager to be offered choice where there is none to speak of. AT&T offers "the right choice"; Wendy's asserts that "there is no better choice"; Pepsi is "the choice of a new generation"; Taster's Choice is "the choice for taste." Even advertisers don't understand the phenomenon. Is there a relationship between the number of soft drinks and television channels—about 27? What's going to happen when the information pipe carries 500?

I have no idea. But I do know this: human beings like things. We buy things. We like to exchange things. We steal things. We donate things. We live through things. We call these things "goods," as in "goods and services." We do not call them "bads." This sounds simplistic, but it is crucial to understanding the power of Adcult. The still-going-strong Industrial Revolution produces more and more things, not because production is what machines do and not because nasty capitalists twist their handlebar mustaches and mutter, "More slop for the pigs," but because we are powerfully attracted to the world of things. Advertising, when it's lucky, supercharges some of this attraction.

THINGS

This attraction to the inanimate happens all over the world. Berlin Walls fall because people want things, and they want the culture created by things. China opens its doors not so much because it wants to get out, but because it wants to get things in. We were not suddenly transformed from customers to consumers by wily manufacturers eager to unload a surplus of products. We have created a surfeit of things because we enjoy the process of "getting and spending." The consumption ethic may have started in the early 1900s, but the desire is ancient. Kings and princes once thought they could solve problems by amassing things. We now join them.

The Marxist balderdash of cloistered academics aside, human beings did not suddenly become materialistic. We have always been desirous of things. We have just not had many of them until quite recently, and, in a few generations, we may return to having fewer and fewer. Still, while they last, we enjoy shopping for things and see both the humor and the truth reflected in the aphoristic "born to shop," "shop 'til you drop," and "when the going gets tough, the tough go shopping." Department store windows, whether on the city street or inside a mall, did not appear by magic.

We enjoy looking through them to another world. It is voyeurism for capitalists. Our love of things is the *cause* of the Industrial Revolution, not the consequence. We are not only *homo sapiens*, or *homo ludens*, or *homo faber*, but also *homo emptor.*

Mid-20th-century American culture is often criticized for being too materialistic. Ironically, we are not too materialistic. We are not materialistic enough. If we craved objects *and* knew what they meant, there would be no need to add meaning through advertising. We would gather, use, toss out, or hoard based on some *inner* sense of value. But we don't. We don't know what to gather, we like to trade what we have gathered, and we need to know how to evaluate objects of little practical use. What is clear is that most things in and of themselves simply do not mean enough. In fact, what we crave may not be objects at all but their meaning. For whatever else advertising "does," one thing is certain: by adding value to material, by adding meaning to objects, by branding things, advertising performs a role historically associated with religion. The Great Chain of Being, which for centuries located value above the horizon in the world Beyond, has been reforged to settle value into the objects of the Here and Now.

CONSUMPTION

I wax a little impatient here because most of the literature on modern culture is downright supercilious about consumption. What do you expect? Most of it comes from a culture professionally hostile to materialism, albeit secretly envious. From Thorstein Veblen on there has been a palpable sense of disapproval as the hubbub of commerce is viewed from the groves of academe. The current hand-wringing over dumbing down is not new. It used to be Bread and Circuses. Modern concepts of bandwagon consumption, conspicuous consumption, keeping-up-with-the-Joneses, the culture of narcissism, and all the other barely veiled reproofs have limited our serious consideration of Adcult to such relatively minor issues as manipulation and exploitation. People surely can't want, ugh!, things. Or, if they really do want them, they must want them for all the wrong reasons. The idea that advertising creates artificial desires rests on a profound ignorance of human nature, on the hazy feeling that there existed some halcyon era of noble savages with purely natural needs, on romantic claptrap first promulgated by Rousseau and kept alive in institutions well isolated from the marketplace.

We are now closing in on why the dumbing down of American culture has occurred with such startling suddenness in the last 30 years. We are also closing in on why the big complainers about dumbing down are me and my paunchy pals. The people who want things the most and have the best chance to acquire them are the young. They are also the ones who have not yet decided which brands of objects they wish to consume. In addition, they have a surplus of two commodities: time and money, especially the former. If you can make a sale to these twentysomethings, if you can "brand" them with your product, you may have them for life. But to do this you have to be able to speak to them, and to do that you have to go to where you will be heard.

The history of mass media can be summarized in a few words: if it can't carry advertising, it won't survive.

Books are the exception that *almost* proves the rule. Books used to carry ads. Initially, publishing and advertising were joined at the press. Book publishers, from William Caxton to modern university presses, have advertised forthcoming titles on their flyleaves and dust jackets. No doubt publishers would have been willing to bind other material into their products if only there had been a demand. While we may have been startled when Christopher Whittle marketed his Larger Agenda series of books ("big ideas, great writers, short books") by inserting advertising into what was essentially a long magazine article bound in hardcover, he was actually behaving like a traditional book publisher. When Whittle published William Greider's *Trouble with Money*—94 pages of text and 18 pages of Federal Express ads—book reviewers turned away, aghast. But when Bradbury & Evans published Charles Dickens's *Little Dorrit* in 1857, no reviewer or reader blanched at seeing the bound-in ad section touting Persian parasols, smelling salts, portable India-rubber boots, and the usual array of patent medicines.

BOOKS

The reason why books were not an advertising medium is simple: there wasn't much to advertise, and once there was a surplus of machine-made parity items, there was a cheaper medium—the magazine. The death knell of book advertising is still being rung not by publishers but by the postal service. Put an ad in a book and it no longer travels at fourth-class book rate but at third-class commercial rate. A prediction: advertising will return to books. UPS, Federal Express, and the other commercial carriers make no such distinction about content, only about weight and size. In addition, since Dr. Spock fought Pocket Books to have cigarette ads removed from his baby-care book in the late 1940s, the Authors' Guild has advised writers to have a no-advertising clause inserted in the boilerplate of their contracts with publishers. What would it take to reverse this? Not much, I suspect. Put a few ads in, drop the price 10 percent, and most people would accept it. Of course, the real reason books are currently ad free is that the prime audience for advertisers, namely the young, is functionally illiterate.

Here is the history of magazine and newspaper publishing on a thumbnail. All the innovations in these media were forced on them by advertisers. You name it: the appearance of ads throughout the pages, the "jump" or continuation of a story from page to page, the rise of sectionalization (as with news, cartoons, sports, financial, living, real estate), common page size, halftone images, process engraving, the use of black-and-white photography, then color, sweepstakes, and finally discounted subscriptions were all forced on publishers by advertisers hoping to find target audiences.

From the publishers' point of view, the only way to increase revenues without upping the price, or adding advertising space, is to increase circulation. First-copy costs in magazine and newspaper publishing are stupendous. Ironically, the economies of scale are such that to increase the "reach" of this medium and lower your last-copy cost, you must also run the risk of alienating core readership. This is not advertising-friendly. What amounts to a Hobson's choice for the publisher has proved a godsend for the advertiser. It means that papers and magazines will tend to self-censor in order to provide a bland and unobtrusive plasma as they, on their own, seek to maximize their profits. They dumb down automatically. Look at the *New York Times* and you can see this operating in slow motion. The increase of infotainment and the presence of movie ads, the jazzy "Style" section of Sunday, and, of course, the use of color, to say nothing of the appearance on the front page of stories that used to be deemed tabloidlike and were therefore relegated to the back sections—were attempts to find the "proper" readership, not to find all that is "Fit to Print." If newspapers want to survive, they will have to think of themselves not as delivering news or entertainment to readers but delivering readers to advertisers.

PRINT MEDIA One might even see newspapers and magazines, in the current bafflegab, as members of a "victim" class. They are remnants of a print culture in which selling was secondary to informing. To survive, they had to replace their interest in their reader as reader with the more modern view of the reader as commodity. Still, print media might have maintained their cultural standards, had not radio and television elbowed them aside. Ironically, print had to conglomerate, to fit itself into huge oligopolies such as Scripps-Howard, the Tribune Company, the New York Times Company, Gannett, the Washington Post Company, Times Mirror, Meredith, and the rest, in order to sell advertising space profitably. As advertising will flow to that medium which finds the target audience cheapest, the demographic specialization of print is a direct result of the rise of Adcult.

This struggle to find targeted audiences has led to two interesting extremes. On one extreme are magazines that are pure advertising, such as *Colors from Benetton, Le Magazine de Chanel,* and *Sony Style,* which erase the line between advertising and content so that you cannot tell what is

text and what is hype. At the other extreme are magazines such as the reincarnated *Ms.* or *Consumer Reports,* which remain ad free for political or economic reasons. Meanwhile, the rest of magazine culture aspires to the condition of women's magazines, in which the ratio of advertising space to print space is about 10 to 1, and to the editorial condition of newspapers, which is as bland as vanilla.

The electronic media have turned the screws on print, have made it play a perpetual game of catch-up, have forced it into niches so that only a few national magazines and newspapers have survived. Broadcasting has forced print to narrowcast. Television is usually blamed, but the real culprit is radio. Radio started with such high hopes. It has achieved such low reality. Rush Limbaugh and Howard Stern are not stars of this medium by accident.

After World War I, Westinghouse found itself with a surplus of tubes, amplifiers, transmitters, and crystal receivers. So in November 1920, it started KDKA in Pittsburgh on the Field of Dreams principle ("If you build it, they will come"). It worked. Once transmitters were built, Westinghouse receiving apparatuses could be unloaded. You could make them at home. All you needed was a spool of wire, a crystal, an aerial, and earphones—all produced by Westinghouse. Patience and a cylindrical oatmeal box were supplied by the hobbyist. By July 1922, some 400 stations had sprung up. *ELECTRONIC MEDIA*

Rather like users of the Internet today, no one then seemed to care "what" was on as long as they were hearing something. When stereophonic sound was introduced in the 1950s, at first the most popular records were of the ordinary sounds of locomotives and cars passing from speaker to speaker. People used to marvel at the test patterns of early television as no doubt monks stood in awe before the first printed letters. However, in the 1920s, great plans were being hatched for radio. Universities would take advantage of this new way to dispense their respective cultures by building transmitters. The government would see to this by allocating special licenses just for universities. This medium would never dumb down, it would uplift.

The problem was that everyone was broadcasting on the same wavelength. When transmitters were placed too close together, the signals became mixed and garbled. AT&T suggested a solution. It would link stations together using its existing lines, and soon everyone would hear clearly. AT&T envisioned tying some 38 stations together in a system it called "toll broadcasting." The word "toll" was the tip-off. Someone was going to have to pay. The phone company suggested that time could be sold to private interests, and it called this subsidy "ether advertising." The suggestion was not an immediate success. Secretary of Commerce Herbert Hoover, considered a presidential possibility, warned that it was "inconceivable that we should allow so great a possibility for service . . . to be drowned in advertising chatter," and that if presidential messages ever "became the meat in a sandwich of two patent medicine advertisements it would destroy broadcasting." Such Cassandras were uniformly ignored. This would never happen. The universities would see to it by their responsible use of the medium.

In 1922, AT&T started WEAF (for wind, earth, air, fire) in New York. The station tried all kinds of innovative things, even broadcasting live from a football stadium. It tried letting companies buy time to talk about their products. Such talk was always in good taste: no mention of where the products were available, no samples offered, no store locations, no comparisons, no price information—just a few words about what it is that you offer. At 5 P.M. on August 28, the station manager even let a Mr. Blackwell step up to the microphone and say his piece about a housing development. He spoke only once. This is what he said, and it is every bit as important as "Mr. Watson, come here, I want you," only a bit longer. It was to be the Mayday distress call of high culture:

It is 58 years since Nathaniel Hawthorne, the greatest of American fictionists, passed away. To honor his memory the Queensboro Corporation has named its latest group of high-grade dwellings "Hawthorne Court." I wish to thank those within sound of my voice for the broadcasting opportunity afforded me to urge this vast radio audience to seek the recreation and the daily comfort of the home removed from the congested part of the city, right at the boundaries of God's great outdoors, and within a few miles by subway from the business section of Manhattan. This sort of residential environment strongly influenced Hawthorne, America's greatest writer of fiction. He analyzed with charming keenness the social spirit of those who had thus happily selected their homes, and he painted the people inhabiting those homes with good-natured relish. . . . Let me enjoin upon you as you value your health and your hopes and your home happiness, get away from the solid masses of brick, where the meager opening admitting a slant of sunlight is mockingly called a light shaft, and where children grow up starved for a run over a patch of grass and the sight of a tree. Apartments in congested parts of the city have proved failures. The word "neighbor" is an expression of peculiar irony—a daily joke. . . . Let me close by urging that you hurry to the apartment home near the green fields and the neighborly atmosphere right on the subway without the expense and trouble of a commuter, where health and community happiness beckon—the community life and the friendly environment that Hawthorne advocated.

Three weeks later, the Queensboro Corporation had sold all its property in Hawthorne Court (named for "America's greatest writer of fiction," who clearly had never been read by Mr. Black-

well) in Jackson Heights, Queens. The genie was out of the bottle.

Giving the public what it wants had its price. Like television today, the messenger was soon being blamed for the message. Commercial radio broadcasting was "dumbing down" American culture with its incessant repetition of mindless humor, maudlin sentimentality, exaggerated action, and frivolous entertainment. Proving yet again the power of Gresham's Law when applied to culture, radio programming by the 1930s was selling out to the lowest common denominator. Typical of highcult outrage was James Rorty, erstwhile advertising copywriter turned snitch for such leftward-leaning periodicals as the *New Republic:*

American culture is like a skyscraper: The gargoyle's mouth is a loudspeaker [the radio], powered by the vested interest of a two-billion dollar industry, and back of that the vested interests of business as a whole, of industry, of finance. It is never silent, it drowns out all other voices, and it suffers no rebuke, for is it not the voice of America? That is this claim and to some extent it is a just claim. . . . Is it any wonder that the American population tends increasingly to speak, think, feel in terms of this jabberwocky? That the stimuli of art, science, religion are progressively expelled to the periphery of American life to become marginal values, cultivated by marginal people on marginal time?

But wait! What about those universities? Weren't they supposed to make sure the airwaves would be full of "the best that had been thought and said"? While there were more than 90 educational stations (of a total 732) in 1927, by the mid-1930s there were only a handful. What happened? Surely, the universities would never participate in any dumbing down. Alas, the universities had sold their radio licenses to the burgeoning networks—called "nets" or, better yet, "webs"—emanating from Manhattan. In one of the few attempts to recapture cultural control from commercial exploitation, the National Education Association (NEA) lobbied Senators Robert Wagner of New York and Henry Hatfield of West Virginia to reshuffle the stations and restore a quarter of them to university hands. These stations would forever be advertisement-free, making "sweetness and light" available to all. The lobbying power of the NEA met the clout of Madison Avenue. No contest. The Wagner-Hatfield bill died aborning, defeated by a margin of almost two to one.

One of the reasons the Wagner-Hatfield bill floundered so quickly was the emergence of a new cultural phenomenon, the countrywide hit show. Never before had an entertainment been developed that an entire nation—by 1937 more than three-quarters of American homes had at least one radio—could experience at the same time. "Amos 'n' Andy" at NBC had shown what a hit show could do. NBC thought a "hit" was the way to sell its RCA receivers, and the network was partially right—more than 100,000 sets were sold just so people could hear the minstrel antics of "The Mystic Knights of the Sea." But CBS knew better. Hits could make millions of dollars in advertising revenue. Although they were not yet called "blockbusters" (that would come with the high-explosive bombs of World War II), the effect of hits was already acknowledged as concussive. One could support hundreds of programming failures.

In truth, CBS or not, television never had a chance to be anything other than the consummate selling machine. It took 25 years for radio to evolve out of wireless; it took much less time for television to emerge. And while it took a decade and an economic depression for advertisers to dominate the radio spectrum, it took only a few years and economic expansion for them to do the same with television. Advertisers had rested during the war. They had no product to sell. No surplus = no advertising.

TELEVISION Even though radio not only survived but prospered during the war, the new kid on the block was too tough to beat. From the first narrow broadcast, television was going commercial. The prophetic Philo T. Farnsworth presented a dollar sign for 60 seconds in the first public demonstration of his television system in 1927. Once Hazel Bishop became a million-dollar company in the early 1950s based on television advertising, the direction of the medium was set. It would follow radio. Certain systemic changes in both broadcast media did occur, the most important being the networks' recapture of programming from the agencies. Although this shift away from agency control took scandals to accomplish (notably, the scandals involving quiz shows rigged under pressure from ad agencies), it would have happened anyway. Simple economics made it cheaper to sell time by the ounce than by the pound. The "nets" could make more by selling minutes than by selling half- or full hours. magazines maximized ad revenues by selling space by the partial page; why not television? The motto of this new medium became, "Programs are the scheduled interruptions of marketing bulletins." How could it be otherwise?

We need not be reminded of what is currently happening to television to realize the direction of the future. MTV, the infomercial, and the home-shopping channels are not flukes but the predictable continuation of this medium. Thanks to the remote-control wand and the coaxial (soon to be fiber-optic) cable, commercials will disappear. They will become the programming. Remember, the first rule of Adcult is this: given the choice between paying money or paying attention, we prefer to pay attention.

What all this means is that if you think things are bad now, just wait. There are few gatekeepers left. Most of them reside on Madison Avenue.

Just as the carnival barker doesn't care what is behind the tent flap, only how long the line is in front, the poobahs of Adcult care only about who's looking, not what they are looking at. The best-seller lists, the box office, the Nielsens, the various circulation figures for newspapers and magazines, are the meters. They decide what gets through. Little wonder that so much of our popular culture is derivative of itself, that prequels and sequels and spin-offs are the order of the day, that celebrity is central, and that innovation is the cross to the vampire. Adcult is recombinant culture. This is how it has to be if advertisers are to be able to direct their spiels at the appropriate audiences for their products. It's simply too expensive to be any other way.

Will Adcult continue? Will there be some new culture to "afflict the comfortable and comfort the afflicted"? Will advertising, in its own terms, lose *it*? Who knows? Certainly, signs of stress are showing. Here are a few: (1) The kids are passing through "prime-branding time" like a rabbit in the python, and as they get older things may settle down. The supposedly ad-proof Generation X may be impossible to reach and advertisers will turn to older audiences by default. (2) The media are so clogged and cluttered that companies may move to other promotional highways, such as direct mail, point-of-purchase displays, and couponing, leaving the traditional avenues targeted at us older folks. (3) Branding, the heart of advertising, may become problematic if generics or store brands become as popular in this country as they have in Europe. After all, the much-vaunted brand extension whereby Coke becomes Diet Coke, which becomes Diet Cherry Coke does not always work, as Kodak Floppy Disks, Milky Way Ice Cream, Arm & Hammer antiperspirant, Life Saver Gum, and even EuroDisney have all shown. And (4)—the unthinkable—mass consumption may become too expensive. Advertising can flourish only in times of surplus, and no one can guarantee that our society will always have more than it needs.

But by no means am I predicting Adcult's imminent demise. As long as goods are interchangeable and in surplus quantities, as long as producers are willing to pay for short-term advantages (especially for new products), and as long as consumers have plenty of disposable time and money so that they can consume both the ad and the product, Adcult will remain the dominant meaning-making system of modern life. I don't think you can roll this tape backwards. Adcult is the application of capitalism to culture: dollars voting. And so I say to my melancholy friends who bemoan the passing of a culture once concerned with the arts and the humanities that the only way they can change this situation is if they buy more Fast-Moving Consumer Goods, change brands capriciously, and cut the kids' allowances. Good luck.

Unit 5

Key Points to Consider

❖ What aspects of new media technology are the most attractive to you? Do you predict that new media forms will be more attractive for information or entertainment uses? Why? What attributes do new media forms need to win mainstream adoption?

❖ It has been argued that spectrum scarcity, the driving force behind FCC regulation of electronic media, is no longer an issue. Is there a need for regulation of Internet access? Of Internet content? Why or why not?

 **Links** | **www.dushkin.com/online/**

These sites are annotated on pages 4 and 5.

In 1926, U.S. inventor Lee De Forest, the "father of the radio," noted, "While theoretically and technically television may be feasible, commercially and financially I consider it an impossibility, a development of which we need waste little time daydreaming." In 1946, Darryl Zanuck, head of the 20th Century-Fox motion picture studio, predicted that "[Television] won't be able to hold onto any market it captures after the first six months. People will soon get tired of staring at a plywood box every night." De Forest and Zanuck have been proven wrong. Contrary to their predictions, television established itself as a mass medium with unexpected speed.

The articles in this section provide their own predictions of changes to come. As described in articles in unit 1, media corporations are clearly positioning themselves to be players in an interactive media environment that integrates computers, fiber optics, and cable systems into a delivery system for multimedia content. Early adopters have moved from frequenting chat rooms to creating virtual palaces, getting their news from Matt Drudge and personalized on-line news services, while technophobes resist figuring out how to get their VCRs to stop blinking 12:00. Advertisers are taking new media increasingly seriously and are particularly intrigued with the target marketing potential of the Internet (see "Now It's Your Web"). In 1997, General Motors invested $5.8 million in Internet advertising, an increase of 390 percent over its 1996 Net-ad commitment; Ford spent $4.92 million, an increase of 315 percent, and Toyota $4 million. From May of 1996 to May of 1997, 152,000 Web users typed in their name and address to request a Toyota sales brochure or video. Toyota later matched those names with buyers at its dealerships, reporting that the ads led to sales of 7,329 cars—a truly impressive 5 percent conversion rate.

Not surprisingly, the current trend toward media mergers, maverick spinoffs, and narrowcast advertising has been viewed from varied perspectives. Some fear the impact of consolidated corporate structures on independent news reporting and the loss of multiple independent voices reflecting diversity of opinion. Some voice concern over misguided target-marketing schemes and consumer privacy. Some predict merely a coming of more avenues competing for audiences via similar content produced in similar bad taste. Others foresee an exciting evolution that turns today's passive media forms into a two-way, interactive information highway offering endless variety, convenience, and flexibility (see "The Daily Me").

Most media futurists admit that one important unknown factor in the portrait of media to come is the direction of government regulatory policy. Merger mania among media industries has been fueled by an extended run of deregulatory sentiment in Washington. Restrictions enacted in 1970 to restrain the three major television networks from monopolizing the production and distribution of programming expired in November 1995. Regulations pertaining to the reach and satur-ation of any one media owner's holdings are being systematically relaxed. Legal battles are yet to be fought. Issues of free speech, equal access, and pro-tection of children have become hot topics in anti-cipating the nation's transition to media interactivity. J. D. Lasica ("X-Rated Ratings?") contends that every regulatory solution proposed to date poses more pro-blems than advantages. According to Jeff Baumann,

executive vice president and general counsel of the National Association of Broadcasters, "Things are happening so quickly in the marketplace, regulatory-wise and technologically, that it's difficult to get a grip on it. I don't think the public is aware and I don't think the Congress and the FCC have taken time to reflect on what these innovations really mean."

A second unknown factor in predicting the shape of things to come is media consumers' ultimate, long-term acceptance of new media technology, for just as a marketplace orientation has shaped present-day media, it will influence media of the future. *Business Week* magazine notes that top-20 advertisers such as General Motors, American Express, Walt Disney, and Procter & Gamble are betting on the Web's growing use: "For starters, the sheer number of Netizens prowling the Web, some 24 million today, is becoming too large for companies to ignore. Forrester Research Inc. expects that number to double to 52 million by 2000, putting the Web on a fast track to coveted mass-media status. What's more, in the past 2 years, the Net has gone from being a haven for nerds and academics to a hangout for professionals, teenagers, and grandmothers alike. This rich demographic shift . . . [has] finally turned the Web into a hip place to pitch." Other futurists caution that noise and congestion is making it hard for Web sites to attract visitors and keep them coming back. According to Kim Polese, chief executive of Marimba Inc., "People want their computers to be as easy as their television. They want just a few channels that they can turn to." Her company is devoted to creating software that simplifies Web browsing while maximizing narrowcasting capabilities.

The future of other highly touted new technologies, such as digital high-definition television and digital video disks also depends on consumer acceptance. On November 1, 1998, 42 television stations in major markets began transmitting their first digital broadcasts; however, even the few potential viewers who had shelled out upwards of $5,500 for HDTV sets could not decode the signals without an additional $1,500 set-top converter box. Does the public want high-definition technology enough to pay for it? And why should broadcasters spend $10 billion or so to convert their stations to digital simply to show their viewers the same old programs? Research indicates that Net users are more affluent and better educated than the population as a whole: more than 42 percent have household incomes greater than $50,000 and 73 percent have attended college. Will NetTVs, designed with both cable and Internet connection ports, find the average couch potato interested in waiting for a Web page to download when *NYPD Blue* provides far more action? Michael Noll, dean of the Annenberg School of Communications at the University of Southern California, suggests that the level of satisfaction with current technology is likely to keep most consumers from making sizable investments in new electronics.

The results of a recent Harris poll indicate that at least two-thirds of Americans currently do not know what the information highway is, much less what they think of it or whether they want to travel it. Media futurists, however, estimate that between 5 million and 30 million households will be using new media by the year 2010. By tracking the preferences and reactions of these change leaders, media providers will come to understand the kinds of innovations that will ultimately be accepted by the mainstream.

The Shape of Things to Come

199

The Net is moving toward one-to-one marketing—and that will change how all companies do business

Now it's YOUR WEB

7 A.M. Stumble out of bed and log onto MyExcite (www.excite.com), which greets you with a cheery "Welcome Harry," for your local weather and info on your personal stock portfolio.

ILLUSTRATIONS BY CHRISTOPH NIEMANN

Soon after Jeri Capozzi logged onto the online nursery Garden Escape Inc. last winter, she was hooked. And it wasn't just because the World Wide Web site offered unusual plants, such as hyacinth beans, firecracker, and dog's tooth violet. It's because Garden Escape created a personal store just for her. Greeted by name on her personal page when she visits, Capozzi can take notes on a private online notepad, tinker with garden plans using the site's interactive design program, and get answers from the Garden Doctor. So far, the 41-year-old insurance caseworker from Litchfield, Conn., has spent $600 at Garden Escape and has no plans to shop at any other nursery. With service that personal, she says, "I probably will never leave it."

Personal service on the Internet? Isn't that an oxymoron? For most Web surfers, the Net has been just another aloof mass medium like television, radio, and newspapers,

dishing up a morass of information that you then have to sift through. But as consumers such as Capozzi are discovering, the Net is finally beginning to cast off the mistaken identity of its youth and deliver on its original promise—the ability to tailor itself to every one of its 100 million users.

Don't think "mass." Think "me." Like no other mass medium or marketplace, the Net offers merchants the ability to communicate instantly with each one of their customers. The Net also lets those customers talk back, so that they can demand unique products and customized services. Until now, few Web-site operators have taken full advantage of this intimate link, but that's changing. According to a survey of 25 top online merchants by New York market researcher Jupiter Communications, 40% say they have begun to offer personalized features, with 93% saying they will within a year.

If personalization pops up all over the Net, it could usher in a new era in electronic commerce—one that threatens to shake the foundations of conventional mass marketing and mass production. Indeed, the real kick from the Net's personal touch will go far beyond marketing and sales. Ultimately, it could transform not just merchants' contact with customers but all their operations, from how they research and design products to how they're manufactured.

CHANGING FOCUS. For most of this century, mass marketing and production have held sway, thanks to both the exploding population and the incredible production efficiencies of the Industrial Age. It just didn't make economic sense to provide products and services customized to each buyer. And without a cost-effective way to track the purchases and preferences of individuals, marketers had to resort to

9 A.M. In the office, you're running low on floppy disks and printer paper. Log into your personal account on the company intranet with Office Depot (www.officedepot.com), click a few boxes, and the stuff's on its way.

10 A.M. Calling up your department's intranet page, you print out market research reports on rivals you had asked a software "agent" to search for.

11 A.M. American Airlines (www.aa.com) just sent an E-mail with a special fare on your usual business route next week.

2 P.M. An E-mail from Amazon.com (www.amazon.com) tells you the John Grisham book you asked to be alerted about is out. You hit the hyperlink, land at Amazon.com, and with one more click, the book is on its way to you.

12 P.M. While you're at the deli, your cell phone beeps. The digital readout says some stocks you own hit predetermined sell prices. Tap in your sell orders, and they go out instantly over the Net to your broker.

3:30 P.M. An alert on your customized contact service at PlanetAll (www.planetall.com) says your dad's birthday is next week. Log onto the comparison shopping service MySimon (www.mysimon.com), which sends out a personal "bot" to scour the Net for the lowest price on the Sinatra boxed set.

7:30 P.M. The kids want a dog. Surf over Ralston-Purina's breed finder www.purina.com), fill out the questionnaire on your lifestyle and the kinds of dogs you like, and the site provides a ranked list. Yikes—a St. Bernard's at the top.

9 P.M. You'll need a bigger house to fit that St. Bernard. Log onto Coldwell Banker's Personal Retriever homebuying site and peruse your personal portfolio of homes that meet your criteria.

5:30 P.M. While listening to a supplier drone on about widgets, you surf Garden Escape (www.garden.com), check out landscaping plans you did online for your garden, click the Plant Finder for what will grow in that sunny border, and order the suggested marigolds.

10 P.M. Time to relax. At Imagine Radio (www.imagineradio.com), click on "Harry's Jazz Station," a Web audio feed programmed with your favorite artists, and let Miles Davis blow your tensions away.

inexact measures, such as demographics, to sell their wares.

Now, the Net—and its ability to reach the masses individually yet economically—may mark a historic swing back to one-to-one marketing. That could change merchants' focus from gathering a mass of customers for their products to getting products that fit individual customer demands. "The technology has caught up to the number of people in the world, and we've come full-circle," says Steve Kanzler, chief executive of LikeMinds Inc., a personalization technology company with the slogan: "Every individual is a market."

Early signs show personalization has a huge payoff. Jupiter reports that customization at 25 consumer E-commerce sites boosted new customers by 47% in the first year—and revenues by 52%. Even at a cost of $50,000 to $3 million for the personalization software, along with computers to store the customer profiles, personalization generally pays for itself within a year.

Music retailer CDnow Inc. already is signing its virtues. On Sept. 16, it launched My CDnow, which lets customers get a page designed just for them with music suggestions based on their stated preferences, past purchases, and ratings on artists and CDs. CDnow has seen an immediate benefit in consumer interest: The number of pages viewed on one of

its features, called "Wish List"—which appears on the customized pages and lets shoppers name CDs they may buy later—jumped 200% almost immediately. "It really is a music store for each of our 600,000-plus customers," says Jason Olim, CDnow's CEO. "At the end of the day, it will mean more revenues."

Only if cybernauts are of the same mind as merchants, who think the upside of personalization outweighs the downside. So far, the answer to that is decidedly mixed. Because customizing requires people to cough up personal information and fill out sometimes lengthy forms, only a small fraction of Netizens have done so.

Worse, there are rising concerns about privacy, which could prove the Achilles' heel for personalization. Too often, sites step over the fine line between being personal and being nosy. And many Web surfers chafe at the very underpinnings of personalization: To build customer profiles, Web merchants often monitor an electronic trail that reveals all sorts of things about users—say, that you're a 28-year-old female Los Angeles office worker who likes vegetarian food, Jackie Chan movies, and mystery novels. "Personalization to many Web sites means, 'How can I sell you out to an advertiser so I can charge more for ads?'" says Steve Tomlin, CEO of PersonaLogic Inc. of San Diego, which makes personalization software.

Alarmed, government officials are threatening federal regulation that could severely limit the use of personal details merchants so badly need to offer tailored products. One encouraging sign: Most E-merchants seem increasingly aware that they have to be upfront with customers, and they are devising ways for cybernauts to surf incognito (see box, "Fending Off Those Pesky Snoops").

SNEAKY PEEPERS. Even if fears of sneaky peepers are assuaged, personalization faces yet another hurdle. For all its promise, it still is crude and cumbersome. Personal-recommendation technology, which uses complex mathematical formulas to match people's likely interests, has a long way to go before it lives up to your most trusted critic's suggestions. Buy a gift for someone whose tastes you abhor, for instance, and your future customized recommendations may never recover. And separate databases on your habits aren't always matched up: Amazon.com, for instance sometimes suggests books you have already bought there (see box, "Some Matches Are Not Exactly Made in Heaven").

Still, those who have taken the plunge seem pleased. Portal site Excite Inc. says people who use personalization come back five times as often as others and view double the number of pages. They also tend to stick around when they come. "It

NET PERSONALIZATION: A PRIMER

WHAT IT IS:
Personalization is what merchants and publishers do to tailor a Web site or E-mail to a consumer based on past behavior, tastes shared with others, age, or location. Surfers either give the data to the site operator, or it can be gleaned by their movements or purchases on the site. Customization involves the active choices that Web site visitors make to specify which news, products, or other features they want to see regularly. The goal for merchants: One-to-one marketing.

HOW YOU USE IT:
Shoppers can use a program called an intelligent agent—also known as a bot—that automatically scours the Net for information, such as prices on products. For customer service, a few Web sites feature a humanlike chatterbot, an intelligent agent that can answer questions in a conversational style. Many retail sites offer customers a recommendation service, which uses complex mathematical formulas to suggest products that match customer preferences.

THE TECHNOLOGY:
Collaborative filtering compares customers' purchase history, stated preferences, or clickstream—where they go on a site—with those of other buyers to determine what they're likely to buy next. Another matching technique is neural networks—sets of programs and data that mimic the human brain to recognize hidden patterns in complex data, such as correlations between buyers of seemingly unrelated products.

has kind of contained my surfing," says Hollywood producer Chris J. Bender, who has his stocks, movie news, and local weather on his customized MyExcite page.

How does personalization work? Buy a book at on-line retailer Amazon.com, and the next time you visit, the opening screen will welcome you back by name. Using recommendation software that analyzes your previous purchases, plus any ratings you have made on other books, it will suggest several new books you might like. And it will remember your personal information so you can buy a book with a single mouse click.

Or surf over to portals Yahoo! Inc. and Excite. Click on lists of what you want to see and do on the Net, and type in some personal information. Viola! Your MyYahoo! or MyExcite page displays your name and personal E-mail box, news you request, sports stats, the weather, and an alert about your spouse's birthday next week.

It's happening at work, too, where businesses are getting just as up-close with each other online. This month, Office Depot Inc. began offering small-business buyers personalized online catalogs. And new software from Trilogy Development Group Inc. in Austin soon will enable these customers to craft unique Office Depot catalogs for each of their employees—based on their buying authority—and created instantly on demand.

There's a lot more to come. This fall, many of the best-known consumer sites, such as computer-seller Cyberian Outpost and N2K Inc.'s Music Boulevard, will launch personalized features to help kick off the holiday selling season. N2K, in a trial run of personalization this year, found that the recommendations prompted people to buy CDs 10% to 30% of the time—a huge leap over the average 2% to 4% rate on the rest of the site.

IN THE RED. Cybermerchants need just that kind of boost. After paying millions of dollars for real estate on portals and other high-traffic sites, few E-merchants are actually making money. Some big ones, such as Amazon.com, are expected to lose money until well after 2000. To earn profits, they have to get customers to buy not just once, but over and over.

For that, a personalized Web experience is critical. To keep coming back—or even to hazard an online purchase for the first time—customers need to feel they're getting something no one else in the brick-and-mortar world can offer. That's what Amazon.com is trying to do. By offering personal recommendations, which can change after every purchase and every visit, it hopes to get people to keep coming back. It worked for Christopher Mills, a market manager for a Torrance (Calif.) software company. He keeps buying at Amazon because, he says, "it has a real personalized touch." Indeed, repeat buyers accounted for more than 60% of Amazon's $203 million in sales in the first half of 1998.

Brand-building is just as important as sales for many merchants. They're finding that personalizing attracts more people and keeps them on their sites longer. Ralston-Purina Co., for instance, has a Breed Selector on its purina.com site that guides people through a series of questions on their lifestyle and what canine qualities they prize. It then spits out a ranked list of dogs that fit their personal preferences. Since the feature was installed in June, the number of visitors has jumped 25%, and they stay twice as long—exposing them to more Purina marketing messages, says Mark S. Whitzling, director of Purina Interactive Group.

Loyal users are just as critical for merchants. They can use the data that members have revealed to help advertisers target the most likely buyers—and charge more for the ads. Right now, an untargeted Web site banner ad averages about $17 per thousand people reached—less than half the rate of consumer magazines. Kent Godfrey, CEO of the San Francisco Web marketing technology firm Andromedia Inc., thinks ad-driven sites need some ads to top $300 per thousand viewers. "To do that, you have target on an individual basis," says Godfrey.

It will be an uphill struggle—and not because it can't be done technically. So far, few advertisers target ads online with any more precision that they do in conventional media because segmenting too finely may produce scant customers. "We can show ads to golfers in Kentucky with two kids," says Charles Ardai, president of Juno Online Services, which offers free Net access to people willing to accept ads. "But is it really worth your while doing a lot of work and analysis to target three people?"

Even so, early trials show some promise. Kraft Foods, Bristol-Myers Squibb, Kellogg, and others, for instance, saw an average 27% increase in sales when they ran a targeted banner ad on the grocery-shopping

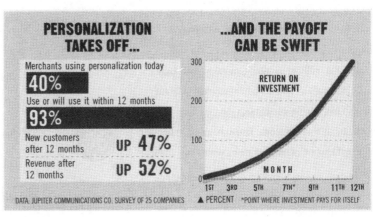

PERSONALIZATION TAKES OFF...

Merchants using personalization today
40%

Use or will use it within 12 months
93%

New customers after 12 months **UP 47%**

Revenue after 12 months **UP 52%**

DATA: JUPITER COMMUNICATIONS CO. SURVEY OF 25 COMPANIES

...AND THE PAYOFF CAN BE SWIFT

RETURN ON INVESTMENT

300

200

100

0

MONTH

1ST 3RD 5TH 7TH* 9TH 11TH 12TH

▲ PERCENT *POINT WHERE INVESTMENT PAYS FOR ITSELF

CHART BY JEAN WISENBAUGH

FENDING OFF THOSE PESKY SNOOPS

You're 55 years old, you make $50,000 a year, and you've been surfing the Web for athletic-shoe supports. Suddenly, Amazon.com starts urging you to buy safe-sport guides for aging joggers. Even more irksome, CDnow Inc. is recommending you buy '60s oldies by such artists as Iron Butterfly. Jeez. It's bad enough CDnow thinks you're a heavy metal fan. Do you really want these sites to know your salary, your age, and all about your fallen arches?

The trouble is, most of them already do. Consider "cookies," the deceptively sweet name for software that's downloaded into your PC's hard drive, usually without your knowledge. Sent by online merchants, advertisers, and Internet services, they quietly record your Web habits. Each time you visit a site, cookies are uploaded for review by the people who put them there, so they can pitch you products you may find too good to pass up.

Some cookies simply track what you read and buy on a single Web site. But more powerful software, called "tracking cookies," follow you everywhere. These hard-drive supersnoops, often used by advertisers, let marketers combine data from the cookie on your hard drive with the personal information you volunteer when filling out registration forms. Armed with such profiles, cybersalesmen may be able to get at your credit-rating, salary, and lifestyle.

BLOCKERS. What to do? You can block cookies entirely, using the preference settings in the pull-down menus of the two leading browsers, Netscape Navigator and Microsoft Internet Explorer. Or you can curb their snooping. With Netscape Navigator 4.0, you can set preferences so that your browser accepts only cookies that get sent back to the "originating server"—no more tracking

cookies. The result: E-merchants and services are kept from tracing anything you do beyond their site. And there are other ways: Software, such

TAKE CONTROL

JUST SAY NO Browsers by Netscape and Microsoft let you turn off cookies, data files that track your movements online and are placed on your hard drive when you first visit a site. But much of the Web then is rendered off-limits—and you won't get customized information.

PICK AND CHOOSE COOKIES Trust Labels, a free browser plug-in from Engage Technologies, Inc., filters out cookies that might identify who you are or where you live, so you can personalize sites yet remain anonymous. Netscape may put the software in its next browser.

CREATE YOUR OWN PROFILE Software makers are working jointly on a much broader filter called P3P, which would let you tell your browser how much data to divulge.

CHRISTOPH NIEMANN

as Kookaburra Software's Cookie Pal ($15), lets you list sites from which you'll accept cookies. And for $60 a year, Netizens can subscribe to The Anonymizer, a San Diego-based service that lets you surf the Web and send E-mail anonymously.

Some Net marketers argue that as long as your real name, address, and phone numbers are protected, it's impossible to overly intrude. "We don't need to know who a person is to customize the experience," says Dan Jaye, chief technology officer of Engage Technologies Inc., which sells anonymous user profiles to online marketers. Over the past five months, Engage has amassed a database of 38 million user profiles, which it sells to advertisers and E-retailers. Jaye says these "can't be used to track you down. If the government subpoenaed our database, we couldn't tell them who you are."

For those still worried, Engage is developing "trust labels," which reject any cookie that marketers or advertisers use to expose a Web surfer's real identity. Engage demonstrated the tool to the Commerce Dept. in June, and Netscape may add it to the next version of its browser, due late this year.

But the most ambitious privacy effort so far is called the Platform for Privacy Preferences (P3P). Software companies are working on a P3P standard that would let cybernauts choose how much personal information to disclose. Under the plan, cybernauts—by setting their browser preferences—may choose to block out everything or agree to disclose only some data, such as their zip code and gender. Progress is slow, however, so consumers may have to wait a while for relief. Until then, the best advice might come from your mom: Don't accept cookies from strangers.

By Paul C. Judge in Boston

service, Peapod Inc. Even more impressive, San Francisco electronic coupon company Planet U found in a trial at Dick's Supermarkets in Wisconsin and Illinois that Web coupons targeted to shoppers' preferences were redeemed 20% of the

time—more than 10 times conventional coupons.

For many earthly merchants, the Net's ability to personalize products and services with pinpoint precision adds up to a bowling ball aimed at the very foundations of modern-day

commerce. It heralds wrenching change for how manufacturers, distributors, and retailers will be organized and run. Today, most companies organize themselves by products: Product managers are the basic drivers for marketing. In the future,

SOME MATCHES ARE NOT EXACTLY MADE IN HEAVEN

Our reporter finds customizable Web sites are fun, but also a pain in the neck

I admit it. I'm a bit of a privacy freak. I memorize a fake phone number for nosy video-rental clerks. And I don't participate in supermarket rewards programs for fear of revealing my personal data (say, my weakness for Cheez-Its). So even if Web sites promise me personalized news or product recommendations, I often hesitate, or at least fudge data on the registration forms—O.K., so I lie. But to keep our readers informed (and to keep my job), I have sacrificed my privacy to check out customizable sites.

I began my search for My Web where just about everybody else does—at the Internet portals. Since last year, Yahoo!, Excite, Infoseek, Lycos, and others have offered ways to customize their sites in hopes of making you forget they were just supposed to be doorways to everywhere else. I tried MyYahoo first and, to my relief, it didn't ask for much personal info. But I got a cramp from spending a couple of hours scrolling through screen after screen, picking which news, sports scores, stock prices, and other features I want to see on my personal start page.

FIRST-NAME BASIS. An easier way comes from Excite. Instead of forcing you to fill out a form, it asks that you type in your zip code for local weather, your birth date for your horoscope, and so on. Before you know it (that's the idea), you build up a profile that allows Excite to tailor material for you. You still have to make some choices to personalize areas such as news and stocks. But at least MyExcite has manners: It greets me by my name—not "robh56," like MyYahoo.

But I really came here to buy stuff on the company dime. Uh, I mean, I want to find out how well the so-called recommendation services work. Merchants like online bookseller Amazon.com use software that logs my interests and purchases and, using complex mathematical formulas to match them to other customers' habits, spits out suggestions for products people with similar tastes have bought. I've ordered only a few books from Amazon, on cooking, the Internet, and Jack Kerouac. So when I ask it for recommendations, I can't blame it for suggesting more books on the Net and cooking (but nothing, oddly, on Beat Generation writers).

To refine my profile, I drive into Amazon's ratings section and, on countless pages of book lists, click either "I own it" or "Not for me" under each book. There's seemingly no end, so after 20 pages of this, I stop, rub my eyes, and ask for recommendations. In the literature and fiction category, the

CHRISTOPH NIEMANN

HURRY UP AND WAIT
Personalized Web sites can test your patience. You'll spend a couple hours clicking and scrolling, for example, with MyYahoo's page set up

first six suggestions are by John Steinbeck, many of whose books I told Amazon I own. Not exactly rocket science. The nonfiction category brings up more Net and cooking fare, plus *Nightwork: Sexuality, Pleasure, and Corporate Masculinity in a Tokyo Hostess Club.* Whoa! Where did that come from? Several intriguing choices do pop up, one of which I buy (*Silicon Snake Oil*, by Clifford Stoll). But I bet the service would be more accurate if I could just type in some favorite books.

Still, Amazon does better than the competition. At barnesandnoble.com. the personal recommendation area is nowhere to be found on the site's first page. No wonder. Once I find it, I work through a dozen screens but find mostly contemporary fiction and only a few books I've read. Sure, make me feel like a philistine. Finally, a black screen appears. What now? I go back and try the "Get recommendations" button—and it asks me again to rate all those books. Think again.

JOHN DENVER? I hope to have better luck with compact disks. My CDnow almost blows it by recommending a John Denver CD immediately after I register my music preferences. I suppose it couldn't know I hate John Denver, but it does know I chose neither country nor folk as a preference. However, after energetically clicking "not for me" on that one and clicking on others I did like—I also could type in my favorite artists and rate records I already own—the suggestions quickly improved. Otis Redding? Bingo.

Emboldened, I move on to movies. Video merchants such as cinemax.com and bigstar.com offer a few good suggestions but also some head-scratchers: C'mon, does *anyone* actually like the golf farce *Happy Gilmore*? That's why Reel.com Inc. is so refreshing. Instead of hoping that buyers will rate enough movies to build up an adequate database, a staff of 20 real people rates and matches movies before plugging them into a recommendation program. I ask for movies similar to *Pulp Fiction,* and "close" matches spit out *Get Shorty* and *Reservoir Dogs.* Nice. But the "creative" matches were even better: *Fargo, Trainspotting,* and *Blue Velvet* (though after watching all those in succession, I might welcome *Happy Gilmore*).

Now, I'm ready for the big kahuna—buying a house. Coldwell Banker's Personal Retriever makes a decent attempt. Clicking through a series of choices on the type of house I want, the price range, the location, and the like, I create my personal portfolio of house listings in the locales I'm interested in. Hmmmm—only four in my price range? (How about a raise, boss?) Once I find a listing I like, I click on a calculator to figure what my mortgage would be (ouch!) and get some information on local schools. I can save the listings and get updates via E-mail. It's handy, but limited to Coldwell Banker listings, and it's not all that tailored to my financial situation.

I'll have better luck once I have the house and can get started on a garden. Garden Escape's garden.com offers a raft of appealing personalized features, starting with a home page tailored to my climate (which it knows from the zip code obtained during a short registration). I also can store orders for plants and tools in a "wheelbarrow" for later purchase, jot notes about plants in an online notebook, and launch a Garden Planner program that lets me plug in plants on a grid representing my garden. A Garden Doctor even answers questions personally. **CHATTERBOTS.** For pure fun, though, my favorite customizable site is Imagine Radio. It lets me create my own online radio station on the site, which can be heard by anyone through a PC using Real Networks Inc.'s latest player. Clicking away on a long, though limited, list of artists (no classical, for example), I create my own personal station with just the music I like. No Yanni or Michael

Getting Personal

Like any new technology, the software behind personalization of Web sites can have some rough edges when it comes to getting your personal page set up or getting back what you want. Our review surveyed a few sites to see whether the experience was a pleasure, a pain, or just so-so.

WEB SITE	RATING
AMAZON.COM	☹
BARNESANDNOBLE.COM	☹
GARDEN.COM	☺
IMAGINERADIO.COM	☺
MY CDNOW (cdnow.com)	☺
MYEXCITE (excite.com)	☺
MYYAHOO! (yahoo.com)	😐
PERSONAL RETRIEVER (Coldwellbanker.com)	😐
REEL.COM	☺

Bolton for me. Curious? Check out "Radio Rob": Click on the site's "personal" music button, and it's in the "Carnival" section.

Although these services are supposed to make the Web feel more personal, almost none of it feels as if there's someone at the other end of the wire. For that, I try a prototype service from Big Science Co.—a so-called chatterbot, or artificial intelligence character. One named Andrette is being tested as a possible cyberconcierge at Access Atlanta, a Cox Interactive Media city guide. Here's a sample (typed) conversation:

Andrette: "Tell me what you are looking for."
Me: "I'm looking for love."
Andrette: "Say that again, please?"
Me: "What are the best bars in town?"
Andrette: "To discover some great restaurants, click here."
Me: "O.K., how about music clubs?"
Andrette: "Click here for the Access Atlanta music calendar."

Not bad, I suppose, but a entertainment listings index might work better.

What I initially feared most from all these personalization efforts was a deluge of junk E-mil. So far, that hasn't been a problem. I get more spam from two posts to a single Usenet group a year ago than from all my personalized Web adventures. On the other hand, the E-mail pitches I have received don't seem to make use of the personal information I've divulged. American Airlines Inc., whose frequent-flier program I signed up for online, has sent me several E-mails on last-minute Net SAAver Fares and hotel deals—none targeted to my home airport, let alone routes I specified.

Clearly, Web personalization has a long way to go. Navigating the Web's vast resources still required a steady mouse hand, a big browser bookmark file, and a lot of patience. Oh, and I almost forgot, a good memory. I've created so many sign-on names and passwords for security on various sites that I can't remember them all. So I have to write them down—the worst security breach of all. Even so, my personal Web already is useful. I do get things done faster and sometimes discover things I didn't know I wanted—to the detriment of my credit-card balance. I tend to stick around some sites more consistently and even feel a little warm and fuzzy toward a few. Your results may vary. But then, that's the whole idea.

By Robert D. Hof in San Mateo, Calif.

companies instead will have customer managers, predicts Martha Rogers, co-author of *The One to One Future: Building Relationships One Customer at a Time* and a professor at Duke University. Their job: Make each customer as profitable as possible by crafting products and services to individual needs. **HALLOWED GROUND.** The upshot is that actual customer demand—not forecasts—will drive production. Dell Computer Corp., for instance, has created some 1,500 customized home pages for its best customers so they get direct access to corporate-specified personal computers, negotiated discounts, and records of orders and payments. This is a big reason Dell's PC unit sales are growing over 70% a year, light-years ahead of the industry average of 11%.

The Web even allows customers to directly influence the most hallowed province of corporatedom: product research and design. Consider the case of Sapient Health Network. The site offers personalized information for some 115,000 sufferers of 20 different diseases, from breast cancer to hepatitis C. After filling out an extensive questionnaire on their unique conditions, each patient gets a personal "bookshelf" full of symptoms, treatments, and the like, specifically related to their unique ailments.

Originally, Sapient charged subscription fees—but patients balked. So now, Sapient makes money from collecting patient data anonymously, compiling it into population studies, and selling it to drug companies. It also conducts focus groups and recruits willing patients into clinical trials of new treatments—often with unheard-of targeting, such as people who are incontinent and wet one pad a day. Asks Sapient product marketing director Michael S. Noel: "Where are you going to find these people in the real world?"

Ultimately, these ever-widening electronic links to the customer will lead to the Holy Grail for manufacturers and service providers: mass customization of products. For an early example, look to artuframe.com. The art and framing site based in Lake Forest, Ill., started offering 1 billion possible combinations of posters and frames last May. Using recommendation software from Net Perceptions Inc. in Minneapolis, customers narrow down the vast choices—eventually coming up with their unique product. "We're giving total control to the customer," says artuframe.com President William A. Lederer. He expects $3 million in sales this year.

The Net's ability to reach millions instantly and individually is even creating products that couldn't be sold economically before. American Airlines Inc. recently beefed up its frequent-flyer member site using one-to-one marketing software from BroadVision Inc. Members can streamline their booking process by creating a profile of their home airport, usual routes, seating and meal preferences, and the like for themselves and their families. With these profiles and a way to reach members instantly, American can offer, say, parents whose children's school vacations start in a few weeks discounts on flights to Disney World. Says John R. Samuel, managing director of interactive marketing: "We're now able to create a product that couldn't have existed before."

As the Net's ability to personalize products and services spreads, terra firma businesses will have to follow suit. How long will Compaq Computer Corp.'s customers, for instance, remain willing to wait longer for shipments and get less-customized PCs than competitors buying from Dell? "Consumers are going to have the big stick," says Eileen Hicken Gittens, president of Personify Inc., a San Francisco maker of Web customer-analysis software.

Does all this mean the end of mass marketing? Of course not. Many merchants aren't even ready to go online in a big way, let alone market one-to-one. But for all the perils of personalization, the real danger is pretending the Net is just another marketing channel. After all, why do you think they call 'em *custom*ers?

By Robert D. Hof in San Mateo, with Heather Green in New York and Linda Himelstein in San Mateo

WITHOUT A RULEBOOK

Cyberspace presents journalists with an entirely new set of ethical dilemmas.

IN FEBRUARY, 1997, FRED MANN, GENERAL MANAGER OF PHILADELPHIA Online, addressed 37 of his colleagues in the auditorium of the Poynter Institute for Media Studies and set the tone for the four-day ethics conference that was to follow.

Online journalism, he said, is a quagmire of conflicting interests and new ethical dilemmas. It raises questions even the most seasoned journalists have yet to consider. "And if I was asked to speak tonight because I could answer all of these confusing questions, well, they screwed up," Mann said. "I can't."

It was his hope, he continued, that the conference would produce some common understandings. "I look to this gathering for guidance and support," he said.

Mann, who oversees the Philadelphia Inquirer and Daily News' Web site (*www.phillynews.com*), may have found both. But what he didn't get was consensus.

Despite long days of heated debate, and the drafting of a set of guidelines for making ethical decisions online, participants left St. Petersburg with more questions than answers:

➤ Are news sites responsible for the information they link to?

➤ How does a site remain credible and accurate in the face of minute-to-minute deadlines?

➤ Are online sites responsible—legally or ethically—for what goes on in their chat rooms?

➤ Are "cookies" (online tracking devices) and registration requirements an invasion of users' privacy?

➤ And perhaps most troubling: Is the long-standing church-and-state relationship between editorial and advertising morphing into an overly accommodating partnership?

"We failed to reach consensus on many issues and, in some cases, to even agree on the nature of the problems," wrote participant Anne Stuart, managing editor of WebMaster magazine (*www.web-master.com*), in her column on the conference.

Almost a year later, not much has changed.

Web editors around the country say there is little consistency across the profession—even between one situation and another in a single

BY DIANNE LYNCH

"Online is different," says SPJ's Staci D. Kramer. "But if I'm a reporter, I still shouldn't be printing a story without sending it first through an editor. It can't go directly from me to my computer to the Web...."

newsroom. And while most journalists contend that traditional values remain relevant online, they disagree sharply about how those values play out in a medium defined by immediacy, interactivity, burgeoning competition and unflagging pressure to produce revenue.

Such ethical uncertainty has not slowed the rush to cyberspace. AJR/NewsLink (*www.ajr.org*) reported in October that more than 2,000 American newspapers publish regularly on the Web, and—despite the 100 or so publications that abandoned their online enterprises last year—the number continues to grow.

With 71,000 new users logging on to the Internet every day in 1997 and newspaper readers twice as likely as average Net users to spend money online, the question for most media outlets is not if but how to establish a strong Web presence—though many acknowledge that it is fear of obsolescence rather than enthusiasm that drives their efforts.

But as the online landscape evolves from an unsettled frontier into, perhaps, a commercial boomtown, professional attention remains fixed on technology and economics.

The problem, say some editors and ethicists, is that the online environment changes rapidly and unpredictably. Decisions are made in a culture still uncertain of itself, and the clamor for profits too often drowns out other concerns.

"In the case of new media, people are going 100 miles an hour, both to get up to speed and to stay ahead of their competitors," says Bob Steele, director of Poynter's ethics program. "We need to ask ourselves, 'How do we make good decisions in an environment that has neither a long journalistic tradition nor an opportunity for reflection?'"

Steele suggests that online newsrooms look to their print counterparts as models. But the very nature of the online audience changes the terrain, argues Doug Manship Jr., new media director of the Advocate in Baton Rouge.

Print newspapers adhere to community standards as they make ethical decisions, he says. "Most papers know their readership very well and make

editorial and advertising decisions based at least in part on their readers' sensitivities."

But how does an editor gauge an audience that could be national, even international, in scope?

That's just one of the challenges that traditional approaches to ethics may not cover, according to Brooke Shelby Biggs, columnist for Hotwired (*www.hotwired.com*) and producer of the site's commentator page.

"The ideals put forth in the ethics codes still hold true and are very valuable online," Biggs contends, "but this particular medium has so many ingredients that the codes don't take into account. It makes things a lot more complicated."

Biggs argues for a new media watchdog group, a coalition of journalists to serve as a touchstone for the industry. Not a news council, the group would be a "cross-section of representatives of the online community talking about these issues in a more formal way." At minimum, she says, online journalists need a better understanding of their audience and its culture.

The Web community is antiestablishment and skeptical of the status quo. It assumes that information should be free-flowing, unrestrained and open to interpretation—assumptions that thwart the old media's traditional role as gatekeeper and protector of the public's right to know (see "Net Gain," November 1996).

"The people who have been great at communicating information to a mass audience will continue to be great at it," she says, "but they're going to have to be more open and creative about it, even while they're protecting their credibility and authority."

If there is anything about which most editors and observers seem to agree, it's that good ethics is good business. In the increasingly chaotic and fragmented world of online media, newspaper sites have brand names to protect and defend—brand names that

set them apart from a ravenous pack of wannabe news providers.

"I do have one important answer," Mann told the ethics conference last year. "If we hope to prosper online, it is because, amid the thousands of Web sites—from Yahoo! to the two guys in their garage in West Philly—we journalism sites are paid attention to because we have brand recognition that says we are credible sources of information."

But how do you foster credibility online? Through roundtable discussions, Staci D. Kramer, a freelancer and chair of SPJ's Task Force on Online Journalism, is helping to define issues in new media, ranging from credentialing to copyright to ethics. The organization's traditional code of ethics is a good place to start, Kramer says. Its tenets are direct and clear: Seek truth and report it; minimize harm; act independently; and be accountable.

For trained and experienced journalists, the SPJ values are working assumptions, Kramer says. But that may not be true for the new breed of online publishers and writers. "There is a feeling that the difference between people who were trained as journalists and people using the Internet to act

Philadelphia Online's Fred Mann says credibility is the key to prospering as an online news site.

as journalists is that the first group adheres to a common set of ethical guidelines, and the second doesn't feel that it has to," Kramer says.

In addition, independent journalists don't benefit from the institutional checks and balances built into newsroom routines. The daily news cycle sends a story through a series of internal checkpoints before it arrives on a reader's front porch or computer screen. That's not always the case in an environment in which anybody with a computer and a modem can publish.

"Online is different," Kramer says. "But if I'm a reporter, I still shouldn't be printing a story without sending it first through an editor. It can't go directly from me to my computer to the Web, the way it does with so many people who are pamphleteering online."

Kramer says it's important to remember that despite the differences between old and new media, the fundamental issues remain the same. "We need to remember: Common sense doesn't leave the room when online journalism comes in," she says.

Who could argue? But one newsroom's common-sense decisions can depart dramatically from another's, which results in widely varying policies on such fundamental issues as linking, the use of cookies and advertising relationships. In the forefront—and coming under fire for some of its decisions—is the venerable, traditional and authoritative New York Times.

LINKING

ON SEPTEMBER 15, 1997, THE NEW YORK Times, in both its print and online versions, featured an in-depth story by reporter Nina Bernstein about the use of electronic data-gathering techniques that have "turned private detectives into a vanguard of privacy invasion."

"At a time of growing public alarm over the erosion of privacy by technology and data commerce, electronic dossiers have become the common currency of computer-age sleuths, and a semi-underground information market offers them much more: private telephone records, credit card bills, airline travel records, even medical histories," Bernstein wrote.

The print version of the story named the businesses that provide these services. The online version provided direct links to their Web sites.

On October 21, the New York Times on the Web (*www.nytimes.com*) carried a story about a new Web site devoted to establishing the innocence of convicted killer Charles Manson. Under the headline "Manson Family Web Site: History Rewritten by Losers," the story described the prosecutor's concern that the Web site "obviously is sucking in unsuspecting young people who have no idea what a bad person Manson is."

At the close of the story, the Times provided links to Access Manson and three other sites espousing his innocence.

The links in these stories probably led readers to less-than-credible organizations or information, acknowledges Rob Fixmer, editor of CyberTimes, the section of the Times' site featuring orig-

inal material. But, he adds, the Times is providing its readers a service, not assuming responsibility for the information at the other end of the click.

"Our job is to share as much information as possible," he says. "We have to have enough faith in our readers that, when we send them to a site, they will make an informed, intelligent decision about what they're seeing."

That doesn't mean the Times has no standards for linking, Fixmer adds. He has written guidelines based on the Times' tradition as a family newspaper: no links to sites that "celebrate violence" or present sexual content; no links that promote or extol bigotry or racism.

In addition, when a reader clicks on a link embedded in a story, a "disclaimer" page appears, explaining that

the user is leaving the Times' site for destinations over which the newspaper has no control. "In a way, that's a legal disclaimer to the point that we're telling you you're going somewhere that has some affinity to the story," Fixmer explains, "but we don't know what you're going to find when you get there."

The Washington Post's site (*www. WashingtonPost.com*) has adopted a similar approach: a combination of vetting links and informing readers when they're leaving Post territory. Staffers make every effort to review links and let readers know what to expect.

Even so, the site posts an Editor's Note in the margin of linked pages, reminding readers that their clicks are taking them away from *Washington-Post.com*. Many sites rarely link to con-

---

Online Ethical Challenges

LINKING, COOKIES (ONLINE TRACKING DEVICES) AND ADVERTISING RELATIONSHIPS are among the most pressing ethical issues confronting online journalists. But they are far from the only situations raising new questions:

CHAT ROOMS: Online journalism is all about interactivity. So most online news sites have opened chat rooms. In many cases, however, the discussion often centers around name-calling and body parts. Is a site ethically or legally responsible for what's being posted? And what's the impact on a site's brand name when chat room users are bombarded with obscenities?

IMMEDIACY: Forget about the news cycle. Online users want information now—and that means deadlines around the clock. Some editors say that's simply what wire services have been doing for years. Others argue that the pressure to publish has never been greater—and with that comes new questions about accuracy, credibility and balance.

CORRECTIONS: Most daily newspapers regularly run corrections so readers know they've been misinformed. Most online news sites have yet to adopt the practice. Some say that's because they haven't made mistakes. Others simply correct the mistake when it comes to their attention. Others follow the wire service model and post write-throughs. Do news sites online have an obligation to inform their users when they've gotten it wrong?

ARCHIVING: Thanks to online archives, it's possible to track down information published months, even years, ago in a few keystrokes. What kind of ethical and legal responsibility does a site have for the information stored in its archives, easily and permanently accessible to its readers? What are the privacy implications of a system in which a story is available indefinitely?

DATABASES: One of the great strengths of the new medium is interactivity. Users can access huge databases and cull out the information particularly relevant to them: their taxes, their school spending, their neighborhood crime rate. But at what point does that access allow users to invade their neighbors' privacy?

PLAGIARISM: The cardinal sin of traditional journalism, plagiarism takes on new dimensions online. Downloading code is as easy as pointing to "view code" in a browser; images can be copied by a simple click of the mouse. The culture of the Net is based on openness and sharing; the culture of the newsroom abhors copying of any kind. How can these two cultures be reconciled when it comes to reasonable or fair use of information and images?

—D.L.

"What exists in newspapers and what we've got to translate into online is that we're independent and not for sale...," says Tim McGuire of Minneapolis' Star Tribune. That means "that you must not fool readers about what is advertising and what is news and information."

tent outside their own pages, a practice some Net users say exemplifies the old media's failure to exploit or understand the unique features of the new medium.

But among sites that do embed links in their editorial content, disclaimers are often touted as a workable solution: They create a safety zone between a site and the rest of the Net, thereby protecting its brand name and credibility.

That's a practical answer but not an ethical one, says Poynter's Bob Steele. "We cannot just say 'Buyer beware,' " Steele says. "That alone does not mitigate against the harm that can come from tainted information."

In his view, sites are ethically responsible for the information they provide to readers, even if that information comes through a link. "I've never liked the word 'disclaimer,' " he says. "It means, 'I do not claim responsibility.' I don't believe that's an appropriate position for a news organization to take."

Steele says there's nothing wrong with warning readers "when we are leading them to something that might alarm them," but, "to say 'disclaim' and wash our hands of it to me seems to be both arrogant and irresponsible."

COOKIES

CLICK ON *WWW.NYTIMES.COM* AND SEVERAL things could happen:

If you're new to the site, you'll be asked to register. You'll need a user name and password. You'll be asked for your age, your gender, your Zip Code and how and where you buy the Times; you'll also be asked for income information, but that's optional. And you'll be asked whether you want to receive e-mail about site features and advertisers.

Fill in the blanks and *nytimes.com* is open for business.

Unless you've configured your browser to reject cookies.

Then you'll find yourself back at the registration page, cycling through the same process. Over and over. Until you decide to let the Times embed in your home computer a bit of data—commonly called a cookie—that allows it to track where you go on its site (see "The Cookies Crumble," July/August 1997).

In short, the Times' policy is clear and unequivocal: No cookies, no access.

In an online collection of replies to frequently asked questions, the Times explains the rationale. Cookies are used to save your log-on information. They keep tabs on which of the site's paid services you can access, and they allow the Times to track your clicks, either for advertising or editorial content.

So what's the big deal?

Despite the fact that most sites—including the Times'—assure readers that cookie information is used only in the aggregate and won't be sold or provided to other companies, privacy advocates argue that cookies infringe on Web users' right to surf the Net anonymously and privately.

In addition, they argue, many Web users don't even know that cookies exist. They're not sophisticated enough to set their browsers to warn them about cookies, or to delete the files in their hard drives where cookies are stored.

And it's all too easy to imagine scenarios in which cookie data could be used to track a Web user's personal proclivities and site preferences. For example, a Tennessee newspaper filed suit in October claiming that local government employees' cookie files are covered by open records laws; the newspaper wants the files to determine whether city workers have been spending work hours visiting entertainment or adult-oriented Web sites (see Free Press, page 15).

"If I were to gather this kind of information about a student or colleague, I probably would be guilty of stalking under current law," University of Illinois journalism professor Eric Meyer said in a posting in an online news forum. "Online, we call it intelligent marketing, and we clamor to sign up as part of such networks. Why? Because it's money, and money is in particularly short supply online."

However you spin it, say cookie opponents, using software to track users'

Web activities reeks of George Orwell—Big Brother in cyberspace. Except in this scenario, the motivation is profit.

The potential for abuse is there, acknowledges Kevin McKenna, who is on leave from his post as editorial director of the New York Times Electronic Media Company while on a Knight Fellowship at Stanford University. "But cookies are not intrinsically good or evil," he says. "It's how they're used. And we use them for good reasons."

The Times is highly sensitive to its users' concerns about privacy, McKenna says. That concern prompted the site to post a privacy policy that articulates exactly what it will do with the information it's collecting.

The Times is not the only news site to require registration and cookies. The Wall Street Journal Web site (*www.wsj.com*), which charges an annual subscription fee, also demands that readers provide personal information before accessing its services.

But many other news sites—even those whose editors argue that cookies aren't as threatening as many people believe—are very sensitive to the public's general antipathy toward them, at least for now.

Hotwired's Brooke Shelby Biggs says online journalists need a better understanding of their audience and its culture.

McClatchy's *Nando.net* is one. Executive Editor Seth Effron says the staff is still divided on the use of cookies, both within its site and in advertising content.

Christian Hendricks, the site's president and publisher, says advertisers are just trying to measure the effectiveness of their banner ads, not infringing on the privacy of users. But it's a distinction that readers sometimes miss, he says. And that makes cookies as much a public relations issue as an ethical one.

"I actually had someone tell me a cookie knows everything about the user," Hendricks says. "Things like where the user has been on the Web, their credit card numbers, all kinds of things."

Incorrect though that perception may be, it's that kind of public image of cookies that makes them more trouble than they're worth, in his view. "One must remember that a cookie by itself is meaningless," he says. "It's the information that is attached to it in some databases—and how that information is used—that is problematic."

TRANSACTION FEES

READ A BOOK REVIEW AT NYTIMES.COM, click a Barnes & Noble link, and order the book. You get quick service, the giant bookseller makes a sale, and the Times gets a commission.

Is it just good business—or an inappropriate melding of a respected news site's advertising and editorial content? The answer depends upon whom you ask. (See The World of New Media, December 1997.)

Bernard Gwertzman, editor of New York Times on the Web, says his staff debated the arrangement and consulted with the Sunday book editor and senior editors at the paper before it was approved. He also ran it by a group of people at "one of those interminable Internet conferences" and found opinions decidedly mixed.

"I wasn't at all sure on this one, either," he admits, "so we had demos, we kicked it around."

There was easy consensus, Gwertzman says, that the Times reviews weren't going to pander to the bookseller. But there were two issues to consider, according to McKenna: "The first was our own integrity, which we don't intend to compromise. The second is user perception, which is equally important."

The arrangement's success depends upon the site's ability to convince readers that advertising isn't affecting editorial content, according to McKenna. The Times came out of its deliberations convinced that it could strike the balance.

"In the end, I decided it was a service for our readers," Gwertzman says. "We need to explore avenues of revenue since we don't charge for our product, but we need to do it in a respectful way."

Nytimes.com is far from the first or only news site to establish transaction-fee relationships with online vendors. Salon (www.salon.com), one of the best-known Webzines, has a deal with Borders Books, and Amazon.com has a growing "associates program" in which it contracts with online publishers who earn up to 15 percent on sales resulting from consumer clicks off their Web sites.

But common practice doesn't make an arrangement valid or ethical, say some observers.

SPJ director Kramer says appearances are just as important as reality. "If the New York Times can live with the fact that there appears to be a conflict of interest there, they have to realize that somewhere down the road, those appearances may come back to haunt them," she says.

The site's most sophisticated users will assume that the traditional firewall between advertising and editorial content remains intact, Kramer says. "But your ethical responsibility is to program and present information to your broadest audience, not your most sophisticated user," she adds.

In response to suggestions that agreements like the one between Barnes & Noble and the New York Times are simply a service to readers, journalism professor Meyer scoffs outright. Under many such arrangements, he wrote in an online posting, news organizations "have an active financial stake" in the topics they cover. He added, "Any way you cut it, however many rationalizations you try to make, coverage becomes an unethical shill for a product."

Most of the editors contacted for this article were more open to the idea that the new medium demands—or at least allows—new relationships with advertisers. After all, they argue, they're providing their products free of charge; the money has to come from somewhere.

"You can't apply the ethics from the old media to the kinds of information and editorial content you'll find on the Web," says Hotwired's Brooke Shelby Biggs. "And you can't do it in advertising either."

Nevertheless, it's the tension between revenue and readership that most concerns online editors. The challenge is to keep advertisers happy even as a news site maintains its traditional—and ethical—obligations to objectivity, fairness and credibility.

"What exists in newspapers and what we've got to translate into online is that we're independent and not for sale," says Tim McGuire, editor and senior vice president for new media at Minneapolis' Star Tribune. "That means advertising cannot and will not affect coverage. It also means that you must not fool readers about what is advertising and what is news and information."

That doesn't mean sites shouldn't accept transaction fees, McGuire argues. It does mean they need to be honest with their readers about what they're doing. "When you click on that button that takes you to the Barnes & Noble site, the nytimes.com site should say, 'You may click to Barnes & Noble and order this book, and when you do, the New York Times gets a cut of that,'" McGuire argues.

Even murkier, says McGuire, are sponsorship arrangements in which advertisers actually pay for the presentation of some kinds of editorial content.

"That's going to be a very touchy area," he says. "We need to look at what television has always done and say, 'Can we do this kind of thing in a way that makes it very clear to readers what the role of our sponsors is?'"

ANNE STUART'S OBSERVATION ABOUT THE state of new media ethics remains as true today as it was a year ago: There's no consensus about whether the Web poses new problems and issues, much less how they should be addressed.

McGuire says the profession needs to relax about the fact that guidelines for online journalism have yet to be written. "Some people forget that it took us a long time to work our way to a firm understanding of newspaper rules," he says. "We're going to have to work our way to a set of rules about online, and they may not be the same rules."

But Jim Willse, editor of Newark's Star-Ledger and 1997 chair of ASNE's New Media Committee, says the traditional rules and values work just fine, even in the online world. Most of the new situations presented by the Web are practical—not ethical—concerns.

"Most of these issues don't bother me very much..." he says. "You've got common sense, you grew up with good values, you're not going to invite incursions into your editorial integrity. There doesn't seem to be any reason for any great hand-wringing about it."

Publishing the news is basically the same, whether you're doing it once a day or once every 15 minutes, Willse suggests.

"I don't see any new ethical issues online that are fundamentally at odds with traditional journalism," he says. "I guess I'm just less anguished about these things than some of my colleagues."

Dianne Lynch teaches journalism at St. Michael's College in Burlington, Vermont. She is on sabbatical this year while working on a research project on online ethics.

BY CHRISTOPHER HARPER

THE DAILY ME

Brad Bartley is not the only student from Oklahoma at the Massachusetts Institute of Technology, but he is the only one from Quapaw. His tiny hometown, population 985, lies in the northeastern corner of the state. When Bartley arrived in Cambridge, he wanted some news from back home but couldn't find much in the Boston-oriented media. Maybe you get an occasional score of a game involving the local football or basketball teams. Maybe you get a glimpse of the weather in Oklahoma when a local television station shows the national radar map. But Boston is Boston, and Oklahoma is not exactly on the radar screen of the media in Beantown.

Bartley is a clean-shaven, jut-jawed, no-nonsense kind of guy who might have been cast in the play or movie "Oklahoma," in which Gordon MacRae sang about the winds sweeping across the Plains. But Bartley was able to do something about his info-gap. He and seven other freshmen set out to solve the problem as part of a class at the MIT Media Lab. That's where Nicholas Negroponte, the author of "Being Digital," holds court in a futuristic building constructed from an odd array of ornamental cement, white tile and glass. The building is named for Jerome Wiesner, the eccentric late MIT president and science adviser to John F. Kennedy who helped Negroponte start the lab 11 years ago.

If Mohammed were to go to a mountain in the age of new media, it would be the MIT Media Lab in Cambridge. The lab is Mecca for those who want to know what the new millennium will bring, be it the newspaper of the future, virtual reality or any other current buzzword.

Fortunately, the Media Lab's ayatollahs also listen to good ideas, and Bartley and his fellow freshmen had a good one. Together with researcher Pascal Chesnais, the freshmen devised a customized, personal news service, named FishWrap,

Customized online news services allow readers to receive news content tailored to their interests. But do readers risk missing important developments that don't fit their profiles?

which is updated continuously via computer.

Today—three years after the creation of Fish-Wrap—the mainstream media from the Wall Street Journal to Time Warner offer dozens of variations of what the MIT freshmen conceived. The San Francisco Examiner and Chronicle's Internet edition, The Gate, actually uses the personalized computer structure developed at MIT, as do newspapers in Italy and Brazil.

But there are questions about customized news services, sometimes called the "Daily Me." The services are egocentric; a user chooses what he or she wants to read and can filter out other information. The roles of the newspaper reporter and editor—the traditional gatekeepers of information—are limited, if not eliminated altogether, in deciding what news the user receives. The user may become isolated from his or her neighborhood, city, state and nation because he or she has filtered out any information about the global village. "It's more isolation and less real life," says media critic Edwin Diamond, a former MIT professor who writes about online issues.

THE ROLES
of newspaper reporter and editor—the traditional gatekeepers of information—are limited, if not eliminated altogether, in deciding what news the user receives.

WHILE THERE ARE A NUMBER OF VARIATIONS OF personal news services, here's how the original, FishWrap, works. More than 700 people subscribe. A computer program asks three questions. First, the computer needs to know the zip code of the user's hometown. Second, the computer asks about the subscriber's academic interests and then his or her personal interests. From that profile, computer programs seek out key words, such as "computers" or "Oklahoma," to construct a daily news and information site from news stories filed into the computer's database by the Associated Press, the Boston newspapers, Knight-Ridder, Zagat's Restaurant Guide and a host of other news providers.

The main page shows what news sources have provided the information. The reader can then focus on a news category and view summaries of stories. If a summary seems interesting, the reader can call up the full text with graphics or audio. As a navigation aid, FishWrap displays a bar at the top of each computer screen that indicates the

But this problem is addressed, in part, by FishWrap's unusual front page. Readers decide what news they'd like to see at the top and what news they think is important for others to read.

"It's really about control, decision making," says Chesnais, a bearded ex-New Yorker who has been working on projects about news in the future since 1986. "We have no editors making decisions involving what people should read. The readers do that."

reader's current location in the document.

Like its printed cousins, FishWrap has a front page called Page One. But unlike other personalized services, in the spirit of democracy—perhaps news editors would call it anarchy—each of the 700 FishWrap users can determine what goes on the front page. If someone thinks that the group should read a particular story, that individual can put it on the front page. There is no limit to the number of front page stories that FishWrap can handle. These selections allow the reader to enjoy the breadth of community interests and force the user to be exposed to ideas outside of his or her personal choices.

Today, the lead story is about a Turkish politician who was physically attacked in Hungary. "I'd read that," says Bartley, an electrical engineering student. "It's weird enough." But if there are not enough people who read the story, it falls down to the bottom of Page One and then off the front page after 36 hours. The addition of the Page One stories came after a survey found that students were indeed concerned about becoming isolated from events outside their own interests.

But democracy can create some distinctive news decisions. When the Oklahoma City bombing occurred, for example, the disaster story placed second on page one behind a story about the mugging of Big Bird on the same day. "The icon of your childhood getting pummeled was more important to the students," Chesnais says. "It struck a chord among [them]."

After the front page, the MIT subscriber can access a constant stream of up-to-the-minute stories from the Associated Press. When the bombing in Oklahoma City happened, for example, Bartley turned to his computer to monitor what was happening in his home state and watched television on CNN from the corner of his eye. "Generally, I like to read more than watch television because it's more complete," he says. "It's better here on the computer because it was more restrained. I get this when I want it on the computer, and it's up to date."

The next section provides local, national and international news from a variety of sources. Bartley's local news comes from Oklahoma. Most of the time, Bartley does not find much that interests him, but he's glad to know that the weather in his hometown this day is better than in frigid Cambridge.

For his personal page, "Stuff That I Like," the MIT student has chosen computer technology, book reviews, architecture and photo essays. Today he gets nothing that interests him in the book review section, which includes books about Fergie and Oprah Winfrey and a reading by singer Johnny Cash. Under the photo essays, he retrieves photographs of George Gershwin and from South Africa.

When Bartley finishes reading his FishWrap, the computer retrieves all the articles he has scanned and offers him an opportunity to save any stories. After he logs off, the computer will reorganize the personalized edition if Bartley has changed his reading choices or has added new topics to his personal choices.

The computer program also responds to changes in reading habits. For example, Chesnais' sister was in Rwanda when the genocide began in 1994. As he started reading more about Rwanda, stories about the country moved up in importance as the computer determined he wanted more news about what was happening there. When his sister left Rwanda, the computer program pushed the stories down in importance as he selected fewer of them.

The customized news service at MIT, which is available only to students and faculty, also offers travel information. If a user is going to Finland, for example, news about that country appears on his or her FishWrap 48 hours before he or she travels and ends after the user returns.

FishWrap also tries to provide more detail and context for readers about specific stories. PLUM, which stands for Peace Love and Understanding Machine, is a software program that augments news on natural disasters reported in FishWrap. By placing news events in the context of a reader's home community, PLUM helps the reader better understand distant disaster news.

Here, for example, is the Reuters dispatch from June 30, 1995, about floods in China:

"China fears its worst flooding disaster this century with rising waters already killing hundreds of people and devastating farms and fisheries in its eastern region. Spring rains which annually bring calamity to tens of millions have been compounded by the effects of global warming and some meteorologists predict the worst inundation in a hundred years."

After reading the lead, most users would say: "What a pity!" Then the reader would move on. But FishWrap makes the story more relevant to people in Cambridge by incorporating a variety of data easily accessible on the Internet, such as material from the CIA Fact Book. The MIT news service pulls out the details on the worst floods in the United States. FishWrap points out that more than 14,000 people in Boston speak Chinese. The service creates a graphic of the area in China affected by the floods and places it on a map of Boston, showing that nearly all of the Boston suburbs would be under water if a similar flood occurred in Massachusetts. The damage of $500 million would cost every person in Boston $2,200, or about 7.5 percent of the average yearly income in the city. The number of households affected by the Chinese flood—220,000—would mean roughly all the houses in Boston.

NONE OF THE CUSTOMIZED NEWS SERVICES PROvides as many options as FishWrap. Some cost money. Others are free. You have to drop by a World Wide Web site to view some—known as "pull" technology, like pulling you to a local newsstand to buy the newspaper. Others send electronic mail messages to your computer—known as "push" technology, like pushing your newspaper onto your doorstep once you subscribe.

The Wall Street Journal's interactive edition costs $49 a year for those who don't subscribe to the printed version of the newspaper, or $29 for subscribers. Interactive Journal lets a user select stories from a number of categories of news and also flags stories that mention companies in the user's stock portfolio, providing a daily accounting of how investments performed. The Interactive Journal also offers briefing books about companies and a variety of stories related to business throughout the world. Articles that appeared during the past two weeks can be easily searched and retrieved.

Mercury Mail offers NEWSpot, a daily e-mail of headlines and brief customized story summaries on a wide variety of topics. Because the personal edition comes as e-mail, it's like getting your newspaper delivered at home rather than buying it around the corner or going each day to a World Wide Web site.

Personal News Page is the newest offering from Individual, Inc., a company that was one of the first to offer customized news. PNP offers news from more than 700 publications, emphasizing science and technology, with secondary focuses on medicine, media and general business.

Pathfinder, Time Warner's online service, is arguably the deepest and most intimidating site on the Web. For free, a reader can search Time, Fortune and People, or learn about problems with old houses and progressive farming. For a fee of $4.95 a month or $29.95 a year, Pathfinder sorts through the material and provides the user with information on specifically requested subjects.

PointCast offers news and information from CNN, Time, People and Money magazines, Reuters, AccuWeather and a host of local newspapers. The service allows the user to select topics of interest, delivering matching stories by displaying them as a screen saver.

While some customized services like FishWrap force users to read headlines about international, national and local events, other services offer only those subjects the reader selects. That troubles some editors, particularly because of their reduced role as gatekeeper and the isolation it creates for readers.

"Say you have a user who has set up a customization agent so that he or she gets favorite sports teams' news and selected stocks," says Leah Gentry, managing editor of Excite, a search engine and information service. "OK, the president is assassinated. That's a gimme. You override and give them that headline regardless of stated news preferences." But even Gentry is not certain if she would immediately flash a bulletin

WHILE SOME *customized services like FishWrap force users to read headlines about international, national and local events, other services offer only those subjects the reader selects.*

Customized News Services

Do you want good news? Sports news? Trekkie news?
Tired of the same old headlines about murder and mayhem?
Welcome to the "Daily Me," and you're the publisher. If you
don't like what you read, the only one to blame is you.
Here are some of the customized news services:

Newspapers

NEWS.COM
www.news.com
Cost: Free

*The Los Angeles Times
Hunter*
www.latimes.com
Cost: Free except for
archival material

*The Philadelphia Inquirer
and Daily News Clipper*
www.phillynews.com
Cost: Free

*The San Jose Mercury
News NewsHound*
www.sjhound.com
Cost: $7.95 a month

*The San Francisco
Chronicle and Examiner
The Gate*
www.sfgate.com
Cost: Free

The Times of London
www.the-times.co.uk
Cost: Free

The Wall Street Journal
www.wsj.com
Cost: $29 to $49 a year

Magazines

Time Warner's Pathfinder
www.pathfinder.com
Cost: $4.95 a month or
$29.95 a year

Ziff-Davis ZDNet
www.zdnet.com
Cost: Free

E-mail

Farcast
www.farcast.com
Cost: $9.95 a month

*Individual, Inc.
Personal News Page
(Also available on the
World Wide Web)*
pnp.individual.com
Cost: Free to $6.95 a
month, depending on
service requested

Mercury Mail
www.merc.com
Cost: Free

Netscape In-Box Direct
www.netscape.com
Cost: Free

MSNBC
www.msnbc.com
Cost: Free

Screen Savers

After Dark Online
www.afterdark.com
Cost: Free

PointCast
www.pointcast.com
Cost: Free

WorldFlash News Ticker
www.scroller.com
Cost: Free

Search Engines

Excite
live.excite.com
Cost: Free

Infoseek
www.infoseek.com
Cost: Free

Yahoo!
www.yahoo.com
Cost: Free

on a plane crash or a hijacking. "At what point do you stop respecting the wishes of the user and start feeding them what you think is important?" she asks.

If a company provides the option for an exclusive, personal news service, then the provider should stick to its commitment, maintains Melinda McAdams, a former content developer for the Washington Post's Digital Ink. "I am a user who absolutely does not want that allegedly important news flash. I will *never* have only one source of news on my desktop or in my life," she says, "and these news flashes would surely, certainly, undoubtedly be redundant and thus unwelcome for me."

Several editors suggest that the user should be asked to specify if he or she is absolutely certain that the news editors should not override the desire to be left alone when big news breaks. Steve Yelvington, editor/manager of the online edition of Minneapolis' Star Tribune, thinks the other customized services will eventually gravitate toward a shared community experience much like FishWrap. "There's a belief that computers are changing the ground rules, but those ground rules aren't what we thought they were, and when we look closely at the World Wide Web experience, we find that computers aren't very good at handing power over to individuals anyway," he says. "They're incredibly clumsy devices for navigating through information space. They're slow and unreliable. I think the market will demand that broad-but-shallow 'Daily We' element in any customizable environment."

What impact will these customized news products have on the future of the printed page? No one really knows. The Wall Street Journal says its online edition attracts a younger audience than the print edition. And many of the online edition's readers do not subscribe to the print version. Perhaps it's useful to go back to Bartley, the MIT student who helped create the "Daily Me," who will be one of the news users in the future. "I think it would probably be fine if personalized news replaced newspapers," he says. "You get it in a lot more convenient form. You get it where and when you want it. It's easier to keep it around rather than clipping it and watching it get yellow."

Bartley sees an upside for newspapers. "Costs can go down for a newspaper, like maintaining a warehouse full of paper and a fleet of truck drivers. You can get the quick response time of television with the completeness of text. It will get easy to compare things by reading news from different sources side by side. It just seems like a big win situation."

But with only nine percent of America's homes wired to the Internet, it's likely that many people will still find their daily newspaper at the drugstore, on the doorstep or in the rose bushes.

Christopher Harper teaches journalism at New York University. His book on digital journalism will be published next fall by NYU Press.

X-RATED RATINGS?

W HEN PRESIDENT CLINTON CHALLENGED THE HIGH-TECH INDUS-
try this summer to create a "family-friendly Internet" by
cleaning up cyber-smut and other offensive content, newspaper editorials applauded the president's decision to forgo
government regulation and let private industry police the Net.

Few realized that the White House's "parental empowerment initiative"
would plunge online news publications headlong into the thorniest thicket
of free speech issues in the history of cyberspace—and lead to the news
media's rejection of the president's proposal when it comes to their own
Web sites.

The fate of an Internet self-rating system, however, remains far from
settled. And the online news media's actions in recent weeks have been riddled with more intrigue than a John Le Carré thriller—with the final chapters still unwritten.

Consider the questions the online news world took up after the president's call for an Internet ratings system: How would Web news sites rate
themselves for violence, language and sexual frankness when publishing
stories involving war, murder, rape, gang shootings, domestic abuse, hate
crimes and teenage pregnancy?

If an exception is carved out for news sites, which
sites would qualify? Where do you draw the line between news and information, entertainment, propaganda and opinion? And who decides?

If news sites refuse to rate themselves, will they be shut off from a growing number of parents and others who are demanding filters on their Web
browsers?

Finally, will the entire ratings scheme transform the Net from a global
democratic village into a balkanized, regulated medium where foreign
despots can easily censor any material that strays from the party line?

Questions like these are now being vigorously debated by online journalists who've barely had time to catch their breath after the U.S. Supreme
Court slapped down the Communications Decency Act in June (see The

*The Clinton
administration
and the Internet
industry have
championed
voluntary ratings
for Web sites
to create a
"family-friendly"
environment in
cyberspace. Their
campaign nearly
led online news
organizations
to create a
licensing system
for Web
journalism.*

BY J.D. LASICA

World of New Media, September).

The Clinton administration has adopted the approach championed by the Internet industry, which fears another effort by Congress to clamp down on "indecent material" in cyberspace. At the July 16 Internet summit at the White House, the president called on such companies as Netscape, America Online and IBM to give parents the tools needed to shield children from obscenity, violence and antisocial messages on the Net.

"We need to encourage every Internet site, whether or not it has material harmful to minors, to rate its contents...to help ensure that our children do not end up in the red-light districts of cyberspace," Clinton said.

The assembled captains of industry obliged. Netscape indicated it would support Internet ratings in its next browser, meaning that about 97 percent of all browsers will support Internet ratings. (Microsoft's Internet Explorer 3.0 already includes ratings as an option for parents to turn on.) The search engines Lycos, Excite and Yahoo! also fell into line, pledging to ask for ratings labels for all Web sites in their directories.

The technology that permits Internet ratings—and the linchpin of the industry's plan for self-regulation—is a labeling language called PICS, or Platform for Internet Content Selection. Operational since last year, it allows Web pages to be rated and blocked according to their content. In theory, dozens of rating systems could be used with PICS—anything from the Christian Coalition rating system to the National Organization for Women rating system—but to date, only two groups have devised self-rating systems: SafeSurf and the de facto industry leader, RSAC.

Short for the Recreational Software Advisory Council, RSAC is a computer industry group set up in 1994 to rate video games. In April 1996 its mission was expanded to devise a ratings system for the Net. The nonprofit group in Washington, D.C., is backed by industry heavyweights such as IBM, Dell, Disney, CompuServe and Microsoft.

RSAC's Internet rating system (RSACi) works like this: You connect to its site and fill out a form rating your site for sex, nudity, violence and offensive language. Then you're assigned a tag to slap into your Web page's HTML code. The tag is invisible to anyone looking at your Web page, but it can be read by PICS-enabled browsers, search engines and software filtering products like Cyber Patrol and SurfWatch.

Under this rating system, the user can set a tolerance level of 0-4 for each content category. The higher the ratings number, the greater the number of restrictions. The ratings guidelines are very specific; for example, using the word "pig" for a police officer qualifies as an epithet, which invokes a level 3 rating for "strong language." If you adjust your rating filter to screen out sites with strong language, those Web pages will be blocked from your computer screen.

In theory, it all makes for an idyllic, family-friendly, Frank Capra kind of browsing experience. But a ratings plan originally devised for computer games like Mortal Kombat doesn't necessarily translate well to online news sites.

MSNBC experimented in self-rating its news site with the RSACi system beginning in late 1996. The task proved cumbersome, with editors having to review and rate each story and fend off complaints by readers who wondered how stories about bombings and murders could rate a "0" for violence. Finally, MSNBC abandoned the effort in March. "The news is not something that can be rated," explains Debby Fry Wilson, director of public relations for MSNBC. "The news is what it is, and often it is gruesome and disturbing, but it's based in reality rather than entertainment-based."

HOW, THEN, TO DEAL WITH THE PROBlem of running a news site that's blocked by filtering software that screens out unrated sites?

A handful of media executives have been addressing that question since February 1996, when James Kinsella and Maria Wilhelm, then the editor and deputy editor of Time Inc.'s Pathfinder site, began mobilizing online publishers and Internet representatives to oppose the CDA and to champion the cause of content providers.

"We were concerned that nobody was representing the voice of the producers, distributors and creators of original content on the Web," says Kinsella, now general manager of MSNBC on the Internet.

Kinsella and Wilhelm founded the Internet Content Coalition, a nonprofit association that grew to include the Wall Street Journal, New York Times, Washington Post, Los Angeles Times, NBC, the Newspaper Association of America, Sony, MIT, MSNBC, The Weather Channel, Playboy, Ziff-Davis, AdWeek, CMP magazine group, Warner Bros. Online, Wired and CNET, the online computer network.

Wilhelm, now president of the WELL online community, says, "A parent wants to turn on the ratings system in a browser. At the same time, news sites feel a queasiness in applying a rating scheme of violence, nudity and language to news."

The coalition originally proposed this solution: In addition to the RSACi categories of sex, nudity, violence and language, a fifth labeling system called RSAC News would give readers the option of allowing in or screening out all news sites; the reader would simply switch the news label on or off. It would be tantamount to a sort of "ratings clemency" for news organizations: They would not have to rate their sites, but they'd still be seen by the online user.

There was just one sticking point: What constitutes a news site?

"There is a long tradition of what qualifies as

"WE NEED
*to encourage
every Inter-
net site,
whether or
not it has
material
harmful
to minors,
to rate its
contents...,"
President
Clinton said
at the July
16 Internet
summit at
the White
House, "to
help ensure
that our
children
do not end
up in the
red-light
districts of
cyberspace."*

acceptable, standard practices from newsroom to newsroom," Wilhelm said. She and other coalition members suggested that it would simply be a matter of hammering out criteria that would win backing from a broad cross-section of the news industry.

Indeed, the coalition members seemed so confident that such a consensus could be reached that RSAC's governing board embraced the "news" label concept and charged the ICC with the task of devising criteria to determine which sites would qualify for the "news" designation. RSAC went so far as to get Microsoft to give preliminary approval to include the "news label" in the next version of its Internet Explorer Web browser.

In July, RSAC Executive Director Stephen Balkam envisioned the process by which he saw news organizations rating themselves: "The nytimes.com would click on the RSAC News Web site, fill out the form and answer questions. That form would then be sent to the ICC to determine whether it met the criteria. Then it comes back to us. If the criteria are met, we send out the approval. If they're not, we'll inform them of that." Sites turned down for the news designation could appeal to a joint committee of RSAC and the ICC, Balkam said.

Balkam said the RSAC news label would be awarded to "legitimate, objective news" sites, but that Webzines focusing on analysis and opinion, like Salon or Slate, would not. "We'll follow a similar line to television ratings, where soft news programs are rated."

Publications with extremist agendas needn't bother to apply, Balkam suggested. "If we came across a publication called the Nazi News, we would certainly, undoubtedly turn them down."

In July, the coalition began the herculean chore of trying to set down criteria that would apply to all news organizations on the globe. To broaden the discussion, it encouraged feedback from a score of other news organizations, including ABC, CNN, U.S. News & World Report, Newsday, the Houston Chronicle and Minneapolis' Star Tribune.

Its missive received a withering response.

In August, Time Inc. came out flatly against creating a standard for news labeling and said it will not self-rate its Pathfinder site, which includes Time, People, Money, Fortune and other publications. "We believe that the First Amendment...would be endangered by any effort to apply ratings to the suitability of journalism," Time said in its statement.

"It gets to be such swampy territory that we'll all wind up drowning in it," says Daniel Okrent, editor of new media for Time Inc. New Media. "The Net industry is running around scared of the next version of CDA. But I'd much rather trust the Supreme Court to strike down whatever nonsense comes out of Washington than to trust a bunch of Netheads to determine what people in this country are able to read."

"You can't define news on the Web since

MARIA WILHELM *was cofounder of the Internet Content Coalition, a nonprofit group of online publishers who opposed the Communications Decency Act and voluntary ratings of news Web sites.*

CHRISTOPHER BARR, *editor in chief of CNET, was criticized for supporting voluntary self-ratings. "Our intent was to keep the government out of regulating content on the Internet."*

everyone with a home page is a global town crier," says Joshua Quittner, news director of Pathfinder. "Ratings—a software 'solution' to the 'problem' of objectionable content—is good for the software business but nonsense for journalism."

Other critics expressed alarm at the specter of major media organizations sitting in judgment of small, alternative, activist publications. Still others suggested that setting up an official body to determine which Web sites were "bona fide" news organizations amounted to an unconstitutional licensing system for journalism.

Paul Steiger, managing editor of the Wall Street Journal, publicly distanced his newspaper from the coalition's actions. If there must be a news label, he suggested that the only acceptable process would be for Web sites to decide for themselves whether they're a news outlet.

Netizens, too, cried foul. When CNET's editor in chief, Christopher Barr, called in his July 21 column for voluntary self-ratings and an exception for sites run by "real news organizations," he was met with a barrage of negative e-mail from users who saw no need for a ratings system.

"I took a lot of heat for it," says Barr, who sits on the coalition committee that considered news labels. "Our intent was to keep the government out of regulating content on the Internet. As onerous as voluntary ratings are, it's better than the alternative."

That, at any rate, was the prevailing view among coalition members until the backlash hit in August. Says one high-ranking online news insider: "What happened is that the ICC got on the phone, called a bunch of Web editors and got them to agree to their original plan of carving out a news exception to Internet ratings. But when word filtered up to their bosses at Time and Dow Jones and MSNBC, they said, 'Whoa, we're not doing this.' The more experienced journalists saw the dangers in that approach."

The ICC quickly began backpedaling. Meeting in New York on August 28, representatives from about 25 news organizations voted not only to drop its plan to create a news label, but it went on record opposing Internet ratings for news sites. The closed-door vote was nearly unanimous.

By the next day, the Wall Street Journal—one of the few papers to rate itself—had removed the rating labels from its entire site.

Neil Budde, editor of the Wall Street Journal Interactive Edition and a key player on the committee that was studying the news label approach, summed up the coalition members' sentiments this way: "We couldn't support a body that would rule on who did or didn't get a news label, so it seemed pointless to support a news label at all. In the end, we decided that none of this stuff really fit very well with the basic tenets of news and journalism. We decided not to rate our sites at all and support the free flow of information."

"THE INTER-net is not just another medium choice, like television or the movies," says Jaron Lanier, a visiting scholar at Columbia University and computer scientist. "It's the future of all communi-cation that's not face to face. To say that we're going to rate all commu-nication is a criminal idea."

Budde, chastened by his boss Steiger's public rebuke of the ICC's news label proposal, says, "I must admit some of us involved early on got pushed a little by the technology rather than thinking through all the implications."

So what now? The coalition's vote puts news organizations squarely at odds with the president's call for a universal rating system. Were the coalition members troubled by taking a stance opposed to the president? "I don't know that news organizations have ever taken their cues from politicians," Budde says.

News organizations, of course, remain free to rate their own sites. And some may choose to do that. "In the short run," Budde says, "the economic interests are weighted in favor of sites that self-rate." But it seems likely that most news organizations will adopt a wait-and-see policy. The coalition members did not suggest an alternative to a news label, and while they opposed ratings for news sites, they did not oppose Internet ratings in general.

"It is a perplexing issue for all of us," says Merrill Brown, editor in chief of MSNBC on the Internet. "As a parent of small children, I'm strongly in favor of tools that let me control my children's access to certain things. On the other hand, news does not fit neatly into any ratings scheme."

Budde says one alternative, which would keep Internet ratings alive but allow organizations to decline to rate themselves, is to give users control over which unrated sites to allow into their homes. "Microsoft can craft its browser in a way to allow rated sites plus a list of individual sites determined by the user or by a trusted source: anyone from a cousin to the Newspaper Association of America."

The problem with that approach, Budde acknowledges, is that well-known news sources like the New York Times and USA Today are sure to qualify, while less mainstream publications like Suck or Brock Meeks' muckraking CyberWire Dispatch are less likely to make the list.

The difficulty of a one-size-fits-all Internet ratings system goes well beyond news sites. Thousands of other Web sites face the same dilemma: medical and scientific sites that discuss body parts in clinical detail; art museums that display online exhibits with partial nudity; government sites that contain information about safe sex or terrorist groups, leading to the irony of citizens who set their ratings to an ultra-chaste "0" being barred from entering a government site.

With so many loopholes and drawbacks, the question arises: Are Internet ratings workable? Many critics believe that ratings threaten not just news sites but free speech on the Net.

David Talbot, a former arts and features editor at the San Francisco Examiner who's now editor of the prestigious online magazine Salon, says that Internet ratings pose an implicit financial threat to vibrant online journalism.

"Commercial sites like Salon are already under pressure to tone down our writing and subject matter," he says. "We are obviously not a pornographic site, but we often publish frank discussions about adult subjects. This was supposed to be the very promise of the Web—that communication could be more freewheeling and less mediated by commercial interests. If sites like ours start to get R ratings or whatever tag some in-the-box bureaucrat chooses to slap on us, it could very well scare off advertisers who've made an across-the-board decision not to place ads on any sites that don't have the Good Housekeeping Seal of Approval.

"Web ratings are a slippery slope that will lead to a handful of formulaic corporate sites soaking up all the ad dollars, while independent sites with rougher creative edges are financially marginalized," Talbot adds. "Most will live short and brutish lives and then go out of business. That's when the Web is dead, in my book. The news media should be joining forces to fight the ratings juggernaut."

While few, if any, newspapers have come out editorially against Internet ratings, other groups have not been so reticent. The American Library Association opposes any form of intermediated restrictions on Internet content. The Electronic Privacy Information Center (EPIC) in Washington, D.C.—a lead plaintiff against the CDA—is spearheading an assault on Net ratings. And in August the ACLU issued a white paper titled "Fahrenheit 451.2: Is Cyberspace Burning?," a scathing indictment of Internet ratings.

MUCH OF THE FERVENT OPPOSITION to PICS-based ratings systems boils down to one factor: The reader may not be the one making the decision on what material is screened out. And that's the essential difference between filtering and censoring: Who decides what you can see?

"PICS ratings will have a devastating effect on free speech all over the world—and at home," declares Lawrence Lessig, a professor at Harvard Law School. "The problem is that the filter can be imposed at the level of the individual user, the corporation, the proxy server, the Internet service provider, or the national government. This is disastrous, because you can have invisible filtering done at any level of the distribution chain."

PICS filtering allows self-labeling, where you embed labels into your Web site, but it also allows a third party to rate your site any way it deems fit. A software filtering company, a Christian Coalition ratings board or a foreign government could rate sites according to their own agenda and distribute their ratings online.

"We're creating a versatile and robust censorship tool, not just for parents but for censors everywhere," Lessig warns. "It will allow China and Singapore to clean up the Net. It will let companies control what their employees can see. It makes it easy for school administrators to prevent students from viewing controversial sites."

This is no exercise in academic conjecture. Already, Australia, Japan and Dubai are weighing labeling plans to muzzle the Net by enforcing "national content controls." At home, third-party intermediaries—from employers, libraries, universities and access providers to the Internet cafe down the street—may soon substitute their judgment for yours. And that's the biggest potential for abuse: You may never know that a particular article or work or idea even existed.

Indeed, ratings and filtering systems are already blocking access to political organizations, medical information and unpopular viewpoints. David Sobel, legal counsel for EPIC warns: "Once voluntary standards are in place, statutory controls will surely follow."

Several "son of CDA" bills have been floated in Congress, ranging from government-mandated labels to criminal penalties for those who mislabel their site. One proposal, the Online Cooperative Publishing Act, was put forward by SafeSurf to ensure that families "may feel secure in their homes from unwanted material."

SafeSurf, which is lobbying mightily to become the ratings system for Netscape, goes well beyond RSAC's sex, nudity, violence and language categories and five levels of access. Instead, it offers nine categories—including gambling, "glorifying drug use" and "homosexual themes"—and nine rating levels. The company, which started out in 1995 as a two-person parents' group, recently moved into plush offices on Wilshire Boulevard in Los Angeles, thanks to large investors.

"A lot of parents we hear from are more concerned with gangs and gambling and neo-Nazis than with Playboy," says company President Wendy Simpson, who says more than 60,000 people have self-rated their Web sites under the SafeSurf ratings system.

For its part, Netscape is sanguine about the prospects for global censorship. Peter Harter, the company's global public policy counsel, says Netscape is "value neutral" on the subject of censorship. "Netscape has responsibilities as a global information company. Other countries don't have a First Amendment, and we don't believe it's our right to force our values down the throats of other cultures and countries. If Singapore or China or other nondemocratic countries choose to set up massive filters to restrict the information flowing into their country, it's their right."

So why would media organizations consider consenting to a voluntary ratings system that has such potential for censorial abuse? The law of maximum eyeballs. The foremost concern of Web site operators is how to drive traffic to their site. Even those who disdain ratings have acknowledged they may be forced by the

NEIL BUDDE, editor of the Wall Street Journal Interactive Edition, says, "In the short run, the economic interests are weighted in favor of sites that self-rate."

Salon Editor **DAVID TALBOT** *calls Web ratings "a slippery slope that will lead to a handful of formulaic corporate sites soaking up all the ad dollars, while independent sites...are financially marginalized."*

marketplace to self-rate if their sites become inaccessible to tens of thousands of potential readers. To date, of more than a million Web sites, over 43,000 have rated themselves under the RSACi ratings system. That number is expected to grow rapidly as the high-tech industry and the Clinton administration join forces to push the ratings plan.

Sobel and others see a bleak future for controversial online journalism if ratings become widely adopted. "Unfortunately, a lot of people think we need to knock down everything to the common denominator of this mythical six-year-old who surfs the Net. Do we really want that kind of sanitized content?"

Consider one image, the Pulitzer Prize-winning photo of a young, naked, terrified Vietnamese girl whose village was napalmed by an American jet. Surely, that would have scored high on the violence and nudity rating scales.

"The image of a child running down the road, skin burning with napalm, is horrifying, and potentially traumatic, to a child," Thomas Leavitt, a computer industry employee, said in an online posting. "At the same time, how many careers, how many idealists and crusaders have developed as the result of seeing the unvarnished truth at a young age?"

If Internet ratings catch on, says Leavitt, "no journalist would be free of this conflict of interest between reporting the truth and pleasing the ratings police. Every article, report and photo would be influenced by the question, 'What rating will this receive?'"

In the stampede to protect children in cyberspace, there's a natural tendency to look for a technological solution. But every solution to date has spawned more questions than answers—and more pitfalls.

"These efforts to rate the Net result from a real misunderstanding of what the Internet is all about," says Jaron Lanier, a visiting scholar at Columbia University and computer scientist who coined the term "virtual reality." "The Internet is not just another medium choice, like television or the movies. It's the future of all communication that's not face to face. To say that we're going to rate all communication is a criminal idea."

Lanier says ratings will blind us to many of the quirky, idiosyncratic, vibrant voices that make the Internet so astonishing. "The Internet creates a giant mirror where we see the whole of humanity—the bad with the good. If you start creating these narrow rating channels by precensoring opinions and ideas before you've even been exposed to them, then our lives will be dimmed and narrower and the sky a little less bright."

J.D. Lasica is AJR's new media columnist and the copy desk chief for San Francisco Sidewalk, Microsoft's online city guide. His last AJR feature article, in May, was on push technology and the news.

INTERNET

THE NEW RATINGS GAME

For all the techno-savvy out there, measuring traffic on the Web remains a very inexact science

When executives of SportsLine USA Inc. sat down in March to review their marketing deal with America Online Inc., they didn't anticipate spending an hour poring over conflicting data on how many people visit their Web site. After an exasperating session, both sides decided to break off that part of the review, crunch the numbers from different rating companies, and come back later. "We weren't getting anywhere—we weren't even looking at the same measurements," says Kenneth Dotson, SportsLine's vice-president for marketing.

Such knock-down fights over measuring Internet traffic are all too common. While the Web has been trumpeted as a digital marketplace where advertisers could target precise demographic groups and gather reams of data on buying habits, the reality is altogether different. Today's technology just isn't up to snuff, and advertisers still can't aim their Web ads any more accurately than they can glossy magazine ads. Worse, even basic measurement techniques for sizing up the most popular Web sites are so varied that a list of the top 25 sites is instantly disputed.

DEVILISHLY DIFFICULT. The problem this creates is more than just data frustration. Reliable measurement methods are essential for the Net to become the advertising bonanza Web-site operators are banking on. By 2002, online ad revenues are expected to hit $9 billion—a ninefold jump from the $1 billion spent in 1997, says Jupiter Communications. Advertisers say they have been holding back, in part, because of differing tallies. "It affects ad spending when you see wide discrepancies in numbers," says Norman Lehoullier, managing director at Grey Interactive Worldwide, an ad agency with 71 clients, including Dell Computer, and Procter & Gamble.

> The next 18 months should shake out which services—and techniques—win out

Web sites measure their own popularity, largely by the number of "hits," or the times a page or parts of a page are called up. Sites then try to convert that into "unique visitors," so that one person calling up several pages is not counted more than once. That's an inexact science, and advertisers want precise—and impartial—data.

That's devilishly difficult. Figuring out how to zero in on specific groups of buyers is improving, though the Holy Grail of laser targeting by age, income, and past buying habits is generally still out of reach.

Even the easier target of measuring the number of people visiting a Web site is a tough slog. For the past couple of years, Media Metrix Inc., founded by market research firm NPD Group Inc., was the only game in town for tracking the popularity of sites. Now, the company is being challenged by a band of rating-service wannabes. Last fall, upstart RelevantKnowledge Inc. began nipping at the leader's heels. On Mar. 30, NetRatings Inc., a startup backed by Hitachi Ltd., launched a rival service. And this summer, PC Data Inc., which tracks hardware and software sales, and Nielsen Media Research, of TV research fame, are joining the fray.

The snag: Each uses different methods for monitoring usage, which produces conflicting results. Consider February's tallies: The lists of the top 25 Web sites put together by RelevantKnowledge and Media Metrix shared only 19 names. And while both ranked the search engine Yahoo! in the top three, they varied on the other two top slots. "I think no data is better than wrong data, especially when the industry is saying we can be an effective medium," says Marshall Cohen, president of Marshall Cohen Associates, an entertainment and Internet consultant.

The differences start with the survey groups. Each service has a group of people, or "panel," who agree to install software on their PCs to monitor their movement online. Media Metrix recruits its panel by buying population lists and conducting random mailings and phone

Reprinted from the April 27, 1998 issue of *Business Week*, pp. 73-74, 78 by special permission. © 1998 by The McGraw-Hill Companies, Inc.

RATINGS HERE, THERE, AND EVERYWHERE

MEDIA METRIX
TOP-RATED PROPERTIES:*

1.  AOL.COM

2. YAHOO!

3. Microsoft *Where do you want to go today?*

The pioneer of Web ratings relies on a survey group of 30,000 people who have software installed on their PCs to track usage. Ratings are based on reach—the percentage of visitors at a Web site each month vs. the total number of Web users.

* Group of sites rated from home in February

NETRATINGS
TOP-RATED PROPERTIES:†

1. YAHOO!

2. Netscape®

3. WELCOME TO OUR COMMUNITY GeoCities

Uses the Web to recruit a sample group that's expected to rise within a year to 25,000 people, from 2,000 at launch. Presents data in a variety of ways, such as listing top sites by most page views (or times a page is loaded into a browser) per person.

† Group of sites rated week of March 15

RELEVANTKNOWLEDGE
TOP-RATED PROPERTIES:**

1. YAHOO!

2. Netscape®

3. eXcite

Signs up survey group, now made up of 11,000 Net users, via phone. Plans this year to expand to 20,000 people, in part by going international. Its data show the number of first-time users who visit a site each month.

** Group of sites rated in February

NIELSEN MEDIA RESEARCH
Plans to begin offering data this summer. Survey group now numbers 3,500 and is expected to reach 10,000 by yearend. Group selection made through random-digit phone calls. Hasn't decided yet how it will slice data. Plans to track Net usage on non-PC devices, like TV set-top boxes connected to the Internet.

---

calls. Some 45,000 people have agreed to take part in its surveys, but only 30,000 actually do. Of those, 9,400 were Web users in February. Media Metrix executives say that by enlisting PC users who are not all Netizens yet, they can track people as they start to come online.

NO-NOs. RelevantKnowledge, in contrast, relies on random phone calls to recruit people who already use the Web. While 11,000 have agreed to be part of RelevantKnowledge's survey group, only 4,000 usually participate.

The size of the sample can be crucial. While the Nielsen TV panel of 5,000 people is plenty for the 52 cable and network channels it monitors, small sample sizes for monitoring the Web make it difficult to track usage beyond the top 200 to 300 sites. Ad agencies and Website operators say that, ideally, they would like to see panel sizes of at least 10,000 people.

The latest company to join the measurement game, NetRatings, already is drawing criticism. Its sample group of 2,000 pales next to that of Media Metrix, although NetRatings expects within a year to have 25,000 participants. And some potential clients fret that its group is re-

cruited off the Web—which can tilt results toward heavy users, rather than a cross-section. Self-selection for survey groups also is considered a no-no, because it means the process of selection isn't random. "Those of us who are conservative researchers wouldn't call something that's self-selected a sample," says Jim Alexander, vice-president of consumer and strategic research at the Weather Channel. NetRatings defends its practice of recruiting right off the Web, saying a savvy panel gives more useful results.

The varied sample groups are only one of the ingredients that contribute to conflicting data. Another issue is that none of the services adequately factors in people who use the Net at work. Tracking firms miss up to one-third of Web usage if they focus only on the home, says IntelliQuest Inc., a technology market-research firm. "The tough thing is that so much of what we do is business-to-business advertising, and none of the services do a good job giving information on that," complains Alan May, media director at Anderson & Lembke Inc., the agency that handles Microsoft Corp.'s Web ads. In March, RelevantKnowledge included about 700 Web users at work, while

Media Metrix included 850. All three plan to expand work coverage, but admit difficulties.

The problem lies in convincing companies that it's O.K. for employees to install tracking software on their computers. This software is more sophisticated than cookies, the tiny software programs commonly used by individual sites to monitor usage. The fear is that the software can potentially trace identities, as well as confidential data, such as memos or sales information. "If people are concerned about cookies, imagine how they would feel about this technology," says Manish Bhatia, vice-president for interactive services at Nielsen, which won't audit work usage initially, although it's developing technical solutions aimed at making the software less intrusive.

International Web users also get short shrift. RelevantKnowledge began working with a Swedish partner in March, and the other services have plans in the next year to attack the problem. "That's important to us," says Sean Pfister, director of research and analysis at CNET Inc., whose technology news and search sites get between 8% and 15% of their traffic from international users.

TRACKING WHO SURFS WHERE

The Internet hasn't delivered on one-to-one marketing—yet. But a raft of services are becoming even more sophisticated in helping advertisers target ads and track their effectiveness. "We're constantly learning more about which eyeballs are going where," says Norman Lehoullier, managing director at ad agency Grey Interactive Worldwide.

To do this, advertisers rely on a variety of services. They mix and match the ratings information from companies such as Media Metrix Inc. with data from other companies such as Excite Inc.'s MatchLogic, or AdKnowledge. These services let advertisers and Web-site operators serve up ads to specific audiences and then assess the response. **FOLLOW THE LINKS.** How is the information used? Ask Fragrance Counter, a Brentwood (N.Y.)-based cosmetics retailer, which during the past two quarters used ratings info from Media Metrix and RelevantKnowledge to select sites that were popular with women. Fragrance Counter then added its proprietary technology to figure out how successful its ads were.

The result: Ads linked to keyword searches, such as "perfume" or "Estée Lauder," as well as to the shopping areas on search engines, were among the most effective. Ads in the Yahoo! Inc. shopping area, for example, had a "click rate," or percentage of people who clicked on the ad, of 4%—compared with less than 1% in the Yahoo! local-content area. And the percentage of people who bought a product was 3% in the Yahoo! shopping guide, vs. less than 1% in the local-content area. "From what we've learned, we'll pay significant cash for the placement we want," says Eli Katz, vice-president for marketing at Fragrance Counter.

Still, the information advertisers can get is limited. Most of the ad-tracking services are confined to collecting such data as which browser a cybernaut uses and what country he or she lives in. That's pretty slim, although it does the trick for technology news service CNET Inc., which uses such data to target Windows-based-software ads at Windows 95 users. Another way to aim ads is through a method called "context"—monitoring the overall content a cybernaut is viewing and serving up ads accordingly. If someone is searching on the keyword "car," for example, a General Motors Corp. ad might pop up.

Getting precise demographic information is the most difficult. That's because it's still hard to get wary consumers to provide personal data such as age, income, and sex. One way Excite is attacking that problem is by running online sweepstakes—a gimmick that puts cybernauts in the running for prizes like vacations to Florida in exchange for personal information. "This helps advertisers introduce more knowledge into their decisions," says Craig Donato, Excite's vice-president for database marketing.

Other services are attacking the problem more broadly by trying to track usage across many sites. CMG Information Services Inc.'s Engage plans later this month to introduce an ambitious service called Engage.Knowledge, which will start off with 10 million profiles of Web users. These profiles will be collected from a host of sites, including search engine Lycos Inc., that monitor usage on their Web sites. The data collected by Engage.Knowledge can be sliced into 800 categories, including sports and hobbies, for advertisers and Web-site operators. It's far from advertising nirvana, but it's one step closer.

By Heather Green in New York

The new ratings services may be muddying the waters for now, but the added competition is expected to lead to more reliable measurements. Media Metrix already has been forced to slice data in ways comparable to rivals. By June, the company plans to offer home and work data combined. That's something RelevantKnowledge already provides. NetRatings and RelevantKnowledge also are beefing up their ability to track America Online Inc.'s subscribers, while its rivals have limited access. The reason: AOL executives say they are hesitant to give carte blanche to new tracking companies without details on their methodologies.

EARLY BETS. Other forces also are at work to standardize ratings. This month, the Advertising Research Foundation formed a committee of companies that use the ratings services. The objective: to look into how the services operate. "At the minimum, the idea is to understand what the companies are doing. It's unclear now," says James Spaeth, president of the foundation, a nonprofit group that encourages marketing and ad research. Media Metrix also has met with the Media Rating Council, which accredits ratings services that disclose their procedures and abide by them.

So, which method will win out? In the next 12 to 18 months, a frontrunner is bound to emerge. For one, the sheer cost of using the services, which can range from $40,000 to hundreds of thousands of dollars annually, will force Website operators to be selective. "Our tactic this year is to buy all the data that looks valuable, get really knowledgeable about it, and then next year drop what we don't think is worth paying for," says Karen Edwards, Yahoo! Inc.'s vice-president for brand marketing.

Early bets are on Media Metrix, because it leads the pack, with 150 clients, and has the biggest survey group. And although Nielsen is late to the party, its brand name and resources have caught advertisers' attention. "Media Metrix is the frontrunner, but nobody has got it right yet," says analyst Chris Charron of Forrester Research Inc. That means there will be more data angst before the Web measures up.

By Heather Green in New York

AE Article Review Form

We encourage you to photocopy and use this page as a tool to assess how the articles in **Annual Editions** expand on the information in your textbook. By reflecting on the articles you will gain enhanced text information. You can also access this useful form on a product's book support Web site at **http://www.dushkin.com/online/.**

NAME:

DATE:

TITLE AND NUMBER OF ARTICLE:

BRIEFLY STATE THE MAIN IDEA OF THIS ARTICLE:

LIST THREE IMPORTANT FACTS THAT THE AUTHOR USES TO SUPPORT THE MAIN IDEA:

WHAT INFORMATION OR IDEAS DISCUSSED IN THIS ARTICLE ARE ALSO DISCUSSED IN YOUR TEXTBOOK OR OTHER READINGS THAT YOU HAVE DONE? LIST THE TEXTBOOK CHAPTERS AND PAGE NUMBERS:

LIST ANY EXAMPLES OF BIAS OR FAULTY REASONING THAT YOU FOUND IN THE ARTICLE:

LIST ANY NEW TERMS/CONCEPTS THAT WERE DISCUSSED IN THE ARTICLE, AND WRITE A SHORT DEFINITION:

ANNUAL EDITIONS revisions depend on two major opinion sources: one is our Advisory Board, listed in the front of this volume, which works with us in scanning the thousands of articles published in the public press each year; the other is you—the person actually using the book. Please help us and the users of the next edition by completing the prepaid article rating form on this page and returning it to us. Thank you for your help!

ANNUAL EDITIONS: Mass Media 99/00

ARTICLE RATING FORM

Here is an opportunity for you to have direct input into the next revision of this volume. We would like you to rate each of the 39 articles listed below, using the following scale:

1. **Excellent: should definitely be retained**
2. **Above average: should probably be retained**
3. **Below average: should probably be deleted**
4. **Poor: should definitely be deleted**

Your ratings will play a vital part in the next revision.
So please mail this prepaid form to us just as soon as you complete it.
Thanks for your help!

RATING

ARTICLE

1. TV without Guilt: Group Portrait with Television
2. The Context of Television Violence
3. Anything Goes: Moral Bankruptcy of Television and Hollywood
4. Gendered Media: The Influence of Media on Views of Gender
5. Boys Will Be Girls
6. TV's Frisky Family Values
7. So Big: The Telecommunications Act at Year One
8. The Global Media Giants
9. "You News"
10. Do You Believe What Newspeople Tell You?
11. A Matter of Trust
12. Challenging the "Liberal Media" Claim
13. The Rise and Rise of 24-Hour Local News
14. Parachute Journalism
15. Tell It Long, Take Your Time, Go in Depth
16. The Rise of Solutions Journalism
17. Spoon-Fed News
18. Assembly-Line Journalism
19. Tales from the Trail
20. Myths of the Global Information Village

RATING

ARTICLE

21. Missing on the Home Front
22. Consumer Alert
23. Secrets and Lies
24. Too Much Information?
25. The Intervention Dilemma
26. Starr Turn
27. Spot News: The Press and The Dress
28. Inventing the Commercial
29. Blowing Up the Wall
30. Sex, Lies, and Advertising
31. The Squeeze: Some Major Advertisers Step Up the Pressure on Magazines to Alter Their Content. Will Editors Bend?
32. Television Is Losing Its Largest Viewing Audience
33. The Last Gasp of Mass Media?
34. "But First, a Word from Our Sponsor"
35. Now It's Your Web
36. Without a Rulebook
37. The Daily Me
38. X-Rated Ratings?
39. The New Ratings Game

(Continued on next page)

ANNUAL EDITIONS: MASS MEDIA 99/00

BUSINESS REPLY MAIL
FIRST-CLASS MAIL PERMIT NO. 84 GUILFORD CT

POSTAGE WILL BE PAID BY ADDRESSEE

**Dushkin/McGraw-Hill
Sluice Dock
Guilford, CT 06437-9989**

Ill....ll...l..l..l..llbl...lll.l..l.l..l..l.l.l..lbl

ABOUT YOU

Name _____   Date _____

Are you a teacher? ☐ A student? ☐
Your school's name
_____

Department
_____

Address _____ City _____ State ____ Zip ____

School telephone #
_____

YOUR COMMENTS ARE IMPORTANT TO US !

Please fill in the following information:
For which course did you use this book?
_____

Did you use a text with this *ANNUAL EDITION*? ☐ yes ☐ no
What was the title of the text?
_____

What are your general reactions to the *Annual Editions* concept?
_____

Have you read any particular articles recently that you think should be included in the next edition?
_____

Are there any articles you feel should be replaced in the next edition? Why?
_____

Are there any World Wide Web sites you feel should be included in the next edition? Please annotate.
_____

May we contact you for editorial input? ☐ yes ☐ no
May we quote your comments? ☐ yes ☐ no
_____